FOLLOW, COMMUNICATE, LEAD

Creating Competent Connections

Michelle Terese Violanti

University of Tennessee, Knoxville

Cassandra Ann Ray

University of Tennessee, Knoxville

cognella®

SAN DIEGO

Bassim Hamadeh, CEO and Publisher
Todd R. Armstrong, Publisher
Michelle Piehl, Senior Project Editor
Alia Bales, Production Editor
Abbie Goveia, Graphic Design Assistant
Trey Soto, Licensing Coordinator
Natalie Piccotti, Director of Marketing
Kassie Graves, Vice President of Editorial
Jamie Giganti, Director of Academic Publishing

Cover image copyright © 2019 iStockphoto LP/Florent Rols.
Design Image: Copyright © 2015 Depositphotos/lovemask.

Printed in the United States of America.

3970 Sorrento Valley Blvd., Ste. 500, San Diego, CA 92121

BRIEF CONTENTS

DETAILED CONTENTS

ACTIVE
LEARNING

This book has interactive activities available to
complement your reading.

Your instructor may have customized the selection of activities
available for your unique course. Please check with your professor
to verify whether your class will access this content through
the Cognella Active Learning portal (http://active.cognella.
com) or through your home learning management system.

PREFACE

F ollow, Communicate, Lead: Creating Competent Connections offers a distinct approach to the leadership/followership communication course. We set out to write this book because we were having a difficult time teaching leadership without addressing followership in a more substantive way than other textbooks. If you are looking for a textbook that addresses all of the theories in individual chapters and devotes separate chapters to the components of leadership communication, this is not the textbook for you. However, if you are looking for a textbook that addresses leadership and followership as equal parts of the effectiveness equation, marries theory and practice throughout, and weaves communication competencies throughout the text, then this is a book worth considering.

Message creation, enactment, and interpretation serve as this textbook's core. Leadership and followership are about both communication and relationships; one cannot exist without the other. Competent leaders are aware of the context in which they communicate (audience as well as situation) and recognize that their communication efforts have consequences for everyone involved. When followers are absent from the discussion, assessing leaders' effectiveness becomes a one-sided coin. Over the course of time, leadership has moved from a one-way pistol in which the leader shoots orders into the work lives of followers to an interactive chessboard where both leaders and followers contribute to the co-creation of effective communication and goal achievement. While some organizations are becoming more bureaucratic, many are looking for ways to become more empowering and lessen the number of management layers. Technological advances increase the likelihood of leaders and followers not sharing office space, a trend likely to increase as more organizations build global satellite "offices." As today's headlines impact leadership and followership, we are going to see increasing levels of responsibility and accountability for everyone involved in both formal and informal organizations. These additional responsibilities and accountability standards require strengthening people's communication and organizational competency.

Acknowledging the World in Which We Live

Daily, issues of leadership and followership appear in our information-saturated society, whether it is the inappropriate behaviors of public leaders, followers on Facebook or Twitter creating a grassroots movement, or groups of people coming together to effect change in their communities. While these aspects of leadership and followership appear in the headlines, a large majority of leaders and followers operate under the media's radar in formal/informal, for-profit/not-for-profit, and/or instrumental/relational types of organizations. With those leaders and followers in mind, the purpose of this book is to build competent communicators by bridging historical and contemporary perspectives, leaders and followers, theory and practice. Comprised of followers who act as leaders, leaders who need to know when to step back and be followers, and people whose work lives fluidly transfer between leader and follower, today's organizations seek to hire people who are both knowledgeable about, and capable of, adapting to a wide variety of communication situations.

The evolving nature of our world, the organizations in which people work, and the local communities in which people live illustrate this book's timeliness and applicability for tomorrow's leaders and followers. While students' grandparents and great-grandparents likely grew up in communities where people shared cultural heritages (ethnicities, races, genders), current and future United States' communities will be increasingly multi-cultural and require both leaders and followers to understand the perspectives of people with different world views and ways of interacting. Those same grandparents and great-grandparents worked in few organizations, often changing careers or workplaces less than three times in their work lives; today's and tomorrow's leaders and followers will be significantly more mobile, members of global workplaces, and adaptable to the changing workforce. Finally, as our world evolves and technology continues to connect people, today's and tomorrow's leaders and followers must understand how technology and their online presence affect others' perceptions of their competency.

Features and Benefits

As the project started to take shape, we realized there were other components we desired in a textbook. Let us introduce you to the pedagogical elements we chose to include in the book and why we believe you will find them useful in your classrooms.

- **Building Communication Competencies.** Competent communication is specific to the context in which it occurs; teaching students to assess the situation and the factors that influence a given situation is critical to their future success as both leaders and followers. Focusing on both leadership and followership competency also enhances students' potential success because being able to see a situation from multiple perspectives allows people to develop more competent messages as well as perform when they find themselves in each role. No one is *always* a leader or *always* a follower. Discussion questions, self-assessments, and activities help strengthen students' competency. Each chapter also provides leader and follower development practices that students can use as pro tips to become career-ready and successful.

- **Underlying Processes Woven Throughout the Text.** Chapter one introduces the reader to the similarities and minor differences between leaders and followers when it comes to communication. It also highlights the values and practices we believe exist across leadership situations (culture, diversity and inclusion, ethics, power and social influence). There are no chapters with titles such as "Ethics" or "Diversity" that often end up at the end of a textbook or term and are the first to go when time runs short.

- **Traditional and Contemporary Theories.** Two chapters take students on a journey through classical leadership theories and introduce them to recent conceptualizations of both leadership and followership. To supplement these theories, we have included a relevant communication-related theory in each of the chapters to help students understand the connections between theory and practice.

- **Case Studies.** Each of the case studies included in the text is built from actual events in an actual company. Because of that, the answers are not always neat and tidy and offer the potential for students to utilize content from multiple chapters to address the issues. All of the cases involve both leaders and followers so they can be approached from either or both perspectives as well as a combined approach. All of these cases come with electronic resources for background information not included in the case. This is an opportunity for them to use their devices in class for educational purposes (avoiding withdrawal symptoms from too few electronics). Each electronic resource comes in the form of a QR code they can scan or a shortened electronic locator they can type into a browser.

- **Memory Devices.** Visual representations are an important way to reinforce and help students remember what they read. In each chapter, we have created an opening image that ties the chapter's content together and triggers students' memory about the important chapter concepts. Additional visuals are embedded in each chapter to highlight important concepts and connections among constructs.

xvi   Follow, Communicate, Lead

Resources

It takes a community to teach well—scholars who are willing to share their research, practitioners who are willing to share their experiences, and instructors who are willing to share their success stories. We bring our community to you with the following resources and encourage you to share your resources with us and others (for credit of course).

- **Typical Items.** Like almost any other textbook you will find on the market, this one has sample syllabi, sample assignments, a test bank, discussion questions, customizable slide decks, and sample classroom activities in the instructor resource manual.

- **Distinct Resources for Instructors.** A test bank that represents all levels of Bloom's taxonomy, including asking students to write about content from multiple chapters in a single question. Accessible Syllabi for multiple types of courses (semester, quarter, condensed sessions of three or five weeks; face to face, hybrid, and online delivery). Access to the authors as part of your teaching community (reach out and ask questions, share success stories, brainstorm ways to handle classroom situations that arise, provide feedback and what is and is not working for your classes so that we can improve or develop additional resources for you). If you like entry or exit tickets, there are recall/comprehension practice quizzes that can be used or customized in your course management system.

- **Online Resources for Students.** Discussion questions and activities are available in the online environment and easily migrated to your course management system. Links to self- assessments and case-study resources are available at the online course site. Bonus materials not found in the text can also be found here (e.g., links to videos, current events, and research summaries). All students have access to practice quizzes that test their recall and comprehension.

Acknowledgments

Textbooks such as this do not materialize out of nowhere. Many people helped make our adventure a reality. First, we could not have done this without our families' support; unbeknownst to them, there are examples in the book that we took from observing them and their workplaces. Second, we must thank Todd Armstrong at Cognella for believing in this concept, and our ability to carry it out, when there were no other books that addressed both leadership and followership on the shelves. Third, we must thank our reviewers who provided invaluable feedback during the process to make this a stronger book: Jennifer L. Fairchild (Eastern Kentucky University), Kyle B. Heuett (Ball State University), Jessica D. McCall (University of North Carolina, Greensboro), and Raymond R. Ozley (University of Montevallo).

We wish you the best of luck as you continue to cruise the followership and leadership seas to help develop the next wave of competent communicators. Please encourage your students to read the Introduction. We are here to support you in whatever way we can.

Michelle and Cassie

CHAPTER 1

DEFINING LEADERSHIP AND FOLLOWERSHIP

"Followers are more important to leaders than leaders are to followers."

—BARBARA KELLERMAN

"He [sic] who cannot be a good follower cannot be a good leader."

—ARISTOTLE

Write down the first three words you think of when someone says leader.

_____ , _____ , and _____ .

Write down the first three words you think of when someone says follower.

_____ , _____ , and _____ .

L ook at the similarities and differences between your lists. Generally speaking, the leader list has positive and prosocial (beneficial to those around the leader) items on it because we assume that leaders are effective. On the other hand, the follower list likely has a negative connotation, or at least, less positive. Throughout history, culture has taught us to place more value in leadership than followership. If we think of historical views of leadership and followership in terms of underwear, leadership is in the sexy lingerie section, whereas followership gets shoved into a poorly lit corner of granny panties and muumuus. Put another way, leadership is the Ben Franklin $100 bill and followership is the Abraham Lincoln penny—some would argue leader and follower wages also reflect this difference. What it means to be a follower has been less than, inferior to, or plain boring compared to meanings and perceptions associated with being a leader. Yet, followers and leaders are equally important.

Sandy beach and water, milkshake and ice cream, and leadership and followership—in each pair, you need the second for the first to exist. Beaches without water are simply big sandboxes in which preschool children play, milkshakes without ice cream are simply whipped milk, and leaders without followers are simply individuals talking in a forest where no one can hear them. Without followers, there are no leaders and without leaders, the followers are a group of people with no purpose or goals.

While leadership and followership have often been defined based upon organizational titles or positions, those definitions are incomplete. For example, in the military, people determine whether you are a leader or a follower based upon the rank you hold and who else is present (a person with a higher rank or a group of people in a lower rank). Titles or positions are the most common defining feature of followership and leadership in hierarchical organizations. In more communal organizations, leadership and followership may be determined by expertise or resources. In these places, the person who has expertise in a specific area (e.g., planting crops) may be the leader for the fruits and vegetables production tasks; the person who has the cows and pigs may be the leader for the protein production tasks while the fruits and vegetables' leaders become followers. Because leadership and followership exist in relation to each other, they must be defined in ways that allow people to be both leaders and followers as the situation necessitates.

Followers, Leaders, and Managers

If defining leaders and followers were not enough, enter the concept of managers who are also necessary organizational members. Interestingly, we rarely distinguish leaders from managers. Those who are in positions where they oversee others may be referred to as team leaders or managers; the two terms are often used interchangeably. In reality, there are some distinct differences between leaders and managers. Looking at the ocean floor picture below: 1. Which are the leaders (label them with L)? 2. Which are the followers (label them with F)? 3. Which are the managers (label them with M)?

Typically, people will choose the fish at the front of the school as the leader—the person who guides the rest of the group moving forward; they similarly choose the rest of the fish school as the followers. Others may choose the isolated fish who sits in the corner office and rarely interacts with others as the leader. Do you think anyone would choose the person in the middle of the school as the leader? Why? How about the fish swimming

FIGURE 1.1 Followers, Leaders, and Managers

away from the school—the person who trusts the organization members to do their jobs while focusing on crafting the organization's future?

There are no right or wrong answers for which fish are managers, leaders, or followers. For example, the person in the middle of the school might be the leader because that is an excellent vantage point for seeing what all of the followers are doing while still being able to connect easily with all of them. The fish looking back at the school of fish may be a follower who is new to the organization and using observation skills as part of the socialization process to learn how things work around this reef. Those on the bottom may be managers who are making sure all of the mundane tasks are being accomplished or they may be followers who have been assigned to complete those tasks. The fish swimming away from the school may be emerging leaders who are carefully developing a vision for how the fish will work together in the future; those fish may be followers who are heading to the leader's or manager's office to share the latest innovation the team has developed. How we choose to label the fish is a direct result of implicit leadership (ILT) and followership (IFT) theories.

Implicit theories focus on the cognitive processes people use to form images of and attach meanings to people, places, and things (managers, leaders, and followers in this case). Interacting with media, peers, parental figures, and coworkers influences our beliefs about leaders and followers.

Look at the letters on your fish and think about what messages you have heard or seen that would steer you to label them in that way. The cognitive representation we create of what it means to be a follower, leader, or manager helps us not only interpret a specific interaction, but also influences our behaviors, messages, and evaluation.

Prototypes, our cognitive images of what it means to be a typical or ideal leader, follower, or manager, allow us to label someone without having to recall all of the characteristics we associate with the label. For example, if your terms at the beginning of the chapter included reserved, supportive, and obedient for a follower, then you could choose "follower" rather than having to think to yourself "someone who is reserved, supportive, and obedient." These prototype shortcuts save our brains significant amounts of processing energy each day. **Normative prototypes** indicate our attitude, belief, and behavior expectations for what is typical. **Valence prototypes** indicate whether we evaluate the person positively or negatively in a given situation. Together, people use these prototypes to label someone as follower-not follower, leader-not leader, or manager-not manager and adjust their behavior to match the prototype label they have created for each of the people involved in the interaction (Phillips & Lord, 1986).

Think about Nelson Mandela as a leader in the peace movement. Some of the normative prototype characteristics might be strong, influential, and well-spoken; while no one is perfect, almost no one labeled Mandela as having a negative valence. On the flip side, Adolf Hitler possessed the same normative prototypes and primarily a negative valence because he used those characteristics for anti- rather than pro-social behavior.

RESEARCH SUMMARY

Study 1: Braun et al. (2017) set out to study implicit followership theory by examining the extent to which organization members associate women's social roles with follower roles. They conducted one experiment and one implicit association task to test two hypotheses: "Typical female followers are rated higher on ideal IFT [implicit followership theory] scales than male followers" and "Typical male followers are rated higher on counter-ideal IFT scales than female followers" (p. 380). German workers participated in the two studies. In the first study, participants read a scenario in which they were the leader of a new team and asked to rate a typical male or female follower they would encounter on that team. In the study, leaders rated typical female followers as having a more relational orientation while also rating typical male followers as having a more task orientation and counter-relational orientation. In the association test, people clicked on either a male or female follower for each term (e.g., educated, intelligent, rude, uncooperative) as it came up on the screen. Both men and women reacted faster when clicking on good follower terms with a woman and bad follower terms with a man. Interestingly, the woman-follower prototype was stronger for female than male participants in the study—females rated women in the follower role more strongly than males did. While this study was conducted in Germany and not the United States, there are no comparable studies here and little reason to believe that the findings would be significantly different.

Implications: Both men and women are being socialized through their interactions with media, peers, parental figures, teachers, and coworkers to believe that typical women make better followers and typical men are not ideal followers. What does this mean for interactions in the workplace? First, women are more likely to be pushed toward follower roles and positions in most organizations. Second, men are more likely to be pulled into situations that demonstrate leadership ability. Long term, three outcomes occur: 1. Men, who may be excellent followers, end up in leadership positions for which they may not be well suited; 2. Women, who may be excellent leaders, end up in followership positions for which they may not be well suited; and 3. Organizations suffer because they have people in the wrong positions and may not hear and take advantage of the innovative ideas of the women who never make it to the leadership roles. Overall, organizations and society suffer a tremendous loss because people who are well qualified end up leaving the organization to find a place where they are appropriately respected and feel as if they are making a valuable contribution; therefore, innovation that advances our society becomes a slower process.

Study 2: Carnes et al. (2015) set out to examine the relationships among a person's implicit leadership theories, personality, and decision to choose someone as a formal leader. Using simulation and interviews, the researchers had people play the role of either the applicant or the evaluator to test two hypotheses:

- Applicants' personality characteristics (extraversion, conscientiousness, openness to experience, and agreeableness) positively predict their ratings of a leader candidate, even when interview experience and intelligence are controlled.

- Raters' personality characteristics (extraversion, conscientiousness, openness to experience, and agreeableness) positively predict their ratings of a leader candidate, even when interview experience and intelligence are controlled.

- Raters select applicants based upon their perceptions of an ideal leader.

(continued)

Almost all of the raters had at least one year of work experience and over 85% of the applicants had experience being the interview applicant. Raters and applicants were matched to create a total of 284 pairs. Applicants were applying for a leadership development program at a simulated campus career fair. Raters assessed the quality and content of their answers to typical interview questions and both groups completed a personality survey. Results indicated that applicant extraversion, conscientiousness, and openness to experience predicted interview rating scores for applicants; agreeableness was not a significant predictor. Applicants who had these personality traits were more likely to be chosen for the leadership development program. For raters, only conscientiousness scores predicted their interview rating scores; raters with higher conscientiousness scores were more likely to rate the applicants more highly. Finally, raters' perceptions of the ideal leader and their ratings of whom they would choose for the leadership development program were not related to each other—that is, the researchers could not support implicit leadership theories with their data; the raters used other means to determine who should enter the program.

Implications: When selecting applicants for organizational positions, interviews are effective tools. While interviews are effective tools, they may not be sufficient for choosing future leaders. Interviewers would likely benefit from a realistic description of exactly what tasks the leader will be performing, what skills are needed, and a description of the ideal leader with respect to the organization's mission, vision, goals, and values. At a time when computers are increasingly screening applicants' résumés, finding additional ways (personality tests, video-captured interactions, simulations) to screen applicants to choose those who have the most leadership potential is critical.

According to implicit theories of followership and leadership, how people make sense of behaviors is not the same as the behaviors themselves. Thus, four people working on the same team could have vastly different perceptions of the leaders' and followers' behaviors. Interactions are most effective when leaders, followers, and managers have shared perceptions or interpretations in a given situation. Starting from the connectionist perspective of implicit theories emphasizes that all organizational members are intertwined and all interactions are contextual (Foti et al., 2017); as such, culture, ethics, diversity, and social influence all play a role in how people make sense of other people's communication behaviors.

Followership and Leadership Themes

We introduce the four themes below as a foundation for material upon which we expand throughout the book. They are four aspects woven into the fabric of leadership and followership. Culture involves the life experiences leaders and followers bring to the situation; culture impacts the way we create and interpret messages. Diversity and inclusion have become two buzz words in American society where we attempt to balance recognizing differences across people and groups of people while also seeking mechanisms to connect those same people and groups of people. Ethics, simply put, assesses a person's, group's, organization's, or society's character and ability to behave in what is considered a right or just manner. Finally, power and social influence include the bases from which people develop their ability to persuade others and the messages they use to encourage others to think about something in a new or different way, behave in a new or different way, or adopt a new or different belief or value.

Culture

Culture, which exists at the international, national, regional, organizational, and interpersonal level, is often so embedded in our attitudes, beliefs, behaviors, and values that we hardly recognize it. In simple terms, culture is "the way we do things around here" (Deal & Kennedy, 1982). If only it were that simple. Cultures are deeply entrenched in their membership. Edgar Schein spent most of his academic life examining organizational culture, but his analogy is just as relevant for organizations as it is for nations.

> Culture operates at many levels and certainly how we do things around here is the surface level. I like to think of culture to be like the lily pond. On the surface you've got leaves and flowers and things that are very visible; a visitor would see them. That's the 'how we do things around here;' but the explanation of why we do things in that way forces you to look at the root system, what's feeding it and the history of the pond, who planted what. If you don't dig down into the reasons for why we do things this way you've only looked at the culture at a very superficial level and you haven't really understood it (quoted in Kuppler, 2014, par. 4).

Drilling down through the crust, mantle, and currents to the organization's core is difficult and time consuming; without an understanding of how those various layers interact, followers and leaders find themselves questioning organizational decisions and wondering about others' communication behaviors.

While everyone generally agrees that cultures and subcultures exist, a precise definition of culture has been elusive. For our purposes, **culture** is the shared assumptions that impact people's behaviors, feelings, perceptions, and thoughts. **Subcultures**, segments that create a smaller set of their own assumptions, support and do not contradict the more widely shared assumptions. For example, around the world, there are fandom subcultures that support a sustained loyalty to any shared interest—Fortnite, Candy Crush, or even Harry Potter. Fandom subcultures cross geographical and other boundaries, without upsetting the shared assumptions within those geographical boundaries. That is, Harry Potter fandom does not upset the shared assumptions of freedom of speech in the United States or the importance of periods of silence during a conversation in Africa.

Countercultures, segments that create a smaller set of their own assumptions, work in opposition to the more widely accepted and shared assumptions. Countercultures bring about change in the larger culture. What began over 10 years earlier with a woman in the Bronx, New York, became a firestorm when Alyssa Milano used #MeToo to encourage people to post it as their status if they had been a victim of sexual assault or sexual violence. The social media campaign's goal was to bring awareness and seek to change the status quo culture that turns a blind eye to these behaviors.

At the organizational level, researchers characterize cultures as actors, objects, and a metaphor (Smircich, 1983). As an actor, cultures dictate the behaviors of organizational members. As part of a larger interdependent system, culture acts upon organizational members and influences the shared values that then impact behaviors. Culture is an active agent in the organizational processes. As an object, culture is something that can be created, managed, and changed. It is external to the organizational members and can be manipulated by them, particularly management, to lead people to behave in desired ways. Finally, as a metaphor, the subjective experiences of organizational members are understood as the culture; it is not an entity with human qualities that can act or be acted upon, but rather the shared knowledge, meanings, and generative processes that allow members to act in an organized manner.

Diversity and Inclusion

Diversity and inclusion have been buzzwords in business and society for as long as many of us can remember, almost to the extent that you rolled your eyes when you saw this heading. If we define diversity as difference and inclusion as making others feel as if they are a part of the group, we risk making the words meaningless. Just because two people have different skin colors, sex organs, socioeconomic classes, countries of origin, or any other demographic difference does not guarantee they think, behave, or believe differently.

Many forms of diversity are actually invisible to the naked or trained eye and therefore difficult to detect. For example, people with chronic illnesses (e.g., auto-immune diseases) or physical ability limitations (e.g., sensory processing disorders, color blindness) may come to work every day and never reveal the extent to which that illness impacts their work lives. That is, those physical ability limitations may make it difficult to follow a multi-media presentation during orientation and the chronic illnesses may make it difficult to sit through an all-day meeting. Leaders and followers who consider these potentially invisible differences that make a difference are labeled as more communicatively competent because they design appropriate and effective messages for a wide variety of audiences.

Assume we start from the point where diversity is necessary for progress rather than diversity is an opportunity for one person to offend another by not accepting or respecting the ways in which the two differ. For followers and leaders to move forward and grow, they must be willing to expose themselves to people who have different backgrounds, experiences, and viewpoints. Over 75 years ago, Maslow (1943) defined sense of belonging as one of the higher-order needs all humans possess. When we first meet people, we make judgments about the extent to which they are similar to or different from us—which makes us ask, "do they belong in our group?" Fortunately, this shorthand mechanism allows us to make quick decisions; unfortunately, we base those decisions upon outward appearances and explicit characteristics without taking the time to get to know the other person. Once we have labeled the other person as "not belonging," the process to reverse that judgment remains an uphill battle. People fight these battles every day and the organizations in which they work or volunteer can help or hinder that process.

In America, organizational leaders and managers make decisions about whether they are going to develop and operate under a purposeful diversity and inclusion strategy or a diversity compliance policy (Lee & Kramer, 2016). As a philosophy, **purposeful strategies** permeate every aspect of the organization by seeking multiple perspectives or approaches and encouraging people to remain open to myriad possibilities during decision making; they serve to strengthen the organization's culture. On the other hand, **compliance-based policies** seek to shield the organization from being involved in discriminatory practices, especially due to ability (physical or intellectual), age, color, gender identity, genetic markers, marital or family status, nationality, race, religion or spiritual affiliation, sex, sexual orientation, and/or socioeconomic class.

What difference would it make if you followed or led in a compliance-policy versus purposeful-strategy organization? In policy compliance organizations, leaders and followers operate in clearly delineated situations with specific answers to what is right and in fear of violating the written rules; in purposeful strategy organizations, followers and leaders must be willing to handle significantly more ambiguity because right and wrong is more of a continuum, where organizational members determine what is right and wrong for the situation.

FIGURE 1.2   These scales represent the decisions we make each and every day about diversity and inclusion as well as what it means to behave in an ethical manner.

Ethics

What is the difference between right and wrong; was the action right or wrong? People answer this question to determine whether someone has acted ethically. If only it were that simple. What constitutes "right" differs based upon one's background, experiences, attitudes, beliefs, values, and the context in which the interaction occurs. As a branch of philosophy, entire courses and full encyclopedias are devoted to ethics. Thankfully, we are going to hit the highlights here and see how the various approaches play out in other contexts throughout the book.

All of the theories or approaches about which we are going to talk involve normative ethics. **Normative ethics** concern distinguishing right from wrong and choosing to behave in the manner that is considered right. For example, growing up you likely heard from your teachers that it was not right or acceptable to cheat on tests or homework; in college, you have heard about following an academic integrity policy or not engaging in plagiarism—all forms of normative ethics in action (the little devil on your shoulder usually says, "Just don't get caught!"). **Ethical duty theories** focus on people's actions and what behaviors are considered right and wrong based upon the obligations one has to others. **Ethical consequentialist theories** focus on the extent to which the behavior's outcomes are beneficial or good. Finally, **ethical virtue theories** focus on the extent to which one possesses a moral character.

Generally, people prefer one version of normative ethics over others, which is why a single situation can be viewed through the various ethical theory lenses. Let's use the example of telling an instructor that the paper assignment is not done because the computer crashed, when in fact the student simply did not leave enough time to complete the paper.

- From an ethical duty perspective, the behavior is considered a lie and immoral because the motivation behind telling the lie is to garner an extension.

- From an ethical consequentialist perspective, the behavior is considered immoral because the outcomes of creating an external excuse for what happened to the paper do not promote the greatest good for the greatest number of people, provide serenity for the person creating the excuse, or lead to long-term health and well-being.

- From an ethical virtues perspective, the student lacks moral character by not demonstrating moral or intellectual virtues or empathizing by seeing the situation through the instructor's eyes.

While one of those perspectives might ring true for you now in this example, you may find yourself making different choices as the situation changes and whether you are a leader or follower in that situation. Table 1.1 provides an overview of the most common ethical approaches based upon people's actions, situational outcomes, and character.

TABLE 1.1   Ethical Perspectives

Focus	Approach	Key Assumptions
Actions	Immanuel Kant's Categorical Imperative	▪ We label people as good or bad based upon the motivation for their behaviors rather than the consequences or goodness of the actions.
		▪ Moral worth comes from behaving in a way that fulfills one's duty to others because it is the right thing to do, even if it does not bring happiness.
		▪ People only behave in ways that they believe all others in society should be able to act.
	Thomas Hobbes, John Locke, John Rawls' Contractualism	▪ People are willing to give up some rights to preserve social order.
		▪ People are primarily self-interested and rationally choose to behave in ways that maximize their self-interests (avoid harm) by acting morally to preserve authority.
		▪ Social contracts are renegotiated when they no longer meet the culture's needs.
		▪ Moral acts are those we would agree to if we were all unbiased.

(continued)

TABLE 1.1   Ethical Perspectives *(continued)*

Focus	Approach	Key Assumptions
Outcomes	John Stuart Mill's Utilitarianism	▪ People should choose to act in ways that promote the most good (pleasure) for the greatest number of people.
		▪ All people's happiness and pleasure are equally important.
		▪ Cultural, spiritual, and intellectual pleasures are more important than physical pleasures.
	Epicureanism	▪ Goal is to act in ways that bring tranquility for oneself, limit one's physical pain, and minimize anxiety about what may happen in the future.
		▪ Happiness, the highest good, is intrinsically driven and valued for its own sake.
		▪ Must focus on a behavior valued for its own sake. Short-term pleasure.
	August Comte's Altruism	▪ People have a moral obligation to act in the best interest of others, sometimes at the expense of their personal best interests.
		▪ Builds social connections and has positive health and well-being benefits for the individual actor.
		▪ Emotions drive moral judgments.
Character/ Individual Actors	Aristotle's Golden Mean	▪ Virtues are habits or qualities that allow one to achieve their purpose.
		▪ Moral virtues include justice and temperance; intellectual virtues include theoretical and practical wisdom.
		▪ Moral virtues serve as the middle ground between two unwanted extremes.
	Carol Gilligan's Ethics of Care; Michael Slote's Ethics of Care and Empathy	▪ The extent to which people are dependent and interdependent varies from person to person.
		▪ Assessing how people are dependent and interdependent varies from person to person.
		▪ Empathy and compassion are more important than duty and consequences.
		▪ Care involves attentiveness, responsibility, competence, and responsiveness.

Power and Social Influence

When you hear the word "power," what comes to mind—having strength or force, the amount of energy produced in a given amount of time, possession of control, or authority over others? While all of these are potential definitions, for our purposes **power** is having the personal qualities, resources, and/or situational characteristics necessary to engage in social influence.

After refinement and further definition, the original power bases created by French and Raven (1959) and later refined by Raven (1965) have stood the test of time. First, **coercive power** involves using communication to manipulate or threaten force against another; its counterpart, **reward power**, involves using communication or other tangible objects to provide incentives. Second, **expert power** stems from having the necessary knowledge, skills, or experiences. **Information power**, possessing the knowledge sought by others, differs from expert power because the knowledge is wanted or needed by others to accomplish their goals. **Legitimate power** derives from one's position within the organizational structure; even in a group of peers, the person designated as the leader possesses legitimate power. Fifth, **referent power** focuses on the positive social relationships one has built with others; others feel a sense of loyalty, respect, admiration, friendship, and positive affect for this person. Generally, power bases grow out of personal characteristics (referent, expert), positional characteristics (legitimate), or a combination of both (coercive, informational, reward). With the exception of legitimate power, both leaders and followers can utilize any of the power bases.

Those who have power can use it for both good and evil—power can be used as well as abused. Power bases can also work in combination with each other. For example, a person who has referent power in a particular situation may also possess reward or informational power. Just because a person has legitimate power does not guarantee the person possesses expert or informational power.

With the possible exception of legitimate, power is relational and a function of the extent to which the people involved grant power to others. For example, followers with informational power, because they have been in the organization for a long time and know the institutional history, may call on that knowledge (unethical behaviors of previous leaders were not made public even though the people were relieved of their duties or fired) to influence a newer leader to support a particular change or policy (eliminating the possibility of retribution for whistle blowing) in the organization. If the leader or other followers do not believe the follower's long-term organizational tenure does not constitute informational power, then the power base cannot be used to engage in social influence.

Others' opinions and actions impact those around them; people respond to the pressures or discomforts they feel in these situations. **Social influence** is the process of using socialization, obedience, compliance, persuasion, and conformity (Flanagin, 2017) to alter another's attitudes, behaviors, beliefs, and/or values in the short or long term. Often, people assume that social influence only occurs when one's attitudes, beliefs, behaviors, or values are changed as a result of a behavior or message; in reality, those changes may require repeated exposure and reflection.

If you took a public speaking course, how many of the persuasive speeches moved you to change your attitudes or behaviors (becoming an organ donor, wearing a seat belt all the time, adopting a particular stance on a controversial topic such as the death penalty)? Similarly, how many times have you been at work and listened to managers explain how they were changing a process that worked completely well to one that seemed unlikely to work—how long did it take you to buy into the change? The reason is because social influence is a process that occurs over time; it occurs as leaders and followers gain knowledge about what it means to work in a particular organization, hear different coworkers using compliance-gaining strategies, and attempt to fit in by mirroring the behavior of others.

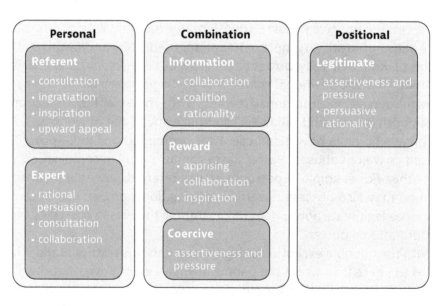

FIGURE 1.3   Power Bases and Social Influence Strategies

Eight strategies have consistently emerged as workplace social influence strategies (Schriesheim & Hinkin, 1990; Yukl et al., 2005).

- **Upward Appeal/Coalition:** Messages that create a network of people to impact the attitudes, behaviors, beliefs, and values of others.

- **Rationality/Rational Persuasion:** Messages that use logical appeals (*logos*) to encourage attitude, behavior, belief, or value changes.

- **Inspiration:** Messages that indicate personal fulfillment associated with the request.

- **Ingratiation:** Messages that indicate a friendship, or at least a positive relationship, exists between, or among, the people prior to making the request.

- **Consultation:** Messages participants use to negotiate a more acceptable request.

- **Collaboration:** Messages that offer to provide resources or assistance if the other person completes a request or approves a proposed change.

- **Assertiveness/Pressure:** Messages that compel a person to change one's attitude, beliefs, behaviors or values.

- **Apprising/Exchange of Benefits:** Messages that explain how the person will profit OR remind the person about having profited in the past.

In many ways, these influence strategies correspond to the power bases. Leaders and followers with referent power bases have consultation, ingratiation, inspiration, and upward appeal social influence tactics available to them. Followers and leaders with reward power are most likely to use apprising (exchange of benefits), collaboration, and inspiration messages. Leaders with a legitimate power base may rely on assertiveness/pressure and persuasive rationality as social influence tactics. Working with an informational power base often leads to collaboration, coalition, and rationality strategies. Organizational members with expert power may utilize rational persuasion, consultation, and collaboration. When followers and leaders possess a coercive power base, they tend to draw exclusively upon assertiveness or pressure. Because any leader or follower may have access to multiple power bases in a given situation, the person may use a combination of social influence tactics.

Leadership and Followership Behaviors

As the implicit theories discussed above indicated, followership and leadership are contextual and based upon the perceptions of those involved in the situation. With that in mind, seven core leader and follower competencies are necessary, but not sufficient, for success. The eighth one is unique to leaders (see Figure 1.4 for a summary).

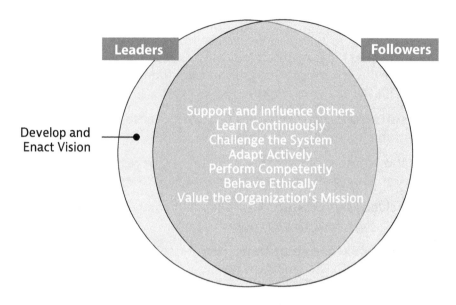

Develop and
Enact Vision

Leaders

Followers

Support and Influence Others
Learn Continuously
Challenge the System
Adapt Actively
Perform Competently
Behave Ethically
Value the Organization's Mission

FIGURE 1.4   Communication Competencies of Followers and Leaders

Support and Influence Others

Followers and leaders share expressing support and spreading influence. In general, expressions of support cultivate relationships and influence others. Leaders and followers express support to, and for, each other with messages intended to confirm, encourage, and/or protect the other in different ways. Imagine a "horrible boss" situation where a leader does not know your name or position within the company, offers superficial feedback on performance reviews, and often reminds you of how easily replaceable you are. In this case, your value as a person and a follower is disconfirmed rather than confirmed, superficial feedback discourages you from striving to improve, and you feel unprotected and vulnerable in terms of job security. Chances are slim that a follower in this situation would then interact with the leader by expressing positively glowing remarks about this leader's ideas or encourage other coworkers to support the leader's initiative. In fact, followers in this type of situation may go as far as to recruit and rally against the leader. While this is the exact opposite of expressing support to confirm, encourage, or protect, it highlights the wide-reaching effects of social support and influence of both leader and follower behaviors.

One of the most glaring advantages of supportive communication is the way it creates a trusting climate, a safe place, within leader-follower relationships to use open communication and extend mutual influence. The outcomes of supportive communication are especially important for leaders' and followers' willingness to openly offer and receive feedback (e.g., constructive criticism) as well as ask and answer questions.

Learn Continuously

Leaders and followers learn what makes doing the job a success versus a failure, making learning another behavior leaders and followers share. Learning refers to the process of gaining knowledge. Through interaction, leaders and followers alike learn what works and what does not work by using knowledge gained through education, personal experiences, and observing how others do things. Learning is how implicit theories are developed and shaped over time.

In terms of leader-follower communication, leaders learn from followers just as much as followers learn from leaders; learning is contextual. While a leader may coach followers on how to perform certain tasks, followers may teach leaders new ways of using technology to complete tasks more efficiently. Who enacts the role of teacher versus learner is not concrete; it is ongoing, fluid, and shifting. Beyond learning how to accomplish tasks, leaders and followers must learn how to communicate with each other effectively and appropriately to achieve goals in a variety of contexts. Most of our first learning experiences within organizations occur during the onboarding (i.e., socialization) process. From interviewing to socialization to celebrating a 30-year employee anniversary, leaders and followers must learn how to support, challenge, and adapt behaviors toward one another while maintaining ethics that identify with the organization's values and mission.

Challenge the System

People and organizations value leader and follower behaviors that constructively challenge one's self, each other, and the organization to improve. **Constructive challenging** involves 1) engaging in behaviors that critique the ideas, agenda, strategy, or policies of oneself, others, or an organization in a way that supports the learning and growth necessary to make something better, and 2) becoming better as an individual member of the collective. Although leaders are expected to challenge their followers and organization to improve while achieving goals, followers are not always granted this same luxury. For followers, challenging a leader or the organization can be like walking on a tight rope 50 feet in the air without a safety net, balancing on the fine line between risk and reward.

Followers are often more exposed to the front–line aspects of the job (products, sales, customer interaction, etc.) then leaders (Carsten et al., 2014). For example, let's consider a "challenge or crumble" scenario from Yamaha, a boat manufacturing company leading the watercraft industry since 1989. Alesha, a team leader in the small parts production department of Yamaha, received a list of parts to build every morning in her department. Alesha knew the parts list did not include the parts needed for production. Instead of using the list she was given, she built parts based on her expertise and experience regarding what she knew was needed. The plant manager, Tim, found this behavior unacceptable and told her to build based on the list schedule he gave her. Using Tim's schedule of parts for the first 4 hours of the day ended up almost shutting production down completely. Reluctantly, Alesha decided to confront Tim to explain why she did the job the way she had instead of Tim's way. Alesha and Tim ended up writing a new program to make the list schedule for the correct parts to ensure production met the organization's goals.

This type of "challenge or crumble" situation is a common experience across many organizational industries where an overall plan or the daily task operations required to fulfil a leader's vision and the goals of an organization rely on constructively challenging the system for optimal effectiveness. While the above real-life example has a happy ending, it would be naïve to think there is not a dark side to these types of situations.

Offering constructive criticism to others can be a challenge in itself. Since challenging others' ideas, agenda, strategies, or policies is often uncomfortable and difficult to navigate, the second part of this book considers factors related to constructive challenging in various contexts. What awaits you in the final chapter of this book is an opportunity to analyze the dark side of these behaviors, *destructive challenging*, when leadership and followership behaviors are toxic. Overall, constructively challenging a leader, a follower, or the system is more difficult when you do not value the organization's mission, know how to competently perform the other's job, perceive a lack of support, or the parties have underdeveloped situational adaptation skills.

Perform Competently

Both leaders and followers engage and enact behaviors to "do the job." Doing the job behaviors refers to the way people do and say things while completing tasks. Rewinding to ancient history, without modern technology or machines, the Great Wall of China was built by followers to prevent barbarian invasions based on a leader's vision. Fast forwarding through history to today, the construction of the bridges and roads we drive on, the houses we live in, and the stores or technology used to buy and sell goods and services are results of followers and leaders doing the job.

People engage in doing the job behaviors in different ways. For college students, the different ways of enacting doing the job behaviors are most visible in group projects. Some members of the group or team perform competently (i.e., effectively and appropriately), some skate by doing the bare minimum, and others fail to do the job at all. To do the job, learn, support, or constructively challenge competently is valued by employers and important to organizational success. As such, we need to understand what competent performance means, what it is, and what it is not.

Performing competently is defined as expressing messages and behaviors in a manner that is both appropriate and effective to complete tasks and achieve goals. **Appropriateness** and effectiveness serve as the dual criteria for competent performance. Behaviors are considered appropriate when messages and actions match a given situation. **Effectiveness** is defined as producing a desired outcome. One can achieve effectiveness without appropriateness and vice versa; however, performing competently requires satisfying the dual criteria of competent behavior.

Satisfying the dual criteria of competent performance also involves understanding the difference between knowing and doing. A person may know how to do something; knowing how to perform does not guarantee that person will actually do it. For instance, if your goal is to score an A on an upcoming exam, then you know what material needs to be studied and by now you should know how to study for exams. It would be appropriate for you to take the time necessary to use this knowledge and complete the task of studying (create flash cards, review information, memorize content, etc.). Knowing what to study and knowing how to study do not mean you will actually sit down and use this knowledge to engage in the behavior of studying, or "doing" the task of studying.

Let's say you studied and scored an A grade on the exam. In this case, you performed competently; the behaviors you enacted were both appropriate and effective. However, if you studied and scored a B on the exam, your behaviors were appropriate but not completely effective—your desired outcome of scoring an A was not produced. As we learn how to perform a job competently, we hone the ability to actively adapt to the surrounding circumstances based upon our experiences.

Adapt Actively

Actively adapting drives leader and follower behaviors such as learning, supporting and influencing, challenging the system, and performing competently to successfully achieve goals. **Active adaptation** refers to adjusting and controlling in-the-moment communication behaviors to align with the situation and attaining short-/long-term goals successfully. We can easily see that leaders or followers who lack the skills to actively adapt communication behaviors are no longer in gear to drive; they are parked, stuck in neutral, or rolling in reverse on the road to success expressway.

In the previous example, the success of Yamaha's production plant hinged on both leader and follower—Alesha's and Tim's ability to actively adapt while engaging in the discussed leader and follower behaviors (supporting and influencing, learning, and performing competently). The example about support and influence behavior shows how active adaptation can determine success in terms of employee engagement, productivity, and organizational climate. Therefore, actively adapting is important at the individual, dyadic, and collective levels of interaction.

Behave Ethically

As previously discussed, ethics is a recurring theme throughout leader and follower experiences. An **ethical end-game** refers to the principled philosophy/perspective one assumes when communicating to pursue goals. There is no one-size-fits-all ethical perspective because determining what is ethical and effective in one situation may not work in others. Understanding your own ethical end-game can raise awareness regarding how well you identify with and prioritize an organization's values and mission. Therefore, examining how far you need, and are willing, to stretch your position to meet a leader's vision or an organization's mission is an ongoing behavior critical to leader and follower communication processes and outcomes.

Develop and Enact Vision

Before talking about the last behavior, we need to discuss the one behavior unique to leaders: developing and enacting vision. Leaders inspire the efforts of others to achieve by generating and setting the goal and direction for those efforts. Having a vision and setting a vision are distinct, yet complementary and interdependent processes. On one hand, developing a vision focuses on questions about the "where" in terms of an overarching goal's direction. Where do we want to be in 5 to 10 years? Where do we see our efforts taking us? Enacting a vision answers questions regarding more personal aspects of the direction of our efforts asking "what." What do we want to become? What should we focus our efforts and attention toward?

The purpose of a vision is to inspire and motivate others to look forward, see the bigger picture, and give meaning to how their efforts of today will achieve the goals desired five years from tomorrow. It almost goes without saying then, followers need leaders to develop and enact a vision to follow, and leaders need followers to bring that vision to life. If the goal is to inspire and motivate, then both leaders and followers must understand the qualities that differentiate a "dud" vision from a "stud" vision.

The three primary characteristics of an effective vision, include: clear forward thinking, expansiveness, and active engagement. First, a vision must be based in forward thinking that is expressed in a clear and concise manner. Creating and expressing a plan that explicitly shows anticipated and forecasted concern for the future outcomes of an organization,

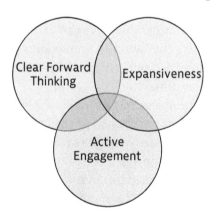

FIGURE 1.5 Characteristics of an Effective Vision

followers, customers, and one's self assists in gaining the support of your intended audience.

The vision must be broad enough for anyone within the intended audience to buy in. A vision must expand the abilities and efforts of each individual within the collective to allow all members the opportunity to engage and be a part of fulfilling the vision. Said another way, an effective vision is an equal opportunity employer; it doesn't discriminate based on skill, position, expertise, or experience. Followers who feel they are capable of making a valuable contribution to an overall goal will be more likely to *want* to achieve a vision.

Third, a vision must be active. The most significant and the most trivial of humankind's accomplishments would never be achieved without followers actively working to make a leader's vision a reality. Therefore, promoting active engagement for those who bring a vision to life requires listening and being attentive to followers' mental and emotional needs, motivations, goals, and values. An effective vision generates a deeper sense of purpose, serving as a compass navigating the day-to-day efforts of followers as individuals and as a collective toward a common goal.

Value the Organization's Mission

Bringing a vision to life is at the heart of an organization's mission. Organizations create mission statements targeting questions about "why" and "how" daily operations in the present contribute to a desirable future. Why are we doing this? Why do we care? How does the way we do things support our ultimate purpose? Effective leaders and followers value their organization's mission. When people identify with an organization's values and mission, they tend to work in the best interest of that organization's mission. Many top companies have found ways of tapping into this idea to enhance organizational life and employee output. For example, Zappo's mission statement is "To provide the best customer service possible. Deliver 'WOW' through service." The productivity, engagement, effectiveness, and satisfaction of a Zappo's employee who does not personally value providing "WOW" quality customer service will be significantly less than someone who does.

An environmentalist working for an oil rig company is another example of how the values between an employee and an organization's mission fail to align. Therefore, it is important for leaders and followers to be interested in, research, and understand how their own values align with those of potential or current employers. Alignment begins early and carries through all communication aspects of the entire employment process. Although this idea is simple, it can be easily overlooked when other organizational features (e.g., salary, benefits, training, career growth) appeal to leaders and followers. Regardless, how followers and leaders communicate is a direct reflection of the extent to which they align themselves with the organization's mission.

Leaders and Managers

At the beginning of the chapter, we talked about distinguishing between leaders and managers, yet never mentioned it again. Managers are necessary for an organization's day-to-day functioning. Looking back at the ocean example, managers are most likely to be the snails, shrimp, and clams known as bottom feeders. Without these fish "cleaning" the ocean floor, the other fish would not be able to perform. They oversee the necessary tasks and represent people who complete them as well as perform behind the scenes.

Henri Fayol (1916), French management theorist, developed a typology of manager characteristics that can be broken into five categories: planning, organizing, commanding, coordinating, and controlling. Created over 100 years ago, these principles remain as relevant today in a mediated, technology, and knowledge-driven society as they did then in an industrial society.

- **Planning** involves developing the strategic design necessary to accomplish upcoming goals. For example, if you were planning to earn an A in this course, reading all of the assigned materials, asking questions, and participating actively in class would be part of your strategic plan.

- **Organizing** includes recruiting, training, and structuring the work activities of one's employees. For the purposes of this course, you might engage in organizing by creating a study group, choosing who will participate, and determining who will make what contributions to the group.

- As part of **commanding**, managers oversee the everyday task accomplishment of workers as well as communicate all organizational policies and procedures to the employees. In the study group, you would develop a set of guidelines members use when creating materials for the group members and ensure that everyone completes their tasks in a timely manner.

- If the organization is going to move forward, all efforts of the different groups must work together to better the final output (**coordinating**). In the study group, your management efforts should strengthen all group members' performance by making sure they have the material available in the way they learn best (visually, auditorily, etc.).

- **Controlling** is as much about overseeing the environment in which people work as it is the people. Managers safeguard the organization by making sure anyone who does not comply with the organizational policies and procedures corrects the deviations and returns to the path necessary to achieve the organizational goals. In the study group, this would be making sure the person who creates a half-hearted, last minute study guide recognizes the group's goal of strengthening their knowledge and comes to the next meeting with appropriate materials to remain a member of the group—no one should benefit to a greater extent than the other members.

Fayol's management functions have some overlap with the followership and leadership behaviors discussed above; however, effective leaders and followers are distinguishable from managers because of the depth and breadth of their communication-related behaviors.

Communication Styles (DISC)

When people identify with an organization's values and mission, they tend to work toward the organization's mission. Many top companies have found ways of tapping into this idea to enhance organizational life and employee output. The way you do things, how you dress, express your thoughts and feelings, and how you think (e.g., attitude or approach) is unique to you as an individual; it is your style. A style is a preference—a natural tendency to behave in a way that is comfortable to you.

Communication styles, the manner in which leaders or followers express or enact behaviors, vary among individuals. The messages people produce and the way we interpret messages indicate our communication style. Understanding a leader's or follower's communication style and having the ability to adapt our own communication style are important effectiveness skills. Marston (1928), an American psychologist from Harvard University, developed the theoretical underpinning of the DISC communication styles: driver, influencer, supporter, and contemplator.

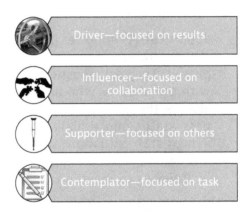

FIGURE 1.6   DISC Styles

Communication scholars have updated the DISC assessment, making it one of the most widely used tools for assessing communication styles of today's employees (Hartman & McCambridge, 2011; Mok, 1975).

- **Driver:** A driver is results-focused. Drivers are task-oriented and desire information as a means to accomplish tasks. They feel a need to understand and ask "what" questions (e.g., what is the purpose? or what should be done to reach a given goal?). The objective is completion or crossing the finish line to produce results. Questions asking, "how," "who," or "why" are secondary in terms of information-seeking and information-giving communication. Others perceive drivers as doers, direct, dominating, demanding, determined; in high-stake situations they may be considered pushy as they attempt to achieve goals and rely on dictating communication (Hartman & McCambridge, 2011). Therefore, the goal for a driver *is* the outcome.

- **Influencer:** Interactive by nature, influencers are "people-persons" and thrive in social settings. They value relationships and desire information to inform their understanding and approach regarding the way something is done when pursuing a goal. They address questions asking "how" (e.g., how does the purpose of the plan achieve our goal? or how can we work together to achieve a given goal?). Influencers can come across as exciting, motivating, inspiring, opinionated, expressive; in high-stake situations, they may use assertive communication that comes across as attacking (Hartman & McCambridge, 2011). The goal for influencers is social interaction; they value enthusiasm and primarily focus on collaboration.

- **Supporter:** A supporter is other-focused. The value relationships and desire information to identify or understand others' roles during goal pursuit. They ask questions concerned with "who" (e.g., who agrees with the plan? or who has the knowledge and expertise needed to achieve the goal?). Alternative aliases for supporters include steadiness, status-quo, amiable, reliable, accommodating, and emotional; in high-stake situations they are most likely to conform (Hartman & McCambridge, 2011). Supporters value sincerity with the ultimate goal of achieving cooperation.

- **Contemplator:** A contemplator is a thinker. Contemplators are task-focused and desire information to understand the reason or logic for something. They primarily address the "why" questions (e.g., why is this plan important? or why did you do it that way?) out of curiosity. Others perceive contemplators as conscientious, analytical, cautious, orderly, and perfectionists; in high-stake settings, they may appear compliant by retreating to their personal knowledge/expertise comfort zone (Hartman & McCambridge, 2011). The goal of a contemplator is quality, valuing excellence and contributing work that meets the highest standards. They prefer to enact behaviors in the most comfortable way, not restricted to only one style of communication.

The way you prefer to interact and how you choose to interact can be different. In a leadership role, being able to analyze the different ways your communication style impacts others and being able to shift communication styles competently are valuable skills. Effective leaders and followers adjust their own style by using DISC knowledge to identify and analyze style preferences of one's self and others. These style-identifying and style-flexing skills are particularly important for communication situations involving leaders and followers who have different communication styles (Hartman & McCambridge, 2011).

CASE STUDY   **Morning Star Company**

Morning Star, a company based in California, is the world's largest tomato processing company. They process tomatoes that become diced or crushed tomatoes, tomato paste, and tomato sauce on your grocery store shelves, among other tomato products. The company, founded by Chris Rufer in 1970, operates under a philosophy of self-management. According to Morning Star,

> "We envision an organization of self-managing professionals who initiate communication and coordination of their activities with fellow colleagues, customers, suppliers and fellow industry participants, absent directives from others. For colleagues to find joy and excitement utilizing their unique talents and to weave those talents into activities which complement and strengthen fellow colleagues' activities. And for colleagues to take personal responsibility and hold themselves accountable for achieving our Mission."

Beyond the organization's self-management philosophy, they articulate their organizational vision, mission, values, and commitment to sustainability.

- Vision: "To be an Olympic Gold Medal performer in the tomato products industry. To develop and implement superior systems of organizing individuals' talents and efforts to achieve demonstrably superior productivity and personal happiness. To develop and implement superior technology and production systems that significantly and demonstrably increase the effective use of resources that match customers' requirements. To provide opportunity for more harmonious and prosperous lives, bringing happiness to ourselves and to the people we serve."

- "Our Mission is to produce tomato products and services which consistently achieve the quality and service expectations of our customers in a cost effective, environmentally responsible manner."

- Values: "To work with fellow colleagues, customers, suppliers and industry participants within a framework of solid integrity and openness in pursuit of voluntary and mutually beneficial transactions and relationships. To maintain our facilities in a clean and orderly condition with a pleasant appearance."

- Sustainability: "Our goal is to ensure a healthy environment. In partnership with our suppliers, we use economically viable practices to protect sensitive areas, improve air, water, soil, and wildlife resources and conserve non-renewable mineral resources. The Morning Star Packing Company and its affiliates reduce waste and pollution through technological innovation, recycling, energy conservation, and limits use of water, pesticide, and nutrient inputs to those biologically required for a successful crop."

(continued)

In an era where people request organizational transparency, Morning Star delivers. On its website, viewers can find an open letter from Rufer that details a dispute between Morning Star and Operation Rotten Tomato. In the letter, Rufer talks about the fact that the organization fell victim to employees who embezzled and stole intellectual property. Similarly, they make available their response to a State of California Water Board $1.5 million dollar fine. While the fine was rescinded, the response was clearly written by Rufer himself and remains posted on the website even though there are errors such as "through the book at us."

As one peruses the documentation available, the reader encounters what happens when an organization chooses to operate outside the societal norms. While they choose not to use titles internally, they still must operate within a culture where titles are valued. For example, Rufer refers to himself as founder, president, operator, and owner in various places. Similarly, on the organization's careers page, it states that "Our company is operated by colleagues without titles or an appointed hierarchy of authority." Yet, like every organization, they have a list of job positions available for potential applicants (truck driver, grower representative, and distribution/warehouse manager).

The company continues to operate under its original self-management philosophy today as it did five decades ago. What remains to seen is whether it will continue to be audacious and an outlier in an age of traditionalism or whether other organizations will adopt similar standards.

DISCUSSION QUESTIONS

1. In our society, labeling is an important process. To what extent would you be able to label followers, leaders, and managers at Morning Star?

2. This chapter discussed seven communication-related behaviors enacted by leaders and followers. To what extent is each present at Morning Star? For the ones that you do not see, are they necessary? Why or why not?

3. Given your own work experiences, how realistic would it be for you to work for an organization such as this one?

ANALYSIS OPTIONS

A. Even in an egalitarian organization such as this one, someone has to be legally responsible for the organization (signs contracts, legal proceedings, etc.). Morning Star's founder has been diagnosed with Alzheimer's disease and can no longer function in that role.

B. Because this organization is the exception rather than the norm, the process of vetting, hiring, and socializing new organizational members is critical to its success. You have been hired to oversee these processes.

C. *Inc.* has referred to Morning Star as an organization with all leaders and no bosses (managers). The organization has begun receiving negative press for operating like a cult. Headlines include "Everyone drinks the poison and is willing to accept lower wages because they do not have a title"; "Self-management is another name for blind follower"; and "Someone has to have final authority in any organization." Because of this press, Morning Star finds itself in a position where the only applicants are friends and family members of current employees, which potentially hinders the organization's ability to remain innovative.

ANALYSIS PROCESS

- Brainstorm a list of options for addressing the issue.

- Make a list of strengths and challenges for each of your brainstormed solutions.

- Choose the best solution for the issue.

- Develop an implementation plan for your chosen solution.

- Additional resources:

I, Tomato: Morning Star's Approach to Self-Management on YouTube
https://tiny.utk.edu/FCL1_1

Morning Star Farms self-management site
https://tinyurl.com/y27579zx

Morning Star Farms corporate site
https://tinyurl.com/mjhcb23

DISC Assessment
https://tiny.utk.edu/FCL1_2

DISCUSSION QUESTIONS AND ACTIVITIES

1. How would you define the culture on your campus? What subcultures and countercultures exist on campus? What are the similarities and differences between the cultures with which the administration and the students identify?

2. Of the approaches to ethics, which do you believe is most important for leaders and followers in today's organizations? Why? Would your answers be different for different types of organizations? Why?

3. Go to https://tinyurl.com/y29f9yqa to complete your free DISC assessment. Based upon what your assessment says, what are your followership and leadership strengths and areas for improvement? If you were going to work on changing one of these areas, which would it be and why? What can you do to better prepare yourself for the world of work that lies ahead?

4. Being able to develop and implement a vision is the primary communication difference between followers and leaders. Create an organization that interests you (no cheating by making it similar to something that already exists). What you would propose as the vision? Why? What types of followers would be most likely to be part of your organization? Why?

5. Pair up with another student and choose one local and one national organization or workplace. Based upon the information you can find online and/or your personal experiences, would you define the person in charge as a leader or manager? Why? How well do the followers enact the communication competencies? Provide specific examples to illustrate your ratings.

Fig. 1.6a: Source: https://pixabay.com/photos/classic-car-blue-classic-car-76401/.

Fig. 1.6b: Source: https://pixabay.com/vectors/silhouette-joining-together-puzzle-3425581/.

Fig. 1.6c: Source: https://pixabay.com/illustrations/crutch-support-medical-care-health-2717745/.

Fig. 1.6d: Source: https://pixabay.com/vectors/checklist-task-to-do-list-plan-1295319/.

CHAPTER 2

HISTORICAL APPROACHES TO LEADERSHIP

"I am not afraid of an army of lions led by a sheep;
I am afraid of an army of sheep led by a lion."

—ALEXANDER THE GREAT

"I suppose leadership at one time meant muscles;
but today it means getting along with people."

—MAHATMA GHANDI

When you think about a famous historical leader (from at least 100 years ago), who comes to mind? _____, _____, and _____. What are the first three characteristics that come to mind? _____, _____, and _____. If you subscribe to the same philosophy as the early leadership theorists, your list probably contained qualities such as male, tall, attractive, intelligent, and even muscular, as Ghandi said. We have come a long way in the last 100 years of leadership studies; it is important to understand where leadership, and for the moment we mean leadership without considering followership, research began.

FIGURE 2.1   Two Sides of the Same Coin

The coin pictured above illustrates the early leadership studies. We only focused on leadership with the leaders being considered the actors in the play of life and the followers as passive recipients of their influence, authority, and positional responsibilities.

Historical Overview

A historical overview of leadership approaches can become monotonous and boring to read, just as history can be boring if it is presented as a series of dates, events, and people. Appreciating a historical perspective is all about the story someone tells. To help with the leadership historical perspective, we have chosen the wild world of animals to illustrate the various ways classical leadership has been conceptualized.

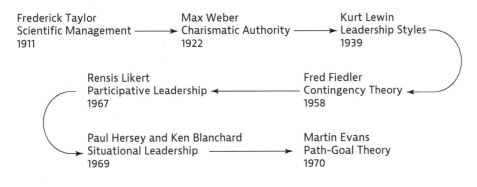

FIGURE 2.2   Historical Timeline

Scientific Management

While it is not considered a leadership theory, Frederick Taylor's (1911) theory of scientific management served as the foundation for early leadership theories. **Scientific management** focuses on finding the most efficient means to complete a task. According to Taylor, employees who are working on the front lines are in the best position to help an organization innovate and find the procedures that use the least number of resources. Resources may be the amount of time, the amount of energy or electricity, or the number of steps a specific process takes. Scientific management has four basic principles:

- Use the scientific method to determine what processes are most efficient instead of using the "tried and true" method that has been in place.

- All workers should be matched with the job or piece of the process for which they are best equipped; being equipped for a job means that they have the necessary skills (or can learn to do them in the most efficient manner possible) and the motivation to do the job.

- Oversee all employees to ensure they are performing the tasks most efficiently and provide appropriate instruction or training when necessary.

- Divide the work between workers who do the physical work and managers who do the mental work, so that they are each contributing to completing the task in the most efficient manner possible.

Think about an assembly line as that was the classical example of scientific management in action. Everyone had a specific task on the assembly line, and they were required to do it in the one best way as determined by researching all possible ways of doing the task to determine the most efficient one. The one best way went so far as to tell employees how much time they had to do each task and subtask, exactly how each body part (hand, head, arm, leg) was to move to complete the task, and what the quota was for each shift.

When music came on CDs instead of being downloaded from the cloud, each case sold in stores had to be assembled by hand. One person was responsible for opening the plastic cases and sliding them down to the next person who inserted the cover art. That person passed them to the next person who snapped the CD in place, so it did not move or get scratched during shipping and handling. The next person received the open case and was responsible for closing it and passing it on to the finisher, who loaded them into cases of 24 for shipping to stores.

After the boxes were loaded, a group in another department was responsible for creating the boxes, taping the loaded boxes shut, adding the shipping labels, and making sure they went to the appropriate place for shipping. All of this was done with cameras in place so management could watch to make sure that people were performing the tasks as they were designed, remaining efficient, and meeting their quotas. As you can imagine, manual laborers were not happy with management watching them and many of them went out on strike for better working conditions and more satisfying employment.

Few people talk about or practice scientific management in its pure form today; however, the idea of managers and employees working together has become the basis for teamwork in today's organizations. Over time, we have also learned that there may be more than one way of doing each task instead of only ONE BEST WAY. Finally, scientific management has clarified the relationship between rewards and productivity.

Charismatic Authority

Max Weber (1922), a German sociologist, proposed charismatic authority long before the notions of charismatic leadership, a contemporary approach, existed. Charismatic was originally a religious term in which certain members of the church received divine intervention, a gift from God, to be predestined to become leaders (priests, pastors, ministers). Weber took these religious inclinations and generalized them to apply to a variety of leaders.

Specifically, **charismatic authority leadership** involves possessing certain exceptional or supernatural qualities, including being male, that set one apart from other organizational members; on the basis of possessing those qualities, others deem that person to be the leader. Nearly 40 years later, this became known as referent power. Because power and authority are instilled in a single individual, a succession plan must be created to minimize the possibility of the organization, government, or society ceasing to exist upon the leader's death or inability to continue leading.

While he led more than 25 years ago, David Koresh headed a splinter group of the Branch Davidians and serves as an excellent modern-day example of charismatic authority. He and his devout followers of the "Doctrine of David" lived at the Mount Carmel Center near Waco, Texas. After the authorities raided the compound in search of illegal firearms, a 51-day standoff ensued. Federal agents died. Koresh stalled his surrender as he continued to write his doctrine for the next generation of followers and released children who were not his direct blood descendants who would become the next generation of leaders.

Ultimately, Attorney General Janet Reno approved an ATF (Alcohol, Tobacco, and Firearms) tear gas raid to smoke everyone out of the compound. The compound caught fire and everyone inside died, including children. People were willing to follow him because they believed he was their savior and died because they blindly, without question, followed his charismatic authority and teachings. His succession plan completes the charismatic authority circle.

Leadership Styles

One of the difficulties when multiple people in different disciplines study a topic is that the same word can be used to mean different things. During our journey through leadership time, styles will be used in different approaches to leadership to mean different things. We will do our best to help you keep them straight; just know that you have to be specific about whose version you're referencing when you use the phrase, "leadership style." In this case, Kurt Lewin (1939) defined three leadership styles: autocratic, democratic, and laissez-faire. While many of us prefer to have a leader who uses one of these styles, they are each appropriate for different types of organizations.

Autocratic leaders use communication to exert power over their followers and behave in a dictatorial manner. Followers are passive recipients of their leaders' orders. The relationship between leaders and followers is viewed as a transaction in which the leader provides instruction and compensation in exchange for following commands and productivity: "Come to work, do the job as I tell you to do it, and you will receive a paycheck at the end of the week." In these types of organizations, leaders and followers primarily discuss the task at hand if they speak to each other at all. Autocratic leaders are often successful in bureaucratic organizations where followers need significant help with the task at hand (i.e., the military), in new organizations where the founders are the only ones with the knowledge necessary to move the organization forward (e.g., a local small business), and in organizations with employees who lack the motivation to complete the task (e.g., minimum-wage jobs at fast-food restaurants or crop harvesters in the heat of the summer sun).

FIGURE 2.3   Mountain gorillas are similar to autocratic leaders.

Mountain gorillas (western lowland gorillas and silverback gorillas) illustrate what it means to be an autocratic leader. As the leader, the dominant gorilla is male, the oldest, and the strongest. He is the protector and primary decision-maker for his troop. He takes on the responsibility of protecting the troop from enemies, finding sites to feed and rest, resolving conflict, and deciding when to eat and sleep. In exchange, the male gorilla leader has exclusive rights to mate with the females in his troop and receives dominant portions of food. He is both feared and adored by the females and infants in his troop.

Democratic leaders use communication to invite followers to participate in the decision-making process and share power. Followers are active contributors to the day-to-day organizational happenings; leaders solicit their input when decisions must be made that affect everyone involved in the organization. The relationship between leaders and followers is viewed as an interaction or transaction in which they engage in mutual influence as well as use communication to advance task, relational, and identity goals. Democratic leaders are often successful in communal organizations (food cooperatives), organizations with few layers between the top and bottom (e.g., a customer service call center), teams with structured goals and long-term knowledgeable members (e.g., synagogues, churches).

FIGURE 2.4   American buffalo are similar to democratic leaders.

In the animal kingdom, democratic leadership is demonstrated by American buffalos (i.e., bison). Members of the herd vote for their travel preferences by standing up and staring in the direction they want to go toward, then laying down again. The group follows the leader if he/she initiates movement in the direction preferred by most members. If the leader chooses to initiate movement toward a less popular direction, then few members follow.

Laissez-faire leaders have been labeled as un-leaders because of their hands-off approach to followers. The term laissez-faire comes from French and roughly translates as "let others do as they choose." In **laissez-faire leadership**, neither leaders nor followers use communication to influence each other or engage in decision making processes. Very little communication transpires between leaders and followers regarding task goals; while there may be communication regarding relational and identity goals, the hands-off approach of laissez-faire leaders does not promote communication. Laissez-faire leaders may exist in any type of organization, often because they do not know how to promote a vision and interact with followers; however, they are generally most effective in organizations where the followers are mature, knowledgeable, and motivated. Warren Buffet of Berkshire Hathaway has surrounded himself with competent individuals who serve as leaders, which allows him to take a hands-off approach and remain the face of the organization. Steve Jobs of Apple also successfully used laissez-faire leadership by telling his employees what he needed and allowing them complete freedom to make decisions and use their creativity to develop innovative products and solutions.

FIGURE 2.5   Despite their King of the Jungle moniker, lions actually exhibit laissez-faire leadership.

When we see or think about the lion, many of us are struck by the majestic mane, robust body, or the fear-inducing roar. Despite the lion's ferocious and powerful looks (and sounds), the lion portrays laissez-faire leadership quite well once we understand its behavior. Lion prides typically consist of approximately six related lionesses, their dependent cubs, and two or three males (i.e., coalition). Within the coalition of male lions, there is a leader. As the leader, the lion protects their territory from other coalitions (other groups of males), but they don't hunt or take the lead on making decisions for the pride. Lions patrol, eat, sleep, and mate. It is the lionesses that hunt, make decisions, and protect their territories against other females and enemies (e.g., hyenas, wolves, wild dogs) for the pride. As the leader, the lion gets to eat first; however, they spend very little time interacting with the majority of the pride. It is this hands-off approach of the lion and their minimal communication (or influence) with other members of the pride regarding tasks that captures the essence of laissez-faire leadership.

Trait Approaches

Leadership traits theory became known as the "great man theory" because researchers only studied men and believed that only men could be leaders. Historically, at the beginning of the 20th century, after women were no longer considered the property of their husbands and before they gained the right to vote in America, men held almost all of the public leadership positions. Over 100 years later, we have yet to see a women president in America and the majority of Fortune 100 and 500 company leaders continue to be men (approximately 5% of Fortune 500 companies are women; Wiener-Bronner, 2017). Thus, being born male and being born to be a leader were at the top of the traits list. In the 1940s and 1950s, two researchers compiled similar lists after examining the trait theory literature: social, self-confident, responsible, persistent, masculine, intelligent, insightful, initiator, extroverted, dominant, conservative, adaptive, and alert (Mann, 1959; Stogdill, 1948).

After looking at over 100 more studies, Stogdill (1974) created a list of the traits most commonly found in leaders. These included: 1. Drive to be responsible and complete tasks; 2. Vigorous pursuit of goals; 3. Take risks and engage in novel problem solving; 4. Take the initiative in social situations; 5. Demonstrate self-confidence and self-identity; 6. Accept consequences for one's decisions and actions; 7. Ready and able to handle stress; 8. Tolerant of frustration and delay; 9. Able to influence others' behaviors; and 10. Capable of structuring systems of social interaction. Take a careful look at Stogdill's list—how many of those characteristics are actually traits with which people are born? In reality, all of them are qualities that people can develop over time AND if they were truly traits, then there would be no reason for you to waste your time and money enrolled in a class about leadership—that is why trait theories and approaches to leadership have not withstood the test of time. When trait research failed to elicit the magic bullet combination of traits necessary for being an effective leader, researchers turned their attention to specific behaviors that effective leaders may use.

Even though dinosaurs lived in prehistoric times, our anthropological indications of their traits match the classical leadership approach. First, dinosaurs are almost always male in every rendition we see of them. We know there had to be females to procreate and keep the species alive; however, we do not see that indicated in modern renditions. Second, dinosaurs were tall, often standing above many treetops. Dinosaurs, when standing on their hind legs stretched 40 to 85 feet in the air. Third, like the trait approaches that have become extinct as we have recognized leaders are not born with a set of traits they are meant to use in their leadership roles, dinosaurs no longer walk the earth.

FIGURE 2.6 Dinosaurs and classical leadership traits are similar.

Behavioral Approaches

Two research studies conducted at The Ohio State University (1940s) and the University of Michigan (1950s) served as the basis for behavioral theories of leadership. Through a series of studies in which the researchers narrowed down a list of over 1800 behaviors to approximately 150, they determined that leaders are more or less focused on initiating structure and more or less focused on consideration. **Initiating structure** behaviors involve providing clear expectations for the leader-subordinate relationship, creating formal lines of communication (usually verbal or written), and determining how tasks will be performed (a remnant of scientific management). **Consideration** behaviors involve establishing a warm and welcoming climate for subordinates, building trust, and showing concern for subordinates. At this point in history, even though consideration is specifically about building interpersonal relationships, the term "subordinates" continues to be used to indicate the power differential and hierarchical differences between leaders or managers and their employees.

At approximately the same time, studies at the University of Michigan set out to determine what leader behaviors and styles contribute to productivity and employee satisfaction. From these studies René Likert and his colleagues identified task-oriented behaviors and relationship-oriented behaviors. **Task-oriented behaviors** included providing needed resources, coordinating people's work efforts, and planning how the work would get done. **Relationship-oriented behaviors** included offering help and support, providing guidelines to achieve goals, and recognizing the value of internal reward systems (not everyone is motivated by external rewards such as pay, but may complete a task because it makes them feel valued, important, and a part of the team). It should not be surprising that the researchers set out to examine what contributes to productivity and satisfaction and came up with task (productivity) and relational (satisfaction) behaviors—today we would call this confirmation bias (finding what we set out to find). Rather than dismissing these studies for failing to meet basic research standards, they complemented The Ohio State University studies well and became the foundation for the Managerial/Leadership Grid.

TABLE 2.1   Behavioral Leadership

	Low Initiating Structure or Task Orientation	⟶	High Initiating Structure or Task Orientation
High Consideration or Relationship Orientation	Country Club or Accommodating Leader		Team or Sound Leader
↓		Middle of the Road or Status Quo Leader	
Low Consideration or Relationship Orientation	Impoverished or Indifferent Leader		"Produce or Perish" or Dictatorial Leader

Country Club Leaders

Blake and Mouton (1974) combine the findings from The Ohio State University and University of Michigan studies to develop what they labeled as the managerial grid. While the title includes managerial, the labels within the grid focus on leadership styles. A **country club or accommodating leader** shows a high concern for the employees' well-being and a low concern for productivity. They believe that being friendly and supporting their followers leads to increased productivity. These leaders rely upon reward power to keep their followers satisfied. In what situations do you believe you would want a country club leader? Maybe a small group bible study where the goal is less about completing a specific, time-oriented task and more about building rapport among the members. What about a service project leader for a sorority or fraternity—could a country club leader be effective there?

FIGURE 2.7 Dogs are awesome pets because they almost always accommodate their humans and make them feel as if they are at the country club.

Dogs are considered humans' best friend. What makes them similar to accommodating or country club behavioral leaders is their low focus on the tasks at hand and their high focus on the relationship. Think about it— dogs have few task-oriented needs: being walked (or at least let out in the yard to run around), being fed/hydrated, and occasionally being groomed. On the relationship side of things, everything is about their connection to their humans. No matter how bad a human's day was, the dog is there to snuggle, cuddle, or play. Dogs themselves rarely have a bad day so humans can always count on them to be cheerful, positive, and eager to reconnect at the end of a long day.

Team Leaders

Team or sound leaders show a high concern for the employees' well-being and a high concern for productivity. They believe that the task and relationship must be balanced to achieve the best outcomes for both the organization and the relationship. Because they seek balance, they are open to using a variety of power bases, including expert, informational, referent, reward, and legitimate. Because coercive power is likely to damage the relationship, they generally avoid it. If you were to ask 10 people on the street, how many of them do you think would like to have a team leader? On the surface, their concern for individual employees and their concern for the task at hand seem like an ideal combination. In reality, they have their place in organizational life just as all other leadership styles do. Sound leaders are most effective in growing organizations where the followers still need guidance about how to do the task and appreciate the individualized attention. They are also the leaders who are most likely to burn out because they expend significant amounts of time and energy on the task and relationships with little down time for themselves.

FIGURE 2.8   Bottlenose dolphins show us what it means to be a team leader.

Bottlenose dolphins serve as an example of team (or sound) leaders. There is a social hierarchy in bottlenose dolphin pods (i.e., groups). When the pod hunts or needs to swim to safety away from enemies, the leader is responsible for guiding the direction of travel. Their social nature of interacting with each other creates close bonds and further contributes to their task productivity, which includes hunting, mating, and defending themselves. This balance between the relationship and task that reflects the team-leader style can be seen in nursery pods (mothers and offspring), juvenile pods (youth leaving the nursery pod to join other young dolphins), and adult male pods (male partnerships created for cooperation purposes).

Middle of the Road Leaders

Moderate concern for the task and moderate concern for the relationship characterize middle of the road leaders. In their effort to balance attention to the task and attention to the individual, status quo leaders seek to avoid conflict while promoting harmony and rarely rely upon their power bases. For example, if confronting an employee about not making the required number of potential sales calls is likely to promote a defensive climate in the office, the status quo leader refrains from discussing the issue in the hopes that it will resolve itself. As a compromiser, middle-of-the-road leaders focus

FIGURE 2.9   Meerkats split their time between tasks and relationships.

enough attention on neither the task nor the relationship. Consequently, neither is adequately addressed. These leaders tend to be most effective in mature organizations where the employees know how to complete their tasks in a timely and efficient manner, there is little variation in the tasks, and they possess enough efficacy to know they are making a meaningful contribution to the organization. Workplace acquaintances and friends, as opposed to the leader, fulfill the employees' relational goals.

Meerkats are indigenous to African desserts. They live underground in groups of approximately 30. As burrowers, their primary task is to continue creating an underground maze that serves as their habitat. During the day, especially during the heat of the day, they leave the underground to search for food and water. When members of the underground colony leave, others perform the task role of standing guard to warn others of predators; if a predator signal is sounded, all meerkats from the colony find the closest entrance and return home to safety. The importance of being social is illustrated when they groom each other and even when they take in other animals to protect them from predators.

Impoverished Leaders

Impoverished or Indifferent Leaders have low concern for production and low concern for employee well-being. Because impoverished leaders have maintaining their organizational position as the primary goal, they avoid becoming involved so that they cannot be blamed for any mistakes or errors that occur. When risk taking is minimized by the leader and the followers, less innovation occurs, and the department or organization stagnates. Indifferent leaders evade interacting with others, so they are unlikely to use any of the power bases; if they do use one, it is most likely to be legitimate power. Given that they have become leaders, there had to be a time when they were not withdrawn from the organization's mission and their followers' satisfaction. By delegating what needs to be done to competent followers, impoverished leaders ensure that their unit's work contributes to the overall organization's needs. While indifferent leadership would not work for many organizational members, followers who are solely focused on the task and have little interest in developing workplace relationships prefer this leadership form. Some professions that might fit this bill are computer programmers, long-haul truck drivers, and sales representatives who spend the majority of their time outside the office.

Everyone knows about sloths being slow, which makes them significantly less task-oriented than many of their counterparts in the wild. What few people know is that sloths are also solitary animals who prefer to be alone rather than with other animals, including other sloths. Their idea of a perfect day is leisurely hanging out in a tree watching the world go by; impoverished leaders are very similar in that they are quite content to sit in their offices,

FIGURE 2.10   Sloths are known for being slow, solitary, and sedentary.

read reports from their followers, and send an email or two each week to make sure the followers know what they should be doing.

Produce or Perish Leaders

Finally, **"produce or perish" or dictatorial leaders** have high concern for productivity and low concern for employee satisfaction. Because the task is their primary concern, dictatorial leaders are more likely to use coercive, expert, informational, reward, and legitimate power—whatever it takes to make sure their followers complete the task correctly and in a timely manner. Relationship building, follower motivation, and communication are low priorities for produce or perish leaders; instead they focus on planning, developing procedures, and how task completion contributes to the larger organizational mission. These leaders tend to be most effective in organizations operating in crisis mode with highly structured, short-term tasks. If you think about an operating room, a house on fire, or a hostage situation, you are going to want a dictatorial leader who can save the patient, make sure the family escapes from the burning building, and the hostages walk out of the situation unharmed. These leaders are also highly effective in organizations that find themselves in crisis situations. In 2017, United Airlines needed a leader who could help them recover from video of a passenger forcibly being pulled off of an overbooked airplane.

FIGURE 2.11   Tigers are the true dictators in the jungle.

While many claim that lions are the king of the jungle, the real kings, and queens, are tigers. Male tigers are solitary animals who interact primarily for mating purposes; female tigers are also solitary, except for when they are caring for their offspring. Rather than interacting with others, tigers focus on protecting their territory—the most important task in the jungle. They spend their days making sure that other animals understand where they may complete their required survival tasks, and that does not include being in a tiger's space.

Contingency Theory

Fred Fiedler (1967) created a theory of leadership effectiveness. Unlike the other theories in this chapter, his primary concern was not about how leaders communicated or interacted with followers, but rather about making sure leaders understood their preferred leadership style and used it to be the most effective leader they could be. For Fiedler, leadership was not a set of skills that should be taught—it was a way of life that grew out of a leader's experiences. Rather than trying to change the leader, leaders should attempt to change how tasks are structured to match their leadership. Restructuring tasks is more feasible in organizations where the leader has significant power over the situation, especially with respect to salary/ promotions (reward power) and discipline (legitimate and potentially coercive power). Another key assumption highlights the role of stress between leaders and their superiors and subordinates. When stressful situations arise, leaders expend more energy on the relationship than on the task and cannot use their expert power or intelligence. In stressful situations, leaders must rely upon their experience rather than their intelligence. Thus, experienced leaders are more effective in high-stress situations and newer leaders are more effective in low-stress situations. In sum, leaders' personal characteristics and motivation should match the team's situation so that leadership effectiveness is no longer about traits, behaviors, or skills.

To assess leadership style, Fiedler developed the **Least Preferred Coworker (LPC) Scale**, which measures the type of people with whom the leader has worked well and poorly over the course of one's lifetime (it is filled out once for each type of follower). Different versions of the scale have been used over time as researchers have refined the items and tried to make it more reliable and valid with fewer items. Regardless of the version, the leader circles a number between two bipolar adjectives that best describes the least or most preferred coworker. All of the adjective pairs address personality and relational characteristics rather than performance and task characteristics: rejecting-accepting, backbiting-loyal, agreeable-disagreeable, distant-close, and quarrelsome-harmonious to name a few. When administering the scale, leaders must understand that there are no right or wrong answers and the more honest they are the more likely they are to end up in leadership situations where they are going to be most effective.

At the end of the scale, the leader receives a total score based upon the numbers circled. Higher scores indicate a more relational orientation to leadership and lower scores indicate a more task orientation to leadership. If you were asked to describe someone you disliked working with on a group project, how many positive adjectives would you use to describe the person? Would you even use any? If you answered no, you are like the majority of the human race. In rare instances, when leaders are focused almost exclusively on the relationship, or lying, do they choose more positive characteristics for a least preferred coworker? This scale assumes that leaders who do not prefer to work with a person will choose numbers closer to the negative adjectives and leaders who do prefer to work with a person will choose numbers closer to the positive adjectives; the scale is more about leaders and their motivations than about followers.

Once leaders have completed the scale and know with whom they prefer and do not prefer to work, it is time to match them to the appropriate situation. Only when leaders can control the situation can they be confident the followers will listen to them and carry out the tasks they assign.

Organizations need both high- and low-LPC leaders to be successful because both the task and relationship are important. To determine which type of leader is most appropriate for the situation, three situational factors must be considered: leader's position power, leader-follower relations, and task explicitness. Based upon combinations of those three aspects, a continuum exists between the most favorable and least favorable conditions for leadership; extreme favorable and extreme unfavorable conditions are best for a low LPC leader who focuses primarily on the task.

Unfavorable	Favorable
Unstructured	Highly Structured
Low Legitimate Power	High Legitimate Power
Weak Leader-Follower Relations	Strong Leader-Follower Relations

For every other combination of situational characteristics (one or two characteristics are favorable, and one or two characteristics are unfavorable), a high LPC leader who is more interested in the relationship is going to be more effective. Given that extreme conditions are rare in most organizations, being a *natural* high LPC leader is beneficial (remember, Fiedler argued that we cannot teach you to be high or low LPC; it is part of who you are).

Think about leaders you have had or seen over the years. For how many of them would this theory have worked? How often do you find yourself in a highly favorable or highly unfavorable situation? Most of our lives do not work at the extremes; we often find ourselves caught somewhere in the middle. When was the last time everyone scored between 95 and 100 or between 0 and 5 on an exam? When was the last time you or a parent/guardian worked in an organization where the task was always highly structured, followers had a strong relationship with the leader, and the leader had control over resources such as pay and promotions? Can you think of a volunteer situation in which the task is completely unstructured and there are poor relationships between leaders and followers? Life, and interactions, are messy or complex and that is why Fiedler's contingency theory does not translate well into most workplaces.

Rats are smarter, and likely more relationally driven, than we humans tend to give them credit for or ever knew. Their social hierarchy (pecking order) consists of an alpha rat (the leader), beta rats (second in command), followed by other lower level rats. Beta rats and other lower level rats in the hierarchy are considered helper-rats to the alpha. Like Fiedler's contingency theory, alpha rats recognize whether a helper-rat is a high-quality helper or a low-quality helper. Alpha rats have been shown to remember acts of kindness by other rats and reciprocate, reward, or favor them accordingly (Martin, 2015). Because alpha rats have a large effect on how other members of the group complete daily tasks, function as a group, and generally feel, being a high LPC alpha may be a key factor in the effectiveness and longevity of that particular alpha rat's group.

FIGURE 2.12   Rats are similar to leaders who adopt a contingency approach to leadership.

Path-Goal Theory

Bellbottoms, roller skates, sideburns, music festivals, and path-goal theory—all of these burst on the scene in popularity during the 1970s. The 1970s in American culture has been labeled as being the time of "sex, drugs, and rock 'n' roll." It comes as no surprise that scholars became interested in how leader behaviors influence followers' satisfaction and motivation at work. Indeed, the 1970s have long passed; however, path-goal theory remains a rockin' (maybe with a slower roll, but definitely still a rockin') theory of leadership today. Path-goal theory assumes leaders select and tailor behaviors (directive, supportive, participative, and achievement-oriented) depending on the characteristics of the follower and the situation, paving a path that leads to follower satisfaction, competence, and overall goal attainment.

The story of path-goal theory begins with Martin Evans' (1970) notion that a leader's behavior (path) relates to followers' outcomes (goals); the extent to which the path (behavior) is perceived to help or hinder followers in goal attainment. The work of House (1971) and House and Mitchell (1974) expanded upon this foundational idea proposing effective leader behavior is: 1) satisfying to followers when followers see the behavior as satisfying or as a source of satisfaction and 2) motivates followers when the behavior meets followers' individual needs and facilitates effective performance by providing coaching, guidance, support and rewards to complement the environment of followers. As such, House and Mitchell (1974) identify four types of leadership behavior focused on meeting these criteria in a given situation: directive, supportive, participative, and achievement-oriented.

Directive behavior focuses on offering and explaining structure for followers by expressing expectations, offering relevant guidance for task completion, providing task instructions and timelines, and explaining policies and procedures (House, 1996). The goal of directive behavior is clarification. Directive behaviors reduce role ambiguity (Cote, 2017) and can serve as an expectancy yard stick for followers to understand how and to what extent their efforts measure up to expectations concerning performance, rewards, and organizational goals.

Friendliness and showing concern for followers' well-being characterizes **supportive behavior**, which aims to satisfy followers' needs and preferences. The goal of supportive behavior is psychological support. Supportive behaviors effect followers' performance by tapping into one's individual and social needs. For example, if a follower is completing a task that is unsatisfying or frustrating, a leader's supportive behavior can boost confidence, mitigate stress and frustration, and generally provide positive effects on overall satisfaction (Cote, 2017). In the music business, the effects of supportive behavior enacted by Goddard Lieberson, the 1970s' head of Columbia records, encouraged the self-esteem and creativity of his followers, music artists such as Pink Floyd, Billy Joel, Carolos Santana, Barbara Streisand, and Aerosmith (Vandegrift & Matusitz, 2011).

Participative behavior encourages followers' voice, to openly offer opinions, suggestions, and criticisms as well as partake in decision-making. The goal of participative behavior is engagement (involvement). Participative behavior serves to increase satisfaction and goal achievement by providing followers the opportunity to think innovatively, collaborate, and utilize voice to successfully complete tasks. We see participative leadership behavior occur within the matriarchal (female-led) societies formed by African elephants. Leaders are typically the oldest and most dominant females. This is because they are well-connected, charismatic, and wise, especially when it comes to remembering locations for rare food and water resources. As the leader, she has a strong influence on what other members do, but also expects other members to speak up and participate in decision-making. There are cases when a matriarch loses her argument to the collective will of other members in the group after she has made a suggestion about a decision that balances the needs of the group (avoiding unnecessary travel while remembering when and where good resources are available) or what anti-predator strategy the family should adopt.

Achievement-oriented behavior stimulates optimal performance by setting performance goals challenging followers to improve, strive to meet standards of excellence, and boost confidence (House, 1996). The goal of achievement-oriented behavior is competence in both performance and ability. Understanding the personal characteristics and abilities of a follower is particularly important for achievement-oriented behavior. Pushing a follower's limits and challenging within reason of their unique capabilities can heighten their confidence and motivate them to achieve goals with higher standards; however, pushing too hard or unrealistic challenging will be ineffective and likely cause the reverse effect.

FIGURE 2.13 Llamas are the perfect path-goal animals. They adapt well to the world and people around them.

Llamas are relatives of the camel and both are similar when it comes to their ecosystem roles. Llamas are known for being very goal- and achievement-oriented as they transport goods for people in South America. However, do not let that fool you, because they are still social creatures and will only engage in tasks up to a certain point. Llamas have been known to "fall down" on the job because they need some "me" time away from the task at hand. When this happens, other llamas come to their rescue and the sense of community is restored. They have voices, or at least behaviors such as sitting down and not moving that act as voices, to let their leaders know when they have had enough.

Situational Leadership

Originally called the life cycle theory of leadership, Hersey and Blanchard (1977) later renamed it as situational leadership theory. This theory serves as the transition between theories and approaches focused solely on the leader, and more contemporary theories in chapter three where followers are recognized, celebrated, and active participants in the leader-follower relationship. This theory is the first one to take followers' needs seriously and explicitly acknowledge that different followers may have different leadership needs. Imagine having worked in an organization for all of your time in high school/college and still having a leader who treats you as if you do not know how to do the job. Most followers would become frustrated, question their ability to do the job and be successful there, have a serious discussion with their leader, and/or leave the organization in favor of one where they will be treated better. As you read the theory's description below, you will see that Hersey and Blanchard's theory is more about managers than leaders (they wrote specifically about the supervisor-subordinate relationship); this is another reason why it is so critical to understand and use terminology to promote shared meaning and understanding.

According to situational leadership theory, followers mature during their time in the organization from newbies (think about first-year students on your college campus) to experienced workers (think about seniors on your campus). At each stage in the process, the leadership they need differs and leaders must adapt their leadership communication to meet the needs of their followers. When followers first arrive at the organization, they are considered to be at the first level of maturity. M1 followers are willing to perform the task and unable to do so without someone providing directions. L1 Leaders should communicate almost exclusively to meet the situation's instrumental goals as they teach the new person how to do the job. Assume you are a new intern at a local radio station. When you first arrive, you are excited about the prospect of learning about the business, practicing your communication skills, and being surrounded by your favorite musical genre. At this point, you know almost nothing about producing a broadcast, transitioning between advertisements or public service announcements and music, and handling various media (phone, social media, internet web page) listeners use to communicate with the station. The goal is to learn how to do all of these things during your semester as an intern. On day 1, the leader may show you all of the equipment and introduce your responsibilities for the next few weeks of your internship. Each day will bring additional knowledge about the way things work at this radio station.

As followers progress, they become more familiar with the tasks they must complete each day and week to achieve the team's and organization's goals. **M2 followers** are still learning how to do the necessary tasks even though they have built more confidence. **L2 leaders** act as coaches by continuing to provide any remaining task-oriented communication and also engaging in relationship-oriented communication to ensure the followers remain confident in their abilities to do the task. If we go back to our internship example at the radio station, you have learned the basics necessary to handle communication with listeners, understand how to use the equipment to transition between songs and advertisements or public service announcements, and produce a show that is pleasing to the listeners. Your confidence is building and your "coach" is there whenever you have a question to instill more confidence and help you work through the situation so that you will be able to do it alone next time.

A second level of moderate maturity also occurs at this point in the workplace life cycle. **M3 followers** possess the necessary skills to complete the job and lack the motivation or willingness to do the job. This can happen because the job has become routine and boring, nothing new is being learned, or the followers determine this is not the job they are interested in doing over the long term. **L3 leaders** focus the majority of their communication on relationship-oriented goals to help followers understand the importance of continuing to make meaningful contributions to the team or department and supporting their motivation both externally (reward power) and internally (helping them see how and why they can be self-motivated). Back to our internship example. This is the point where the novelty of being an intern at a great location has worn off and it becomes the daily checklist of tasks to complete. It may be at this point that you determine working at a radio station is not what you thought it would be (somewhere in the back of your mind you saw the celebrity status of being "on the air" and that has not happened or did not go as well as you hoped). What was excitement at the beginning of the internship now seems like drudgery as you get up each day and drag yourself to work.

As you can see in Table 2.2, the second and third levels are listed interchangeably. While Hersey and Blanchard conceived the theory as it is presented in the table and text, others have questioned whether someone who is motivated (willing) and lacking skills (unable) should be considered more mature than someone who is unmotivated (unwilling) and possess the skills (able). When we think about teaching students, we would much prefer to have someone who is willing and unable than someone who is able and unwilling. As a teacher (or leader), we can help students (followers) develop their skills; what we cannot typically do is motivate someone because external rewards do not generally lead to long-term behavior changes. That is, a grade can only motivate a student until it is time for the next assignment or exam. The same is true of followers—a raise is a short-term motivator that wears off quickly; generally, only when followers have internal satisfaction from a job well done will they continue to perform that job to the best of their ability.

TABLE 2.2 Situational Leadership Life Cycle

	Level 1	Level 2/3	Level 2/3	Level 4
Follower Maturity Levels	Novices	Confident	Capable	Established
Leadership Styles	Directing Telling Guiding	Coaching Selling Persuading	Supporting Participating Problem-Solving	Delegating Observing Monitoring
Communication	One-way communication in which the leader provides primarily task-oriented communication	Two-way communication in which the leader continues to provide task guidance when needed and the two have high relationship-oriented communication	Two-way communication focused primarily on relationship-oriented communication as the leader attempts to motivate the follower	Minimal task- and relationship-oriented communication as leaders expect their followers to be assigned a task and carry it out to the best of their ability with little oversight

At the final stage in the life cycle, followers have reached their highest maturity level. **M4 followers** are established workers who know how to perform their tasks and are both comfortable and confident doing them. For these followers, **L4 leaders** engage in delegating communication where they provide the follower with a set of responsibilities and allow the person to develop the path necessary to complete those tasks. M4 employees can solve problems on their own and do not need significant amounts of relationship-oriented communication. They are both willing and able to perform the job. Having said that, leaders still need to provide appropriate amounts of positive feedback and challenges to make sure the followers remain willing and able. If we go back to the internship example, as an M4 follower, you may find yourself in a situation where the leader allows you to do a half-hour broadcast by yourself—you get to create the song line-up, handle social media posts from the audience, and run the equipment on your own. The leader may be in another room or another part of the building listening to the broadcast and there to congratulate you on a job well done when it is over.

As you saw earlier, the theory has problems in terms of whether M2 or M3 is more advanced. Similarly, it assumes that every leader wants followers to reach M4 and every follower wants to reach M4. In some organizations, employees are happy to know how to do the task, come to work, complete the task, and take home a paycheck. They will never be internally motivated to do the job and are there simply because they need to meet their basic safety needs of having a roof over their heads and food on their table. The other potential issue with this theory is that not everyone progresses through all of the stages or remains at M4 once they reach it—followers may skip M1 if they are coming from another organization in which similar work is done; they may skip M3 if they never get bored with their job; they may regress to M3 if they are nearing retirement and counting the days until they can be travelling, enjoying their grandchildren, or taking up new hobbies; and they may get stuck in M3 if they are millennials who favor meaningful work over what appears to be a series of busy-work tasks.

FIGURE 2.14 Orcas are able to adapt to their environment in ways others cannot.

Orcas (i.e., killer whales) are led by a matriarch. Female orcas stop giving birth when they are about 40 years old, but they can live well into their 90's. The older females who become the leader of a group have the knowledge and experience needed to find food and help teach younger whales hunting techniques. Because better hunting abilities among members of a group of killer whales is more effective, the matriarch orca may encourage learning and skill development by nudging or coaxing young whales to try new techniques. Like the life cycle of situational leadership, the leader progresses from directing, coaching, and supporting to observing as young whales become more skilled and established.

RESEARCH SUMMARY

Study: This study (Drea Zigarmi & Roberts, 2017) set out to test the basic propositions of situational leadership theory by examining directive (task, initiating structure, or instrumental) and supportive (consideration or relational) communication. They looked specifically at four combinations of directive and supportive communication (high/high, low/low, high/low, and low/high). Their hypotheses were that:

- All four styles will be reported as received [by followers].

- All four styles will be reported as needed [by followers].

- Followers reporting a fit between their needed leadership style and the leadership style they received from their manager will demonstrate more favorable scores on selected employee outcome variables.

Over 500 working professionals participated in the study with approximately three-quarters of them residing in the United States and Canada. All of the people participating in the study completed measures about their leaders' behaviors (goal setting, showing and telling how, listening, and facilitating problem solving). They also rated the extent to which they needed each of these behaviors. Other scales included the work intention inventory regarding their intention to endorse the organization, perform at higher than average level, use discretionary effort, stay in the organization, and be an organizational citizen (perform behaviors that are not contractually required and receive no compensation); the positive and negative affect scale to assess their feelings toward their job; and a trust scale that measured their affective and cognitive trust in the leader. In their sample, followers reported receiving low directive and low supportive communication (n = 239) most often even though the largest number of people indicated they needed high directive and high supportive communication (n = 325). Of all of the participants, 295 reported receiving the leadership communication they needed. The first two hypotheses were supported by the data. While the differences were not always statistically significant, followers who reported receiving the leadership communication they needed had higher scores on the positive outcomes (work intentions, positive affect, cognitive trust, and affective trust) and lower scores on the negative outcomes (negative affect).

Implications: Because organizations were trying to flatten their hierarchical structures, it is possible that the span of control for many managers has grown so great that they are not able to provide the level of supportive communication needed by many employees. That may be why so many people reported receiving low supportive and low directive

(continued)

communication. Recent pushes toward charismatic and transformational leadership (see chapter 3) may explain the desire for high directive and high supportive communication. Leaders need to be aware that their followers hold implicit theories about the leadership communication they need and those implicit theories likely include a combination of directive and supportive communication behaviors. Finally, delegation (low supportive and low directive communication) has its place; if too many leaders rely upon this style, they may be seen as abdicating their responsibility and also receive lower performance from their followers.

Classical Leadership Style
https://tiny.utk.edu/FCL2_1

DISCUSSION QUESTIONS AND ACTIVITIES

1. Of the classical approaches to leadership, for which one would you prefer to be a follower? Why?

2. What are the similarities and differences across classical leadership approaches? Make a list of them. Given the lists you have created, in what ways might we be able to combine these approaches into something simpler to remember, teach, and execute?

3. If you were guessing, which classical leadership approach do you think would be most comfortable for you? Go to https://www.businessnews-daily.com/10492-management-theorist-quiz.html and take their quiz to see how accurate your prediction was.

4. Choose a leader—not manager—you have observed in the past (boss, politician, religious or spiritual, extra-curricular activity). If you were going to offer this person advice about being a stronger leader, what would you encourage the person to do differently? What should they continue doing? What leadership approach suits them best?

5. Assuming you want to be a leader at some point in your career, what are the three steps you can take between now and then to be a stronger leader? Think about your preferred approach to leadership as well as the approach you think followers would appreciate most. Do you see yourself sticking to a single approach or using different approaches as the situation warrants? Why?

FIGURE CREDITS:

Fig. 2.1: Source: https://commons.wikimedia.org/wiki/File:2006_Quarter_Proof.png.

Fig. 2.3: Source: https://pixabay.com/photos/silverback-gorilla-male-gorilla-271002/.

Fig. 2.4: Source: https://pixabay.com/photos/buffalo-oklahoma-bison-american-1436182/.

Fig. 2.5: Source: https://pixabay.com/photos/lion-lion-king-forest-king-lion-794962/.

Fig. 2.6: Source: https://pixabay.com/photos/dinosaur-dinosaur-park-model-1310676/.

Fig. 2.8: Source: https://pixabay.com/photos/bottlenose-dolphin-dolphin-swimming-590537/.

Fig. 2.9: Source: https://pixabay.com/photos/meerkat-animal-wild-wildlife-255564/.

Fig. 2.10: Source: https://pixabay.com/photos/sloth-three-finger-sloth-jungle-2759724/.

Fig. 2.11: Source: https://pixabay.com/photos/tiger-wilderness-predator-nature-3543108/.

Fig. 2.12: Source: https://pixabay.com/photos/roof-rat-rat-rodent-animal-961499/.

Fig. 2.13: Source: https://pixabay.com/photos/alpaca-animals-grass-grassland-1845919/.

Fig. 2.14: Source: https://pixabay.com/photos/killer-whales-orcas-breaching-591130/.

CHAPTER 3

CONTEMPORARY APPROACHES

"True leadership stems from individuality that is honestly and sometimes imperfectly expressed ... Leaders should strive for authenticity over perfection."

—SHERYL SANDBERG

"A follower shares in an influence relationship among leaders and other followers with the intent to support leaders who reflect their mutual purposes."

—RODGER ADAIR

When we talked about classical approaches, it was a one-sided coin because only leaders mattered; as we move to contemporary approaches, we use a double-sided coin to represent the importance of both leaders and followers. The double-sided perspective is prevalent throughout the remainder of the book. Both sides of the coin are necessary for it to be accepted as currency just as both leaders and followers play an active role in making sure everyone's communication goals are met.

Leadership theories and practice have come a long way since the early days of trait approaches and a transactional view, in which a leader engaged in behaviors that led to follower behaviors. As we think about contemporary approaches to leadership and followership, our attention shifts from more of a stimulus-response model to frameworks that provide guidance on utilizing people's cognition and affect. As we chronologically look at leadership and followership approaches, take note that we begin with a transformational approach to leadership, pick up with various approaches to followership, and end with more recent trends that fall under the large umbrella of responsible leadership. Followership has become sandwiched between transformational and responsible leadership as it has pushed scholars to address the importance of people and their active engagement.

FIGURE 3.1 Double-Sided Coin

Transformational Leadership

As the name implies, transformational leadership scholars sought to change the way in which we thought about leadership. Their goal was to move from viewing leadership as a transaction in which leaders "paid" followers to engage in particular behaviors to seeing leadership as way to use inspirational strategies to accomplish mutual goals (Bass, 1985). In essence, transformational leaders effect change in both followers and social systems by inspiring them to achieve remarkable or unexpected results. These positive follower changes create a path toward being better prepared to become a leader; managers, on the other hand, seek to keep them as followers to maintain one's own job security and someone to lead. Transformational leadership is only effective to the extent that it is perceived as authentic; as long as it is authentic, increases in motivation, morale, and performance result.

What skills are necessary to be a transformational leader? One of the most important skills is being organized and paying attention to details. Transformational leaders need to be aware of what all of their followers are doing at the granular level and still be able to take all of those pieces and see the big picture. Another important characteristic for transformational leaders is respect—they must respect their followers and, in turn, earn the followers' respect. Because of the mutual respect that exists, both leaders and followers can engage in social influence while appropriately using referent power. The last characteristic is concern for the team. Transformational leaders expect followers to be creative, work together to achieve the best possible results, and provide constructive feedback.

All of this sounds really positive, but what does it mean in practice? First, leaders and followers work together to develop a vision. Second, because the followers have participated in developing the vision, they are usually more motivated to carry it out and seek success. Third, leaders and followers know each other well enough to capitalize on their strengths and ask someone else to help them in areas where they are not as strong, so that they have more efficacy or confidence the next time around. Fourth, leaders focus on their teams, providing them with opportunities to take on increasing levels of responsibility, even though the leader remains accountable to those higher up in the organization—sometimes the leader has to be willing to take one for the team when things do not go as planned. Finally, creating alignment among leaders, followers, and tasks optimizes everyone's performance and creates opportunities to achieve more than everyone thought might be possible at the outset.

Central Concepts

At its core, transformational leadership involves four components (Bass, 1996; Yaslioglu & Selenay Erden, 2018); note how nicely they fit into the 4 "I"s.

- **Idealized Influence:** Leaders engage in ethical behavior while serving as role models with referent power that benefits the collective rather than the individual leader.

- **Inspirational Motivation:** Leaders use optimism to stimulate the followers in working toward the vision.

- **Intellectual Stimulation:** Leaders encourage followers to become partners by voicing their opinions, developing solutions, and taking risks, all of which are rewarded.

- **Individualized Consideration:** Leaders strengthen their relationships with followers by respecting differences, recognizing abilities, listening to their needs, and developing their potential.

FIGURE 3.2   After 50+ years of transactional leadership, it was time to change our thinking.

At the same time as Bass' initial conceptualization, Kouzes and Posner (1987) were working on a practitioner version of transformational leadership that they used to challenge practicing leaders to do things differently. Each of the five components has two specific principles transformational leaders enact. The model had five components. As you read about them, think about the ways in which they overlap with the ones Bass developed.

- **Model the Way:** Two aspects of modeling the way are to 1) set the example that shows how your actions match the organizational/team values and 2) clarify as well as affirm organizational/team values. In this area, one's words and actions must match (what we say about organizational values and how we enact them).

- **Inspire a Shared Vision:** Two aspects of inspiring a shared vision are to 1) envision the future by thinking creatively and 2) enlist others to join you in achieving the shared vision. In this area, Leaders, and their followers must be willing to think outside of the box in which they have typically operated.

- **Challenge the Process:** Two aspects of challenging the process are to 1) search for opportunities to become stronger individually and as a team and 2) experiment with risk taking. Followers and leaders must be willing to learn continuously and adapt to the environment so that they can become more innovative and agile.

- **Enable Others to Act:** Two aspects of enabling others to act are 1) foster collaboration by building trust and 2) strengthen others by increasing their confidence and efficacy. Leaders and followers must work together to develop a culture in which everyone is able to act competently in the team's best interest without fear of retribution.

- **Encourage the Heart:** Two aspects of encouraging the heart involve: 1) recognizing people's contributions and 2) celebrating the small wins. Too often, in organizational settings, people forget to take the time to say genuinely "thank you for helping with this project" or "great job"; transformational followers and leaders remember that everyone matters, wants to be appreciated, and needs to belong to something bigger than themselves.

Interestingly, the practitioners framed their model with respect to action (all of their components begin with verbs) and the academics framed their model with respect to being (all of their components are nouns). That may say something about the difference between your teachers/administration and your workplace leaders. As you can see, there are significant similarities between the two lists. Idealized influence and modeling the way are extremely similar to each other. Inspirational motivation and inspiring a shared vision have very similar processes and outcomes. Intellectual stimulation and enabling others to act both focus on followers' ability to have upward influence and a voice in how things work. Bass' individualized consideration and Kouzes and Posner's enabling others to act and encouraging the heart do not map as cleanly with each other. Bass focuses more on the relationship-building process while Kouzes and Posner focus more on the communication processes necessary for the team to function well.

The Dark Side

Even though transformational leadership was being touted as the next best thing after television and alongside the internet, there were also potential problems associated with transformational approaches. First, the behaviors associated with transformational leadership require large amounts of emotional energy, which can lead to exhaustion initially (Lin et al., 2019), and burnout eventually. Because most people's natural tendencies are not to exhibit strong positive emotions for long periods of time and they may not genuinely feel those emotions (Venue et al., 2013), effective transformational leaders must be willing and able to regulate their emotions to avoid these detrimental outcomes.

Let's see what this means in practice. If leaders are working with their followers to develop a vision, providing motivating messages, and building relationships with other leaders and followers, then there is significantly less time left in a day to do the mundane tasks that leaders must complete. Now, you might be thinking that they should not be doing those tasks because part of transformational leadership is delegating and increasing people's responsibilities. While that is true, remember that everyone has to learn those new responsibilities and who is teaching them ... the leader! Additionally, there are some tasks related to personnel issues that can only be completed by leaders or managers. Hiring managers to do these tasks is also a double-edged sword because it puts another layer between the leader and followers, which goes against the basic principles of transformational leadership.

Second, people began referring to **pseudo-transformational leadership**, which occurs when leaders use inspirational messages to promote their own or the organization's self-interests rather than the collective's interests (Lin et al., 2017). If you think back to the College Admissions Scandal in 2019 where celebrity, and other rich, parents were paying coaches to "recruit" their children to an athletic team because the standards for college entry were lower for athletes than the general student population. These parents were able to use the celebrity leadership status to influence the coaches and people who administered the college entrance exams to set aside the organization's collective interests. Short-term riches overrode the long-term organizational goals.

The same thing can happen within a higher education institution if you have people who are very charismatic leaders. In the wake of the #MeToo Movement, we have seen campuses where these leaders were able to hide sexual harassment, sexual discrimination, and sexual assault claims under the proverbial "rug." How were they able to accomplish this? Followers who experienced these behaviors were, and still are, often swept away by the leader's inspirational message not to report the behavior or told that it is being taken care of, when in fact it is not. You have seen these leaders—people believe anything they say, even if it does not appear to be true, and comply—out of loyalty to the leader, dependence upon the leader for a job or to complete graduation requirements, and a belief that the leader would not be manipulative (Lin et al., 2017).

Advantages and Disadvantages

Just as classical approaches have a time and place in which they work well, so does transformational leadership. Transformational leadership works extremely well in smaller organizations where people have to work together out of necessity to be able to get things done. In smaller organizations, engaging in empathy, seeing a situation from the perspective of others, is easier because people tend to know each other better. Transformational approaches can also work in large or small organizations that want to change and adapt to an anticipated change in the industry or market.

Transformational leadership approaches push followers and leaders to balance long-term and short-term goals. The organization can no longer focus exclusively on short-term profits at the expense of protecting the environment or building relationships with their various stakeholders. Because the vision drives all decision making, short- and long-term goals are evaluated in relation to the extent that they meet or make progress toward achieving the vision. Because not just surviving, but also finding ways to thrive, are important for long-term success, transformational leadership inspires followers and leaders to build coalitions inside and outside the organization; coalitions cannot be built without also building trust.

As we indicated in the dark side of transformational leadership, there are downsides to choosing this approach over others. Transformational leadership does not work well in organizations with little or no structure. Interestingly, we might expect an organization such as Google where flexibility is front and center to benefit from the charismatic nature of transformational leadership; yet, their lack of structure overrides the benefits of leaders engaging in transformational behaviors. Why might that happen? If leaders do not have specified followers, it is significantly more difficult for them to build the

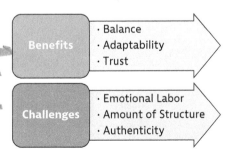

FIGURE 3.3 Benefits and Challenges of Transformational Leadership

relationships, trust, and empathy that go along with engaging in transformational behaviors. At the other end of the spectrum, it also works poorly in highly structured organizations such as the military. In these types of organizations, the reasoning is that there is an expectation of social and psychological distance between followers and leaders—they do not engage in the self-disclosure that tends to build relationships and enhance trust.

Ideal, Effective Followers

What does it mean to be an ideal follower? Answers to this question are like the varying responses you would get when asking people "what would your ideal romantic partner (or hook-up) be like?" It depends on what you're looking for. Some people have a "type," which attracts them to a certain set of characteristics and/or behaviors. For others, it is more about finding someone who fits or fulfills a particular role in their life. There are also people who don't have or aren't looking for a type of partner or someone to fulfill a role. For these open opportunity kinds of people, their ideal partner just happened through interactions over time. Followership approaches offer typology, role-based, and constructionist perspectives for better understanding what followership is and what it means to be an ideal follower.

Follower Styles

Let's talk about follower typologies. Robert Kelley (1988) developed one of the first follower typology models to describe people's core style of following as relatively independent of leaders' influence. The focus of Kelley's followership styles model is effectiveness, making it useful for understanding leader preferences for certain follower behavior(s). According to Kelley (1988), followers can be characterized based on two dimensions: behavior (critical thinking) and motivation (passive versus active). These dimensions distinguish five different types of followership styles: sheep, yes-people, alienated, star, and pragmatic.

Let's look at each type. Sheep followers do not think critically and do not participate, contributing a negative energy for the organization. Sheep rely on the leader (or others) to do the thinking and to motivate them. This style

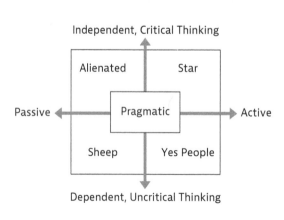

FIGURE 3.4 Kelley's Effective Follower Style Model

places more demand on leaders to think about what they want followers to do and how to get them to do it.

Yes-people do not think for themselves either; they rely on leaders to do the thinking, providing direction and vision. Unlike the sheep follower style, yes-people are active participants in the workplace. Yes-people believe they are doers, they are the type of followers who finish tasks and then ask what the leader wants them to work on next (Kelley, 2008). Because leaders do not need to think about how to motivate yes-people to get things done, their active participation is believed to generate positive energy.

Star followers can also create positive energy and are considered go-getters, characteristic of a sports team's MVP or a leader's right-hand person. They are critical thinkers who are actively engaged. This type of follower offers full support to and for the leader(s); when they believe it is necessary, they provide constructive support for achieving an organization's mission or leader's vision.

In contrast, **alienated followers** think critically, yet their skepticism or cynicism about tasks or a leader's plan of action hinders their participation, which can generate negative energy. Alienated followers are the type of people others might categorize as a "Debbie-downer" or "negative Nathan," as they feel a personal responsibility to stand up to and/or critically evaluate their boss.

Finally, **pragmatic followers** also think for themselves; like their label, their level of engagement is practically calculated. Pragmatics see themselves as exemplifying the status quo; they do enough as they see fit and wait to see whether they should do more. When it comes to achieving the organization's mission or leader's vision, a pragmatic follower is neither the first, nor the last, to jump on board.

Which follower style do you believe leaders are most likely to prefer? Generally, leaders prefer the yes-people follower style or a mix of these styles with yes-people and pragmatics making up the majority, followed by a small group of star followers, and a sprinkling of alienated followers to keep their leaders honest (Kelley, 2008).

Courageous Model

Ira Chaleff developed a courageous follower model, a second follower typology with a more relational view of different follower styles. The model's focus is understanding how leadership styles produce different types of follower styles because followers act in relation to their leader (Chaleff, 2016). A follower may act in one follower style with leader A and act in a completely different style with leader B. Because leader A and leader B use different styles, followers adjust their style to complement the leader's style. This model is most useful for leaders to assess support, empowerment, and organizational culture development.

Followers are evaluated on two dimensions of courage: 1) the courage to support the leader and 2) the courage to challenge the leader's behavior or policies (Chaleff, 2008). Based on where followers fall along both of these dimensions, four of the following types of follower styles can result: resource style, individualist style, implementer style, and partner style.

Followers operating under a **resource style** are present and do their work, yet they are uncommitted, or their priority is somewhere else (kids/family or other outside work). They tend to do just enough to keep their position—no more and no less. Resource style followers are not willing or able to offer their leader constructive feedback, whereas individualist style followers do not hesitate to speak up to leaders (or others).

Individualists can be confrontational, independent thinkers, and forthright. Even when individualist followers accept going along with the rest of the group, they cling to their doubts. This can be valuable; it can also be destructive when their unwillingness to support their leader or organization causes them to marginalize themselves. Focusing on ways for resource and individualist followers to grow their willingness to support their leader should be a top priority for both leaders and these types of followers (Chaleff, 2009).

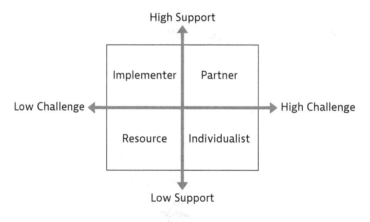

FIGURE 3.5   Chaleff's Courageous Follower Styles Model

Implementers are highly supportive of their leader, dependable, and considerate. The downside, for leaders, of the implementer style is they cannot count on them to speak up with they believe something is not right. Leaders do count on, however, **partner** style followers' courage to express both support and constructive challenging when necessary. Followers who operate under the partner style value cultivating peer-like relationships with leaders, hold complementary views to leaders, and assume full responsibility for both the leader's and their own behavior.

Engaged Follower Model

Kellerman's (2007) engaged follower model highlights levels of involvement. This model is most useful for assessing the extent to which followers buy into a leader's vision and/or an organization's mission. Unlike the previous follower typologies, Kellerman uses follower engagement as the one and only dimension categorizing five different types of follower styles: isolates, bystanders, participants, activists, and diehards.

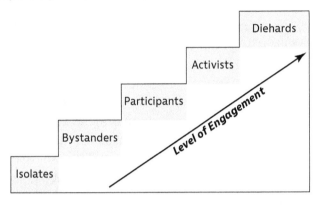

FIGURE 3.6   Kellerman's Engaged Follower Model

We think you'll find Kellerman's (2007) one sentence summary for each follower style in her model refreshing:

- **Isolates** are completely detached.

- **Bystanders** observe but do not participate.

- **Participants** are engaged in some way.

- **Activists** feel strongly one way or another and about their leader or organization, and they act accordingly.

- **Diehards** are prepared to go down for their cause—whether it's an individual, an idea, or both.

If you think about any group you have been a part of, for school or work, you can probably quickly draw connections between your own experience with group members and how they reflect one of the follower styles in Kellerman's model. Think about a group you have been in where group members' approaches to finishing the project were largely different from each other. Who was the leader of this group? Now, was there a group member who nobody heard from for the entire semester until a few days or weeks before the project was due? If so, then that person portrays the isolate style. The group member illustrating the bystander style may have seemed informed about the group's status, however, rarely pitched in, and only if and when it was desirable. The participant style may have been demonstrated by a group member who offered clear and immediate feedback about whether they agreed or disagreed with an idea, plan, decision, or the division of work.

Are these follower engagement styles starting to sound hauntingly familiar yet? Now, who would you say enacted the activist's style in your group the most? This person was likely highly dependable, initiated group discussion or chats, and took the lead on making sure everyone had a specific task to complete to fulfil the leader's vision for the project. Last, but certainly not least, who out of your group would you say most aligned with the diehard style? The diehard is the person who finished most of the extra work that some other member(s) said they would finish but didn't. Whether the diehard adored or despised the leader was never up to question. They made where they stood clear, maybe even uncomfortably so, and stopped at nothing.

The two types of followers most likely to drag down the rest of a group or organization are isolates and bystanders. Isolates put in an honest day's work and have zero enthusiasm for doing much more of anything that would attract attention. Isolates are totally unaware of what's going on around them, whereas bystanders are aware of what's going on but selectively choose when and why they will (or will not) engage (Kellerman, 2007). To become more engaged, both isolates and bystanders rely on leaders (or others) to motivate them.

In the middle, we see the **participant** follower style. Participants are dedicated to making some sort of impact, as they either obviously support or obviously oppose their leader and organization and it is clear where they stand.

Activists are highly committed to either support or undermine their leader and organization. They are loyal, dedicated, and work hard to see their goal accomplished. While both activists and diehards are results-oriented, diehards stop at nothing. **Diehards** make up the most extreme and rare type of follower engagement. They are completely and utterly consumed with commitment to either deeply support or expel their leader and/or organization. For leaders, participants, activists, and diehards can be valuable assets or their worst nightmare; it is no wonder isolates and bystanders go unnoticed—they pose far less of a threat.

Role-Based Approach to Followership

According to Uhl-Bien et al. (2014), a role theory approach sees followership as a part played by people in a junior hierarchical position to understand:

- What mix of followership characteristics and followership behaviors creates effective outcomes?

- Followership from the perspective of followers themselves, not to better understand leadership from the follower perspective.

- How followers influence leader behaviors, by looking at followers as causal agents (as independent variables) and leaders (or leadership) as outcomes of followership (as dependent variables).

A role is defined as a set of appropriate behaviors for a position that people enact (Baker, 2007). One way of understanding a follower role is by looking at the different types of follower styles from followers' perspectives. Follower styles, as we've discussed above, are categories that clump together certain characteristics believed to align with certain follower behaviors. The premise: if we understand follower styles, then we can better understand how followers enact a followership role. This means seeing things, like follower styles, in the way that followers see them to discover how they are most useful for followers, not just leaders.

The role-based approach also recognizes the importance of, more or less, pulling followership characteristics and followership behaviors apart to understand how each relate and contribute to the overall followership process. This offers us another way of understanding a followership role, by looking at other kinds of followership characteristics. They are isolated from, yet still related to, follower behaviors. So far, followership research has primarily looked at two of these followership characteristics: follower role orientations and followers' implicit followership and/or leadership theories.

Do you remember when we talked about implicit theories of leadership and followership? Follower role orientations are related to implicit followership theories. Role orientations are cognitive representations we create of what it means to perform a certain role. Follower role orientation is defined by a follower's beliefs about their role—beliefs about responsibilities, activities, and behaviors—which includes personal definitions of what is important and what it means to be effective while working with leaders (Carsten et al., 2014). They indicate there are three common follower role orientations.

- A passive role orientation occurs when people believe the follower role requires adherence to leaders' orders, deference, and loyalty. Passive followers believe they advance their leaders' initiatives by going along without question, listening and following while remaining silent.

- A co-production role orientation occurs when people believe the follower role involves being an actively engaged partner (solving problems, constructive challenging, relaying information) of their leader.

- An anti-authoritarian role orientation develops when followers believes they should avoid, disregard, and/or oppose a leader's control or authority.

Because followership is a relatively young area of research compared to leadership, there remains much unexplored terrain. For example, it is likely other follower role orientations exist. How would you describe followers who believe their role requires performance that is neither completely passive nor actively engaged all the time? What other follower role orientations do you believe we can expect to find? Follower role orientations are also context sensitive (activated by context). We should anticipate followers, especially more experienced followers, are equipped with more than one follower role orientation.

Overall, follower role orientations capture follower expectations about what followers should do (how followers should perform), implicit followership theories capture expectations of who followers are (Epitropaki et al., 2013). Both of these followership characteristics will be useful for understanding how followers' perceptions of their own behavior and perceptions of their leader's behavior guide the way followers think about and behave (act, react, or interact) with a leader. This knowledge allows us to better understand:

- how followership characteristics influence followership behaviors, and

- how followers influence leaders' attitudes and behaviors.

Followership (Following) Behaviors

Obedience is the classical stereotypical behavior that comes with the follower label. We know followers have a long history of being defined by **obedience**, referring to passivity, deference, and blind adherence. **Proactive behaviors** are followers' planned and deliberate efforts to create or control a situation, as they see fit, to align with personal or organizational goals. Examples of proactive behavior rooted in communication include voice, upward delegation, upward influence, and feedback seeking behavior. Proactive behaviors are anticipatory, whereas resistance behaviors are typically reactionary (in response).

Another distinction between the two involves the presence of risk. When followership behaviors are risky (pose a threat for either follower or leader), they are considered resistance behaviors. Followers perform resistance behavior in two ways: constructive or dysfunctional. **Constructive resistance** behavior involves efforts intended to open conversation with a leader (e.g., request clarification and/or negotiation), whereas **dysfunctional resistance** behavior involves passive-aggressive acts or efforts (Tepper et al., 2001). Because upward influence behaviors may or may not involve risk, it is necessary to think about them in context to determine whether they are performed proactively or as resistance.

We can easily see how certain follower styles or role orientations match with followership behaviors, but this is not always the case in real life. For example, there are times when star followers or followers with co-production

TABLE 3.1   Followership Characteristics (and Styles) & Followership Behaviors

Followership (Following) Behaviors	Followership Characteristics of:			
	Kelley's Follower Styles	Chaleff's Follower Styles	Kellerman's Follower Styles	Carsten's Follower Role Orientations
Obedience	Sheep; Yes-people; Pragmatics	Resource; Implementer	Isolates; Bystanders	Passive Orientation
Proactive	Star	Partner	Participants; Activists; Diehards	Co-Production Orientation
Resistance	Star; Alienated	Partner; Individualist	Participants; Activists; Diehards	Anti-Authoritarian Orientation
Upward Influence	Alienated; Star	Individualist; Partner	Participants; Activists; Diehards	Co-Production Orientation; Anti-Authoritarian Orientation

orientation may engage in constructive resistance or passive following behaviors intended to support their leader. In what situations do you believe this may happen? Overall, the role-based approach is most useful for assessing leader-follower relationship development and/or relationship dissolution.

Constructionist Approach to Followership

A constructionist approach is less concerned with hierarchical roles and more focused on behaviors (acts of following and leading). Together, followers and leaders interact to co-create followership and leadership processes from the constructionist perspective. According to Uhl-Bien et al. (2014), a constructionist approach sees followership (and leadership) as a socially constructed process in which people's acts of following and leading combine to co-construct followership, leadership, and their outcomes to understand:

- What and how do following behaviors and leading behaviors mix to co-create leadership, followership, and their outcomes?

- Followership (and leadership) as a dynamic relational process.

- Followership (and leadership) as mutual influence.

The constructionist approach is most successful for leader-follower interaction related to the role of interpersonal communication in the evolving nature of leader-follower relationships, identity construction and development, and relational features of leader-follower relationships (trust, intimacy, closeness, mutuality, etc.).

Followership Theory

The role-based approach and constructionist approach make up two lines of followership research housed under followership theory. According to Uhl-bien et al.'s (2014, p. 96) followership theory, "followership *is* the characteristics, behaviors and processes of acting in relation to a leader." Both followership approaches operate using the same definitions for the following followership constructs:

- **Followership characteristics** refer to individual qualities impacting one's definition and enactment of followership,

- **Followership behaviors** are actions enacted from the standpoint of a follower role or in the act of following, and

- **Followership outcomes** refer to the results of followership characteristics and followership behaviors that can occur at individual, relationship, and/or work-unit levels.

In Table 3.2, you see some of the followership characteristics, behaviors, and outcomes proposed by followership theory. Some we have discussed and some we discuss in later chapters. Because followership is still a relatively new area of research, there are followership characteristics, behaviors, and outcomes not yet explored. In the spaces below, fill in what you believe are "unexplored" followership variables important for further understanding followership.

TABLE 3.2 Followership Constructs

Followership Characteristics	Followership Behaviors	Followership Outcomes
▪ Follower role orientations ▪ Implicit theories of followership and leadership ▪ Follower Motivation	▪ Voice ▪ Upward Influence ▪ Upward Delegation ▪ Feedback Seeking ▪ Obedience ▪ Proactive Behaviors ▪ Resistance	▪ Individual Follower Outcomes (effectiveness, career advancement, emerging leadership, creativity) ▪ Individual Leader Outcomes (leader behaviors → feedback seeking, decision-making, motivation, burnout, ethics) ▪ Relational Outcomes (trust, relationship quality, leadership style or approach) ▪ Work-Unit Outcomes (goal accomplishment, organizational culture/climate, collaboration)

Responsible Leadership

Responsible leadership is an umbrella term for all of the various approaches to engaging in leadership behaviors that protect an organization's members, natural resources, and the environment. Often, people will talk about an organization's sustainability or corporate social responsibility initiatives when they are talking about the ways in which those organizations engage in responsible leadership (Tsui, 2019). Within responsible leadership, it is not just about the leader-follower relationship, but also about the ways in which those relationships affect a larger community, both internal and external to the organization.

In essence, responsible leadership involves making strategic business and communication decisions that consider all stakeholders' interests and expectations (Violanti & Ray, 2019); those stakeholders include internal employees, external suppliers, shareholders for publicly traded companies, investors for privately held companies, the global and local community, the environment, and future generations. In this model, performance is measured in relation to the impact leaders and followers have on economic, social, and environmental factors. For example, these might include the ways in which one organization contributes to the developing greenways that may become the places in which a state or regional bike race is held. Bringing race participants to the community is an economic boon that may translate into backpacks of food for children whose parents cannot afford to feed their families all weekend long. Greenways have additional social and environmental benefits.

RESEARCH SUMMARY

Study: Liu and Lin (2018) set out to examine what happens when followers experience ethical conflict in an organizational setting. Ethical conflict is defined as feeling pressured to act in a way that is inconsistent with one's moral beliefs; in this case, it would be feeling pressured to behave in a contradictory way at work. Specifically, they examined the following two hypotheses:

H1: Ethical conflict is positively related to intention to leave the organization.

H2: Responsible leadership is negatively related to intention to leave the organization.

H3: Ethical conflict is negatively related to intention to help others in the organization.

H4: Responsible leadership is positively related to intention to help others in the organization.

(continued)

Working professionals in the high-tech industry in Taiwan completed one set of surveys if they were the followers and a different set of surveys if they were the leaders to avoid some of the biases inherent in having everyone complete the same scales. Their findings revealed that there is 1) a positive relationship between ethical conflict and intent to leave the organization; this relationship is stronger when the person does not identify with the organization and when the person is experiencing uncertainty (support for H1). The findings also revealed a negative relationship between responsible leadership and intent to leave; this relationship is stronger when the person identifies with the organization and feels lower levels of uncertainty (H2 is supported). In support of H3, there is a negative relationship between ethical conflict and helping behavior; this relationship is strengthened when the person does not identify with the organization and when the person feels uncertainty. Finally, in support of H4, the data revealed a positive relationship between responsible leadership and intention to help others; this relationship was even stronger when the person identified with the organization. This is one of the few empirical studies specifically addressing responsible leadership and will hopefully serve as a foundation for gathering additional evidence about the role of responsible leadership in organizations.

Implications: Because this study was conducted in Taiwan with high-tech employees specifically, we need additional evidence to generalize these findings to a larger population. The results seem promising for those who want to be responsible leaders as long as they can surround themselves with people who buy into the organizational values associated with paying attention to a wide variety of stakeholders and not just employees, customers, or shareholders. Not everyone has the same view of sustainability as responsible leaders do, so it becomes important to make sure that followers understand, identify, and agree with the organization's values—they have to be willing to accept a strong culture. Leaders also have to be extremely vigilant about making sure the organizational culture and values are communicated clearly.

Dimensions

de Bettingies (2014) defined five dimensions of responsible leadership. They are as important and prevalent today as they were when he first spoke about them. When we talk about these dimensions, they are a combination of qualities leaders have, behaviors they enact, and contextual factors that place the leader in a larger system. Each dimension prompts questions leaders can use to assess their levels of responsible leadership as well as engage in strategic planning (see Figure 3.7).

Awareness

Awareness is a cognitive, reflective process leaders undertake. You may be wondering when leaders have time for this given the constant demands on their time and energy. In reality, they cannot afford not to take the time to be mindful about themselves, their organizations, and the greater societal good if they are going to be responsible leaders. Awareness is the first step in developing a strategic plan for oneself, one's organization, and the larger society in which the first two operate. Taking just 10 or 15 minutes a day to meditate or engage in mindfulness can significantly increase leaders' and followers' awareness of their strengths and areas for improvement.

Being mindful is also an opportunity to think about enhancing all stakeholders' awareness of what is happening in the organization. How valuable is it to implement strategies to conserve natural resources or lower worker stress levels if no one knows about them? Just remember that transparency (responsibility) comes with accountability (being willing to share the good, the bad, and the ugly). Becoming more aware of the world around me means more than scrolling through social media, swiping or liking, or reading the top headlines someone created for you. Global awareness is an active process of seeking out reputable information sources and analyzing the data for yourself.

Vision

For those of you who do not have visual impairments, imagine what they world would look like if you could only see shades of white, gray, and black, or could only see large objects at close distance, or could only sense the world through sound, touch, and smell. How different would your life be? The same thing happens when we live each day without thinking about the future—we engage in tasks, build relationships, and develop our identity only in the moment with no consideration for how that will affect us and those around us next week, next year, next decade.

For responsible leaders and followers, vision encompasses all of our strategic planning efforts for ourselves, our organizations, and the planet on which we live. It is more than just thinking about each of these things in isolation—how we envision ourselves affects how we envision our organizations and the world in which we live as well as the one we plan to leave to those living in the twenty-second century.

Imagination

For leaders who are extremely detail- and bottom-line oriented as well as tacticians who carry out someone else's vision, imagination may be the hardest pillar of responsible leadership. Were you the child who struggled with a blank piece of paper in art class because you could not think of one thing to draw or the child with so many possibilities it was impossible to choose just one? Generating possibilities for oneself, one's organization, and the larger culture is what imagination entails.

Another way to think about imagination is to ponder how you could be a different person, a different friend, a different coworker, a different leader, a different ... Different does not automatically imply better or worse, so avoid engaging in evaluation when you are thinking about what could be different. At the organizational level, are there different values that could be enacted to better various stakeholders' well-being? What do you hope that your great-great-grandchildren will be thanking your generation for putting in place? Have you ever thought about thanking the generations that came before you and developed the technological capabilities that have become social media? How do you want your generation and your organization to be viewed historically?

Responsibility

Responsibility is about making choices. No one can solve all of the problems we face today or will face tomorrow. So, what can we do to be more responsive and for what can we hold ourselves more accountable? How do I extend my reach as a leader, or follower? How can I minimize the potential negative impact I have on others and the world around me? Another way to think about it: what can I do to be a role model *each and every* day? It can be a daunting task if you allow it to overwhelm you, so pick one aspect of how you can have a more positive impact, practice it for 30 to 60 days until it becomes a habit, and then move on to the next positive change.

At the organizational level, we sometimes get so caught up in making sure those who provide us with the cash we need to operate are happy that we forget about the ways our organization is negatively impacting those around us. For example, would you rather be known as the organization that was always open (24/7, 364 days a year—closed only for Thanksgiving) or the organization that had a hot meal for children on free- and reduced-lunch when school was not in session? The first organization is potentially negatively impacting employees with families who are missing holidays and family time, the environment from the increased pollution associated with people shopping when there is no public transportation, and the local small business community that cannot afford to stay open and compete with your hours. While you may argue that is what capitalism is all about, responsible leadership advocates would argue that you have it all wrong because you cannot envision a world in which everyone is responsible for everyone and everything else.

Action

Ultimately, action is the result of having considered the other four pillars of responsible leadership. Action is the place where people are held accountable by those around them and the history that will eventually be written.

Action requires leaders and followers to make sure that what they say they are going to do actually gets done in the way they say it is going to get done. What is worse than being transparent about a new initiative, touting how well it will positively affect the community and environment, and never fully implementing it because the organization decided to go in a new direction?

Action requires courage—the courage to put yourself and your reputation on the line, spending time building trusting relationships, and inspiring others to walk with you down the responsible leadership and followership path. What will it take for people to stop blaming others when things go wrong, avoid acting to minimize the potential consequences, and accept that making mistakes are an important component of being human? How often do you find yourself saying "That will never work" or "We have never done it that way"? Those are phrases that serve as obstacles to acting responsibly.

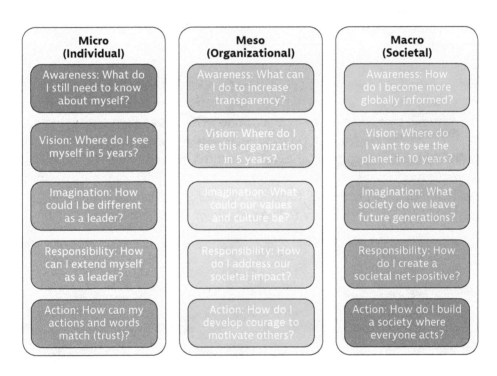

FIGURE 3.7   Questions for Responsible Leadership (adapted from de Bettinges, 2014)

Levels of Analysis

When we talk about levels of analysis, we are recognizing that leadership and followership within a responsible leadership approach cannot occur only at the individual or dyad level, which is where most of the current leadership research has occurred. Looking at the skills, characteristics, and behaviors of responsible leaders themselves is known as the **micro-level** (Tsui, 2019). As the name implies, a micro analysis is often a self-report of what one is doing or an "other" report by followers who indicate their perceptions regarding the leader. This seems extremely curious given that the primary value of responsible leadership is its focus on a variety of stakeholders, with followers only being one of those, See Figure 3.7 for some of the micro-level questions associated with responsible leadership.

Miska and Mendenhall (2018) moved our thinking beyond the micro level and connected responsible leadership to its roots at the meso and macro levels. **Meso-level** leadership occurs at the group and organizational levels, rather than the individual level. The strategies organizations choose to reach their vision and achieve their daily mission must be responsible, ethical, and authentic in the same ways that leaders and followers must exhibit these qualities. That is, responsible leadership contained within the walls of an organizational setting is not going to achieve the communication and business goals necessary to reach all stakeholders inside and outside the organization.

As you likely know from your experiences over time, when one aspect of a system, such as your body, changes, it has an impact on all other systems. If you break your wrist or come down with a virus, then you have to rest and change how you do simple things, such as cooking, so that you do not spread the virus and make things that can be prepared with one hand. The same is true at the macro level. **Macro-level** thinking highlights the importance of considering the larger society and culture in which organizations, and their members, operate. The time for thinking about a local economy has passed; we will never return from the global economy we have created and in which we will continue to live for the foreseeable future, at least until we figure out how to live outside of Earth's atmosphere!

FIGURE 3.8 Today's students will find themselves leading teams made up of both humans and robots. In an age of artificial intelligence, tomorrow's leaders will need to be agile enough to shift between human and robotic followers.

The Future Is Now: Artificial Intelligence

Up until now, we have talked specifically about relationships that involve human leaders and human followers. Artificial intelligence is considered the wave of the future. Tomorrow's workplaces call for leadership approaches that address human-human as well as human-machine relationships between leaders and followers. How much of what we have talked about up to this point does not translate well to the human-machine relationship? What aspects of classical and contemporary leadership approaches are well-positioned to address human-machine relationships? Will we see ourselves cycling back to contingency, path-goal, and possibly even high-task/low-relationship models of classical leadership?

Time will tell exactly how the human-machine relationship evolves. All we can do at this point is speculate about what those workplaces might look like. While our instincts may be that robots do not need much in the way of affect, the future of AI is in developing robots that can use emotional intelligence to reach our internal (employee) and external (customers, clients, suppliers, communities) human stakeholders. Programming is becoming more and more sophisticated each year; leaders will soon find themselves overseeing groups of robots capable of experiencing and expressing emotional intelligence; with these robotic teams comes additional teams of programmers who work with them. Future leaders will have to balance their attention to building relationships with humans and their ability to catalyze ethics and morals in robots, also known as **roboethics** (Smith & Green, 2018).

DISCUSSION QUESTIONS AND ACTIVITIES

1. Find a partner. Using a cloth or towel, make sure that one of the people (the follower) cannot see. The other person must lead the person around for a minimum of 4–5 minutes. Switch roles and repeat the activity. After the activity, write one to two pages about your experience, including how it felt to be in each role, which role you preferred and why, what you wish the other person had done differently, and what you would do differently if you got another chance?

2. Thinking about all of the times you play the role of follower, what will you do differently now that you know about these various approaches to followership? What skills do you still need to develop to be a better follower? What specific steps can you take to develop those skills?

3. Name someone you consider to be a transformational leader. Does this person better align with Bass' or Kouzes and Posner's definition of transformational leadership? Make a list of at least three ways the leader exhibits each defining characteristic (e.g., individualized consideration or model the way). These can include behaviors, characteristics, messages, and mannerisms/ways of treating others.

4. Given what you know about responsible leadership, research Coca Cola and see what you can find out about their worldwide efforts to engage

in responsible leadership (check out their sustainability statements and initiatives). What are some of the challenges they are facing as they try to take care of their human, environmental, and natural resources? How realistic do you think it is for a worldwide organization to satisfy its various stakeholders' expectations and still remain profitable? Why?

5. Recall the different forms of contemporary leadership we discussed in the beginning of the chapter. What mix of following behaviors and leading behaviors do you believe co-create transformational leadership, charismatic leadership, and responsible leadership? What other outcomes could these different mixes of following and leading behaviors generate? Use the activity table below to fill in your answers and organize your ideas.

CONSTRUCTIONIST APPROACH ACTIVITY

Following Behavior(s)	Leading Behavior(s)	Leadership Process	Other Outcome(s)
		Transformational Leadership	
		Charismatic Leadership	
		Responsible Leadership	

FIGURE CREDIS:

Fig. 3.1: Source: https://pixabay.com/photos/coins-dollars-two-dollar-coin-1466263/.

Fig. 3.2: Source: https://pixabay.com/illustrations/banner-header-change-transforma-tion-1076311/.

Fig. 3.8: Source: https://pixabay.com/illustrations/hand-robot-human-machine-for-ward-1571847/.

CHAPTER 4

INDIVIDUAL AND RELATIONAL COMPETENCY

"It's easier to donate a few thousands to charity and think oneself noble than to base self-respect on personal standards of personal achievement. It's simple to seek substitutes for competence—such easy substitutes: love, charm, kindness, charity. But there is no substitute for competence."

—AYN RAND

"Competence is to ensure that your actions put people's hearts at ease when things are in your hands."

—ISRAELMORE AYIVOR

Think of the most competent communicator you know. Using what you know about this person, fill in the blanks below.

The name of the most competent communicator I know is _____.

Imagine or recall a time when this person demonstrated communication competence to constructively challenge a leader (or follower). In this situation, the two most prominent qualities of this person's communication competence were:

1. _____

2. _____

Next, imagine or recall a time when this person demonstrated communication competence to express support to a leader (or follower). In this situation, the two most prominent qualities of this person's communication competence were:

1. _____

2. _____

Last, imagine or recall a time when this person demonstrated communication competence to influence the behavior of a leader (or follower). In this situation, the two most prominent qualities of this person's communication competence were:

1. _____

2. _____

Looking at your lists above, are the communication competence qualities you listed identical for all three situations? The likely answer is "no." Look at your lists again—what are the similarities and differences?

FIGURE 4.1   Jigsaw Puzzle

ommunication competence is much like a jigsaw puzzle. Most jigsaw puzzles are cut with exactly the same tabs (the rounded parts that stick out from a straight edge) and blanks (the rounded indentations on a straight edge) that fit together as an interlocking mechanism. Because a single piece's tab could connect to any of the other piece's corresponding blanks, determining which ones actually connect to each other to form a picture is the beauty of doing the puzzle. Some pictures are easier to create because they have many colors and vivid images. Others are more difficult to assemble because they may have 500 pieces of a shaded blue skyline or varying shades of green in the forest. Regardless of the number of pieces, jigsaw puzzles accurately represent the trial and error processes as well as the accumulated knowledge necessary to communicate in a competent manner. Just as most who do jigsaw puzzles start with the outside edge, competent communicators begin by developing their toolbox of communication strategies. Once the edges are formed, assembling the jigsaw puzzle's interior becomes easier because you know where different aspects of the image are going to be.

Competent communicators use their past experiences (trying different communication techniques to accomplish their goals in a mutually satisfying manner) to strengthen their communication toolbox and also build relationships with those around them to better understand how and when different techniques will be more successful. Most of us are quite familiar with board puzzles made of wood from preschool or kindergarten where only one piece will fit in each hole. We progress to flat, two-dimensional puzzles where the pieces only fit together in one way to form the picture. A completed puzzle picture illustrates people's perceptions of your communication competence;

most of us never complete our communication competence puzzles because there is always more to learn and experience as organizational followers and leaders.

Communication competence is more akin to newer three-dimensional puzzles where the pieces fit together to form an object that can be examined from multiple angles and vantage points. Each vantage point highlights some aspects of the completed object and obscures others. Competent leaders and followers recognize and understand that their perspective is limited by contextual factors such as the relationship, where the communication occurs, background experiences of the participants, etc. This recognition and understanding aids them as they exchange create, deliver, and interpret competent messages.

Communication Competence

Communication competence is the ability to create and choose messages geared toward meeting the a given audience's and situation's needs. Think about your competence with regard to followership and leadership communication. You signed up for this class for a specific reason: you want to strengthen your skills, you are curious about an effective or ineffective leader's/follower's communication strategies, it fulfills a graduation requirement, or even that it meets at the right time for your schedule.

Communication competence is often described as comprised of some combination of three ingredients: motivation, knowledge, and skills. Competence **motivation** refers to the willingness to direct one's energies and abilities to pursue and attain goals (Sawyer & Richmond, 2015). Assuming that you are taking the class for one of the first two reasons—to improve your own skills or understand someone else's strategies—competence motivation is already satisfied because you are here to achieve a specific purpose and willing to devote the time and energy to read the textbook.

Competence **knowledge** involves drawing on information or understanding acquired as part of one's lived experiences that can be transferred to a new situation (Greene & McNallie, 2015). By the end of this course, you should be familiar with the theory and practices that govern effective followership and leadership communication. As you complete the course, you will likely evaluate what the academics and practitioners highlighted here say in comparison to what you have experienced in your own family, education, and/or work experiences.

Competence **skills** are intentional goal-directed, enabling behaviors or sequences of behavior (Spitzberg, 2015). That is just a fancy way of saying that we need to learn and practice how to be effective communicators. Coming to class motivated to learn about followership and leadership is not

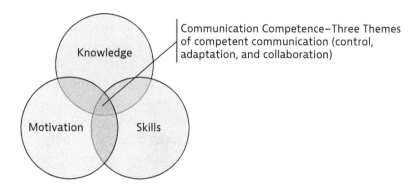

FIGURE 4.2   Features and Themes of Communication Competence

sufficient for becoming a competent communicator. You need to think through how you would communicate in particular situations and practice those strategies to become better at it.

As depicted in Figure 4.2, all three features are necessary to engage in competent communication. For example, a leader may be motivated to create and set a vision, have the knowledge to develop an effective vision, but lack the skills to effectively express that vision to followers. Similarly, a follower may have the knowledge and skills to complete a task and lack the motivation to complete the task by the deadline.

Back to our classroom example. The instructor may assign a group project without a rubric that tells you exactly what needs to be done to earn an A and without providing the content necessary to help students complete the task (e.g., how to work successfully in groups without engaging in division of labor). While the instructor has a vision for helping students see how organizations outside classrooms function, that vision may not be well communicated to the students. Similarly, the students may perceive the assignment as busy work and not be motivated to complete it; they also may not possess the group interaction skills necessary to be successful. Both leaders and followers must commit to some level of all three aspects of competence if the group and larger organization are going to be successful.

Over 100 components define what it means to be a competent communicator (Spitzberg & Changnon, 2009). Table 4.1 lists only some of the most commonly examined and reported components relevant to effective leadership and followership.

Notably, the problem with lists like these is that it would be unrealistic to expect any leader or follower to have or demonstrate all of these components in every situation. Not even competent fictional characters (superheroes, Harry Potter, Katniss Everdeen of *The Hunger Games* series, etc.) exhibit every component listed in Table 4.1 in every situation. Think of communication competence as the superpower effective leaders and followers possess. While they can be successful without it, it is so much easier to accomplish

TABLE 4.1   Components of Communication Competence

Motivation	Knowledge	Skills
Goals (long-term/short term)	Cognitive complexity	Adaptiveness
Basic human needs	Self and other awareness	Altercentrism
Openness (to others and new information)	Problem solving	Interpersonal/Prosocial skills
Self-confidence (self-efficacy)	Situation-specific information	Interaction Management
Agency	Expectations	Listening
Positive Attitude	Interaction rules	Social and Emotional Control
Self-regulation	Self-monitoring	Empathy
Attraction	Analyze/Plan	Expressivity
Tolerance for ambiguity	Language proficiency	Encoding and Decoding (message skills)
Professional commitment, perseverance, and initiative	Knowledge of more than one perspective or alternative interpretations	Nonverbal Behavior

Adapted from Spitzberg & Changnon (2009).

their goals with it. Because not all situations require all competence components, there is no magical check-list of characteristics that automatically make someone a competent communicator in all situations.

Communication competence is intimately linked to context. At the core of communication competence rests three themes: personal control, adaptation, and collaboration. Rather than providing a list of ways to combine the competencies listed in Table 4.1, we discuss baseline competencies capturing these three themes of communication competence: co-cultural communication competence, person-centered communication, and emotional intelligence. Understanding competent communication in this way allows you, our world's followers and leaders of today and tomorrow, to enhance, capitalize on, and piece together different components based upon what is required by a given audience and situation.

Competence as Control: Co-Cultural Communication Competence

As globalization and migration continue to rise, our communities and workplaces become increasingly characterized by cultural unlikeness, thus bringing co-cultural communication competence to the forefront. Previously, we defined culture as the shared assumptions that impact people's behaviors, feelings, perceptions, and thoughts. At work, followers and leaders with various backgrounds shaped by different cultural beliefs and values interact and work together to complete tasks and accomplish goals. At work, when leaders' and followers' behaviors, feelings, perceptions, and thoughts mesh, understanding is achieved; when they collide, conflict often results because of cultural differences.

Rather than seeing diversity (physical, cultural, social, etc.) as something that influences communication, people view it as an inconvenience, imposition, or even wrong (everyone should be like me). However, embracing diversity, and being willing and open to differences, is the essence of co-cultural communication competence. As such, **co-cultural communication competence** involves the processes of exchanging symbolic information between people who, as a result of culture, can simultaneously share the same, similar, and different orientations toward the world.

Think about coffee. Most coffee drinkers fall into one of two camps: those who have a favorite and will stick with it until it is no longer available (those who do not embrace or recognize diversity) and those who like to experiment with a range of coffee (embracing diversity). If you are an experimenter, you may try Chipotle coffee that combines beans from Mexico and Brazil and melds chili peppers, cinnamon, and cacao nibs. Combining disparate viewpoints, or flavors in the case of coffee, falls somewhere on the spectrum from complete failure to complete success; the more you experiment by communicating with diverse others, the more competent you will likely be the next time you encounter someone with different cultural values and world views.

According to communication theory, at the individual level, people who are able to exert personal control and interact in a prosocial manner are more competent communicators (Miller & Steinberg, 1975). Therefore, co-cultural communication competence (CCC) considers an individual's ability to exert as much personal control as possible over an interaction in a given situation (self-regulation) while being prosocially involved (actively adapting aspects of one's motivation, knowledge, and skills) to tailor messages to a given social context. Picture the scene of an event involving a disc jockey (DJ). You may be thinking of a wedding, gala, private party, radio, nightclub, concert, music festival, etc. The situation and audience of such events vary. If your DJ scene were made into a jigsaw puzzle, the audience and the situation of that event would be the outer edge and corner puzzle pieces. When put together, these edge and corner pieces provide a framework in which to fit the other pieces. CCC occurs within this framework to determine how the episode unfolds.

The DJ must exert personal control over self and behaviors to attend to the task (playing music that fits the needs of the situation and audience). The DJ must also be involved pro-socially to gauge the audience and tailor the music played to that specific group of diverse individuals. For example, guests at a wedding reception will appear bored or unenthusiastic if the DJ fails to pay attention to the task (music and transitions between songs) or make appropriate decisions about what type of music to play (playing classical music rather than celebratory dance music to get people on the dance floor). Further, to celebrate the union of the newlywed couple, if the DJ's task is to encourage guests to dance, then the DJ must be prosocially involved to gauge and create a playlist of music tailored to that specific audience. As you may know, guests attending a Greek wedding will be encouraged to dance by different music than guests attending an African, Indian, or American wedding.

Personal Control: Self-Regulation

Self-regulation involves the personal control processes that help or hinder individual responses (thoughts, feelings, and actions) in a specific context (Carver et al., 2015). For example, there are times when followers and leaders must regulate aspects of the self to understand and create competent messages. For example, how often have you received a text and automatically replied "K" without completely processing the message or request? We spend a large portion of our communication time ceremoniously responding to the environment around us rather than paying attention to motivation, beliefs, and consequences. Co-culturally competent communicators regulate messages and actions relevant to goal pursuit and performance.

Co-culturally competent followers and leaders may find themselves in situations where it becomes important to exert control over environmental factors (resources, setting, communication channel, etc.). However, not all personal, behavioral, or environmental aspects need to, or can, be regulated in every situation. While routine or familiar tasks may demand one's attention and monitoring, these types of tasks do not require investing as much energy in making decisions (e.g., the routine task of sending out a company-wide newsletter on the first day of each month). Developing the monthly newsletters, on the other hand, would require one's attention while also taking more motivation control, decision control, and planning. In a similar vein, casual or informal conversation with coworkers or your boss calls for different self-regulatory efforts compared to more formal communication.

Think about the differences in personal control exerted during a conversation about taking a weekend trip or engaging in one of your hobbies compared to asking your boss for a raise or engaging in constructive challenging to improve someone else's (your boss or coworkers) plan or decision(s). Self-regulation is like physical strength—the mental resources used for exerting personal control can become exhausted or depleted, which causes performance to suffer. Depleted self-regulation decreases job performance, prosocial behaviors (upward communication and voice), and positive leadership communication (Lian et al., 2017). Therefore, understanding when, what, and how much self-regulatory control to exert (or reserve) depends on one's goals and abilities, the particular audience, as well as the particular situation.

Two factors influence self-regulatory processes: goals and self-efficacy beliefs. Each time we enter an interaction, whether face-to-face or technology mediated with a leader, follower, co-workers, work groups or teams, we do so with particular goals in mind. Clark and Delia (1979) describe three goals (identity, instrumental, and relational) that appear in some combination in every communicative interaction. **Identity goals** (i.e., self-presentation) refer to the way we want others to see us as well as the way others see us; **instrumental goals** refer to messages designed to accomplish a task or request a favor; and **relational goals** refer to communication that serves to build, maintain, and dissolve connections with others.

Goals, which vary from interaction to interaction, also have differing levels of emphasis across relationships and cultural boundaries. For example, when a follower interacts with a leader, identity and instrumental goals may be more important; relational goals may be more prevalent when interacting with coworkers, work groups and teams, friends, or family. Goals lead people to develop messages designed for a specific audience and context. Exerting control over goal-driven aspects of self, behavior, and the environment influences which messages are developed, expressed, and perceived as competent.

In addition, followers' or leaders' self-efficacy influences goal-driven behavior. **Self-efficacy** refers to a person's beliefs about one's own capabilities to exercise control over the level of functioning or events affecting the experience (Bandura, 1991). Bottom line: self-efficacy is all about one's confidence! How self-assured (or uncertain) leaders and followers are about their ability to exert control in a given situation influences the actual goals leaders and followers set or strive to achieve as well as the way messages are designed to fulfill needs. For leaders, understanding followers' self-efficacy beliefs is essential for evaluating performance and assigning complex tasks and goals.

For example, low self-efficacy (low confidence in one's capabilities) is associated with motivational tendencies related to avoiding goals, choosing lower-level goals (easy tasks) and lower performance, whereas high self-efficacy associates with higher performance and approaching higher-level goals (complex tasks; Lee et al., 2003). Sometimes the differences in efficacy levels are more a function of how long someone has been in a workplace and sometimes they are more a function of ability. Think back to the first time you used a course management system where your assignments and grades all appeared online (no more agendas from elementary school). Because of your unfamiliarity with the software, you likely had low self-efficacy (a function of time and experience). Similarly, if asked to solve a quantum physics problem on the next exam for this class, you would likely

skip it because you lack the efficacy and ability to complete the
task, especially if that was not
included on the study guide!

Self-efficacy beliefs can also
impact leaders' and followers'
**intercultural willingness to com-
municate**, which refers to one's
predisposition to initiate and
invest energy in exchanging messages with diverse others (Kassing,
1997). Followers must understand
how their self-efficacy beliefs
promote or inhibit their willingness to communicate in terms of
upward communication (process of
information flowing from lower to
higher levels of an organizational
hierarchy) and use of voice when
sending or receiving feedback with
leaders and coworkers. Leaders

FIGURE 4.3 Namaste literally means "to bow,
i to you." It is often used in indicate the connections between a teacher and student as a sign
of greeting that we will spiritually work together
or as an indication of thankfulness. Because of
the spiritual connection, it only occurs when
people can engage in self-regulation and social
perspective-taking.

should clearly frame and articulate follower tasks as learning-oriented goals
aimed at acquiring skills and knowledge. For instance, Riley is a software
design developer who feels his recent presentation was not up to par. He
meets with his supervisor, Drew, for feedback on improving his presentation
techniques. From a learning-goal orientation Drew might say, "You should
develop your speaking skills and presentation knowledge by attending two
workshops before we present the next project at the end of this quarter."

Prosocial Orientation

A **prosocial orientation** toward others (i.e., other-orientation) involves thinking in a cooperative and supportive manner to benefit others. Two features
of a prosocial orientation include humility and social perspective-taking.
Humility encompasses being modest or unassuming by embracing a
self-perspective where one is not the center of the universe around which
all others revolve (Randel et al., 2018). Let's be honest, most of us like our
leaders and followers to be confident and inclusive, but not full of themselves
or cocky. **Social perspective-taking** refers to the capacity to assume and
maintain another's point of view (Hale & Delia, 1976).

To better understand the way humility and social perspective-taking give
rise to competent communication, let's briefly talk about two barriers to a
prosocial orientation. First, the opposite of humility, **egocentrism** (excessive
self-focused attention) serves as a direct barrier to fostering a prosocial

orientation. Think about the social media profiles of people you know. The person who posts an excessive number of selfies and boasts mostly about themselves without ever crediting or acknowledging the influence of others, or the way others play a key role in the accomplishments resembles that of an egocentric leader or follower. Do you think you would enjoy working with an egocentric follower or leader? Why? In what ways would you be motivated to collaborate, support, or learn from an egocentric leader or follower? What happens if you are perceived as the egocentric follower or leader?

Similar to the concept of egocentrism is the second barrier, **ethnocentrism**, which refers to considering one's own culture, beliefs, and standards as superior to or more important than others. Ethnocentrism is associated with negative perceptions of leaders' and followers' credibility and managerial effectiveness as well as one's intercultural willingness to communicate (Campbell, 2016). Ethnocentric followers and leaders are more likely to drink only one type of coffee and consider it superior to all others because they fail to think outside the box and experiment with the diversity of roasted beans available today. Embracing a prosocial orientation in ways that decrease egocentrism and ethnocentrism, such as humility and social perspective-taking, influence the way leaders and followers think, speak, listen, act, and the way followers and leaders choose how to adapt communication during interactions. Up until this point, our discussion has focused on understanding communication competence and the control theme of competence at the individual level.

RESEARCH SUMMARY

Study: Steele and Plenty (2015) set out to determine whether leaders' communication competence or followers' ratings of leaders' communication competence would predict communication satisfaction and job satisfaction. They looked at the differences in perceptions of communication competence, communication satisfaction, and job satisfaction by analyzing: 1) between-group differences of leaders compared to followers and 2) within-group differences among leader participants as well as among follower participants. For between-group differences, they hypothesized that leaders and followers would have different perceptions of:

- leaders' communication competence;

- job satisfaction and;

- communication satisfaction.

For within-group differences, they hypothesized:

- followers' job satisfaction and communication satisfaction would be related;

- leaders' job satisfaction and communication satisfaction would be related;

- followers' job satisfaction and communication satisfaction would be related to ratings of leader's communication competence; and

- leaders' ratings of job satisfaction and communication satisfaction would be related to ratings of self-perceived communication competence.

Over 200 working professionals (one fourth leader participants and three fourths follower participants) working at a water utility company in Trinidad and Tobago participated in this study. All participants in this study completed a questionnaire measuring communication satisfaction and job satisfaction. Leader participants also completed measures about their self-perceived communication competence; follower participants completed measures asking them to rate their leaders' communication competence. In their sample, there were no differences between followers' and leaders' ratings of leaders' communication competence, job satisfaction, or communication satisfaction. The first set of hypotheses testing between-group differences was not supported.

Followers' job satisfaction, communication satisfaction, and ratings of leaders' competence were related; however, ratings of communication satisfaction were more strongly related to job satisfaction than ratings of leaders' communication competence. Leaders reported their self-perceived competence equally related to their job satisfaction and communication satisfaction. The second set of hypotheses testing within-group differences was supported.

Implications: Both follower and leader communication competence are important for followers to feel satisfied with communication and their job. However, leaders' communication satisfaction and job satisfaction rely more on the leader's sole perceptions of their own communication competence. Ultimately, both leaders' and followers' communication competence are important for communication satisfaction and job satisfaction at the individual and relational levels; however, communication competence at the relational level is more important for followers than leaders. In an ideal organization, only competent communicators would be hired; in reality, many less competent communicators find themselves in these roles. For future employees interested in job satisfaction, interacting with the leader and assessing the leader's competence is a critical component of the interview process.

Competence as Adaptation: Adaptation Theory of Dyads

The second theme, adaptation, shifts our attention to understanding communication competence at the relational level. Competent communication requires not only adapting to one's own needs, desires, and abilities, but also to those others in a given situation. When your best friend is sad, do you know how to adjust your messages to be consoling or supportive? Think about when you first met your best friend: did you automatically know exactly how to do this, or did you learn how to adapt best after interacting in a social support situation? You may have had a good idea of what to do and say initially, but only through interaction was that idea and particular approach confirmed.

Leaders' and followers' workplace relationships are no different. People have to interact with each other over time to develop a sound understanding of how to adapt messages in the most effective or appropriate way for a particular interaction partner and situation. The adaptation theory of dyads explains the way task-oriented dyads (leader-follower, leader-leader, or follower-follower) adapt communication during initial interactions (Ellingsworth, 1988). The three assumptions of adaptation theory of dyads include:

1. Leaders and followers create their communication messages to achieve a purpose.

2. Context (audience and situation) determines whether followers or leaders initially share the responsibility of altering their communication or carry the burden alone.

3. Communication impacts leaders' or followers' perceptions of self and diverse other(s) for future interaction.

The first assumption emphasizes understanding why task-oriented dyads adapt their communication during an interaction. Whether communicating about a task, plan, or goal, leaders and followers work together and interact to achieve a purpose. How productive these interactions are for achieving the purpose relies on how well people create and choose messages that are sensitive to and supportive of the perceived and actual differences of the other. Adapting communication in this way is especially important for dyads to remain focused on tasks or achieving their designated purpose when the diversity of their beliefs becomes visibly at odds.

For example, Logan and Alex have been working on a project together for the past month. On the Friday before their Monday deadline, they realize the project will require at least another full day of work to be completed. Logan believes they should meet over the weekend to finish by the Monday deadline, whereas missing the deadline is less of a concern for Alex who believes they should wait until Monday to work on finishing the project. If

Logan and Alex become focused on or distracted by their different beliefs regarding deadlines and work, they are more likely to lose sight of the task and their productivity will suffer.

The second assumption focuses on how contextual aspects of interaction (situation and audience) determine whether dyads initially share the responsibility of adapting communication or carry the adaptive burden separately. In general, a competent communicator will be able to consistently adapt messages to fit the needs of the situation and audience while interacting; however, remember that followers and leaders communicate competently in some situations and are unable or unwilling to in others. As such, we can rely on the situation to inform us of where (or within whom) competence can be observed. For instance, in situations where the dyad has a mutual purpose, such as the above example of Logan and Alex, both interaction partners share the responsibility of adapting communication to one another.

In situations where one person wants something from the other, then the responsibility to adapt communication initially rests on the shoulders of the initiator or person making the request. According to adaptation theory, when one person is superior in terms of status or power, the adaptive burden remains with the less powerful person throughout the interaction (Ellingsworth, 1988). Until they develop individually and relationally beyond the constraints of cultural, societal, or psychological perceptions or beliefs, they are unlikely to be successful.

Person-Centered Communication

The second competency, person-centered communication, highlights the adaptation theme of communication competence. Generally, **person-centered communication** refers to messages reflecting an awareness of the context (Burleson, 1987, p. 305). Context includes the affective, or emotional, as well as the relational aspects of the situation. Organizations seek followers and leaders capable of demonstrating both task and relational competence. More specifically, as shown in Figure 4.4, the top relational competency desired by organizations is person-focused competence, a specific types of person-centered communication (PCC).

Within organizational life, followers and leaders undoubtedly find themselves in support and influence situations requiring PCC to achieve goals and perform both individual and relational tasks competently. However, it is not enough to merely establish that PCC is important to organizations. We must also understand why PCC is one of the top relational competencies desired by organizations. The short answer is that it is important for effectiveness, satisfaction, making money, and relationship quality. More specifically, people who use more PCC are more persuasive, found at higher levels of the

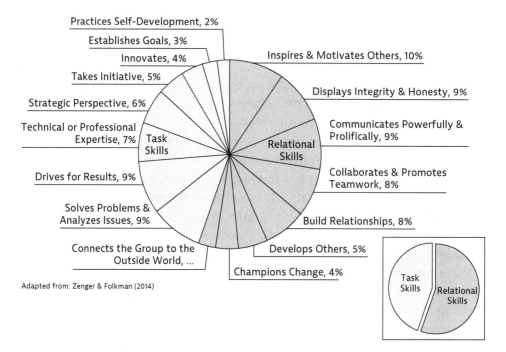

Practices Self-Development, 2%
Establishes Goals, 3%
Innovates, 4%
Takes Initiative, 5%
Strategic Perspective, 6%
Technical or Professional Expertise, 7%
Drives for Results, 9%
Solves Problems & Analyzes Issues, 9%
Connects the Group to the Outside World, ...
Inspires & Motivates Others, 10%
Displays Integrity & Honesty, 9%
Communicates Powerfully & Prolifically, 9%
Collaborates & Promotes Teamwork, 8%
Build Relationships, 8%
Develops Others, 5%
Champions Change, 4%

Task Skills
Relational Skills

Adapted from: Zenger & Folkman (2014)

FIGURE 4.4   Task and Relational Skills Organizations Desire

organization, move up the promotional ladder more quickly, and have higher salaries (Zorn & Violanti, 1996).

PCC highlights the degree to which leaders' and followers' message content is adaptive to the other and encourages the other to reflect, particularly in terms of support situations. The way followers and leaders express, observe, or analyze supportive communication occurs at three levels of person-centered messages (Burleson, 2009).

1. **High person-centered (HPC) messages** acknowledge and legitimize the feelings and viewpoint of the other. They involve focusing on helping the other to articulate, elaborate, and explore those feelings, why they are being felt, and how they fit into the current situation.

   "It must be frustrating to work so hard and not get the programming director promotion (convey understanding). Because you are innovative and smart (support), do you think they didn't choose you because the upcoming creative director opening is a better match for your expertise (think about event in a different way)?"

2. **Moderate person-centered (MPC) messages** recognize the other's feelings and attempt to reduce the other's stress or distract the other's attention away from the troubling situation. MPC messages include

expressing sympathy or offering alternative explanations intended to mitigate feelings of stress or anxiety.

> "Don't feel bad; it's only one of many upcoming promotion opportunities. You'll get the next one. Let's catch happy hour. That will get your mind off of this."

3. **Low person-centered (LPC) messages** are disconfirming by nature; they deny the other's feelings and viewpoint. LPC message features involve criticisms, demands, telling the other how to act and feel, or challenging the legitimacy of the other's feelings.

> "Lots of people wanted that job. You just don't have what it takes. You shouldn't make such a big deal out of it."

Followers' support and influence are needed by leaders and co-workers. Like followers, leaders need reassurance, feedback, and assistance from followers to perform competently. If leaders had all the right answers for every problem, task, or decision placed upon their shoulders, then there would be no need for followers or followership. While the three levels of PCC messages show us *how* competent communicators adapt messages for a particular interaction partner, the situational and behavioral differences among leader-follower dyads can make it difficult for followers to know *when* to engage in PCC to offer support or when their influence is needed.

Followers must consider four situational factors when deciding whether to offer support and influence (Lapierre, 2014).

- **Follower expertise** should be factored into the decision to constructively challenge or voice suggestions for changes or decision-making. Followers must carefully evaluate whether their knowledge and skills will make a valuable contribution to organizational processes or the leader's decision-making process. An important question for followers to ask themselves is, how will voicing my expertise alter the situation or decision and impact the collective interest, compared to refraining or remaining silent? Based on the situation, the choice to "speak up" or "shut up" should be weighed carefully by followers for potential advantages and disadvantages.

- **Leader trust** is a factor promoting or prohibiting followers' decisions to offer feedback. Sometimes leaders explicitly ask for feedback, showing their trust in a follower's opinions or suggestions. It can be less clear whether followers have a leader's trust if feedback is not specifically sought. In that case, followers can observe leader behaviors for indicators of leader trust, including delegating more responsibilities, granting decision-making authority, assigning followers to more important tasks or projects, and less monitoring (Lapierre, 2014). If a leader does not trust a particular follower, then that follower's feedback likely goes unused, overlooked, and may even be perceived as a nuisance, insult, or threat.

- **Time** is a factor for followers to consider when deciding whether to offer support or suggestions. How much time is at stake for a leader's particular problem, task, or decision? When time is limited, there is little room for self-doubt; if followers choose to speak up, then they must be certain their support or suggestion is valuable and necessary.

- The **cost-benefit of change** is a factor for followers to consider when choosing whether their ideas, opinions, or feedback contributes to or detracts from the leader, the leader-follower relationship, and the collective. Specifically, followers can ask themselves journalistic who, what, how, and why questions to evaluate potential costs and benefits as well as assess how well the feedback or use of voice benefits outweigh the costs.

Likewise, leaders are expected to offer task and relational support to followers in terms of learning and development (feedback, guidance, expectations, etc.). Leaders who communicate a sense of inclusion can reduce the uncertainty followers experience in deciding when to offer support. For leaders, PCC is necessary to communicate a sense of inclusion to followers. Leaders who use PCC messages at all three levels strategically, based on the audience's and situation's needs, engage in relationally inclusive behaviors.

PCC is associated with five inclusive leadership behaviors that facilitate followers' perceptions of inclusion (Randel et al., 2018).

- Supporting followers, in terms of PCC, involves understanding what followers like and don't like about their jobs, leadership, and the organization.

- Effective leaders ensure justice and equity by establishing or enforcing policies related to fairness, which are set in place to protect differences in diversity and heighten followers' sense of belonging.

- Competent leaders grant power to followers by encouraging shared decision-making practices. Consulting followers during the decision-making process and integrating follower perspectives creates avenues for learning, growth, and innovation for all members of an organization.

- Leaders who welcome and accept different perspectives and approaches create a comfortable environment for building trust and commitment.

- Helping followers fully contribute involves understanding how followers' expertise is being underutilized, overlooked, or taken for granted. Inclusive leaders who use PCC to support, protect, involve, and help their followers convey respect, value, and community which as a result, stimulates followers' willingness to engage, motivation, belongingness, and feelings of security.

Competence as Collaboration: Emotional Intelligence

The final competency, emotional intelligence, reflects the collaboration theme of communication competence. **Emotional intelligence** (EI) is the ability to monitor and distinguish one's own and others' feelings and use this information to influence or guide the thoughts and actions of one's self and others (Salovey & Mayer, 1990). Think about the character Sheldon Cooper, played by Jim Parson, in the American TV show *The Big Bang Theory*. As a senior theoretical physicist, Sheldon has a genius-level IQ while also severely lacking social and relational skills, contributing to his inability to adequately recognize irony, sarcasm, or engage in empathy. Sheldon shows that high levels of intelligence in sophisticated areas of expertise do not guarantee effectiveness within the social realm. Leaders and followers can be highly successful in using their mental intelligence (IQ) within their particular job, trade, or expertise, yet fail to experience the same success in social interaction.

EI is a critical competency for effective followership and leadership. In fact, it is associated with several desirable workplace attributes and outcomes—communication competence, effective communication, problem-solving, social support, social cohesion, socially appropriate behavior, conflict management, trustworthiness, and cooperation (Troth et al., 2012).

Think about these attributes and outcomes as you imagine the leader-follower scenario in which a leader lacks EI. As a follower, Tae meets with the head supervisor of the company, Sam, to express concerns regarding some recent experiences of being bullied by other employees who work on the same team. Tae becomes emotional and starts to cry while describing feelings of sadness and shame in the way these bullying incidents have negatively impacted not only Tae's productivity, but also the quality and productivity of other team members. Sam's eyes roll, hands fly up in the air, and yells "This is ridiculous. You all need to stop acting like children and do your jobs!" In what ways does Sam lack emotional intelligence? On the flip side, let's think about Sam reacting in a different way. Let's say, instead, Sam begins to sob, face in hands and says "I too was once a victim of bullying at work. It was so severe and traumatic I had to find another job. I can't talk about this!" In this case, in what way is Sam lacking emotional intelligence? If you were a communication consultant, what kind of advice would you give to Sam regarding emotional intelligence? On the other hand, if you were Tae, how would you feel?

For leaders, lacking EI is like buying a one-way train ticket on the ineffective communication express. Effective leaders understand how to collaborate (work alongside) with others to bring out the best in them, and to promote optimal output and healthy working relationships. However, let's put followers on the "hot seat" for a minute. What do you think are the consequences for followers who lack EI when interacting with co-workers or clients? What about when interacting with leaders? Followers are the people on the front line, the people who are doing the bulk of the "heavy lifting" at work to carry out the organization's mission and leader's vision. Followers work alongside leaders, coworkers, and clients, yet it is generally leaders who are either given (or take) credit for followers' work.

Think about it: did Steve Jobs create the first iPhone or iPod all by himself? No, it was the aggregate efforts of Steve and his followers who were led by Steve's vision. Did Mark Zuckerberg create Facebook all by himself? Nope, Facebook was created from the combined efforts of Mark and three or four of his college roommates. In fact, there has been much debate, not to mention legal action, about who out of this group actually developed the vision for Facebook. If Mark were a follower, rather than the leader of this group's work, then did he engage in ethical communication by solely founding Facebook? Moreover, if this is the case, did he have or lack EI?

Thinking back to the above example of Tae and Sam also raises another important communication skill connected to EI: active-empathic listening. For example, if you were Tae, what would you say about Sam's listening behaviors based on Sam's messages? Additionally, in what ways do you think Sam's non-verbal communication impacts Tae's perceptions of Sam's verbal messages? Being able to clearly and accurately send (encode), interpret (decode), and manage both verbal and nonverbal expressions of emotion is the essence of EI. According to Guerrero and Ramos-Salzar (2015), nonverbal and verbal emotional skills aid followers' or leaders' emotional intelligence because 1) emotional sensitivity promotes decoding accuracy, 2) emotional control enhances managing emotions, and 3) emotional expressivity heightens sending (encoding). Each emotional skill relates to one's willingness to listen actively and empathically.

Active-empathic listening refers to the three-phase process (sensing, processing, and responding) of a listener's dynamic and emotional involvement (Bodie et al., 2013). **Emotional sensitivity** is the ability to decode affect, beliefs, and attitudes as well as awareness of how this information impacts thoughts, feelings, and actions (Guerrero & Ramos-Salzar, 2015). For example, has anyone ever tried to cheer you up by using humor? There are times when humor is effective, and times when it is not. Processing (understanding, comprehending, and integrating different factors of the audience and the situation) involves **emotional control**, which is the ability to manage or regulate expressions about one's feelings.

Responding (using verbal and nonverbal communication to indicate active attention) may include asking questions, paraphrasing for shared meaning, or acknowledging understanding another person's perspective. **Emotional expressivity,** an individuals' ability to verbally communicate thoughts and feelings as well as nonverbally convey attitudes and interpersonal cues accurately (Riggio, 1986), plays a key role in responding. People are more willing to collaborate, connect, and/or accept another's influence when

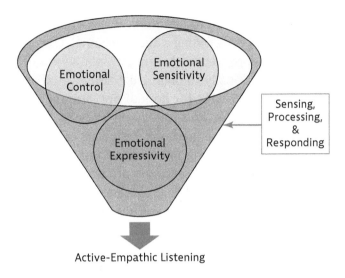

Active-Empathic Listening

FIGURE 4.5   Active-Empathic Listening

leaders' or followers' response messages convey a more precise understanding of the other's experience, beliefs, or attitudes.

Empowerment, Power, and Social Influence

Empowerment, giving another the means to achieve something, occurs when leaders tap into followers' intrinsic motivation, elevating their sense of competence, self-efficacy, and autonomy. Sharing and delegating power or responsibilities as well as supporting followers' learning and development are generally considered empowering leadership behaviors (Amundsen & Martinsen, 2014). Like communication competence, perceptions of empowering behaviors vary from one person to the next and are constrained by contextual factors related to the respective needs and expectations of the audience and situation. For instance, some followers may perceive the act of sharing power during decision making or delegating more responsibilities as an indicator of a leader's trust or developmental support, whereas others may see those acts as evidence of incompetence––that the leader can't or won't lead (Lee et al., 2018a). The key, then, for effective empowerment is tailoring empowering behaviors to fit followers' subjective needs and expectations.

Leaders should consider level of experience as a starting point for understanding follower needs. In terms of task performance, empowering behaviors are more likely to influence the day-to-day performance of less experienced followers, whereas more experienced followers are more influenced by relationship quality (Lee et al., 2018b). Having shared perceptions of each other's needs and expectations allows leaders to engage in appropriate empowering behaviors; followers are less likely to misinterpret these behaviors as over-em-powering or under-empowering (Wong & Giessner, 2018). Of course, obtaining a shared perception does not happen overnight. Followers and leaders must interact and develop relationally to build trust and mutual understanding.

Rather than waiting 365 days for annual performance evaluations to obtain feedback from leaders (and followers), they can create feedback loops for continuous constructive feedback. Followers can create these loops and influence leaders by engaging in upward communication and voice. **Voice** refers to the extent to which followers proactively bring their sugges-tions, ideas, and concerns for change to an organization member's attention (Carsten et al., 2018). As such, follower voice is also a way for followers to influence the behaviors of not only leaders, but also other organizational members. Establishing ongoing feedback loops can increase the frequency of leader-follower interactions, creating greater opportunities for empow-erment because: a) leaders and followers exchange constructive feedback and b) leaders serve as role models, mentors, coaches, or advisors.

Naturally, the role of power comes into play when we talk about ways leaders and followers effectively exert social influence. Given what you know about power, you should be thinking about how followers and leaders can use different types of power (e.g., legitimate, coercive, referent, etc.) to influence, empower, support, or provide feedback. As you think about this, it is also important to consider how the power of language contributes to the way people exercise different types of power. There are times when the extent of influence relies not on what the message is, but *how* that message is expressed.

Leaders and followers can use DISC to enhance influence attempts by engaging in style-identifying and style-flexing (using DISC knowledge to identify and shift communication styles to achieve goals). As a brief review, both the driver and contemplator styles are task-oriented; however, driv-ers are outcome focused whereas contemplators are more concerned with quality. The influencer and supporter styles are both relationship-oriented. The goal for influencers is collaboration (working alongside others to achieve goals), whereas cooperation (working with others to achieve goals) is the main focus of supporters. Misunderstandings are prone to occur in communication situations involving leaders and followers who have different communication styles. When people have a different orientation (task or relational), it can be like interacting with someone who speaks a different language—a language that you do not know, speak, or write. In contrast, having the same orienta-tion is like interacting with someone who has a different accent or speaks a different dialect of the same language. People, leaders and followers alike, are drawn to similarities and therefore more easily influenced when others have a similar or compatible communication style.

CASE STUDY Talent Management at Proctor & Gamble

Have you ever thought about where your home and personal care products come from? What kind of laundry, toothpaste, shampoo, soap, or
grooming products do you use? Chances are you use (or have used) one or
more of Proctor & Gamble's consumer product brands.

TABLE 4.2   Proctor & Gamble Product Brands Examples

Fabric Care	Oral Care	Hair Care	Skin Care & Grooming
Tide	Crest	Head & Shoulders	Ivory
Cheer	Scope	Herbal Essences	Olay
Bounce	Oral-B	Old Spice	Secret
Downy	Fixodent	Pantene	Gillette (and Gillette Venus)
Gain		Aussie	Braun

See https://us.pg.com/brands/ for more product brands and information.

Before Proctor & Gamble's (P&G) current CEO, David Taylor, took over
on November 1, 2015, Alan G. Lafley served as P&G's CEO for 15 years,
from 2000–2015, before retiring in 2016. From 2000 to 2008, the process
of bringing Lafley's vision of innovation to life increased the commercial
success rate of new P&G products from 15 percent to 60 percent. Who
should we thank for developing and improving the P&G product brands
we love to use? We can thank all P&G employees, followers and leaders
alike, and guess what? Some of these people are your age—P&G promotes
developing and improving young talent by hiring university graduates
who were recruited as interns prior to graduating. In 2014, P&G's talent
processes and leadership development efforts consistently received top
recognition in the business world, such as (https://news.pg.com/blog/
pg-ranked-1-leadership-development):

- Best overall company for leadership development—*Chief Executive*
  magazine

- Top companies for executive women—*National Association for Executive
  Women*

- Top MBA employers—*Forbes*

- Best place to work—*Glassdoor.com*

Fast forwarding five years to 2019, P&G continues to be recognized with
top honors for the way they value and invest in their employees, ranking within the top 100 of several *Forbes* magazine's 2018 lists, including
(https://www.forbes.com/companies/procter-gamble/#7b8f98324165):

(continued)

- Top regarded companies

- Best employers for new grads

- Best employers for women

- World's most innovative companies

- Best employers for diversity

So, how does P&G do it? It began with Lafley's vision of innovation honing P&G's talent management processes to focus on investing and nurturing the skills and interest of P&G employees—to broaden innovation capabilities from within. However, Lafely knew that without followers working to achieve a leader's vision and buying in to the organization's mission, that vision would be nothing more than a lost opportunity. In Lafley's words, "As the CEO, I could lead and inspire the company as a whole, but I could not substitute my judgement for that of other leaders who knew and understood the specific businesses far better than I could" (https://www.strategy-business.com/article/08304?gko=b5105). Moreover, Lafely foresaw how the lack of interaction among leaders and followers threatened the success of innovation. In Lafely's perspective, "Often, the root cause is poor social interaction; the right people simply don't engage in productive dialogue frequently enough." Therefore, a key reason for modifying P&G's talent development processes was to increase social interaction among employees.

P&G moved from a traditional approach of investing in employee talent to a more contemporary (interactive) approach over a series of four steps. Step one focused and unified leaders and followers' efforts toward the same organizational mission, thus making purposeful performance a strategy. Employee motivation and capabilities were oriented to a collective common purpose (mission), to improving consumers' lives. At P&G, the consumer is BOSS and "the heart of all we do." Step two emphasized building from within by making innovation personally relevant and directly linked to each P&G employee's job. Innovation is not reserved solely for employees working in R&D or engineering; instead, all P&G leaders and followers, whether in management, sales, marketing, or administration, carry the responsibility to take ownership for the role they play in innovation. Step three concentrated on talent development and growth, competent performance. P&G employees are recruited and cherished not only for their values, intelligence, achievements, and leadership, but also social skills demonstrating agility and flexibility.

P&G specifically stresses the importance of emotional intelligence and social skills relevant to curiosity, connectedness, and collaboration. In fact, people without these social skills are not hired or have been weeded out. As Lafely puts it, "Curiosity, collaboration, and connectedness are easy to talk about but difficult to develop in practice. We have tried to carefully identify and ease out people who are controlling or insecure, who don't want to share, open up, or learn." End-to-end integration is another way P&G values and invests in a global and diverse mix of employee talent. At P&G, employees are challenged by tasks varying in complexity and can expect to experience a wide range of both leadership and followership positions. This way, employees are exposed to a broad array of audiences and situations from which to learn. P&G refers to this as "organizational scalability"—in that leaders and followers are experienced to fluidly scale among positions within the organization's structure. In many ways this reflects Aristotle's idea that "one who cannot be a good follower, cannot be a good leader." Additionally, from day one, employees are granted control and decision-making power in the process of planning how their expertise and skills align with positions that will progress their career at P&G. Employees find themselves working with and alongside leaders who serve as coaches, mentors, recruiters, and trainers. Employees also find themselves working with other coworkers to integrate and fit product ideas (innovation) to local consumers' needs. This highlights the last step in improving P&G's talent management processes, in which employees are expected to engage in integrative thinking. For example, while Febreeze, the odor-eliminating product, saw success and popularity in the U.S., it was rejected in Japan. P&G employees had to think of the consumer and change the product to better fit the needs of Japanese practices and culture. This process required P&G to call upon local consumer surveys and employees knowledgeable in Japanese culture to provide ideas, opinions, and suggestions for tailoring the product to Japanese consumers. This feedback was then gathered and synthesized to refine the Febreeze product launch model. With the exception of the core technology (odor eliminating ingredients) everything about the product was changed—fragrance, bottle design, mist pattern (compared to spray), etc.

Overall, P&G offers a culture fostering individual development and growth. However, since the spring of 2012, major layoffs have occurred to cut costs. In 2012, P&G employed 126,000 employees. Contrasting this number to P&G's 92,000 employees in 2018 indicates about a 27% decrease in its workforce from 2012–2018. In March 2018, P&G announced more major layoffs were coming across all levels in the company, estimating about (https://abcnews.go.com/Business/story?id=88448&page=1):

- Two-thirds of the reductions to come from nonmanufacturing roles and the remaining cuts to come from manufacturing projects.

- 40% of the layoffs to occur in the U.S., the rest coming from P&G's operations in other countries.

(continued)

By August 2018, 3,000 jobs were cut, the current CEO (David Taylor) took a 4% pay cut, and P&G announced even more cuts are coming.

DISCUSSION QUESTIONS

1. Using the information about individual and relational competencies, in what ways do the four steps of P&G's talent development system relate to co-cultural communication competence, person-centered communication, emotional intelligence, empowerment, power, and social influence?

2. Of the four steps involved in P&G's talent development system, which do you believe is most important? Least important? Why?

3. Given the steady occurrence of layoffs and more to come, how do you think this impacts communication among leaders and followers, workplace relationships, and recruitment?

ANALYSIS OPTIONS

A. Given the impending layoffs, you have been hired to develop the criteria for layoffs. Explain and address how the criteria you developed recognize diversity and inclusion, consider ethics, and recognize the importance of communication competence for an individual's and organization's long-term success?

B. Often, when companies experience continuous and/or impending layoffs, employee factors related to competent performance and turnover suffer, are put at risk, or become threatened (e.g., job security, job satisfaction, communication satisfaction, and feelings of belonging, etc.). How should P&G work to address, mitigate, and prevent leaders' and followers' competent performance from deteriorating and voluntary turnover from occurring?

C. P&G CEO, David Taylor, has pledged another $10 billion in cost cuts by 2021. While a large portion of those savings will come from moving to fewer, larger, and more automated factories, P&G also plans to sell off some of its product brands (https://www.cincinnati.com/story/money/2018/08/07/p-g-cuts-worldwide-jobs-lowest-decades/930154002/). As cost cuts dwindle the number of P&G employees and middle management roles, it will dramatically change the leader to follower ratio across business departments. For instance, a leader to follower ratio of 1:100 means for every 1 leader there are 100 followers. Determine how P&G can effectively adjust the current talent development system to accommodate this change.

ANALYSIS PROCESS

- Brainstorm a list of options for addressing the issue.
- Make a list of strengths and challenges for each of your brainstormed solutions.

- Choose the best solution for the issue.

- Develop an implementation plan for your chosen solution.

- Additional resources:

P&G Brands
https://tinyurl.com/y3n6mqfh

P&G Plans to Cut Jobs
https://tiny.utk.edu/FCL4_4

P&G Newsroom: Talent Programs Awards
https://tiny.utk.edu/FCL4_1

P&G Cuts Jobs Worldwide
https://tiny.utk.edu/FCL4_5

P&G Values and Invests in Employees
https://tiny.utk.edu/FCL4_2

New Rules of Talent Management
https://tiny.utk.edu/FCL4_6

P&G Innovation Culture
https://tiny.utk.edu/FCL4_3

P&G Digitizes Talent Management
https://tiny.utk.edu/FCL4_7

(continued)

P&G Website Resources
https://tinyurl.com/y6htvwn6

P&G in the News
https://tiny.utk.edu/FCL4_11

P&G Website Resources
https://tiny.utk.edu/FCL4_8

P&G in the News
https://tiny.utk.edu/FCL4_12

P&G Website Resources
https://tiny.utk.edu/FCL4_9

P&G in the News
https://tiny.utk.edu/FCL4_13

P&G in the News
https://tiny.utk.edu/FCL4_10

 LEADER AND FOLLOWER DEVELOPMENT PRACTICES

1. Strengthen your initiative, ability to work independently, commitment to the common good, and courage. Even if you have the first three, without the courage to voice your perspective and address transgressions in the workplace, your competence is incomplete (Suda, 2013).

2. Be in the right place, at the right time (10 minutes early) with the right attitude (Disque, 2018). Specifically, handle as much as you can and be willing to ask for help when you need it, do what you have been asked to do and not what you want to do. Think like those above you and never force someone into a corner without ample time and space to make a needed decision.

3. Surround yourself with other competent communicators so you have role models who excel in different contexts and relational types. While it is tempting to surround yourself with people who are less competent so that they do not potentially outshine you, continuing to grow means challenging yourself to continuously improve.

4. Understand your purpose, what makes you happy, and have the efficacy to choose when you are going to be influenced and when you are going to be the influencer.

5. Understand those around you well enough to know when they need clear directions, resources, and/or the blessing to do it themselves in their own way. Distributed power allows others to engage in self-regulation and take pride in what they are able to accomplish independently (Giles, 2016).

DISCUSSION QUESTIONS AND ACTIVITIES

1. At the outset, we asked you to think about someone you considered competent in different situations. How would your response be different now that you have read the chapter? If it would not be, what reinforced your initial beliefs about what it takes to be a competent leader or follower?

2. Choose someone whom you consider to be a competent communicator. Find at least 10 messages from this person (think about leaders and followers at work, social or religious organizations, campus organizations, etc.). Using what you know about low, medium, and high person-centered communication, classify each of the messages. What recommendations or commendations would you have for this person as a competent communicator? Be specific about what the person should continue doing and what the person should consider revising when communicating with you and others.

3. Choose an interaction where you are a follower. Engage in active-empathic listening. What was hardest? What was easiest? What would you do differently the next time you found yourself in a similar situation to be as competent as possible?

4. Choose an interaction where you are a leader. Engage in active-empathic listening. What was hardest? What was easiest? What would you do differently the next time you found yourself in a similar situation to be as competent as possible?

5. Using the leader and follower development practices as a starting point, develop a list of at least three things you can do between now and graduation to improve your communication competence and better prepare yourself for the world of work.

FIGURE CREDITS:

CHAPTER 5

RELATIONAL LEADERSHIP AND FOLLOWERSHIP

"Leadership is always dependent on the context, but the context is established by the relationships we value."

—MARGARET WHEATLEY

"If your actions inspire others to dream more, learn more, do more and become more, you are a leader."

—JOHN QUINCY ADAMS

Whether you grew up working/volunteering in formal organizations or simply had chores to complete around the house, each of us has had a boss. They helped us figure out what needed to be done, how best to accomplish the task, and hopefully had the common decency to say "thank you" when the work was done. In these situations, we "obediently" followed directions, or at least pretended we were doing what we were supposed to do. Whereas these boss relationships get the job done, they fail to recognize the importance of the relationships built between leaders and followers.

The V formation is much more calculated and precise than most humans realize. Birds fly approximately one meter back and one meter to the outside of the one in front of them until they run out of birds. In this formation, the birds must also flap their wings in concert for the benefits of the formation to work. That is, when one bird flaps its wings, the air immediately behind it is pushed downward and creates downwash; the air out to the sides and behind that is pushed upward and creates upwash. As long as the bird behind remains in formation, it can fly with significantly less energy by using the upwash to propel it forward and allowing its wing flapping to propel the next bird. The last bird in the formation benefits the most because it does not have to propel another bird. What is most amazing about the formation is that they fly for a relatively predictable distance before resting and creating a new formation. The same bird is rarely the leader (center position) for the

FIGURE 5.1   Birds Migrating in Formation

entire journey because different birds have different levels of energy to take on the task of leading the flock. The same is true when relational leadership practices are implemented well. Leader-follower relationships are strongest when the followers engage, learn, and practice being the leader in a safe environment. When leaders and followers build trust, their mentoring and persuasion/social influence processes are more effective. As we move further into the mediated world of leaders and followers not always engaging in face-to-face interactions, we must focus on the role technology plays.

Relational Perspectives on Leaders and Followers

A relational perspective on followership and leadership focuses our attention not on us, not on the other person, but rather on the connection we make when we interact. Think about a trip to financial aid, human resources, or any other "office" that provides a service to organizational members. When people arrive there, they are often treated as another number added to a log that justifies why the person should remain employed—addressing more people's concerns makes me a more indispensable part of the organization. These routines or ceremonial ways of interacting with others (no concern for the other) are what Buber (1956) refers to as **I-It relationships**. In reality, they are not exactly relationships at all—they are transactions in the same way that you engage in a transaction at a bank (money goes in and money goes out; people come into the office and people go out of the office).

Being relational means elevating connections akin to an **I-Thou relationships** (Buber, 1956). In these relationships, both people focus on strengthening their connection with each other rather than themselves or the other person; they use communication to accomplish relational rather than instrumental or identity goals. Relational approaches require the people involved to engage in competent communication. If people are going to be relational followers and leaders, they need to develop listening, perspective taking, and emotional intelligence skills as well as process-orientation, inclusivity, and ethical mindsets. Sound like someone has to be a superhero to accomplish all of this? You are right! We would be lying if we told you this was easy.

Because we talk about competent communication skills elsewhere, we focus specifically on the mindsets here. Each mindset has three levels (Komives et al., 1998): knowing, being, and doing. At the **knowing** level, people possess the information necessary to adopt the mindset—if you have not learned about a mindset, it is almost impossible to make a conscious choice to use it. At the **being** level, people engage in the reflective processes necessary to make an informed decision about whether to adopt the mindset. At the **doing** level, people carry out the behaviors necessary to show others they have a particular mindset. While many people may know about a particular orientation, significantly fewer engage in being, and even fewer in doing.

Process Orientation

When we adopt a **process-orientation mindset**, we approach each situation as one interaction within a much larger series of interactions that make up the relationship. Think about this from a follower perspective. If Lowanna is upset with the way Bindi, a leader, is handling a particular situation, communication options might include flying off the handle and outright stating how ridiculous the new policy is, creating a coalition of people to approach Bindi, letting it drop in favor of assuming the leader knows best, setting up a meeting to learn more about the situation, and providing constructive feedback about the decision, among others. Followers with a process orientation are more likely to engage in productive dialogue, such as setting up a meeting to discuss the situation or provide constructive feedback.

Let's take a moment to see process orientation at each developmental stage. In terms of knowledge, leaders and followers must understand that they operate in a system where a change in one aspect of the system affects all other aspects of the system. In this case, the saying about the means justify the ends is completely true as the process to accomplish the goal is just as important as the outcome. People must trust the roadmap that was created and engage in high-quality communication (being). Finally, the ways in which we enact a process-orientation include collaboration, engaging in constructive feedback, and promoting civil discourse (doing).

Inclusivity

When we adopt an **inclusivity** mindset, we stress the importance of recognizing and valuing people and ideas that come from different perspectives. Think about this from a leader perspective. Daniela and Pedro are trying to put together a team to handle a new client's business. In the past, they typically put people together who have previously worked well together. While that generally works, it also means that many of those people look and think similarly. Because this client is both multinational (offices in multiple locations around the world) and multilingual, Daniela and Pedro are trying to maximize the team's diversity. They think specifically about the group as more of a web, where everyone has a valuable contribution to make and no one holds significantly more power than others, rather than a pyramid, where power is concentrated at the top and the majority of people holding up the structure are similar to each other.

Each level of an inclusivity mindset improves the organization and its members. At the knowledge level, followers and leaders must realize that different people have different perceptions of reality and different subcultures within the organization, which contribute different perspectives on a particular problem or issue. At the being level, inclusivity requires a commitment to equity and fairness. Fairness involves treating people in a way that respects their differences without advantaging or disadvantaging them in relation to others. You may be thinking: how is that even possible? It is through the doing—more listening and less talking, spending time getting to know each other, developing everyone's talents to maximize their potential, and framing situations in ways other than how the dominant group sees them.

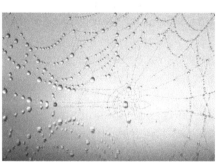

In this organization, everyone understands and appreciates inclusivity.

In this organization, the people who understand and appreciate inclusivity do not possess the power to make change happen

FIGURE 5.2 A-B   Power Concentration

Ethical Standard

Adopting an **ethical standard** mindset means that followers and leaders use a moral or just/care yardstick to determine how to act in each communication interaction. Let's take a look at this from a leader and follower perspective. Danika and Tziamara are trying to determine how to handle a situation in which it appears that Savin is using power to make sure that Jozska's ideas are not heard in the group deliberation processes. Knowing that the two come from very different backgrounds, Danika and Tziamara are trying to determine the best way to indicate that Savin's behavior is unacceptable without disrespecting a culture that values hierarchy. They are also trying to make sure that Jozska is protected from retaliation, additional distancing behavior, during future team meetings.

An ethical mindset may be the most difficult because different people have different ethical standards to determine what is right and wrong, just and unjust, or fair and unfair. In organizations such as this, everyone needs to understand the different ethical models that people use as well as value themselves and others equally (knowing). Thinking about this mindset requires followers and leaders to value high standards for behavior and choose socially responsible behaviors that benefit others, sometimes at the cost of oneself (being). The ways in which we enact an ethical standard mindset include trusting others, being willing to courageously identify issues or point out poor behavior, taking responsibility, and holding each other accountable.

Leader-Member Exchange

What is your one favorite movie or TV show of all time? Most of us have many favorites that we find great pleasure in watching. What we enjoy on-screen is a product of leader-follower relationships. Directors—the primary leader of the film-making creative vision—lead actors and scriptwriters in creating our go-to flicks. They are the reason why we have subscriptions to NETFLIX, AMAZON Video, HULU, DISNEY+, etc. Some directors collaborate with certain actors more than others (see Table 5.1), and they build higher-quality relationships and partnerships. For example, Martin Scorsese and Robert De Niro's working relationship is characterized by a shared passion for bringing together improvisation and venturing into the dark side of the human psyché. In their collaborations, Scorsese created a vision to inspire the goal and direction of each film; both Scorsese and De Niro bought into the mission of bringing those visions to life. Along the way, their behaviors—support and influence, competent performance, learning, challenging the system, actively adapting—built a high-quality relationship.

TABLE 5.1   Director–Actor Dyads with High Film Collaborations

Director–Actor Dyad	# of Films	Film Titles
Martin Scorsese–Robert De Niro	8	*Mean Streets; Taxi Driver; New York, New York; Raging Bull; The King of Comedy; Goodfellas; Cape Fear; Casino; The Audition; The Irishman*
Martin Scorsese–Leonardo DiCaprio	5	*Gangs of New York; The Aviator; The Departed; Shutter Island; The Wolf of Wallstreet; The Audition*
Tim Burton–Johnny Depp	6	*Edward Scissorhands; Ed Wood; Sleepy Hollow; Charlie and the Chocolate Factory; Corpse Bride; Sweeney Todd: The Demon Barber of Fleet Street; Alice in Wonderland; Dark Shadows*
Dennis Dugan–Adam Sandler	8	*Happy Gilmore; Big Daddy; I Now Pronounce You Chuck and Larry; You Don't Mess with the Zohan; Grown Ups; Just go with It; Jack and Jill; Grown Ups 2*
Steven Soderbergh–Matt Damon	8	*Ocean's Eleven; Ocean's Twelve; Ocean's Thirteen; Che Part 2: Guerrilla; The Informant!; Contagion; Behind the Candelabra; Unsane*
Norman Taurog–Elvis Presley	9	*G.I. Blues; Blue Hawaii; Girls! Girls! Girls!; It Happened at the World's Fair; Tickle Me; Spinout; Double Trouble; Speedway; Live a Little, Love a Little*

The idea that some leader-follower pairs develop higher-quality relationships than others is the primary idea behind Vertical Dyad Linkage theory, which later became known as leader-member exchange (LMX) theory. Actually, leader-member exchange's name change is one of many shifts across the theory's lifespan. All aboard the LMX lifespan time warp (imagine really cool music playing right now)!

Think about your own job or class groups. How often do you witness a leader who engages in more effective or interpersonal communication with some followers compared to other followers? These communication differences across leader-follower dyads probably happen more than we realize or like to think about. Vertical Dyad Linkage theory (VDL) was developed to evidence and explain this very phenomenon called **differentiation**. The basic premise of VDL was that leaders develop distinctive relationships with their followers.

The Early Years

In the beginning, VDL focused on discovering differentiation by investigating how leader-follower dyads each behave in situations over time to create an agreed-upon nature of their relationship. Researchers categorized followers who reported having high-quality communication exchanges (high in mutual trust, respect, and obligation) as "in-group" members and followers who reported low-quality exchanges (low trust, respect, and obligation) as "out-group" members (Graen & Uhl-Bien, 1995). Hence, the "member" in the name change from vertical dyad linkage to leader-member exchange.

In the 1970s, the goal for VDL research was to find answers for two major questions.

- Do *all* followers perceive, interact, and respond to their leader in the same way?
- Do leaders behave differently with different followers (i.e., in-group or out-group) to develop different relationships?

The major finding propelling VDL into LMX's evolution over the next few decades was yes, differentiation does exist. In Figure 5.3, the different sizes of the arrows from the leader to each follower illustrate the concept of differentiation. So, how, when, and why does it happen?

Let's warp into the 80s, approximately the time when VDL began taking on its "other" name, like people who start going by their middle name or nickname instead of their first name. VDL became LMX. Leader-member exchange theory focused on explaining the development of relationship quality using the sequences involved in the role making process. The goal was to answer how leaders form unique relationships with followers over time.

According to Graen and Scandura (1987), the role making process involves three phases: role taking, role making, and role routinization.

1. **Role taking** is the testing phase where a leader attempts to discover the abilities, motivations, and limits of a follower over a series of role-relevant assignments and tasks.

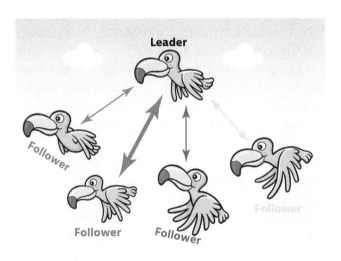

FIGURE 5.3   VDL/LMX Differentiation

2. **Role making** is the phase where a leader and follower begin to define how each will behave in relation to one another in various situations, the nature of their relationship. Here, the idea of social exchange is incorporated and discussed in terms of the leader's resources (information, influence, attention, support).

3. **Role routinization** refers to the united patterns of behaviors that are developed over time through interaction exchanges occurring in the role-making phase. The leader-follower relationship becomes stable as leaders and followers have come to agree upon mutual expectations and behaviors.

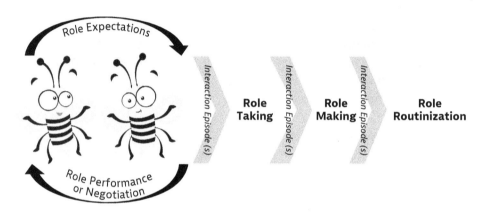

FIGURE 5.4   Role Making Process

The Adolescent Years

For most of us, adolescence represents a relationship-focused shift. The relationships we have with our friends and significant others, and the quality of those relationships, become increasingly important as we brave our teenage years. While LMX is a theory and not a person, a similar shift occurred as LMX went from being a "tween" to a teen during the 90s. During this time, LMX "came into its own" as the prominent relationship-based approach to leadership it remains known for today. LMX research began building on the role-making process by adopting a new attitude based in social exchange theory.

Seeing LMX quality as a result of a process of role negotiation is just as important as understanding how it is impacted by reciprocal influence (two-way social exchange) between leader and follower. This places more emphasis on both leaders' *and* followers' efforts in exchanging resources to develop LMX quality, instead of seeing the leader as the primary driver. As you know by now, leaders can't develop a leader-follower relationship or leadership without followers or followership. We also know that followers are not just passive recipients. It is as complicated as most relationships.

Followers, too, have their own characteristics and behaviors that contribute to the leader-follower relationship (communication exchanges and quality) and the overall leadership process.

Some cultural moments of 1995 America included: eBay's grand debut on the internet, people watching *E.R.*, *Seinfeld*, and *Friends*, the first release of Starbucks's Frappuccino, and the *Toy Story* movie. All of these happened in the same year Graen and Uhl-Bien (1995) moved LMX's attention to integrating the role-making process and social exchange. According to Graen and Uhl-Bien (1995), this integration is illustrative of how partnerships and/or leadership is built by the type of social exchange used to develop LMX quality through three stages that leader-follower dyads experience: strangers, acquaintances, and maturity.

The **strangers stage** involves low LMX and typically occurs during the role-taking phase. Leaders and followers engage in minimal social exchange in this stage, and exchanges are more economical than relationally meaningful. **Economic exchange** refers to more formal and contract-like interactions that occur between leaders and followers. Leaders provide what followers need and followers meet the responsibilities of their job description. A series of economic exchanges provides a foundation for leaders to make an offer to followers for enhancing their relationship. Theoretically, this offer is based on career-oriented social exchange (leaders' resources for advancing followers' careers) and should be presented to *all* followers, not just in-group (high LMX quality) followers.

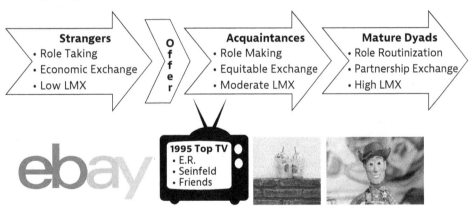

FIGURE 5.5   Graen and Uhl-Bien's (1995) LMX Partnership Model & 1995 Events

The **acquaintances stage** is characterized by moderate LMX and an increase in (or upgrade to) social exchange. Leaders and followers engage in interactions that move beyond purely contractual, representing a more equitable tit-for-tat type of exchange. **Equitable exchanges** involve sharing more information and resources, personally and professionally. Imagine cellular sales specialist Hayden (follower) and Cameron (leader). At the last company picnic, Cameron discovered Hayden worked as an IT specialist before switching careers into sales. A few months later, the company's financial files were at risk of being destroyed when Cameron's office computer caught a virus. Distraught and upset for not making a backup of the files, Cameron called on Hayden's passion and skill (resources) for decrypting computer virus codes to salvage the most important files and documents. A few days later, Cameron made room in their budget to purchase some expensive materials Hayden had requested early in the year to pursue a new project.

The **maturity stage** reflects high LMX and highly collaborated social exchange. Leaders and followers develop a partnership, interacting in ways that show support and reliance on one another. **Partnership exchange** refers to sharing information and resources at both the behavioral and emotional levels, which allows mutual trust, respect, and obligation to grow.

By integrating the role making process and aspects of social exchange, we see how reciprocal influence unfolds.

The Current Trajectory

Ahhh (sigh of relief), 2000-present day, finally something more recent and familiar for most of you. During this time, LMX research has devoted attention to understanding why differentiation occurs by looking at LMX as a process, advancing knowledge about social exchange resources, and expanding the notion of LMX beyond leader-follower dyads. When we think about why LMX differentiation occurs, it is helpful to think about LMX as a process. That is, what causes LMX quality and what are the consequences of LMX quality? Thinking of LMX as a process is the current direction of LMX research.

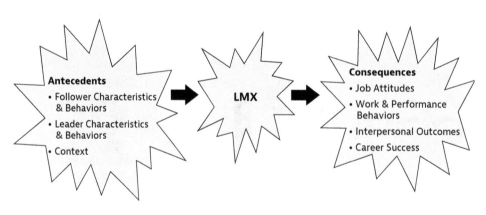

FIGURE 5.6 LMX as a Process

Implicit theories of leadership and followership are antecedents of LMX. For example, when followers' characteristics and behaviors do not align with their leader's implicit followership theory, leaders rate followers' performance more harshly and/or poorly (Whiteley et al., 2012).

We talk about **reciprocity** in interpersonal relationships; **reciprocity** occurs when leaders and followers behave in ways that mirror each other—positive behaviors lead to positive responses and negative behaviors lead to negative responses. When we engage in reciprocal actions, both leaders and followers exhibit low or high LMX, expectations are met, and people remain in balance; when one behaves with high LMX behaviors and the other with low LMX, the relationship is out of balance, which generally has a negative impact on people's attitudes and ultimately their behaviors.

We have talked about the different types of social exchange, but what exactly do followers and leaders exchange? There are different types of resources leaders and followers have at their disposal to exchange as they embark on the process of developing LMX quality. According to Wilson et al. (2010), there are six categories of leader-member resources—affiliation, status, service, information, goods, and money—that leaders and followers may exchange.

- **Affiliation resources** refer to expressions of affection, loyalty, and support. For example, followers may provide affiliation by conveying their commitment or loyalty to a leader. On the flip side, a leader may express words of encouragement to a follower.

- **Status resources** refer to judgements or expressions that impact esteem or prestige. Followers receive status resources from leaders when the exchange of this resource impacts a follower's reputation. Receiving the employee of the month award, for example. Leaders receive status resources from followers when a follower's expression boosts the referent power of a leader (e.g., conveying admiration and respect for a leader).

- **Service resources** involve activities, typically labor, performed for another. In the example of Hayden and Cameron above, they exchanged service resources. Hayden's IT services were exchanged for Cameron's time and effort in adjusting the budget to purchase materials for Hayden's project idea.

- **Information resources** involve advice, instruction, or opinions. Leaders provide followers with information by engaging in mentoring or downward communication. As the people on the frontline, followers may communicate upward informing leaders of activities or issues occurring among their coworkers and peers (fellow followers).

- **Goods** refer to tangible items, objects, or products provided to the other. Followers may provide a leader with gifts, whereas leaders may provide followers with office goods (furniture or computer software) or gifts.

- **Money** is some kind of currency with a standard value. Money as a resource may be exchanged when a leader uses his/her reward power to provide followers with pay raises or bonuses. A followers' performance, on the other hand, may indirectly impact a leaders' pay.

The concept of LMX, the cultivation of trust and social exchange of resources, in workplace relationships is not limited to leader-follower dyads. People have working relationships beyond leader-follower. According to Erdogan and Bauer (2014), the LMX process occurs in:

- Leader-leader exchange (LLX), relationships between two leaders;

- Supervisor leader-member (SLMX), relationships between a leader and follower who is also a leader to other followers;

- Coworker exchange (CWX), relationships between two people who hold horizontal positions.

Regardless of the positions people have in an organization, one of the primary determinants of the relationship's success is the extent to which the two people build trust.

Building Trust

Trust is one of those elusive terms: we know when we trust someone, an organization, or a brand, but please do not ask us to define it. In our information-saturated world, it only takes a quick tweet or post to lose trust and long periods of time to build it. Effective leader-follower dyads have built **trust** because their communicative messages and actions match; both parties show genuine consideration for each other (George & Sims, 2007). Think about trust as relational capital (Jiang & Luo, 2016).

Inviting Followers to Participate in Identifying Needs
Creating Opportunities for Constructive Follower Feedback
<u>+ Providing Useful, Relevant, and Timely Information</u>
Relational Capital (Trust)

When we trust others in the workplace, we are never left wondering why other people performed in a particular way; we are more forgiving when their actions do not meet our expectations, or when they genuinely make a mistake. In addition to the relational benefits, individual and organizational benefits include increased productivity, decreased burnout and intention to leave, lower stress and more energy, higher satisfaction, and increased engagement (Zak, 2017).

Think about your last trip to the grocery store—did you buy the same laundry detergent that was used at home growing up, the one that was on sale or cheapest, or the first one you came to on the shelf? If you chose the one that you have been using for many years, it was likely because you have come to trust that brand as being consistent and always producing clean clothes. If you bought the cheapest one or the first one you came to on the shelf, it was likely because you have not found a brand that has consistently produced the promised or desired results when washing your clothes. The same is true about the relationship between leaders and followers. If a leader and follower have worked together long enough to be able to finish each other's sentences, anticipate what the other is going to want or need in a situation, and forgive one for making a mistake without holding a grudge, they have the level of closeness that indicates trust.

FIGURE 5.7   Trust is the cornerstone of relational leadership and followership.

After conducting numerous experimental studies that examined the neuroscience behind trust in leader-follower dyads, Zak (2017) recommended the following trust-building behaviors.

- **Recognize excellence**: Whether we do it through a simple thank-you or a more formal recognition ceremony, we demonstrate a level of caring and awareness about another's actions. Ideally, recognizing excellence strengthens the trust bond most when it includes the 3 Ps: proximate to the behavior being recognized, peer driven, and public (recognition should be tangible, personal, unexpected, and delivered in a forum where others can celebrate the success as well as hear about the best practices the person used).

- **Induce challenge stress**: We consistently hear about the opioid crisis and people becoming addicted to oxycodone. Imagine being able to produce that same high by going to work—earning money instead of spending it on prescription or black-market drugs. Asking small teams of followers to work together to achieve a goal that is challenging and attainable releases the body's natural feel-good neurochemical oxytocin. Leaders help build trust with their team members when they check in on progress toward the goals and adjust them up or down to continue providing an appropriate level of challenge for everyone.

- **Empower people to decide how they are going to do their work**: When leaders trust and empower followers to make autonomous decisions about how they are going to complete tasks, the followers tend to be more innovative. Citigroup (2014) found that almost half of the people surveyed would give up a 20% raise in favor of more flexible work environments. When leaders and followers trust each other, they can develop a set of goals and have faith that they will be accomplished well within the given timeframe. When leaders and followers do not trust each other, there tends to be significantly more micromanaging and procrastinating or half-hearted efforts.

- **Enable job crafting**: Just as people who share in the decision making are more committed to carrying out the decisions made, followers with a level of autonomy to work on projects that interest them are more productive and motivated. Imagine working for software gaming company, Valve, where you have mobile desks so that you can move freely and choose the projects on which you are going to work. The only way these situations work well is when there are still clearly defined accountability expectations and ways to measure individual contributions.

- **Share information broadly**: Of all the complaints followers make, this has been near the top of their lists since the beginning of time. As more and more followers have grown up in the 24/7 news cycle and with instant access to the internet, their desire for more information has only increased. The more transparent leaders can be with their information sharing regarding goals, strategies, and tactics, the more they can reduce follower uncertainty and stress. Daily contact, face to face or electronically, is a quick and easy way to share information and increase engagement.

- **Intentionally build relationships**: Many leaders and followers associate work with task completion. This approach fails to recognize the importance of building social ties at work, which releases the oxytocin we talked about earlier. Building bridges with other people increases both the quality and quantity of one's work. Even if you think your chosen profession does not value relationships (e.g., computer programming, engineering), stop and think again because no profession or industry is immune from the value of developing a strong professional network.

- **Invest in the whole person**: Low-trust organizations focus almost exclusively on the task at hand; high-trust organizational leaders seek opportunities to help followers develop personally and professionally. Imagine a workplace where annual performance reviews were no longer necessary because leaders and followers were interacting frequently enough to always be looking forward toward the next stage in one's personal and professional growth curve, instead of behind at the tasks one completed over the past year.

▪ **Show vulnerability**: Gone in high-trust organizations are the superpower leaders who never have a bad day or failed attempt; they have been replaced by leaders who are secure enough in themselves and trust their followers to ask for help, admit their shortcomings, and recognize when someone else is better equipped to achieve a goal. Asking for help promotes collaboration and strengthens the bond between leaders and followers. When leaders no longer have to live up to superhero status, they can step back and take the risks necessary to be innovative and progressive.

While we can envision how these trust-building activities occur in a face-to-face environment, more and more leaders and followers are finding themselves in a technology-mediated environment due to geography or flexible work arrangements. When this happens, we must turn to a technology-mediated world in which people connect by developing social presence.

Creating a Social Presence

Employees don't necessarily care how you communicate with them, but they intimately care about the quality of your communications and if you really care about them.
Michael Holland, Executive Coach, 2012
https://www.bishophouse.com/building-my-team/creating-presence-with-your-gdt/
Holland's statement makes communication's centrality in a geographically dispersed leader's (GDL) toolbox obvious. There are plenty of self-help blogs and articles to tell the leader when to use each type of communication when what they really need is instruction on how to connect well with their followers. Which would you rather have over the course of a week—30 texts reminding you about what needs to be done and asking how you are doing OR one email status report and a quick phone call to check on your well-being? In our information-saturated world, most followers choose fewer, clearly purposeful, meaningful messages for quality purposes over a barrage of potentially distracting messages (Buehler, 2017).

To meet GDL communication needs, the following advice addresses using CMC to interact with followers to build/maintain relationships.

▪ Create time to interact with your followers.

▪ Out of Sight should not mean Out of Mind (Buehler, 2017).

▪ Choose the medium that is appropriate for the message and follower (Neeley, 2015).

▪ Use verbal and nonverbal immediacy behaviors (Neeley, 2015).

▪ Storytelling conveys what is important and valued (Grenny, 2017).

- Use language and images to convey what may be lost in the technology (e.g., metaphors, emoticons/emojis/gifs).

- Create non-work social communities for building team spirit and cohesion (Ha, 2017).

- Use open, positive messages (Wright, 2004).

- Be open to feedback and give feedback regularly (DeRosa, 2018).

Select and develop different styles for e-mail. Keep in mind that how you write email messages matters (Byron & Baldrige, 2007). If you want to seem functionally or politically competent, use neutral language, write in sentence case, and avoid emoticons. To convey social or methodological competence, emoticons are useful. If you make the mistake of sending an email with all uppercase, all lowercase, emoticons, or errors, you can change the negative impression the recipient has of your political or functional competence by correcting the infraction in subsequent e-mails. If you want to seem methodologically competent, the only styles that will change the perception are uppercase and emoticon.

Mentoring and Social Support

When we talk about mentoring, we generally associate it with something someone in a leadership position does with someone in a followership position—those who are "in the know" and have experienced things are the only ones who are "qualified" to provide career advice. In reality, mentors can be peers, leaders, or even followers. The reason is because different people have different sets of experiences; ultimately, **mentoring** is the process of using one's own experiences and insider knowledge to help others advance professionally and succeed personally. Think about your own work and volunteer experiences—was someone assigned to be your mentor, did someone take on the role and help you navigate the organizational politics, did you seek out particular people as your mentors?

Formal mentoring relationships are assigned by leaders or human resource professionals in an organization. **Informal mentoring relationships** develop organically as people seek to connect with each other. If we go back to the grocery store, with the possible exception of a vegan version, you cannot buy lasagna without cheese and pasta noodles; this would be formal mentoring (it is predetermined what two ingredients or employees are paired together). It is up to you whether you eat peanut butter and jelly or milk and cookies together; this would be informal mentoring (the people involved decide whether they are going to connect with each other just as you decide whether PB&J need to be eaten together).

Create time to interact with your followers
One on one, in small groups, and as a full team to show you value them as both individuals and part of the larger collective.

Out of sight should not mean out of mind
Be prompt in returning calls, email messages, and texts. You need to work on relationship building personally, not just in texts or emails (Buehler, 2017). Look for ways to rotate your travel to see the followers face to face on a reasonable rotation. Be willing to volunteer to make the trip overseas if you have not seen your followers in that country

Choose the appropriate medium for the message & follower (Neeley, 2015).
Discuss preferred communication methods, make a decision, and stick to it. Agree on standards for frequency and acceptable response times. Take into consideration the follower's culture to ensure you are engaging in communication that is considered appropriate and timely for the culture and individual. Letters, texts, and e-mail are good for sharing information and increasing awareness. Spoken words with tonality help people understand and can be used quickly. Words, tone, and body language together indicate credibility; use together whenever possible.

Use verbal and nonverbal immediacy behaviors
to indicate you are socially present and minimize social distance (Neeley, 2015). Smile, make eye-contact (or appear to), nod, respond positively, ask questions, have strong posture during video conferences, and comment on others' remarks. Look for opportunities to provide informal feedback, check in with leaders and followers to see how you are being perceived, and schedule time to disagree with each other. Just as long-distance friendships and romantic relationships often involve people who avoid conflict because they do not want to waste their time together arguing, virtual leaders and followers can also become conflict avoiders, which hinders relational development and team performance.

Storytelling conveys what is important and valued
When we use vivid and concrete examples, we connect to others in ways that a list of facts cannot. Stories do not need to be long or elaborate; they do need to humanize the point being made and have a clear climax that shows the consequences when people choose not to behave in a particular way or buy into the organizational vision (Grenny, 2017). For example, a leader may use storytelling to convey the importance of following safety procedures before entering the manufacturing facility by talking about someone who had become contaminated and spent time in intensive care at the hospital because the person chose not to check the seal on a clean-room suit. The same might be done with a story about someone who prepared well for a presentation and won a client that the organization and leader thought were completely out of reach.

Use language and images to convey what may be lost in the technology
(e.g., metaphors, emoticons/emojis/gifs). Not all metaphors work cross culturally, so it is important to understand with whom you are communicating to make sure the metaphor works.

Create non-work social communities for building team spirit & cohesion
A Group chat app or closed social media group would allow team members to engage in the conversations that would otherwise occur in a break room, the hallway, or people dropping by each other's offices if they were located in the same building (Ha, 2017).

Use open, positive messages
These lead others to perceive senders as having higher quality communication in internet-based relationships (Wright, 2004).

Be open to feedback and give feedback regularly
Take the time to recognize follower accomplishments publicly and talk to them about areas for improvement privately (DeRosa, 2018).

FIGURE 5.8   Using CMC to Build Strong Interpersonal Work Relationships

Sometimes, mentors help us figure out how to develop a stronger work-life balance that might include using flex-time or teleworking; at other times, they help us determine how to ask the boss for needed resources; at still other times, they are our advocates in a room where promotions are being discussed or raises are being determined. Not all mentors are part of the same organization we are. The stronger your networking skills are, the stronger your mentoring network will become.

TABLE 5.2   Coaching vs. Mentoring

Coaching	Mentoring
Focuses on the task	Focuses on the relationship
Defined and limited amount of time	Evolutionary over time
Addresses performance	Addresses personal and professional development
Can be spontaneous and effective	Requires planning to be effective
Immediate supervisor, manager, or leader is a critical component	Immediate supervisor, manager, or leader is only indirectly involved

Adapted from Fibuch & Robertson (2018).

When we talk about mentoring at the top of the organizational ladder, most corporate presidents and C-suite executives have no one above them to whom to turn for mentoring and social support. For these people, loneliness is a professional hazard—most people are afraid to talk to you in the break or lunch room; employees and followers might also assume that they cannot talk to you unless they want or need something; and because the company's future rests on your shoulders, the task demands of the job often overshadow the relational necessities (Zumaeta, 2019). Additionally, there is a distinct tension created as top leaders attempt to balance their distance and closeness with followers. They feel a need to be distant from their followers because they want to be able to be objective when making decisions that impact people's livelihood and career advancement; at the same time, they need to remain close to their followers so that they can influence and be influenced.

What can top leaders do to avoid loneliness and manage the tensions that arise between one's role and one's self, one's closeness, and one's distance? Zumaeta's (2019) research revealed that the ways to handle potential loneliness include:

- **Disconnect**: Senior leaders need to be willing to disconnect from the role. Sometimes this means getting away from the office to focus on something else. Sometimes it means turning off your brain and all of your electronics—trust your team enough to do the job and do it well. One of the most difficult aspects of this suggestion is to be able to set clear boundaries for work and home lives, connecting with others and remaining distant, or using activities such as meditation or yoga.

- **Be Healthy**: Maintaining a healthy lifestyle that avoids vices, such as smoking and stress eating, and includes exercising helps leaders put their role and potential loneliness in perspective. Taking the time to see medical personnel when there are mental or physical difficulties ensures leaders are at their best.

- **Look Outward**: While a top leader's social support inside the organization may be limited, there are plenty of opportunities to seek social support from leaders in similar positions in other organizations. Using professional organizations is one place where top leaders can find others in similar positions. Technology makes social support opportunities easier from a distance—a quick video conference once a month goes a long way to diminishing loneliness and providing social support.

- **Focus on Fulfillment**: Leaders seek leadership positions because they find it personally motivating to work with others and influence those followers' career and personal development. As long as top leaders remember why they fought to get where they are and use the energy created from living out their passion every day, they will minimize the loneliness and maximize their potential to influence others.

Persuasion and Social Influence

Relational and persuasive leadership no longer occur within the confines of organizational settings. Citizen Influencers (CI) and Citizen Leaders (CL) have hit the online environment in the same way that vaccines hit the medical field—revolutionizing the way people approach medical, consumer, and personal decision making. Think about the last time you were going to purchase something, likely something that was available online. How much attention did you pay to those ratings or review stars? How many blogs or advice columns did you read online to get the best tips available? Did you grow up watching YouTubers opening packages of the latest collectible or taking you on their latest shopping adventure? All of these people to whom we turn

Person	Process	Product
•The Principle of Liking	•The Principle of Reciprocity	•The Principle of Scarcity
•The Principle of Social Proof	•The Principle of Consistency	•The Principle of Optimism
•The Principle of Authority	•The Principle of Trust	•The Principle of Fairness
•The Principle of Self-Efficacy		

FIGURE 5.9   Persuasion Principles

would be considered citizen leaders and influencers, but why? They create relationships with their followers (both literally and figuratively) through their ability to create a social presence (Short et al., 1976), utilize persuasive and social influence strategies effectively, and build trust. They epitomize the communication tactics used by relational leaders.

Communication tactics used by relational leaders and followers are most effective when guided by Cialdini's (2001) six principles of persuasion.

- **The principle of liking**: People like those who like them—uncover real similarities and offer genuine praise. Similarity and praise are two key aspects of building liking and influence. Uncovering and building on common interests or activities creates avenues for leaders and followers to establish and maintain bonds. Compliments or positive remarks create feelings of affection and encourage one's willingness to comply with requests. Praise can also be a way to repair ineffective leader-follower relationships.

- **The principle of reciprocity**: People feel obligated to repay in kind—give what you want to receive. Leaders and followers can elicit the desired behaviors of one another by enacting in the desired behavior first. Trust for example, it takes trust to build trust.

- **The principle of social proof**: People follow the lead of similar others—rely on peer power whenever it's available. Leaders can rely on followers who have referent power with other followers to influence employees to support an initiative, vision, or change. In the same way, followers can rely on a respected colleague, even another leader, to persuade their leader to take a particular form of action.

- **The principle of consistency**: People align with their clear commitments—motivate by making their commitments active, public, and voluntary. Leaders or followers influence will lose traction if the other isn't committed. A leader becomes a manager or just another employee if followers are not committed to fulfilling his/her vision. Influence is enhanced by acting in consistent ways, embracing the power of written or spoken words, and avoiding coercion.

- **The principle of authority**: People defer to experts—expose your expertise; don't assume it's self-evident. Expert power enhances leaders and follower's ability to influence others. Before attempting to influence, be sure to establish your expertise. Leaders or followers are not psychics or mind readers.

- **The principle of scarcity**: People want more of what they can have less of—highlight unique benefits and exclusive information. Leaders and followers are more likely to act when the feel they have something to lose (fear appeal). Influence is also promoted when information seems like it is not broadly available, when it is exclusive. Even if the information itself seems dull, the fact that you can't find it on google or other search engines makes it appear more compelling and special.

Hoy and Smith (2007) recommended adding four additional principles of persuasion important for relational leading and following.

- **The principle of trust**: People follow those they trust—the influence of leaders and followers expands as trust deepens. Leaders and followers are not persuaded by people they do not trust, and influence diminishes when there is a lack of trust in either party.

- **The principle of fairness**: People desire fair treatment—invest in fairness. Followers and leaders are less influential when they act unethically or in ways that are unjust. This reminds us of the golden rule, treat others as you would like to be treated.

- **The principle of self-efficacy**: People who are confident in their own ability elicit confidence in others—believe in yourself and so will others.

- **The principle of optimism**: People gravitate toward optimism—problems are filled with possibilities, just find them. Positivity and constructive thinking motivate followers and leaders to act or show support for the other's plan of action.

The power differential between followers and leaders may, at times, pose as an obstacle to followers' ability to influence. When this is the case, the quality of relationships and followers' referent power becomes critical for effectively influencing others. Relational followers should emphasize their strengths and build immediacy to increase the effectiveness of their communication tactics during influence attempts.

CASE STUDY **Barry-Wehmiller**

Barry-Wehmiller, a private global company based in St. Louis, Missouri, implements manufacturing technology and solutions at companies with items in most grocery store aisles. They have grown exponentially by purchasing struggling companies and turning them around. What differs about their acquisitions from many others is that they do not immediately go in and lay off or fire people; instead, their first order of business is to make sure everyone understands their employment is safe and secure. Their guiding quotation is "You are safe here. We're going to train you on leadership and culture, and we're going to be patient." Additionally, they do not expect these organizations to turn a profit in the first quarter or even the first year; rather, they provide a three- to five-year timeframe because that is how long it takes to implement and see the fruits of their approach, known as truly human leadership. Even though Bob Chapman, company CEO, was trained in business schools and learned management, he came to believe that management practices were more about leaders' and organizations' manipulation of others for individual success, and success

(continued)

focused on money, power, success, and putting yourself before others (Zurer, 2018). Instead, the goal of organizations should be to behave as if they were engaging in parenting behaviors that would prepare employees for adulating behaviors when they needed to use them.

According to Chapman, leadership is about genuinely caring for others; leaders do this by providing opportunities for followers to make decisions, have a variety of experiences, and develop the confidence to be leaders when the time comes. Just as we did in chapter one, Bob distinguishes between leaders and managers: "a leader is someone who is a steward over the lives of the people he is entrusted with, while a manager is a rule enforcer who is focused on the bottom line, not on people" (Morgan, 2016, par. 2). The formula seems simple: focus on followers' personal and professional development and show your appreciation on a regular basis. Enter the difficulty—we are not hardwired or typically trained to be empathic, concerned, or caring about others; we are trained to be nice, polite, and individualistic. Think about someone having a baby in your workplace. If you are nice, you buy a card and maybe a small gift or gift card; if you engage in truly human leadership caring, you help the person determine how their work can be organized to maximize their well-being at work and at home. Empowerment is a critical component of this leadership and followership approach; leaders need to believe they are the stewards of their followers' current and future lives, and followers need to believe they are more than the bread that holds a sandwich together.

When followers feel that their leaders care about them as individuals, they begin to care more about their coworkers and the emotional bonding becomes contagious as everyone celebrates each person's successes and provides support when something does not go well—the same as what happens when a family functions effectively. The most important skills associated with truly human leadership involve being able to engage in dialogue and active listening. When you are a competent communicator who can see the conversation from the other person's point of view (perspective taking) and actively listen without being distracted by a new text message, email message dinging, or the to-do list working its way through your mind, you are going to be a more effective leader and leader-in-training (current follower). Finally, you have to be willing to start from an inverted perspective on trust: rather than the individual leaders and followers having to demonstrate that they are trustworthy, it is up to the organization to demonstrate that each employee is trusted.

Chapman has developed a leadership checklist that guides all leadership behaviors and communication. Leaders at Barry-Wehmiller adhere to the principles included in the checklist and that has led to extremely low turnover, higher satisfaction at work and at home, and increased productivity.

One man in the organization talked about his experience with working for an organization that has adopted a trusting culture. As part of his engagement, Chapman asked one man in the organization "How did this affect your life?" The man responded, "Since we've embraced the idea where I have a chance to make my role better and people ask me what I think, I go home feeling valued and better about myself," Steve explained. "And when I go home feeling better about myself, I'm nicer to my wife. And when I'm nicer to her, she talks to me more."

BARRY-WEHMILLER LEADERSHIP CHECKLIST

I accept the awesome responsibility of leadership. The following describe my essential actions as a leader:

- I practice stewardship of the Guiding Principles of Leadership through my time, conversations, and personal development.

- I advocate safety and wellness through my actions and words.

- I reflect to lead my team in Achieving Principled Results on Purpose.

- I inspire passion, optimism, and purpose.

- My personal communication cultivates fulfilling relationships.

- I foster a team community in which we are committed to each other and to the pursuit of a common goal.

- I exercise responsible freedom, empowering each of us to achieve our potential.

- I proactively engage in the personal growth of individuals on my team.

- I facilitate meaningful group interactions.

- I set, coach to, and measure goals that define winning.

- I recognize and celebrate the greatness in others.

- I commit to daily continuous improvement.

DISCUSSION QUESTIONS

1. According to Gallup, "a good job working with people you enjoy" is the number one determining factor of happiness, ahead of salary or power. In our society where tangible success (money, power, title) has become the gold standard against which all behavior is measured, how would you respond in an organization that was defined more by connections and caring than climbing the corporate ladder and building wealth or power?

(continued)

2. Leader-member exchange, mentoring, persuasion and social influence, and social presence are all important components of the leader-follower relationship. To what extent is each possible, viable, and desirable at Barry-Wehmiller? For the ones that you do not see as consistent with their philosophy, are they necessary? Why or why not?

3. Given your own work experiences, how realistic would it be for you to work for an organization such as this one?

ANALYSIS OPTIONS

A. Even in a truly human organization, there are going to be survival crises and people who do not buy into the philosophy. After his death, you have been hired to be Bob Chapman's successor and ensure the philosophy lives on in the current organizations and future acquisitions.

B. Because this organization is the exception rather than the norm, the process of vetting, hiring, and socializing new organizational members is critical to its success. You have been hired to oversee these processes.

C. Barry-Wehmiller's philosophy of caring, dialogue, and active listening have proven successful in many brick and mortar organizations where leaders and followers see each other every day and can celebrate accomplishments together. The company has just acquired a multinational organization where there is only one physical location and the remaining followers are spread around the world in teleworking situations. Your job is to determine how this philosophy can work for leaders and followers who are not co-located in the same building.

ANALYSIS PROCESS

- Brainstorm a list of options for addressing the issue.

- Make a list of strengths and challenges for each of your brainstormed solutions.

- Choose the best solution for the issue.

- Develop an implementation plan for your chosen solution.

- Additional resources:

Creating Presence (Holland)
https://tiny.utk.edu/FCL5_1

Everybody Matters
https://tiny.utk.edu/FCL5_3

Barry Wehmiller corporate site
https://tinyurl.com/y2wfb6th

**Truly Human
Leadership TedX**
https://tiny.utk.edu/FCL5_5

Truly Human Leadership
https://tiny.utk.edu/FCL5_2

**Truly Human Leadership
Inspired**
https://tiny.utk.edu/FCL5_6

LEADER AND FOLLOWER DEVELOPMENT PRACTICES

1. Always treat people with respect and genuineness—make sure that all of your relationships are authentic.

2. Focus on other people's situation and perspective when interacting with them—empathy and emotional intelligence are keys (Coleman, 2018).

3. Develop relationships with the intent of continuing a mutually engaging game rather than winning (or losing) and never playing with the same person again (Porcelli, 2019).

4. Develop patience—not everything happens in a digital world of "140 characters," or 60-second videos, or thumb swipes. Being effective takes time and effort (Birch, 2018).

5. Make connections by embracing all forms of technology, include face-to-face interactions (jurczak & Violanti, 2019).

DISCUSSION QUESTIONS AND ACTIVITIES

1. From your own college experience, think about the leader-follower relationships developed between you and your professors. Complete this next sentence. The professor that I experienced the highest LMX quality with is _____. Thinking about your relationship with this professor, fill in the boxes in activity below.

Antecedents	LMX Quality	Consequences
Characteristics and/or behaviors of _____ (your name) contributing the LMX quality: _____ _____ Characteristics and/or behaviors of _____ (name of professor) contributing the LMX quality: _____ _____	High LMX	As a result of LMX quality, my attitude about the class was: _____ As a result of LMX quality, my behavior in class was: _____ What interpersonal outcomes did the LMX quality produce? _____ The LMX quality impacted my success in the class because it: _____

In contrast, the professor that I experienced the lowest LMX quality with is _____. Thinking about your relationship with this professor, fill in the boxes below.

Antecedents	LMX Quality	Consequences
Characteristics and/or behaviors of _____ (your name) contributing the LMX quality: _____ _____ Characteristics and/or behaviors of _____ (name of professor) contributing the LMX quality: _____ _____	Low LMX	As a result of LMX quality, my attitude about the class was: _____ As a result of LMX quality, my behavior in class was: _____ What interpersonal outcomes did the LMX quality produce? _____ The LMX quality impacted my success in the class because it: _____

Looking at your completed activity tables, what similarities and differences do you notice?

2. If you are in an online class, find examples of the ways in which the instructor and others in the class create social presence through verbal and nonverbal immediacy. If you are not in an online class, use one of your social media accounts. Do you feel more connected to the students who make an effort to build relationships? How about the teacher? Why?

3. Mentoring and social support can be perceived as behaviors done for someone who is not knowledgeable, motivated, or skilled enough to manage their own professional life. In pairs, have one person build an argument that supports the statement and one that refutes the statement. Share your arguments. Whose position is stronger? Why?

4. Cialdini and Hoy/Smith developed 10 persuasion and social influence strategies. Of those principles, which do you believe is most important? Least important? What factors influenced your decision? Why?

5. Relational leadership and followership are congruent with the contemporary theories discussed in chapter 3. What similarities do you see between the two chapters? What makes them different?

FIGURE CREDITS:

CHAPTER 6

TEAM FOLLOWERSHIP AND LEADERSHIP

> "The leaders who work most effectively, it seems to me, never say 'I.' And that's not because they have trained themselves not to say 'I.' They don't think 'I.' They think 'we'; they think 'team.' They understand their job to be to make the team function. They accept responsibility and don't sidestep it, but 'we' gets the credit … This is what creates trust, what enables you to get the task done."
>
> —PETER DRUCKER

> "Never doubt that a small group of thoughtful, committed citizens can change the world. Indeed, it is the only thing that ever has."
>
> —MARGARET MEAD

I f someone asked you to give an example of a group, what would you say? Maybe it would be a music group or one you belong to on Google or Flickr. You might even mention a group to which you belong on campus (Green Initiative, *a Cappella*, or the people with whom you are working on a class project). How would your response be different if you were asked to name a team? You might pick a high school, collegiate, or professional sports team; you may even name a team that is completing a walk or other event to raise money to find a cure for a disease such as Alzheimer's or Leukemia. Both sets of examples describe an undetermined number of people who come together to accomplish something—make music, communicate with each other, compete, cooperate. So, what distinguishes one from the other? In all honesty, not much separates the two. Teams have become the term of choice in today's business world and groups have become more of the dirty laundry that we stash under our beds, in the back of our closets, and the gym bags in the trunks of our cars. For the purpose of talking about leadership and followership, we are going to draw distinctions between the two terms and then explain how both exist in today's workforce.

FIGURE 6.1   The Olympic Rings

The Olympic Games, which take place every two years and alternate between winter and summer sports, are symbolized by interlocking rings and a torch. Based upon the brief taste you got above about groups and teams, why might we have chosen this image? What could the interlocking rings symbolize? What might a torch tell us about groups and teams? What can we learn from sports about groups and teams? Countries from all around the world compete against each other. The different colors of interlocking rings represent the diversity of perspective that members of the Olympic Committee, which governs all aspects of the Games, bring to the decision-making table. By not labeling the colors, people are free to represent their country from whatever perspective they see fit. To get to the Olympic venue, the torch must take a long journey in which a group of people act as relay runners when they each take a mile of the journey. With the exception of a shared purpose to keep the flame lit and not drop the torch during the handoff, these people will likely never meet each formally or work together again.

At the opening ceremony, all of the athletes and coaches wear a uniform created specifically for their country's athletes to represent their team cohesiveness. Regardless of how athletes compete, they must develop a game plan to maximize their effectiveness and carry it out, even in the face of changing environmental conditions, such as tragedy at home, weather, equipment failures, and human judging errors. During the course of the games, some athletes compete as individuals, some as groups, and some as teams.

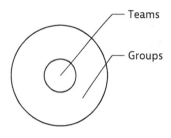

FIGURE 6.2 Groups and Teams

"The thrill of victory ... and ... the agony of defeat," a slogan popularized by Jim McKay from ABC Sports in the 1970s, shows the peaks and valleys of handling conflict. The medal stand at the end of each competition is the one place where language and other forms of diversity do not matter, as we all listen to the winner's national anthem and feel the pride. Who knew something so enjoyable to watch could have so much to say about groups and teams?

Groups and Teams

As the image illustrates, all teams are groups, but not all groups are teams. The characteristics used to describe groups apply to teams; not all of the characteristics used to describe teams apply to groups. For example, both groups and teams may be formal or informal, but only teams are evaluated in terms of collective effort. If we go back to our examples above, a Google group is a collection of individuals communicating with each other because of a shared interest. If a fundraising team does not work together to raise money for the cause, they may all end up asking the same people to donate and not reach their goal.

While baseball, football, basketball, and rowing are clearly team sports, other sports are not as easily classified using this definition. For example, where would you place swimming, tennis, track and field, gymnastics, and golf? In each sport, the athletes compete individually, except in a swimming or track relay. Any individual can earn a trophy or ribbon even if everyone else does poorly; at the same time, it is possible for no one individually to finish in the top three and yet the team could earn a medal if all of the other teams have only one or two elite athlete(s). We will come back and ask the question again after you have a better grasp of what makes a team different from a group.

Many people have tried to categorize the process by which groups and teams form. According to Van de Ven and Poole (1995), there are four ways of thinking about the developmental process.

- **Life cycle models** focus on the stages through which groups come together and come apart. The most famous life cycle model is forming (followers are assigned to work together and begin the uncertainty reduction process by getting to know each other and determining what needs to be done), storming (the rocky road where members seek status/specific roles, such as leader and question the group's structure), norming (righting the ship where members develop guidelines for operating and moving forward to complete the task), performing (light at the end of the tunnel as members complete the task or implement the decision), and adjourning (Tuckman & Jensen, 1977).

- **Teleological models** are based in systems theory and indicate that groups and teams change because of changes in their environment. Environmental changes may come from input factors (purpose, reward structure, goals), process factors (communication, how task and relational conflict are handled, whether team gets caught up in organizational politics), emergent states (norms, cohesion, emotional expression), or output factors (task performance, member satisfaction, or team growth; Bang & Midelfart, 2017).

For example, when a new person is added to the team, it affects the input factors, which may also alter the emergent states (operating norms), process factors (communication), and output factors (team growth). Not all changes in the environment are negative, so a new team member can be either beneficial (helping the team strengthen its process or outcome factors) or detrimental (negatively affecting team cohesion).

- **Dialogical models** highlight the team changes that occur as a result of tension, conflict, or opposing forces. Conflict, tension, and opposing forces are not inherently negative; like most other things in life, they can be beneficial or problematic depending upon how the followers and leaders approach and deal with them. To be beneficial, these changes have to bring about a synthesis that resolves conflict or opposition. For example, we have all used the saying "We will just have to agree to disagree"; if you have used it, the likely outcome is that the argument, conflict, or discussion ended there, which was your goal. In a dialogical model, the team continues to discuss an issue until all of the members have bought into its resolution. Teams seek to reframe the conflict so that they are no longer seen as oppositional.

For example, a team that is trying to develop an innovative solution for handling the lack of parking on a college campus may have two opposing perspectives that focus on maintaining the campus' aesthetic beauty and maximizing the campus' accessibility for commuters who drive to campus. These two solutions cannot exist simultaneously, so the team must determine how to honor both perspectives while still solving the problem—not an easy task! One solution might be to create a parking structure that is consistent with the current campus' look and feel while also creating an off-site parking structure for students who have their cars on campus with them. While this is not the most innovative solution, it is one way that the team can agree to disagree on what is most important moving forward.

Studying groups and teams can take an entire semester by itself, so for our limited purposes here, we are going to focus on the followership and leadership similarities and differences between organizational groups and teams. Table 6.1 lists the primary differences between groups and teams.

TABLE 6.1 Groups and Teams

Groups	Teams
Single leader and multiple followers	Shared followership and leadership
Individual accountability	Individual and team accountability
Purpose/goals created by the organization	Purpose and goals are created by the team
Individual products	Collective products
Meetings and asynchronous communication	Discussion and asynchronous communication
Individual and team evaluations	Team evaluations
Time efficient	Task efficient

Groups

Groups are a collection of individuals who seek to achieve their purpose through a series of discrete contributions. When people come together as a group, the members typically have specific roles they play. That is, one person emerges, wins an election, or has been appointed as the leader. The person has legitimate power, may have expert/information or referent power, and often lacks reward and punishment power. Responsible for calling meetings, creating an agenda of what will be discussed at those meetings, and keeping the group on task, the "leader" performs more of a managerial than leadership role.

If we think about a Bible Study group as an example, someone who is part of the educational ministry program may be appointed to serve as a discussion leader to carry out a mission created by the educational ministry group; followers may be assigned or volunteer to participate based upon when the group meets. As part of each group meeting, followers may be designated, or volunteer, to complete specific tasks. In this case, different followers may be responsible for completing background research or developing discussion questions for a specific passage subset of the larger reading for the following meeting. By engaging in **division of labor**, in which different people are responsible for different parts of a larger task, the group can remain efficient without overwhelming the leader or any of the followers. Even though the leader does not have reward or coercive power, each follower is individually accountable to the group for completing the assigned task; if the group has nothing to discuss the following week, it is not a reflection upon those who did not receive a duty.

Class discussion boards can be an excellent example of groups at work. All students (followers) create posts in response to a prompt (purpose) determined by the teacher (leader) and, typically, they must also respond to some number of posts by their classmates for which they will receive a grade or completion checkmark at the end of the week (individual products and accountability). Each student is free to post whenever it is convenient during the course of the week (asynchronous communication; time efficient). If the ultimate goal of a discussion board is to learn more about a given class topic by addressing a prompt, to what extent do the followers actually accomplish the leader's goal? If you are like our children and the majority of our students, you do not. You read the three posts that are closest to yours when you post and give them a response that meets the quantity requirements (number of words/characters or length) to achieve the desired reward of a completion or other grade in the least amount of time possible. How often do you go back at the end of the week and read the responses others provided to your post, or take even more time and respond to the posts that others made? Do you ever go back and read what other students said about your responses to their posts? Why or why not? Chances are it is because you believe there are no advantages to doing so—it is not going to be on the test, there are no bonus points for addressing responses, and it takes additional time and effort. This is what happens when a group perspective is utilized.

Teams

Teams are an interdependent collective working toward a common goal greater than what any could attain individually. You may be scratching your head and wondering exactly what distinguishes groups and teams because these definitions look ironically similar. The key differences are interdependence, synergy, and collectivity. **Interdependence** indicates that a change to one aspect of the team has an impact, positive or negative, on the team. For example, if you look back at the teleological model above, there are four different factors that can affect a team.

Synergy indicates that the team can achieve more than any of the individuals participating on the team could alone. For example, while it might be possible for one country to solve the problem of world peace, working as a team of countries that represent different perspectives is far more likely to solve the problem because representatives from different countries see the problem and its potential solutions in different ways. **Collectivity** indicates that all of the team members work together to accomplish the goal, share a mutual commitment to a purpose and norms they have created together, and place group well-being above individual well-being. That does not mean that every word has to be written or every aspect researched by the entire team, but it does mean they work together rather than individually; everyone is equally responsible and accountable for the final product or decision. Collectively, people have complementary skills and competencies.

FIGURE 6.3   You have a very large set of dominoes lined up to fall in a particular order from beginning to end. If a child accidently touches one of the dominoes in the middle, then they will fall as two separate sets.

Creating a Space for Groups and Teams

Now that you have formal definitions and explanations for groups and teams, where do each of the following belong?

_____ gymnastics	_____ golf
_____ swimming	_____ track and field
_____ tennis	

There are times when organizations, leaders, and followers need groups and there are other times when they need teams. When the stakes are low in a given situation and time is of the essence, then groups tend to be more effective. Groups can complete a task more quickly because everyone is working on a different aspect simultaneously and assembling them into a final product. Using division of labor with a single leader assigning tasks to individual followers can be effective if someone is not evaluating the end product holistically. Imagine a report to the organization's investors written by seven different people in seven different writing styles. It will be choppy and headings will be the only way to tie the pieces together. Sound like a few group projects you have completed?

On the other hand, if the organization requires an internal report documenting what has been accomplished in the last month, it would be perfectly acceptable for the leader to assign a follower in each department to write a two-to-three-page summary. No one outside the organization is going to see the report (stakes are low) and the task can be completed quickly without people arguing about which font to use or how to present the information (bullet points, numbered list, descriptive paragraphs) because the goal is to get it in the report in the most efficient manner possible.

TABLE 6.2   Choosing Between Groups and Teams

Groups	Teams
Simple tasks or problems	Complex tasks or problems
Cooperation is sufficient	Collaboration or consensus are required
Concrete tasks	Abstract or ambiguous tasks or purposes
Few competencies needed	Differing/competing competencies needed
Quick decisions or task completion	Long-term commitment needed

When the stakes are high and quality is critical, then teams tend to be more effective. Teams tend to produce higher-quality products because they are working together and benefitting from the synergy that comes with those interactions. Cooperation, collaboration, and dialogue take longer to complete well; thus, teams are generally not preferred in crisis or time-sensitive situations. Because leadership and followership roles are interchangeable, members are interdependent, and interaction is critical in team situations, the process becomes just as important as the final product.

Going back to our report example, suppose that a team is creating a visual presentation for a group of investors. They would want to agree on a scheme and structure that works for everyone, including those with visual impairments, work together to develop the content to maintain the presentation's flow, and practice the presentation to guarantee they are meeting the situational requirements (transitioning and connecting speakers, speaking for the proper amount of time, and demonstrating cohesiveness among the team members). How many times have you seen or participated in a group presentation in which everyone completed their slides, spoke for 2–3 (or 6 in the case of the person who did not practice) minutes, and you walked away wondering why they did not each do a separate presentation? Choosing between groups and teams can be best summarized by an African proverb: *"If you want to go fast, go alone. If you want to go far, go together."*

Team Characteristics

If a team is truly going to go far together, then they have to operate as a team. Consistently, five characteristics appear in the literature to define teams. While these are not exhaustive, they do closely align with the communication competencies.

Trust

Just as trust is critical in friendships and romantic relationships, its importance in follower-leader and team relationships cannot be underestimated. Like most relational processes, trust must be built over time; it is not something followers and leaders grant to each other simply because of one's position or area of expertise. Therapists and human resource professionals are not automatically considered trusted individuals before others interact with them. Followers do not automatically trust leaders. **Trust** indicates a willingness to be vulnerable in the presence of others because one expects the other(s) to behave without taking advantage or being opportunistic (Jarvenpaa et al., 1998; Rousseau et al., 1998).

In practice, trust involves allowing people to "do their jobs" without always looking over their shoulders to see if or how they are doing it. Interestingly, when people from collectivist (Russia) and individualistic (United States) cultures work together, their views of trust are more similar than different (McNeil, 2016). The Russians, who generally have a willingness to trust, and Americans, who culturally have an unwillingness to trust, both move more toward a middle ground of willingness to trust in the mixed team. Trust occurs at both the relational and team levels. At the team level, members *share* a general perception that it is acceptable to be vulnerable to others and their work; this perception improves team performance as well as collaboration, information sharing, satisfaction, and open communication.

Three types of trust exist within teams: companion, competence, and commitment (Newell & Swan, 2000).

- **Companion trust**, which takes the longest to develop, indicates that team members will behave ethically and in good faith perform as part of the collective. Similar to friendships, companion trust can develop in face-to-face and mediated environments. Once developed, it is the strongest.

- **Competence trust** indicates that team members have the expertise and ability to perform appropriately and effectively as part of the collective. Developing competence trust in others can come about through past experiences with them or credible external demonstrations (earning a degree, winning an award, etc.). If a team member fails to deliver an expected contribution, competence trust can break down; it is significantly less resilient than companion trust.

- **Commitment trust** indicates a belief that others outside the team have pledged or obligated themselves, formally and/or informally, to the collective. For example, when organizations provide teams with time off from their everyday tasks, they are building commitment trust. Whereas companion and competence trust are based upon individuals and their behaviors, external factors such as the organization and stakeholders play a role in commitment trust.

Of the follower/leader communication competencies, imagine how difficult it would be to support and influence others if you believed they were going to manipulate you. Social influence would be limited to legitimate, reward, and coercive power if the team members did not trust each other; in a trusting environment, referent power works well. Generally speaking, the expectations that allow one to be vulnerable involve positive, rather than negative, behaviors. For example, if a team member believed that others were going to behave unethically by taking credit for an idea that was not theirs, then it would be difficult to be vulnerable in that situation; trust would be broken. To achieve synergy and positive outcomes, the team members must perform competently, challenge the system, and adapt actively to the environment around them.

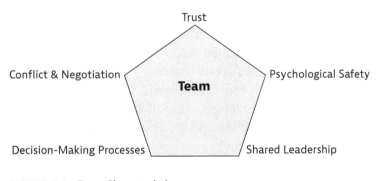

FIGURE 6.4   Team Characteristics

Psychological Safety

Like trust, psychological safety is based upon people's perceptions; trust and psychological safety also tend to be found together in team environments. **Psychological safety**, a belief shared among team members, encompasses relational and identity goals. In a team environment, it facilitates risk taking and authentic behaviors because people do not have to be fearful of how others will respond. Risk-taking behaviors include speaking up when people are behaving unethically, asking for help when needed as opposed to when one does not want to do a job, or taking responsibility when one has made a mistake.

When a leader consistently utilizes reward, coercive, or legitimate power, the followers are less likely to feel psychologically safe because of the negative repercussions of admitting when one sincerely makes a mistake. On the other hand, if followers and leaders work in an environment where expert and referent power bases prevail, the team as a whole is more likely to experience psychological safety. The same is true when teams value both diversity and inclusivity because leaders and followers feel valued for who they are and recognize they can share their perspective without experiencing negative consequences.

With respect to the leader/follower communication competencies, feeling psychologically safe is critical. Team members are capable of recognizing when others are pretending versus being genuinely supportive. For example, a team member says, "That is a really good idea." While you are making eye contact with that team member, the others are rolling their eyes in disbelief. On its face, the comment sounds supportive and encouraging; team members' perceptions, including the person who offered the idea, indicate that the person was actually being sarcastic about the idea's value.

Psychological safety also connects to challenging the system. When one becomes fearful of taking risks, it becomes impossible to challenge the status quo. Without people willing to challenge the system, progress becomes stagnant and organizations eventually wither and die. The same is true about continuous learning. We each have a comfort zone regarding our beliefs and values. When one challenges that comfort zone and tries to stretch it so that we can see a bigger picture or develop a way to strengthen our own arguments regarding our position on a topic, we can become uncomfortable—those who are not competent leaders and followers shut down in the face of that uncomfortableness and fail to learn. Psychological safety allows people to continue learning and trying out new ideas, especially those with whom they may not initially agree. Finally, psychological safety and behaving ethically work together. Engaging in behaviors that one believes are ethical becomes significantly easier when the person is not fearful of the repercussions of those actions.

Looking at two team members, one who feels psychologically safe and another who does not, reveals the importance of psychological safety. Kelly and Peyton both work on the same marketing team for a Fortune 500 company. Kelly feels psychologically safe and Peyton does not. During the course of a team meeting to determine how to market a new product, the *blokwrld* video game to reach a new demographic—parents who use tablets to keep their children occupied—the following conversation might transpire:

Peyton: Let's update the marketing plan we used for our last adult tablet video game app.

Kelly: *From across the table*: We could certainly make that part of our strategy, Peyton. It would be really fun to also develop a campaign geared toward the children who are going to use the app. Children are a captive audience and we can get them to 'beg' their parents to download it. (being supportive and challenging the system)

Peyton: How can we get toddlers to ask their parents for an app? Some of them can barely talk.

Kelly: Children are smart and those who have tablets or phones from an early age learn how to click on the 'get' button at the end of an in-game or video trailer ad. (influencing others, actively adapting the message)

Team
Member: So, you are saying that we could market blokwrld within some of our most popular current apps?

Kelly: Exactly.

Peyton: I still think we are better off to continue marketing to the adults and focusing on the enjoyment and value they get without having to make in-app purchases.

Kelly: I am not saying that we would not do that too. This app could be more successful if we were willing to expand our marketing horizons and reach out to the ones who are going to be playing it. (behave ethically and perform competently while being supportive)

RESEARCH SUMMARY

Chiu et al. (2017) set out to study whether someone's centrality in the social network would predict followers' perceptions of whether the person was a leader. Potential leaders have both positive (teams to whom they provide advice or with whom they build friendships) and negative (teams that they avoid or that their presence hinders the team's progress) social networks.

Study 1: Based in implicit leadership theories, this study examined two hypotheses: 1. Managers who are more central in a positive social network are perceived as leaders; and 2. Managers who are more central in a negative social network are not perceived as leaders. In the student sample, 193 followers and 63 formal team leaders participated in the semester-long team project and two data collections (at the midpoint and near the end of the semester). After controlling for demographics, personality, academic achievement, and initial perception of the formal leader, both hypotheses were supported. That is, student followers perceived the assigned team leader as being more of a leader if that person had built friendships and offered advice to the other team members. Conversely, student followers

(continued)

perceived the assigned team leaders as being less of a leader if that person had hindered the group's progress and avoided building interpersonal relationships with the other team members. While these data are robust because they control for many alternative explanations, they are still student data (student team leaders have little power to reward or punish team members) and it is unclear if they would translate into workplace team situations.

Study 2: This study examined the two hypotheses from study one and two additional hypotheses: 1. Managers who are more central in a positive social network have more social power; and 2. Managers who are more central in a negative social network have less social power. For their purposes, social power is a form of influence in which people can successfully draw upon their expert and referent power bases. Across four organizations (3 in India and 1 in the United States), a total of 69 team leaders and 403 followers participated in the survey research based upon the teams with whom they work every day. The results replicated the findings from study one with positive social networks associated with perceptions of leadership and negative social networks not associated with perceptions of leadership. The last two hypotheses were also supported: leaders who were more central in a positive social network were perceived as having more social power and those who were more central in a negative social network were perceived as having less social power.

Implications: Leaders' informal social networks play a significant role in how followers perceive them. In many ways, this research supports the halo effect found in interpersonal relationships: if followers see the leader as being central to their social network, they are more likely to attribute positive aspects of their leadership prototype to that person, even if they do not observe those prototypical behaviors. This research also indicates that followers who are perceived as central to social network may be seen as leaders, despite not having the formal title of leader. Finally, this research provides insight into how organizations can help train their managers to be leaders by focusing on their referent and expert power bases. The authors summarize their findings very succinctly: "Managers are appointed by the organization, but leaders are anointed by their followers" (Chiu et al., 2017, p. 346).

Shared Leadership

The term "shared leadership" began specifically with respect to teams. More contemporary perspectives on leadership and followership have adopted and adapted the concept of shared leadership as part of their central concepts. **Shared leadership** happens when multiple members of the team collectively engage in social influence, goal attainment, and visionary development. That is, no single person has formal authorization to be "the leader" and various members perform leadership behaviors as the team interactions unfold toward accomplishing their purpose. Engaging in leadership behaviors is not a linear process in which one person takes the leadership role and then hands it off to another. Rather, leadership becomes a fluid process in which multiple members may be enacting leadership behaviors simultaneously.

Because shared leadership requires interaction among the members and open communication, shared leadership positively relates to team cohesion, consensus, and satisfaction (Bergman et al., 2012). **Cohesiveness** is both an individual and collective phenomenon that indicates the extent to which the members feel connected to each other as well as identify with the overall team; when team members feel more connected, they are said to be more cohesive and tend to have more positive performance and relational outcomes. Shared leadership is generally more effective when teams are operating with more contemporary views of leadership and working on a complex task or set of tasks to achieve their goals (Wang et al., 2014).

With respect to communication competencies, shared leadership is the one place where everyone is responsible for developing and enacting a vision. If all of the team members do not buy into the vision, the team will have unproductive conflict. For example, if the marketing team described above has created a vision of being innovative, creative, and using cutting-edge technology, then the conversation that took place between Kelly and Peyton serves as a distraction and could be seen as a waste of time resources given that everyone already agreed they were not going to rely on what has worked in the past simply because it has worked in the past. In conjunction with developing and enacting a vision, shared leadership is an opportunity to work on valuing the organization's mission.

As a team, the members need to always keep the larger organizational mission in mind when making and enacting decisions. For example, if Kelly and Peyton's team worked in an organization where maintaining the status quo were part of the mission, it would be inappropriate for Kelly to propose such a shift in their marketing strategy. Finally, shared leadership is also an opportunity to enhance one's actively adapt competency. Because the leadership roles are fluid and switch between and among team members throughout the process, people need to be ready to adapt their perspective and communication to meet these changing team needs. For example, if a team member with a newborn child comes into a team meeting tired from a long night up with the baby, then another team member has to be confident and knowledgeable enough to step in and run the meeting; making those cognitive changes from being a listener to being a speaker does not always come easily for everyone.

Decision-Making Processes

While researchers label these as group decision-making processes, we are specifically talking about team decision-making processes because in a leader-follower context, they occur in teams rather than groups. **Decision-making processes** occur when a team comes together to evaluate a set of alternatives and choose the best one. Teams determine what is best based upon the available resources (money, people, raw materials, physical space, etc.), time constraints for implementation, organizational bylaws or legal requirements, and the extent to which it matches the organization's and stakeholders' objectives.

Without labeling it as such, you have been engaging in team decision-making processes each time you complete a case study in this textbook. After generating a list of possible solutions or approaches to the situation, each team is asked to choose one and justify why it is best by taking time, resources, and stakeholders into consideration. You may have chosen a solution based upon consensus (everyone must agree to the solution), voting (majority rules), or simply the one that was easiest to justify (not overly effective, but it does allow you to complete the task in the specified amount of time). If you have been doing your work well, you have come to a team, rather than an individual, solution.

Mistakes to Avoid

With the exception of group decision support systems that use technology, decision making is a people process in which the collective must reach a conclusion. Because humans are involved and humans are not perfect, many difficulties can arise in the decision-making process. Effective leaders and followers seek ways to avoid these potential pitfalls by engaging in competent communication practices (Forsyth, 2006).

- **Procrastination:** Rather than interacting and engaging in the agreed-upon process, the team puts off making a decision until it is crunch time. Some will claim they do so because they have too many other demands or obligations; others will claim that they make better decisions under pressure; still others believe that if they avoid the task long enough, an individual will have to take responsibility for making the decision and be the one who is accountable if something goes wrong after the decision is made. Effective team members seek to keep everyone connected to each other, staying on task with set times for interacting about this specific decision, and making sure everyone has a personal stake in the decision being made.

- **Groupthink:** A decision-making practice in which the team members place more importance on maintaining harmony than making a rational or functional decision (Janis, 1972). Rather than critically evaluating a decision, the team members seek to maintain relational and identity goals; they avoid providing dissenting viewpoints and engaging with outside influences. Famous decisions attributed to groupthink include launching the Challenger shuttle, the mass resignation of the Major League Baseball Umpires Association, War on terrorism in Iraq seeking weapons of mass destruction, and social networking such as review sites and "news" sharing. Effective team members make sure a different person is assigned the role of critical evaluator or "devil's advocate" each time a decision is discussed (an assigned role diminishes the potential stigma of providing a dissenting opinion), discuss alternatives with trusted others outside the group to take the pulse of a decision's veracity, and encourage outsiders to participate in the decision-making process when they are the expert.

- **Bolstering**: After making a quick decision, the team emphasizes the positive aspects of the decision and minimizes the negative aspects of the decision. As individuals, we often do this to minimize cognitive dissonance after making a decision. For example, if you have switched majors during your time in college, you likely cannot remember a positive thing about the major you left and spent the first semester, and possibly beyond, in your new major focusing only on the positive aspects. Teams use bolstering to reduce their collective cognitive dissonance. Effective team members minimize the opportunity for bolstering as they do for groupthink; additionally, they listen carefully when someone appears to be engaging in bolstering and ask the person to point out at least one negative aspect or limitation of the decision made.

- **Failure to share information:** Regardless of how hard leaders and followers try, there are always going to be pieces of information that are known by some team members and not known by others. It might be because someone overheard information during a bathroom break or happened upon it through an informal social network. Consistently, research shows that if all team members have all of the available information, they make better decisions than if some people only have partial information (Lu et al., 2012; Stasser & Titus, 1985). Sometimes, failure to share information is inadvertent—the team member did not mean to withhold the information. Effective team members can encourage information sharing by remembering to ask one simple question, "What makes you say that?"

If you are a pessimist, each of these mistakes might be viewed as people being too lazy or incapable to do the work that needs to be done; if you are an optimist, each of these mistakes could be viewed as an opportunity to maintain or strengthen the team's relational and identity goals. In either case, each mistake allows the team to avoid conflict so that they do not have to engage in negotiation processes.

Conflict and Negotiation

Conflict among team members and between followers and leaders generally focuses on task, relational, and identity communication. Most of the organizational conflict literature highlights task and relational communication conflicts at the expense of identity conflicts. **Task conflicts** occur at the group level and concern disagreements regarding how best to accomplish team goals. In some cases, these disagreements can lead to enhanced productivity and innovation because they lead the team to consider alternative perspectives and decision options; in other cases, they can lead to decreased productivity because they lead to relational and identity conflicts (Humphrey et al., 2017).

Relational conflicts occur at the dyadic or triadic level and highlight interpersonal differences in attitudes, beliefs, or values. These differences have the potential to be even more detrimental to the team's functioning because they often remain unaddressed. Finally, **identity conflicts** concern people who *are* in relation to each other and the larger team; these conflicts may play out because people find themselves in competing roles or unable to play the role they desire or believe they are best suited to play. For example, if Alejandro believes that he should be the team information seeker, making sure all of the relevant questions have been asked, and Jayden begins enacting that role during a team meeting, Alejandro is likely to find himself questioning his role, and identity, within the team. Similar to task conflicts, identity conflicts can lead to detrimental relational conflicts.

Because conflicts occur between, and among, people, they must be both expressed and involve affect (Weingart et al., 2015). If people are not invested enough to experience affect, then a simple "difference of opinion" is not going to escalate to the level of conflict. Similarly, if people do not express their positions, they cannot have a conflict. What would it look like to have a one-sided or one-person conflict? Even though you may debate with yourself about whether to stay in lounge pants or get dressed for class, that is not a conflict. Also, if you are mad at your neighbor about how loud the music is when you are trying to study, it cannot become a conflict until you communicate your frustration or desires to the neighbor. How people express their conflict can have a profound effect on how the conflict unfolds (Weingart et al., 2015).

TABLE 6.3   Communicating in Conflict Situations

Conflict	Expression	Reaction	Escalating and Calming Spirals
Very Direct and Very Intense	Shouting, Threatening; Rolling Eyes	Anger; Frustration; Tension	Activated emotional states; Withdrawal or submission
Very Direct and Minimally Intense	Debating, Deliberating, Typically task conflicts	Excitement (positive); Irritation (negative)	Reflective response, Clarifying assumptions; Offering evidence
Minimally Direct and Very Intense	Discounting, Backstabbing, Social undermining to others	Anxiety; Contempt; Humiliation; Hurt	Sensemaking; Trying to save face, Protect personal interests
Minimally Direct and Minimally Intense	Withholding information, Being ambiguous, Engaging in passive-aggressive behavior	Guilt, Hurt; Irritation	Difficult to determine because of avoidant behaviors

Addressing Team Conflict

In an ideal world, all team conflict would be productive and help the team grow while still accomplishing the goals. In reality, we know this is not the case, so it is valuable to develop a toolbox for handling situations in which conflict arises. Communication competent followers and leaders recognize that conflict management is a combination of how people believe they should respond in a given situation and how they do respond; the smaller the gap between what one should do and what one does, the more competent the communicator and successful the interaction. How team members manage their conflicts, positively or negatively, impacts how conflict is handled the next time it arises.

TABLE 6.4   Conflict Management Strategies

	Concern for Others	Concern for Self	Conflict Importance	Relationship Importance	Power
Avoiding	Low	Low	Very Low	Moderate	Unbalanced
Dominating or Forcing	Low	High	High for One Party	Very Low	Very Unbalanced
Compromising	Moderate	Moderate	Moderate	High	Balanced
Accommodating or Obliging	Low	Moderate	Low	Moderate	Very Unbalanced
Collaborating or Integrating	High	High	High	Very High	Balanced

Most of the literature on conflict management styles utilizes Pruitt and Rubin's (1986) dual concern theory—high or low concern for self and other. Based upon the concern for self and other, the strategies have been labeled as win-win, win-lose, and lose-lose. Similar to groups and teams, the strategies each have their own place for being most successful depending upon the conflict's importance, relationship's importance, and power bases available to the team members.

- **Accommodating or Obliging Strategies** involve using no personal or positional power bases because one of the team members simply gives in to the other team member's wishes. This strategy can be effective when there is a longer-term goal and this particular conflict can be foregone. Obliging the wishes of another is not done in a manipulative way so that one can gain an advantage or a chip to call in for the next conflict; rather, it should be done to preserve the relationship and keep the team progressing toward the common purpose. The strategy is considered a win-lose situation because the accommodator loses and the person being accommodated wins; others have labeled it lose-lose because the person being accommodated may not even realize there was a conflict or accommodation made.

- **Avoiding Strategies** involve using no personal or positional power bases because one or both parties are operating as if there is no conflict. You can often hear people talking about "sweeping it under the rug" because when it is hidden there, no one has to deal with it any longer. While this strategy can be effective when the conflict is unimportant, consistently avoiding conflict tends to create animosity and leads to interpersonal conflict. This is known as a lose-lose strategy because the avoider loses by not having any input and the team member(s) being avoided lose because they may never know a conflict existed.

- **Collaborating or Integrating Strategies** focus primarily on personal power bases whereby both parties listen to each other's concerns and work together to reach a mutually satisfying solution to the conflict. To maintain positive relationships, collaboration is recommended when the conflict's importance is high and there is sufficient time for the team to use the strategy. Unlike compromise, they are not both giving up anything, so it is considered a win-win strategy.

- **Compromising Strategies** focus on a combination of personal and positional power bases where the solution is partially acceptable to everyone and completely acceptable to no one. These strategies tend to maintain the relationship, work well when there is not enough time to engage in collaboration with an important issue, and tend to stifle innovation as everyone attempts to maintain at least some of what they wanted. They are considered lose-lose situations because everyone involved must give up something to achieve a solution.

■ **Forcing or Dominating Strategies** involve using legitimate or positional power bases to require someone to resolve the conflict in a desired manner. The person who controls the conflict has little concern for the other(s) in that situation. These strategies can be effective when the issue is unimportant or time-sensitive, and the relationship can be repaired after the fact if need be. This strategy is often referred to as a win-lose in which the person in the power position wins and the person in the subservient position loses.

Which of these sounds most like something you would do? Generally, people gravitate toward one or two primary strategies and attempt to fit them into the situation in which they find themselves. Competent team members take the task and the relationship into consideration and choose the strategy most appropriate for the situation.

Face Negotiation Theory

Stella Ting-Toomey's (2005) face negotiation theory explains how culture (norms and values) impacts the way leaders and followers orient and manage face as well as how they manage conflict situations. **Face** is a metaphor for self-image; it is about "identity respect and other-identity consideration issues within and beyond the actual encounter episode" (Ting-Toomey, 2005, p. 73). Think about the way people (leaders, celebrities) serve as the "face" of a company; these people embody and represent the values, beliefs, and ethics of an organization's identity and culture. At the individual level, you are the "face" of yourself—what you value, believe, how you behave, your communication style, and even the clothes you wear. However, the concept of face is much deeper, psychologically and emotionally, than what meets the eyes and ears at a surface level; it encompasses individual needs and desires in our senses of pride, honor, dignity, prestige, reputation, approval (connection), confirmation, and/or respect.

Leaders and followers engage in facework behaviors to "keep" (face-keeping) or "save" (face-saving) face. **Facework** refers to the strategies (specific verbal and nonverbal behaviors) one uses to maintain, protect, challenge, defend, or restore one's own or another's self-image, the "claimed sense of positive image in the context of social interaction" (Oetzel et al., 2001, p. 235). Engaging in facework is particularly visible when leaders and followers encounter communication situations characterized by face-threatening acts (behaviors that violate identity-related expectations or goals). Broadly, three assumptions of face negotiation theory help us better understand, utilize, and interpret the face and facework of self and others in intercultural encounters:

1. Leaders and followers of all cultures try to maintain and negotiate face.

2. Cultural dimensions influence and shape the way leaders and followers maintain and negotiate face using facework behaviors.

3. The variability and interaction among cultural dimensions, individual, relational, and situational factors influence facework behaviors.

The first assumption emphasizes the ubiquitous and pervading nature of face (self-image) in any culture. At baseline, leaders and followers are human, unique individuals, and regardless of culture we all have face and engage in facework. The second assumption highlights understanding how cultural values influence whether leaders' and followers' primary concern is for self, other, or both (face orientation) as well as tendencies to prefer and use certain conflict communication styles to manage or resolve conflict (Ting-Toomey, 2005). First, at the cultural level, **self-face** (concern for one's own image), is valued more when the culture leans towards individualism (placing higher value on the individual rather than the group), low-context communication (relying on explicit and direct messages for meaning), and low power distance (society accepts that power is distributed equally among members), whereas **other-face** (concern for the other party or persons' image) and **mutual-face** (concern for both your own and another's self-image) is more valued by cultures aligned with certain culture dimensions such as, collectivism (placing higher value on the collective group), high-context communication (relying on implicit language and indirect messages for meaning), and high power distance (society accepts that power is distributed unequally to a select few members) (Sueda, 2014).

An individual level factor related to culture dimensions that influences people's face concerns is self-construal (how the self is defined independent of or interdependently with others). Independent self-construal (IndSC) is the equivalent of the individualistic cultural dimension and interdependent self-construal (InterSC) aligns with collectivism. As such, leaders and followers with a more IndSC tend to have greater self-face concerns when interacting with in-groups and out-groups; leaders and followers with a more InterSC tend to have greater other-face concerns with in-groups, however, focus greater self-face concerns with out-groups, especially in conflict episodes (Ting-Toomey, 2005). Beyond face orientation, culture also shapes leaders' and followers' use of conflict communication styles.

Second, to understand culture's influence on leaders' and followers' preferences for managing and resolving conflict, recall the five conflict management strategies discussed above. Research has found individualism and IndSC are related to using the dominating strategy; collectivism and InterSC relates to using avoiding, obliging, and compromising strategies; and the integrating strategy is associated with both IndSC and InterSC, but more strongly with InterSC (Oetzel & Ting-Toomey, 2013). What is important for us to think about is how this knowledge can be utilized in cross-cultural communication and conflict management. How can followers and leaders build relationships or engage in conflict management without offending one another when contradicting cultural differences and face concerns exist? For example, if your own background and beliefs align with that of an individualistic culture, using a dominating conflict management style would be considered incompetent by someone from a collectivistic culture. This is because it would not allow the other to maintain face. A competent follower or leader would draw upon their ability to recognize the cultural differences that are occurring and adapt to the situation. In that case, they may choose an accommodating style or even an integrating style to manage conflict or preserve face successfully.

Beyond understanding cultural and individual factors separately and as they relate, to complicate things even more, the last assumption stresses the importance of leaders and followers considering the way cultural (individual, relational, and situational) aspects not only vary, but also combine to influence facework. To untangle webs of variation and co-mingled factors, leaders and followers should analyze and distinguish the different layers of face at play when evaluating one's own or others' facework behaviors. Ting-Toomey's (2005) face negotiation theory identifies six layers of face (content domains), including:

1. **Autonomy face**, the need for others to acknowledge our individuality apart from the group and privacy

2. **Fellowship face** (i.e., inclusion face), the need for inclusion

3. **Status face**, the need to be respected for our assets (e.g., prestige, power, position, reputation, appearance, etc.)

4. **Reliability face**, the need for our verbal and nonverbal behaviors to be seen as trustworthy, loyal, and consistent

5. **Competence face**, the need to be recognized for our abilities (e.g., intelligence, expertise, social skills, conflict management skills, team-building skills, etc.)

6. **Moral face**, the need to be valued for one's ethics (ethical approach), honor, and integrity

The power discrepancy among leaders and followers working together across cultures and the variation in cultures' influence on the layers of face that we have to consider can be perplexing without adequate knowledge, particularly in terms of status face. With all the possible combinations of cultural, individual, relational, and situational influences how can we measure the effects of leader and follower communication on teams?

CASE STUDY **Google**

Google—is it a noun, a verb, a word in our everyday talk, or important enough to be included in the dictionary? If you have used a computer, chances are that you have used at least one Google product or service—the search engine, word processing (Google Docs), spreadsheet (Google Sheets), social networking (Google Hangouts), video sharing (YouTube), or any of their other alphabet list of products and services. Initially a private company with no reporting requirements, Google became public and began making their company financials and strategic planning available to a larger community. For as long as we have data, Google has been a team-based organization. As such, they have many different types of teams in their global conglomerate. Some of those teams are co-located in the same building and others are geographically dispersed with people working in different locations around the world.

Creating a team-based organizational structure does not guarantee that the employees are going to thrive on their teams. Initially, Google management believed that if they assembled a "dream team" in each area, they would be successful. That is, if they found the best computer programmer to write the search engine code, best marketing professional to ensure people used the new search engine, best financier to manage the money, and best manager to ensure the employees were satisfied, they would be successful. They found out very quickly that this approach was only successful some of the time.

Because they are a data-driven organization, Google chose its Analytics division to conduct research on what makes effective teams. They chose the name "Project Aristotle" in an effort to highlight one of the philosopher's famous sayings: "The whole is greater than the sum of its parts." They solicited interviews (over 200) and survey data (over 250 items on the annual employee engagement survey) at all levels including over 180 teams that performed both well and poorly. They wanted models associated with qualitative and quantitative metrics, worked for diverse teams across the organization, and consistently explained effectiveness with robust power. Not surprisingly, they found no magic bullet characteristics or qualities that consistently predicted effective teamwork. Instead, they determined that people make the difference; that is, the collective team and how it operates in tandem matters more than the individuals who comprise the team. At Google, the five critical aspects of team functioning include (https://rework.withgoogle.com/print/guides/5721312655835136/):

- Psychological Safety: Team members are willing and able to take risks or be vulnerable.

- Dependability: Team members meet the expectations set for them on time.

- Structure and Clarity: Team members have specific, measurable goals that they can achieve about 60–70 percent of the time; if they achieve all of their goals, then the goals have been set too low.

- Meaning: Teem members are motivated by their work and find it fulfilling.

- Impact: Team members believe they are making a difference in the organization.

Being together in the same office, engaging in consensus decision making, having extroverted team members, seniority, team size, length of time in the organization, and amount of work did not consistently predict effectiveness.

DISCUSSION QUESTIONS

1. Based upon your experiences, how realistic are these five critical aspects of team functioning for other organizations and employees around the world?

2. Of the five aspects of team functioning, which do you believe is most important? Least important? Why?

3. Based upon their research, how do you believe they think about, talk about, and treat leaders and followers?

ANALYSIS OPTIONS

A. Even in organizations that have been crafted to be team based, there are always going to be employees who do not subscribe to all of the ideals of team functioning or find themselves temporarily having difficulty with one of the ideals. For example, in 2017, Google fired an employee for generating a memo that questioned their diversity and inclusion practices (Wakaba-yashi, 2017).

B. After conducting the research, they had to determine how they were going to recognize diversity, promote inclusion, solicit team member support, and implement the research findings.

C. Google has generated mechanisms for promoting psychological safety as well as structure and clarity. You have been tasked with creating similar documents for dependability, meaning, and impact.

ANALYSIS PROCESS

- Brainstorm a list of options for addressing the issue.

- Make a list of strengths and challenges for each of your brainstormed solutions.

(continued)

- Choose the best solution for the issue.

- Develop an implementation plan for your chosen solution.

Google Defines Work
https://tiny.utk.edu/FCL6_1

What Google Learned in Creating Perfect Team
https://tiny.utk.edu/FCL6_4

Understand Team Effectiveness
https://tiny.utk.edu/FCL6_2

KPMG Motivating Employees
https://tiny.utk.edu/FCL6_6

Building a Psychologically Safe Workplace
https://tiny.utk.edu/FCL6_3

Psychological Safety Assessment
https://tiny.utk.edu/FCL6_7

- Additional resources:

 LEADER AND FOLLOWER DEVELOPMENT PRACTICES

1. Use independent teams to solve the same problem so that there are more opportunities for cross-pollination and opportunities for diverse perspectives to be expressed.

2. Work to create an inviting climate where people genuinely feel they belong and are valued members of the team.

3. Use multiple communication media so that everyone can participate in a manner that is comfortable for them to provide input.

4. Be present, free from outside distractions, during team meetings and casual interactions with other team members.

5. Develop flexible, clear team procedures and use them.

DISCUSSION QUESTIONS AND ACTIVITIES

1. Think about your last class project. Were you a group or a team? Why? If you had it to do over again, knowing what you know now, what would you do similarly and differently? Why?

2. Go to https://fearlessorganization.com/?utm_source=google&utm_medium=cpc&utm_campaign=ps_assessment&gclid=EAIaIQobChMIkO3p34G-B6AIVBZSzCh3o9QMnEAAYASAAEgIN-fD_BwE and complete the psychological safety assessment. If you do not work, use your campus environment to assess your psychological safety. What did you learn about yourself and your environment? Given those results, what could you change to enhance your psychological safety?

3. Rank the four decision-making mistakes from least to most problematic or detrimental in your work, school (classes you're taking) and extra-curricular organizations (e.g., student government, religious or spiritual organizations, Greek life, academic honor societies and clubs, etc.). To what extent were your rankings similar and different? Why do you think that was the case?

4. Face negotiation theory was created over 35 years ago. How accurate do you think the different types of face are in today's world? Why? What events have kept them relevant and what events have made them seem less relevant? Think about the ways in which organizational, celebrity, and political leaders have behaved when choosing your events.

5. Knowing what you do about groups and teams, what can you do between now and graduation to better prepare yourself for the team philosophy that awaits you in today's workplace?

FIGURE CREDITS:

Fig. 6.1: Source: https://pixabay.com/illustrations/blue-colors-competition-event-five-81848/.

Fig. 6.3: Adapted from: Copyright © 2016 iStockphoto LP/oatawa.

CHAPTER 7

INTRAORGANIZATIONAL PROCESSES

"If you want to change the culture,
you will have to start by changing the organization."

—MARY DOUGLAS

"It is not part of a true culture to tame tigers,
any more than it is to make sheep ferocious."

—HENRY DAVID THOREAU

U nless you work and live in a vacuum, change is an inevitable part of the process. Organizations are systems with many connected parts (Luhmann, 1955). Without all of the parts, the system does not function at optimum capacity and efficiency; a change in one part of the system affects the other parts of the system. Imagine having a motherboard, battery, case, logo, memory, and a bunch of apps; if all of those pieces are not put together in the proper way, the smart phone does not operate correctly and one cannot play games, make calls, take pictures/video, text, or even read the news. All of those inter-connected parts are the same as you would find in an organization.

The pieces may be different departments that come together to produce a good or execute a service (shipping, marketing, manufacturing, finance, research and development, purchasing); they may also be components of a single department (recruiting, training and development, internal and external communication, health and safety, and benefits under the umbrella of human resources). Within the system, the organizational boundaries separate insiders from outsiders; help new members learn how to communicate, interact, and perform their roles; define the unique organizational culture; and allow people to learn what to expect as part of the system.

What happens in an elementary school? The simple answer is that students learn. In reality, much of what children know as they enter college and,

FIGURE 7.1 A–B   Elementary School Playground and Classroom

ultimately, the workforce, they learned in elementary school. Remember that book *Everything I Needed to Know I Learned in Kindergarten* (Fulghum, 2004)? It is true. In kindergarten, children learn their numbers and letters; as they progress through elementary school, they develop stronger calculation abilities (subtraction, multiplication, and long division) and the ability to spell increasingly complex words. Eventually, they progress to the point of using those same numbers and letters for algebraic equations.

Inside the building walls, teachers, volunteers, and principals formally socialize the children as they learn the organizational culture's values, have opportunities to engage in sense-making when different textbooks present historical facts or literature interpretations differently from each other or the teacher, and see their expectations for earning an A just for trying violated as they earn Bs and Cs.

In the lunchroom and out on the playground, children learn more of the connotative meanings for those all-important sight words in kindergarten. Playing with others in cooperative games, such as kickball or dodgeball, teaches them how to work together with others, that life is not always fair, and what it means to belong to a larger group. As they see children teased and bullied, they learn what it means to be a cultural insider versus an outsider. Time on the playground also provides opportunities to enact the values they have learned inside the school, what to expect from their friends and enemies, the outcomes of trying different responses to a situation, and the importance of strong communication skills when they try to persuade others to play what they want to play or treat another child in a particular way. Each year in school extends their understanding, communication competence, and followership/leadership skills.

In which organization would you prefer to work or volunteer (see Figures 7.2a and b)? Neither is better or worse than the other; each has unique characteristics, ways of interacting, processes for making sense of what is happening, relationships between and among the members, and defining characteristics of the roles people play in those organizations. Think about the top organization as playing a baseball game in which there are specific rules for who bats first (away team), what constitutes a turn (three outs), how play moves from one player to the next (hit the ball and reach base, make an out, or walk), and who wins (the team that scores the most runs).

Think about the bottom organization as playing Pictionary or charades where all of the players share (mostly) equally in the process; while there are still rules about how to play the game and whose turn it is, the ways in which people act out or draw the word/phrase are organic and develop as the turn unfolds. These two different organizational structures have significant implications for the organization's culture, socialization and sense-making processes, members' expectations and how they respond to expectation violations and organizational change approaches.

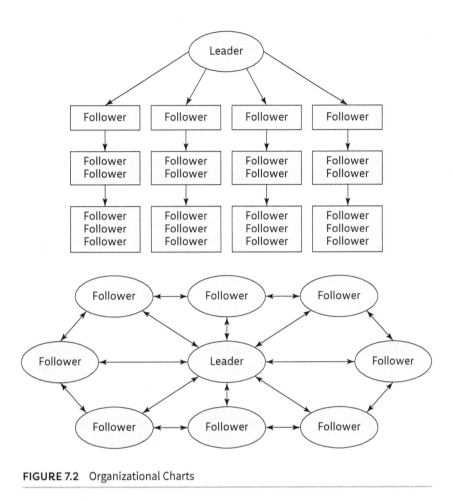

FIGURE 7.2   Organizational Charts

Organizational Culture: The Cultural Metaphor

Rather than seeing communication and organizations separately, the **cultural metaphor** views organizations as communication, with culture as a socially constructed process among leaders and followers. Through interaction, leaders and followers create, maintain, and/or change a shared reality. From this perspective, organizational culture is something an organization is, not something an organization has. Organizational culture theory (Pacanowsky & O'Donnell-Trujillo, 1983) describes workplaces as tribes. All of us are members of different cultures and each culture is comprised of different leaders and followers. As a member of an organization, you are a member of a particular culture, a tribe. For example, as a college student you are a member of a higher-education institution, an academic home (your major), and likely a series of other groups on or off campus.

Pacanowsky and O'Donnell-Trujillo's (1983) web metaphor explains the process and structure of organizational culture. The theory highlights three primary assumptions of organizational culture theory (OCT), including:

1.   Through interaction and its contextual features, leaders and followers create, maintain, and/or change a lived reality, an organizational culture.

2.   Sense-making and the way symbols are used and interpreted among leaders and followers play critical roles in the process and structure of organizational culture.

3.   Cultures vary across organizations, accounting for the variability and variation of leaders' and followers' communicative performances and serving as indicators of organizational culture.

Tribes: Interactive and Contextual Nature of Cultures

The first assumption emphasizes the importance of interaction as well as contextual features influencing interaction. Within any organization, communication among members is the heart of an organization's existence and its culture, making it possible to understand what work life in any organization is like. However, leaders or followers alone are not solely responsible for creating, maintaining, and/or changing an organization's culture. Rather, it is the collective communication among leaders and followers that creates, maintains, and/or changes organizational culture. Within these interactions, the symbols and language used in your tribe, the way your tribe does things or talks about how things are done, differs from others. For example, the organizational life of a particular university or college is not the same at all academic organizations around the world. If you were to visit other campuses, you would get a sense of that organization's culture, what it is like to be a student there, how things work, and how people talk about doing those things. Not only is interaction required, but context also plays a critical role in organizational culture.

As leaders and followers interact, two features of context impact their communication: 1) situational features: who, where, and what and 2) historical features (Pacanowsky & O'Donnell-Trujillo, 1983). During any interactive situation, communication between leaders and followers varies in terms of style, approach, and language use depending on who is involved in the interaction, where the interaction takes place, and what the interaction's purpose is. For example, the language used by a leader and a follower (who) discussing that follower's most recent performance evaluation (what) in the leader's office (where) will differ from two coworkers (who) discussing their performance evaluations (what) during a lunch break in the company break room (where). These contextual features often lead leader-follower communication to be more formal and follower-follower communication to be more informal.

Communication during interaction also depends on historical aspects of leaders' and followers' relationships with one another and the organization. How many years or months have members worked together? How much time have members spent together? How long has each member been a part of the organization? For instance, the language used during a leader-follower interaction regarding a follower's performance evaluation will vary for leader-follower pairs who have a longer history of interaction, say 5 years versus leader-follower pairs who have interacted at work for 6 months. Not only the symbols used, but also the symbols' meaning varies for the leader-follower pair with a longer working history. As a result, both situational and historical contextual factors contribute to an organization's culture as well as how followers and leaders make sense of the symbols and what they mean.

Webs: Process and Structure

Sense-making and the way symbols are interpreted play critical roles in understanding the process and structure of organizational culture. Pacanowsky and O'Donnell-Trujillo rely on the idea of sense-making processes and the web metaphor of culture from Geertz (1973) to describe organizational culture as a process and culture as a structure. As leaders and followers communicate, they are spinning a web; each thread of the web is a product of an interaction among or between leaders and followers. Because the communication among or between leaders and followers is an ongoing process, we see that organizational culture is a communication process.

From these interconnected threads of communication, a web is constructed to represent the structure of an organization's culture. The knowledge that leaders and followers draw on to explain or make sense of their experiences is embedded in the threads weaved by communication and comprising the structure of their web (culture) (Pacanowsky & O'Donnell-Trujillo, 1982). This knowledge includes shared meanings of particular symbols and language used within an organization. Therefore, the organizational culture web is a context in which tribe followers and leaders interact to create, maintain, and/or change a shared reality. As communication continues among and between leaders and followers, meaningful interactions continue to reinforce existing threads or add new threads to either strengthen or modify the design of a culture's structural web.

Variation: Different Tribes Design Different Webs

Different tribes design different webs. The patterns that their communication threads, produced from the collective interactions among leaders and followers, weave different patterns of web structures across various organizations. The last assumption of OCT considers the way cultures vary across organizations, accounting for the variability and variation of leaders' and followers' communicative performances. We develop a better sense of an organization's culture web by examining the way followers and leaders communicate throughout five components of communicative performance.

The five components of communicative performance serve as indicators of organizational culture, including: rituals, passion, sociality, politics, and enculturation. These components offer insightful information regarding questions about "how things work in this place." Each component holds answers or descriptions for different aspects of organizational life to better understand how things work across a variety of organizational cultures (see Table 7.1).

TABLE 7.1   Communicative Performance

Components of Communicative Performance	The "How"
Ritual Performances	How people work in this place
Passion Performances	How work life plays out in this place
Sociality Performances	How people interact in this place
Political Performances	How people use communication strategies in this place
Enculturation Performances	How people become a member of this place

- **Ritual Performances:** Performing cultural rituals reveals the habitual behaviors characterizing the way people use and spend their time. Ritual performances occur on a regular basis (West & Turner, 2018). **Personal rituals** involve routines in an individual's organizational life (e.g., checking email, greeting other members). **Task rituals** involve habitual behaviors that get a job done (e.g., processing paperwork, billing clients, etc.). **Social rituals** concern patterns of interacting with others (e.g., happy-hour gatherings). **Organizational rituals** concern functions including all members (e.g., company meetings, company trips, annual picnics).

- **Passion Performances:** Passion performances, the stories leaders and followers tell about themselves or others, illustrate what organizational life is like. Our stories about organizational life reveal experiences that offer "insider knowledge" on the way customs and shared language play out in organizational life. **Personal stories** are stories about one's self that magnify the experience of a culture. **Collegial stories** are accounts of other members' experiences that tell us "how things *really* work in this place." **Corporate stories** are narratives representing and supporting a leader's ideology (vision). **Passionate repartee** concerns a shared vocabulary and set of meanings (e.g., idioms and metaphors) commonly used among followers and leaders in a given culture.

- **Sociality Performances:** Performances of sociality involve the interpersonal or group aspects of interaction among leaders and followers; they reveal the way members interact with each other and how "smooth" those interactions are. Leaders and followers may perform **courtesies** that confirm another member's presence and usually involve reciprocation (e.g., morning or afternoon greetings in passing). **Pleasantries** concern social performances of self-disclosure ("small talk," "water cooler talk," "elevator talk"). **Sociabilities** reveal or create intimacy among leaders and followers (joking, gossiping, venting, "shop talk"). **Privacies** involve leaders and followers discussing or confessing more private matters that build trust and require support as well as sensitivity from one another (e.g., self-disclosure).

- **Political Performances:** Followers' and leaders' communication strategies for political performances highlight power, control, and influence. They often reveal **personal strength**, or their ability to get things done, by exercising their power. Strategies associated with control reflect the way leaders and followers **cement allies** through loyalty, agreement, and social influence. Influence strategies are also depicted when members engage in **bargaining or negotiating**, an attempt to attain goals perceived as incompatible or contradictory.

FIGURE 7.3 Just as two people must take the time to get to know each other, an organizational newcomer must take the time to get to know the organization, its members, and the way things work there to be successful.

- **Enculturation Performances:** Enculturation performances concern the learning processes required to become a competent member within a particular organizational culture. To become a fully functioning member of a culture, leaders and followers must acquire knowledge and skills by satisfying the expectations related to their role and gaining a deeper understanding of, and appreciation for, organizational life within a given workplace culture—learning the ropes. Even though most of the ropes are learned as a newcomer, understanding an organizational culture is an ongoing process throughout one's tenure or career.

Socialization

While organizational culture focuses on "how we do things," the socialization process focuses on understanding "what we do." Organization **socialization** is defined as "the process through which individuals acquire the knowledge, skills, attitudes, and behaviors required to adapt to a new work role" (Wanberg, 2012, p. 17) and become an accepted member (Jablin, 2001). Both leaders and followers go through socialization processes; however, the mix of knowledge, skills, attitudes, and behaviors needed may differ based upon people's roles and level of experience. Followers and leaders may experience the socialization process when: a) beginning work at an organization as a newcomer or b) entering a new role within an organization (promotion, position transfer/re-assignment, international assignment) (Wanberg, 2012). Three stages characterize the socialization process:

- Anticipatory socialization
- Assimilation
- Metamorphosis

Anticipatory Socialization: Pre-Entry Expectations
Prior to entering any organization, people develop preconceived ideas and expectations related to fulfilling a role, **anticipatory socialization**. Anticipatory stage learning involves our ideas and expectations of what a job is like—what we learn from everyday experiences and job-specific research. Throughout childhood we learn what people do at work, knowledge needed to answer the timeless questions "What do you want to be when you grow up?" and "What do you do with a communication major?" Responses to these questions are typically either job specific (e.g., police officer, lawyer, doctor, teacher, musician, actress, etc.) or industry focused (e.g., law enforcement, legislation, medicine, education, music, etc.).

Rarely (if ever) do we hear people respond to this question by saying "I want to be a follower"; yet, all of us work as followers in some form or at multiple points in our lifetimes. As leaders and followers prepare to enter the workforce, they also learn more about these roles and potential employers by researching positions and organizations of interest to increase their existing knowledge and further solidify expectations prior to going through application, recruiting, and interviewing processes. Much information is gained during this time, even though it is also a time of high uncertainty, ambiguity, and stress.

Assimilation: Becoming One of the Tribe

Congratulations, you're hired! Now what? At this point, leaders and followers go through the **assimilation stage** (aka encounter or entry stage), which is defined as the processes of how people become accepted members (socialized) into an organization's "communication cultures" and make changes to those cultures to meet "their needs and goals" (Jablin 2001, p. 733). Assimilation exposes us to how we are expected to do a job, the way members of the organization do or say things, as well as discover and develop our identity as one of the tribe. For both followers and leaders, assimilation experiences include, but are not limited to, orientation (i.e., orienting, onboarding), training, mentoring, social support, and interactions among employees.

Socialization Strategies. During assimilation, six bipolar pairs of socialization strategies leaders and followers may experience as a newcomer or when assuming a new role (promotion, re-assignment, international relocation, etc.) exist (Van Maanen & Schein, 1975). These bipolar pairs represent "planned" socialization strategies. Each pair is associated with one of three categories—context, content, and social—of acquiring knowledge and skills related to one's role (Jones, 1986). Table 7.2 shows the association among these categories, pairs of socialization strategies, and level at which they are enacted. Institutionalized strategies are commonly experienced when organizations intend to shape peoples' experience to produce a specific outcome. They encourage leaders and followers to learn and enact their roles by engaging in role-taking behaviors. While institutionalized strategies assist newcomers' adjustment within organizations, individualized strategies offer leaders and followers more room for role-making, to add their own design to the cupcake icing (Ashforth et al., 1998).

The first category of socialization strategies (context) focuses on situational aspects in which leaders and followers may find themselves as they are provided and presented with role-related information. This category involves processes for understanding the behaviors and expectations of a job as well as the organization. The collective strategy involves experiences where newcomers go through the same learning experience, which

TABLE 7.2   Socialization Sources and Strategies

	Socialization Strategies		
	Knowledge Sources	Institutionalized	Individualized
Context	The way information is provided	Collective–all newcomers are given the same (institutionalized) learning experience.	Individual–each newcomer is given a unique (individualized) learning experience.
	The way information is presented	Formal–newcomers are segregated from existing members while learning role responsibilities.	Informal–newcomers are integrated with existing members while learning role responsibilities.
Content	Sequence-related information	Sequential–explicit information provided to newcomers about the sequence (stages) of the learning process.	Random–no information provided to newcomers about the sequence (stages) of the learning process.
	Time-related information	Fixed–precise information provided about when newcomers complete a certain stage in the learning process.	Variable–no information provided about when newcomers complete a certain stage in the learning process.
Social	Existing members assigned as mentors	Serial–experienced members are assigned as a mentor for newcomers.	Disjunctive–no experienced members assigned as a mentor for newcomers. Newcomers develop their own definitions for situations.
	Degree of social support	Investiture–positive social experiences with prior members, confirming newcomer expectations about themselves.	Divestiture–negative social experiences with prior members, disconfirming newcomer expectations about themselves.

Adapted from Jones (1986, pp. 262–279).

differs from the individual strategy where each newcomer is put through a more independent and less homogenous experience. At first glance, we may expect followers to experience the collective strategy more, whereas leaders experience the individual strategy more. After all, there are less leadership roles with very different expectations for satisfying those roles compared to follower roles. This line of logic is an example of a logical fallacy (an error in reasoning).

Organizations today recognize the importance of both leader and follower competent job performance . For leaders, one aspect of performing competently is acquiring knowledge about their own role, including the ways leaders are expected to support followers in their roles. As such, leaders must understand follower roles. This is why companies such as Zappos, an online retail company, require all employees undergo the same 4-week training process. During this training experience, task-related information provided for leaders and followers differs; however, the overall process of acquiring information is the same. What makes Zappos even more interesting is how they approach the formal–informal socialization strategy pair. Existing Zappos members meet newcomers at designated training locations to work alongside and answer questions for both leaders and followers during their orientation and training experiences, reflecting a mix of the informal and formal strategies.

The second category (content) also involves understanding the behaviors and expectations of a job as well as the organization. The content category focuses on the way leaders and followers acquire time-related knowledge about assuming their roles. The sequential strategy provides information about the steps one must experience to assume a role. In terms of time, the fixed strategy provides a timetable of when a leader or follower will assume a role. At many organizations, newcomers encounter these strategies as they go through a trial period (i.e., probation period) during their first weeks of work. The purpose of a trial period is for both the organization and leader or follower to decide whether a person's abilities match a role as well as whether a person fits in with the organization's culture.

The third category, social, involves understanding the way organizational members do or say things through different layers of interaction. Leaders and followers acquire information related to a role, the organization, and their own identity through lateral (follower-follower, leader-leader) and vertical (leader-follower) interactions with other members. Social interactions may occur when prior members are formally assigned as a newcomer's mentor, reflecting the serial strategy, or when prior members are not assigned as mentors (the disjunctive strategy). Both leaders and followers serve as formal and informal mentors to guide and teach newcomers as they learn their role.

Beyond experiences of mentorship, social interaction with members offers leaders and followers opportunities to learn about themselves and their identity, what they mean and how they fit in with other members. The investiture strategy captures experiences of positive social interaction with existing members confirming the identity and expectations of a newcomer, compared to the divestiture strategy where negative interactions disconfirm newcomer identity and expectations. These socialization strategies captured in the social category are critical for leaders' and followers' acceptance within organizations, particularly in terms of learning what things mean.

Learning what things mean highlights how socialization functions as a language crash course. For example, the terms "diced" and "capped" to a prison guard may refer to violent behaviors among inmates, whereas employees of the American restaurant chain Waffle House use these terms to indicate the addition of tomatoes and ham to a customer's food order. In fact, understanding the way symbols, words, or phrases take on different meanings as an organizational newcomer involves learning a "foreign" language when people assume international roles. The term "first floor" in the U.S. means a building's ground level and, in the U.K., it means the floor *above* the ground-level floor. The English word referencing the day of the week employees receive their wages, "payday," sounds the same as the term that means "I farted" in Portuguese, "peidei." As leaders and followers learn a place's lingo, they are better able to do their jobs, interact with other members, and determine whether their uniqueness as an individual fits a given organization.

Social experiences with other members also impact the way leaders and followers learn who they are and what they mean to other members in terms of how they fit in within an organization, which influences the way people choose to enact their role. Up until now, we have discussed what scholars consider "planned" socialization strategies set in motion by organizations. These planned socialization strategies capture the way newcomers actively participate in required social interaction of the assimilation phase (and overall socialization process) to acquire knowledge regarding one's role and identity. However, people are not robots and we do not live in a *Matrix* cinema reality where organizations feed knowledge and skills to humans through a plug in the back of our skull base. In real-life, leaders and followers experience planned strategies while also engaging in "unplanned" socialization strategies. Unplanned strategies act as sources of knowledge for leaders and followers during and after the assimilation stage.

Metamorphosis

The metamorphosis stage occurs when a leader or follower becomes an accepted member of an organization. As an accepted member, leaders or followers participate in "learning new behaviors and attitudes, and/or modifying existing ones" (Jablin & Krone, 1987, p. 713). After completing this transition from outsider to insider, unplanned socialization strategies remain active aspects of work-life experiences. There are four unplanned strategies, including: information seeking, information giving, relationship development, and role negotiation (Jablin, 2001).

Leaders and followers may seek information to reduce uncertainty and/ or clarify ambiguous information using Jablin and Miller's (1990) information seeking strategies:

- **Overt questioning:** asking for information in a direct manner.
- **Indirect questioning:** getting others to give information by hinting and using non-interrogative questions.

- **Third-party questioning:** asking someone other than the primary information source.

- **Testing:** breaking a rule, annoying the target, and so on and then observing the target's reaction.

- **Disguising conversations:** use of jokes, verbal prompts, self-disclosure, and so on to garner information from the target without the person's awareness.

- **Observation:** watching another's actions to model behavior or discern meanings associated with events.

- **Surveillance:** indiscriminately monitoring conversations and activities to which meaning can retrospectively be attributed.

Second, as accepted members, followers and leaders offer newcomers information relevant for completing tasks or fitting into the culture. However, followers and leaders can use newcomer information-giving behaviors to assess how well newcomers are adapting to the organizational expectations. Third, relationships continuously develop and change beyond assimilation and throughout metamorphosis, which makes it possible for people to engage in role negotiation. Last, role negotiation involves leaders and followers modifying the behaviors or expectations of their role to better satisfy their individual needs or desires, thus fulfilling the final criteria of the role-making process. Overall, people use socialization processes to learn, enact, and modify expectations for their own behavior as well as the expected behavior of others.

Expectancy Violations Theory

Burgoon (1993; 1995) and colleagues (Burgoon & Poire, 1993) developed expectancy violations theory (EVT) to help explain what happens in communication situations when a person expects one message or behavior and experiences something else. People enter organizations with preconceived attitudes, ideas, and beliefs shaping their general behavior expectancies about leadership and followership roles. As people learn the roles within an organization during the socialization process, these generalized expectancies develop into more specialized communication expectancies for leader and follower roles within that particular organization. **Communication expectancies** are defined as "enduring patterns of anticipated verbal and nonverbal behavior," which contain both: a) predictive expectancies, what we anticipate as typical behavior that

FIGURE 7.4
Expectations can be violated in both positive (someone does something better than you expected) and negative ways (someone does something worse than you expected).

will occur and b) prescriptive expectancies, what is appropriate, desired, or preferred (Burgoon & Ebesu Hubbard, 2005, p. 151).

Expectancy violations occur more often than most of us may think in organizational life. For example, Vanessa is a seasoned surgical technician who recently started working at a new hospital, Reilley Medical Center. In Vanessa's experience, it is typical behavior for followers (nurses, surgical technicians) to address their leaders (supervisors, surgeons, anesthesiologists) by their title and surname (Mr./Mrs. Smith or Dr. Smith). Vanessa believes this behavior is normal, polite, and appropriate. Within her first few weeks of work she notices other nurses and staff greet and talk with the surgeon she works under most, Dr. Johnathan Rose, as John rather than Dr. Rose. Through asking questions and interacting with her coworkers, including J. Rose himself, Vanessa learns John requests all of his colleagues interact on a first-name basis. Given this knowledge, Vanessa sets her predictive expectancies to fit with her normative prototype of follower behavior and acknowledges that interacting with her leader, John, on a first-name basis is different. From this example, we see that people do not always have to engage in outlandish or egregious behavior to violate the expectations of others. Expectancy violations are not always negative—both positive and negative violations occur.

When the behavior of a leader or follower violates or fails to meet our expectations two things occur: 1) we try to make sense of what the behavior means and 2) we attach a positive or negative valence (value) to our evaluation of the violating behavior (White, 2015). Within organizational life, situations characterized by uncertainty and/or ambiguity are particularly susceptible to expectancy violations. More specifically, uncertainty, ambiguity, and stress permeate performance feedback situations for both leaders and followers. Generally, organizations implement annual performance reviews as a method for followers to obtain feedback from leaders.

Think about waiting one whole year to receive feedback from your leader, going to work every weekday for 365 days and not knowing if you are doing something right, wrong, or if there is something you are supposed to be doing but are not. Let that soak in. How would you feel? As a leader, what kind of stress is involved in having annual performance review conversations with *all* of your followers? For followers, EVT predicts that if you prefer annual reviews compared to continuous feedback, then your expectations are met and conversations with your leader will be involved, pleasant, smooth, or reflect generally effective communication. However, if you prefer continuous feedback, your expectations go unmet for 12 months. The outcome, as predicted by EVT, is stiff, unpleasant, or generally ineffective leader-follower interaction patterns. In this case, maybe you wait out the storm within this organization rather than finding a new place to work or maybe your expectations have gone unmet, but "ehh (shoulder shrug) my boss is really great, so the wait isn't so bad." Hold on to your hats and skirts ladies and gentlemen,

EVT's next prediction is like a whirlwind dose of useful common sense. EVT predicts attaching a positive valence with a communicator (e.g., leader, your boss) reduces the size of the violation, whereas a negative valence attached to an evaluation increases the size of the violation. Basically, if you like your boss and see this person in a positive light, you are more likely to overlook or grant a wider space for mistakes if expectations go unmet and vice versa.

Most people do not prefer waiting in limbo for 12 months before receiving feedback, which is important for competent job performance and overall organizational effectiveness. Many top companies like Adobe, GE, Netflix, and Google have abandoned the traditional annual performance review to embrace continuous feedback systems that reduce uncertainty and ambiguity. For instance, at Adobe, a leading software design company, managers do not manage their followers; they serve as coaches for followers. Both leaders and followers at Adobe practice informal "check-in" conversations structured to address expectations, feedback, and growth and development. Adobe has found the heart of success for this informal feedback model rests in the way meaningful and frequent conversations about performance appear to increase employee productivity, engagement, and motivation with less turnover (Burkus, 2017).

Interestingly, companies switching to continuous feedback systems have also raised awareness to the importance of feedback among coworkers to address lateral expectations. Such systems offer platforms for employees to interact, ask questions, and offer feedback with one another in the same way as leaders and followers. Certainly, expectancies are violated or go unmet in situations beyond performance reviews and feedback. Regardless of the situation, when faced with expectancy violation(s), both leaders and followers activate and rely on sensemaking processes.

Sensemaking Processes

People engage in sense-making processes when their expectations do not match their experiences (an expectancy violation has occurred) or when they believe they can no longer function in a particular situation; we bring order and organization to our lives through sense-making (Weick et al., 2005). Whereas expectancy violations theory is concerned with predicting behavior, sense-making theory is concerned with people's meaning-making processes. Situations involving uncertainty, equivocality, and paradox are ripe for sense-making (Sandberg & Tsoukas, 2015).

Sense-making occurs when situations are unpredictable, inconsistent, open to interpretation or multiple interpretations, deliberatively ambiguous, or contradictory—all situations that may lead one to react defensively as a mechanism of self-protection. For example, a new member learns during formal orientation to keep a hard and soft copy of all documents and then learns through informal socialization that as long as the documents are uploaded to the organization's cloud drive a hard copy is not necessary. The situation is likely to require the new member to engage in sense-making to reconcile the two different messages about document preservation. Is formal orientation or informal socialization a more accurate representation of what should be done; whose word should be trusted—those who do it every day or those who simply read from a handbook? How one attaches meaning to these two contradictory messages is the sense-making process. Overall, sense-making is a continuous process that bridges one's past and present experiences with one's expectations.

Think about the student government organization on your campus or another organization to which you belong. The leader, or president of the group, has been awarded legitimate (based upon title), referent (based upon relationships with other members of the group), and informational (based upon attending various meetings and having access to people at all organizational levels) power. The president has always used this power to seek consensus among the student government leaders and with various groups on campus. At the last meeting of the year, the president has a different demeanor as the meeting begins. The goal seems to be how quickly can we get through this agenda, regardless of what it means for consensus and the well-being of other student government members. As one point, the president comments in an almost shouting voice, "I support this resolution and so should you!" even though the president has never voiced an opinion before a vote. Later in the meeting, the senators attempt to engage in discussion about a resolution on the table, and the president attempts to squash the discussion. The senators use parliamentary procedure to their benefit to vote to allow the discussion to continue. At a third point in the meeting, the president presents the budget for the upcoming year with the caveat that "Upper administration and faculty senate have already agreed to this budget and believe it is fair for all student organizations. The faster you approve it, the faster you can get to the end-of-year celebration." With this scenario in mind, the three aspects of sense-making, sense-giving, and sense-breaking are discussed.

Sensemaking

Both leaders and followers engage in sense-making; it can be done individually, dyadically, as part of a group or team, or as a whole organization. **Sense-making** is the process of using past experiences to attach meaning to a current situation that is contradictory, paradoxical, or uncertain. This process of attaching meaning based upon contextual clues occurs every day, even if we are not conscious of it. At its core, sense-making is about answering two questions: "How does something come to be an event for organizational members?" and "What does an event mean?" When people ask the question "What's the story here?" and follow it up with "Now what should I do?" they have recognized the event and indicated they are ready to engage in sense-making (Weick et al., 2005, p. 410).

Below are a set of principles they laid out for the sense-making process.

- **Retrospective and Prospective**: Because we cannot notice patterns over time in the present, all sense-making has to be retrospective, draw upon observations that have occurred over time, and show us a level of contradiction. Our actions associated with the sensemaking can only occur in the present or future and be prospective.

- **Plausibility**: Because sense-making is about the meanings people attach to events, it is never about the truth with a lower case or capital T; it is always about people's perceptions of the truth. We ask ourselves whether the stories being created to explain the contradiction ring true for us based upon our past experiences and any additional data we have access to.

- **Identity**: Who we believe we are, as individuals or an organization at any given point in time, influences how we behave and the meanings we attach to events. We are also influenced by who others believe we are.

- **Socialization**: All of our background experiences (culture, education, norms, attitudes, beliefs, values) help shape how we interpret a situation. These are both individual and organizational experiences.

- **Ongoing**: People are continuously shaping and reacting to the environments around them to enhance the story that will soon be a piece of data in the sense-making process. This shaping and reacting process also influences our identities (how we see ourselves) and image (how others see us).

- **Cues**: Each piece of information we encounter helps us determine what is relevant, a reasonable explanation for the situation, and a link to a broader network of meanings. Each time we speak, or write, we are reinforcing or contradicting the ongoing story.

FIGURE 7.5 Sense-making processes occur when there is uncertainty or paradox. It is often through interactions with others that the light bulb goes on and we are able to reconcile the discrepancies that exist in our work lives.

While this is the sense-making process, other people also influence our interpretations, a process known as sense-giving.

Sense-Giving

Because leaders and followers socially influence each other, both can engage in sense-giving, even though the research has primarily examined how leaders engage in sense-giving. **Sense-giving** is the process of using the meaning one has attached to an uncertain or ambiguous situation to influence the meaning-making process of others. That is, a leader generally hears about an organizational change before the followers. After making sense of the change, the leader conveys the change to the followers; how the leader conveys that change influences how the followers make sense of the change because they trust that the leader is providing them with an accurate representation of the situation. Because people would prefer to avoid dissonance, that uncomfortable feeling we experience following a large decision or change, it is easier to use the leader's interpretation given to the followers than to try and develop other sense-making options.

Another version of sense-giving involves the leader providing the follower with two dialectical (seemingly oppositional) demands and asking the follower to carry out the contradictory processes (Sparr, 2018). Followers might be asked to be open with sharing and closed to protect information; demonstrate that one can work independently in a team-based environment; or innovate in this hierarchical, incremental environment.

Sense-Breaking/Censoring

Sense-breaking is the process of changing the ongoing story through persuasion or inappropriate use of power. In situations where there is extreme uncertainty or contradiction, providing an alternative story to help people make sense of the situation is easier. For example, it would be easier to change the narrative about an organization's commitment to being green and protecting the environment if the employees recently found out that one of the organization's major suppliers is being sued for contaminating the local water supply. Followers in the organization become more likely to question other ethical decisions made by the leaders and work to spin their own story about what the organization and its leaders truly value (maybe the bottom line and profits more than the environment). In that same example, the organization's leaders may choose to engage in sense-censoring—say that three times quickly.

Sense-censoring is the process of creating obstacles to the meaning-making processes in which others are engaging (Whittle et al., 2016). In the green example above, the organizational leaders may look to bury information about the lawsuit against the supplier or they may offer to switch vendors while slowly returning to business with the original supplier under investigation. Because most employees do not read the financial reports or year-end shareholder statements, the organization can slowly go back to its original practices without negatively impacting the narrative created by their "pretend" change to a new supplier—the ethics of this behavior are a different story.

Given what you now know about sense-making, let's return to the student government example above and see what is happening with the president and other members. The members retrospectively think about the way all previous meetings have been run (consensus building) in comparison to the current one (domination and coercion). As the meeting unfolds, they prospectively use this information to consciously respond to the president's behavior by invoking the governing rules. In the example, we are not privy to people's socialization, identity, and plausibility processes even though they are occurring. Each time the president or one of the senators speaks, that message becomes another one of the cues that helps shape the person's identity and the plausibility of the story being created by the individuals and the group.

As this is only one meeting in an ongoing set of interactions among the members, it will simply be another piece in the puzzle of student government. At the social after the meeting, the senators are likely to talk amongst themselves about what occurred during the meeting, speculate about what may have led the president to act so dramatically differently, and build a narrative for how to respond if something similar should occur in the future. Finally, if the president has friends in the group, they are likely to spend some time processing the meeting together to also build a plausible narrative of what just occurred.

Organizational Change

Even though change is an inevitable part of keeping an organization moving forward, some changes are planned (e.g., merging with another organization, the death of a terminally ill CEO or founder, upgrading the organization's technology) and others are unplanned (e.g., sudden death of a CEO or founder, natural disaster such as a hurricane or tornado, crisis in which an organization's product or service does not perform as expected). Regardless of the change, effective leaders are prepared for anything that might come their way; they have contingency plans ready to be put into action so they are not caught flat-footed and do not appear incompetent when they need to address the employees or external stakeholders.

Building a leader's credibility requires significant time, effort, and relationship-building interactions; in a moment, that credibility can be shattered if the leader or founder stands before all of the organization members and cannot calm the employees' fears or address their concerns. Whether planned or unplanned, the organizational conditions under which the change occurs serve as the foundation for how smoothly the process unfolds, the extent to which the followers engage in resistance tactics, and whether the change is destined to fail.

While no one is ever fully prepared for change, primarily because it is unpredictable, certain organizational and individual characteristics indicate that organizational members are as ready for the change as they can be. Trust in one's leaders and followers tops the list of change readiness characteristics (Amarantou et al., 2018). When trust exists in the leader-follower relationship, both parties are willing to work harder for the other person; trust often accompanies referent power and thus people are willing to engage in the uncomfortableness that comes with change because of their respect for each other.

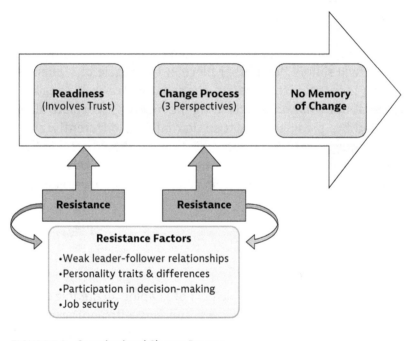

FIGURE 7.6   Organizational Change Process

Change Processes

Practitioners consistently adopt one of the three most common change process models (Bridges, 2003; Kotter & Cohen, 2002; Schein, 2004). Even though they are at least 15 years old, each one remains as relevant today as it was when they created it. In the Bridges model, the three-stage process involves ending/losing/letting go, a neutral zone, and new beginnings. The first stage is the death and decay stage where people recognize that change is needed; the second stage is the calm before the change storm (think about that gray-green sky appearing immediately before a tornado rips through the area); and new beginnings occur when the change has been executed, implemented, and incorporated into the organization's culture.

Schein's three-stage process is similar in that unfreezing is when we need to chip away at the iceberg that has become our accepted and comfortable way of doing things around here, cognitive restructuring is how we mentally prepare all of the organization members for the planned change, and refreezing is where the change becomes so commonplace that we can no longer remember a time when we did not do things that way.

Kotter and Cohen present an eight-stage process model based upon the stories they collected from organizational followers and leaders.

- Play up a sense of urgency

- Create coalitions

- Develop a vision

- Generate buy-in

- Empower action

- Craft short-term wins

- Never let up

- Fold changes into the culture

Regardless of which process model rings true for you and your organization, they all rest on the same basic premises: people must recognize the need for change, engage in the change process, and weave those changes into the organizational fabric.

RESEARCH SUMMARY

Heyden et al. (2016) examined the organizational change process by examining the roles of followers, immediate managers, and organizational leaders or top management. The goal was to determine what contributions each needed to make for the strongest, long-lasting change efforts by testing simultaneously whether the bottom-up or top-down explanations for organizational change work better. Leadership initiates top-down change and followers/immediate supervisors initiate bottom-up change. Internal stakeholders (employees at all three levels) in over 500 organizations implementing a planned change requiring employees to upgrade their knowledge and skills participated in the study. They tested who initiated and who executed the organizational change as well as the extent to which the employees supported the change. The results did not reveal negative support for change when leadership initiated it, regardless of who

(continued)

executed the change. The results did reveal positive support for change when immediate managers initiated it, regardless of whether middle managers or leadership executed the change.

Implications: The strongest support for change occurred when middle managers initiated the change and leadership executed the change—an indication that organizational members play their expected roles. That is, followers, do not expect to be the change agents even though they do want to provide input for change; as middle managers are closer to the organizational action, people expect them to use their expertise to suggest appropriate and effective changes; employees expect leaders to have a vision and be capable of thinking in terms of the big picture, which is necessary for executing a large-scale change. Middle managers possess the proximity and deep knowledge of how things work in the organization; leaders possess the resources and ability to contextualize the change. Interestingly, the best change configuration according to the data appeared the least frequently among the participants. Ultimately, everyone in the organization has a role to play in organizational change and the better they understand and play those roles the more successful the change.

Resistance to Change

One of the most difficult aspects of an organizational change to manage is resistance, whether it is from leaders or followers. **Resistance to change** is any challenge, obstacle, or refusal employed by organizational members to counteract the differences in policies and procedures. Resistance may occur at the individual, group, or organizational level. At the organizational level, resistance often appears when there are organizational-level culture differences, such as subcultures and countercultures, conflict among organizational members, and power differentials. At the group level, resistance appears when people have different perceptions of the task and relational norms, group members engaging in groupthink, and too much or too little group cohesiveness. Finally, at the individual level, resistance occurs when people engage in selective listening, perceive behaviors differently than they were intended, or have poor socialization processes that do not minimize uncertainty or maximize feelings of security.

Four factors best predict resistance to change (Amarantou et al., 2018). First, weak leader-follower relationships predict resistance to change. If you are not happy and do not have a strong relationship with your leaders or followers, helping them work through the change, engaging in the new behaviors, having a positive attitude toward the change, and believing that the change will be beneficial for you as an individual becomes more difficult. Second, personality traits and differences predict resistance to change.

While leaders and followers can have different personality traits (one is risk-averse and the other enjoys living on the edge), they can also have negative personality traits that lead them to see a situation pessimistically, or as a glass half full. They may be people who thrive in predictable environments; change is rarely predictable and that is why so many people resist making changes in their personal and organizational lives. Third, the more leaders and followers participate in the decision-making process, the less likely they are to resist the change. Shutting people out of the process and springing changes on them at the last minute is a sure-fire way to stimulate resistance to change. Finally, the less secure people feel in their jobs, the more likely they are to resist change because the outcomes of those changes are uncertain. For example, if both the followers and leaders do not feel secure in the organization or believe they may soon find themselves on the chopping block once the organizational change is made, they work against the change to preserve the status quo. Overall, handling resistance to change is possible and often successful with planning and competent communication.

CASE STUDY **University of Tennessee**

In February 2017, The University of Tennessee, Knoxville hired its eighth chancellor to lead the flagship (largest) campus (UTK); there are five other campuses around the state. Her first morning on campus, Dr. Davenport entered an elevator of students and said, "Hi, I'm Beverly," introducing herself to the students as the new chancellor. Over the course of the next 15 months, she was visible as a chancellor, interacting with students and various groups on campus.

Four turning points marked her time as chancellor. Within the first month, she hired John Currie as Athletic Director. The decision came down to hiring him or Phillip Fulmer who had previously been the head football coach for many years. Within the first six months, she decided not to outsource facilities services. Outsourcing would mean that a company based in Chicago, IL, with no ties to the university or local community would manage all facilities on campus. In fall 2017, the University fired head football coach Butch Jones; after signing a memorandum of agreement with Greg Schianno to become the next head football coach, UTK cited connections to the Jerry Sandusky sexual abuse scandal at Penn State University as the reason they would reopen the coaching search. After placing John Currie on administrative leave, Phillip Fulmer, who was working in the President's office as a special assistant, became athletic director. Finally, in spring 2018, a white supremacist group reserved space on campus. During this time, Dr. Davenport stood with the students regarding respecting

(continued)

diversity, supported the students traditionally marginalized by such groups, and upheld the First Amendment regarding free speech. After tremendous planning with local, state, and national law enforcement agencies regarding the logistics, the event occurred without incident. Fifteen months into her five-year contract and without warning to the internal stakeholders, President Joseph DiPietro issued a press release to the media firing or demoting Dr. Beverly Davenport as chancellor and later appointed Wayne Davis from the College of Engineering to replace her on an interim basis. Below is the letter President Joseph A. DePietro sent to Chancellor Beverly J. Davenport (quoted in full from https://www.tennessean.com/story/news/education/2018/05/02/beverly-davenport-termination-letter-university-tennessee-ut-president/574328002/):

May 2, 2018

Dr. Beverly Davenport
Chancellor, University of Tennessee, Knoxville
527 Andy Holt Tower Knoxville, TN 37996-0184

Dear Beverly:

I have decided that it is in the best interest of The University of Tennessee to change the leadership of our flagship campus and terminate your appointment as Chancellor of The University of Tennessee, Knoxville.

Your performance evaluation for Calendar Year 2017, a copy of which is being provided to you under separate cover, describes numerous areas of unsatisfactory performance. In several areas, even after I raised concerns early in your tenure and addressed them multiple times since then, you have been either unwilling or unable to improve, including:

1. The relationship between us, as well as that between you (and some members of your cabinet) and some on my leadership team continues to be unsatisfactory. More times than I find acceptable, there has been a lack of trust, collaboration, communication, and transparency in these relationships, and it has been counterproductive to the collective success of the university.

2. You would have benefited from a professional coach, and your unwillingness to routinely engage one, despite my recommendation that you do so, has been frustrating.

3. You have not acclimated yourself to the UT system and still appear unwilling to try to understand or acknowledge the value of the UT system. I continue to detect that you (and some members of your cabinet) have an "us (UTK) vs. them (UT system and UT Board)" mentality.

4. Your one on one, small group, and business transactional communication skills are very poor. I have had multiple people on multiple occasions complain that you do not listen to the person talking to you or pay attention to the details of written communications you receive. I also have received multiple complaints from multiple people about your ability to communicate orally. These complaints are consistent with my personal experience.

5. Regularly, you have problems with lack of organization, attention to details, timely follow-up.

6. You have failed to accept ultimate responsibility in some cases where subordinates make mistakes or errors and publicly have blamed administrators who held positions before you or others in dealing with problems you inherited.

7. You have failed to communicate to the campus a defined strategic vision of where you want to take the institution and a plan for its implementation.

As I indicated to you last Tuesday, I do not think you can be successful as the leader of our flagship campus and have decided that it is best to move forward with a change in leadership rather than putting you on a formal performance improvement plan after considering: (1) the number, magnitude, and fundamental nature of the areas that need to be addressed; (2) the lack of trust in our relationship; (3) your unwillingness or inability to address many of the areas that I brought to your attention early in your tenure and multiple times since then, which leads me to conclude that a formal performance improvement plan would not lead to the required changes; and (4) the broad-based concerns and compelling lack of support from Board of Trustees members regarding your leadership, and my belief that you will have similar problems with the new Board.

Effective July 1, 2018, in accordance with the terms of your appointment letter dated December 6, 2016, your appointment will be converted from your current administrative appointment as Chancellor to your full-time faculty appointment as Professor, with tenure, in the School of Communication Studies. As approved by the Board of Trustees, your compensation as Professor will be $438,750.00 (which is 75% of your initial base salary as Chancellor of $585,000.00) for four years. Beginning with the fifth year, your compensation in your faculty appointment will be adjusted to the average base salary of full professors in the department. Effective immediately, and until June 30, 2018, you will be placed on administrative leave with pay.

Obviously, this is not where either of us hoped we would be when I hired you. Personally, I am disappointed that this action is necessary, but as President

(continued)

it is my duty to make decisions that are in the best interest of The University of Tennessee. I wish you the best as you return to the faculty.

Sincerely,

Joseph A. DiPietro
President

- -

Following the leadership change on May 2, 2018, the following headlines appeared nationwide:

- "A Stunning Ouster in Tennessee Gets Ugly and Feels Like Political Payback" (Stripling, 2018)

- "Chancellor of Tennessee Flagship is Suddenly Fired After Only One Year" (Zamudio-Suaréz, 2018)

- "Tennessee Chancellor Ousted, Blasted" (Lederman, 2018)

- "University of Tennessee Chancellor Being Forced Out of Post" (Megargee, 2018)

- "University of Tennessee Chancellor Fired in Unusually Blunt Letter" (Anderson, 2018)

- "Vote of Confidence for University of Tennessee President" (Burke, 2018)

Follower Perspective

On May 7, 2018, UTK's Faculty Senate had its final regularly scheduled meeting for the academic year. During the meeting, they passed the following resolution (quoted in full from https://senate.utk.edu/wp-content/uploads/sites/16/2018/05/Resolution-for-Censure.pdf):

- -

Resolution for 5.7.18: Censure of UT System President

WHEREAS, University of Tennessee (UT) System President Joe DiPietro has taken administrative actions that directly and negatively affect members of the University of Tennessee Knoxville campuses (the University of Tennessee, Knoxville (UTK) and the University of Tennessee Institute of Agriculture (UTIA) which are both represented by the UTK Faculty Senate) without apparent regard for campus-level concerns; and

WHEREAS, the UT System President has failed to be transparent and responsible in his communications with the UTK and UTIA community and the public regarding matters such as his position on outsourcing and the post-tenure review revision process; and

WHEREAS, the UT System President dismissed UTK Chancellor Davenport with a letter that, according to the *Chronicle of Higher Education*, personalized a national problem of flagship-system tension and attached it to Davenport, and

WHEREAS, these actions have undermined the stability, reputation and mission of UTK and UTIA; and

WHEREAS, the UTK Faculty Senate is committed to the long-term advancement of the University of Tennessee campuses in Knoxville;

THEREFORE, BE IT RESOLVED that the UTK Faculty Senate votes to censure these actions and to call for a discussion to change the structure, leadership and location of the University of Tennessee System to better support the Knoxville campuses in building a positive national reputation for the flagship institution of higher education in Tennessee.

Leader Perspective

On May 10, 2018, The University of Tennessee Board of Trustees for the multi-campus system met with one public item of business—the resolution that appears below (quoted in full from https://trustees.tennessee. edu/wp-content/uploads/sites/3/2019/03/2018-May-10-Special-Meeting-Minutes-Signed.pdf.

THE UNIVERSITY OF TENNESSEE
BOARD OF TRUSTEES
RESOLUTION

Vote of Full Confidence in President Joe DiPietro

May 10, 2018

WHEREAS, President Joe DiPietro has led The University of Tennessee System with humility, honor, and integrity since January 1, 2011; and

WHEREAS, President DiPietro has led the University under a strategic plan, "Defining the Future," to align the University with the state's goal to increase enrollment and graduation rates, enhance economic development, and respond to the changing needs of the state workforce; and

WHEREAS, under President DiPietro's leadership, the University has experienced unprecedented growth in a number of areas, including enrollment, graduation rates, retention, and research; and

(continued)

WHEREAS, President DiPietro has established credibility in the office of President, resulting in support by the Governor and the General Assembly for increased state appropriations which, in turn, have directly resulted in a record-setting fourth year of self-limited tuition increases of three percent or lower for University students and their parents; and

WHEREAS, under President DiPietro's leadership, and due to the Governor's strong commitment to higher education and the support of the General Assembly, the University has experienced an unprecedented increase in capital funding, especially at the flagship campus in Knoxville;

WHEREAS, President DiPietro committed the University to becoming a national model in Title IX compliance; and

WHEREAS, President DiPietro has approached every matter, including personnel matters, with the singular goal of doing what is in the best interest of the University; and

WHEREAS, at the outset of the process concerning outsourcing of facilities management services, President DiPietro, because of his strong concern for and commitment to the employees who do the hard work of maintaining University facilities day in and day out, personally negotiated with state officials to obtain binding contractual language prohibiting employee layoffs and providing total equitable, if not greater, compensation for the employees; and

WHEREAS, President DiPietro publicly and repeatedly committed that each campus would be allowed to make the outsourcing decision based on what was in its best interest, and President DiPietro and the Board have honored that commitment despite the fact that two campuses decided to forego the potential for substantial savings through outsourcing and now must find another way to achieve the savings; and

WHEREAS, despite the honest and transparent actions of President DiPietro and the Board with respect to the outsourcing decision, some continue to foment fear among our employees by repeating false allegations and rumors spread during the outsourcing process and by making the totally baseless suggestion that the Board still intends to impose outsourcing; and

WHEREAS, the Board firmly believes that the faculty as a whole is the University's most valuable asset, and the University is fortunate to have many outstanding and dedicated faculty members throughout the University system;

WHEREAS, President DiPietro, who himself has held tenured faculty appointments at three universities, is a strong advocate for academic freedom and tenure, and because of his desire to protect tenure, created an open dialogue with the University Faculty Council to improve the Board's tenure policy to enhance performance, transparency, and accountability as it relates to the tenure review process and evaluation of tenured faculty; and

WHEREAS, a small number of faculty at the flagship campus in Knoxville, including the Faculty Senate President, voiced opposition to the requirement of post-tenure review of all tenured faculty, claiming that post-tenure review is a threat to tenure despite the fact that it is a well-established practice at several public research universities with top-25 ranking, a status the flagship aspires to achieve; and

WHEREAS, the Faculty Senate at the flagship campus in Knoxville has attempted to harm the reputation of President DiPietro and the University by censuring the President for certain administrative actions; and

WHEREAS, President DiPietro's actions were undertaken with integrity and courage and, as always, in the best interest of the University.

NOW THEREFORE BE IT RESOLVED that The University of Tennessee Board of Trustees, meeting in Nashville, Tennessee, on May 10, 2018:

1. Declares disappointment with the Knoxville Faculty Senate's censure resolution and calls for the Knoxville Faculty Senate and its leadership to seek the truth before making unfounded accusations; and

2. Commends President Joe DiPietro for his integrity, courage, and invaluable service to The University of Tennessee and the State of Tennessee; and

3. Declares a "Vote of Full Confidence" in President Joe DiPietro's judgment and leadership.

DISCUSSION QUESTIONS

1. Using the information about organizational sense-making, sense-giving, and sense-censoring, what do you believe occurred with the various stakeholders (students, campus faculty and staff, alumni and donors, legislators and the Board of Trustees, community members, local/regional/national research and service partners)?

2. Given what you have read about socialization processes, what do you believe occurred during Dr. Davenport's socialization as well as what expectations did her arrival on campus set for students, faculty, and staff?

3. If you were making a list of "unwritten" qualifications for the next chancellor at The University of Tennessee, Knoxville, what would they include?

(continued)

ANALYSIS OPTIONS

A. The University of Tennessee must hire a new chancellor and will likely hire a new President in the next year. You have been hired to oversee these processes.

B. Dr. Davenport is being retained as a faculty member in the School of Communication Studies as part of the College of Communication and Information (CCI). Her salary is reported to be between 3 and 12 times that of all other College faculty. As Dean of CCI, part of your leadership role is to help meet the sense-making needs of your alumni, community partners, donors, faculty, staff, and students.

C. Organizational change is most effective when it is initiated by the followers and middle management (faculty and staff, department heads, deans, faculty senate) and implemented by leadership. Given that premise, your role as part of this group is to initiate changes that ensure the next diverse chancellor (female, not heterosexual, a first-generation college student from a lower socioeconomic class, multiracial or not Caucasian, etc.) is not treated differently from the previous white male chancellors.

ANALYSIS PROCESS

- Brainstorm a list of options for addressing the issue.
- Make a list of strengths and challenges for each of your brainstormed solutions.
- Choose the best solution for the issue.
- Develop an implementation plan for your chosen solution.
- Additional resources:

DiPietro Letter
https://tiny.utk.edu/FCL7_1

Faculty Senate Resolution
https://tiny.utk.edu/FCL7_2

Board of Trustees Resolution
https://tiny.utk.edu/FCL7_3

DiPietro Support
https://tiny.utk.edu/FCL7_6

Davenport Fired Outsourcing
https://tiny.utk.edu/FCL7_4

Davenport Support
https://tiny.utk.edu/FCL7_7

DiPietro Firing
https://tiny.utk.edu/FCL7_5

 LEADER AND FOLLOWER DEVELOPMENT PRACTICES

1. Minimize the use of "but" or "or" and maximize the use of "and" (both/ and or either/and), asking questions, especially in sense-making and sense-giving processes (Sparr, 2018).

2. Seek out opportunities to learn how to execute change and know your followers well enough to help them through the change (Heckelman, 2017). As followers, know yourself well enough to know what you need when there is going to be a change so that you can communicate those needs to your leader or immediate manager.

3. Use the banana principle (Luna & Cohen, 2017) if you want your leaders or followers to change. Given a bowl of bananas and oranges, people will take the bananas first and leave the oranges. Why? The reason lies in their skins—bananas are quicker and easier to peel with less mess; oranges are juicier, messier, and may require a tool to get them started. People want the path of least resistance. During change, pave the way for the followers and leaders so they are not getting a flat tire on the sharp edges of rocks or veering off course because the roadway is unmarked.

DISCUSSION QUESTIONS AND ACTIVITIES

1.   Think back to your first days as part of your current college/university or workplace. Indicate what processes were used to make you part of the tribe. When you were going through it, did you view it as positively or negatively as you do now? Why (be sure to talk about the sense-making processes and expectancy violations that might have impacted your current perceptions)?

2.   How realistic is it for organizational leaders and followers to develop socialization processes that meet every newcomers' needs?

3.   Identify the last large "crisis" that impacted your campus or place of work. Interview someone who was there for the incident and draw a visual representation of the sense-making, sense-giving, and sense-breaking processes as described by the person you interviewed.

4.   Let's look at change through the lens of a classroom organization. Assume that the teacher is the leader and the students are the followers—a role they have come to expect to play in this organization. The teacher comes in about three weeks before the first exam and tells the students that they are going to be in charge of writing the exam questions. Would your classroom organization of followers have built enough trust with the instructor to be ready for the change? What valence would be attached to the expectancy violation? To what extent would you expect yourself or your classmates to resist the change? Why—what conditions are not being met? What would the teacher have had to do according to Kotter and Cohen, Schein, or Bridges to make this endeavor more successful? What contextual factors play a role in how well the change is received? Would it matter if the students generated the idea to write their own exam questions? Read below to see what the research says.

5.   Identify a place you would like to work or volunteer in the future. What sources of information could you consult to complete the anticipatory socialization process (learning about the tribe)? Choose three of these sources and make a list of the most important information you learned from your research.

FIGURE CREDITS:

Fig. 7.1a: Source: https://pixabay.com/photos/kindergarten-playground-swing-1322559/.

Fig. 7.1b: Source: https://pixabay.com/photos/classroom-school-education-learning-2093744/.

Fig. 7.3: Source: https://pixabay.com/photos/person-woman-man-couple-people-3519503/.

Fig. 7.5: Source: https://pixabay.com/vectors/question-questions-man-head-2519654/.

CHAPTER 8

INTERORGANIZATIONAL NETWORKS

I f you have ever lived or visited a large city with a strong public transportation system of subways, trains, buses, and/or elevated rails, the map above probably looks familiar. Sometimes the tracks run parallel to each other, sometimes they diverge, and sometimes their paths just cross. The same is true when it comes to organizations. Two organizations may find themselves on parallel tracks where they both manufacture and distribute similar, complementary products. For example, Mead (paper) and PaperMate (writing utensils) school supplies are both needed and do not compete with each other. At other times two organizations find their paths crossing for a period of time to complete a project together. For example, the Alzheimer's Association and a local business that sells running gear may team up for a fund-raising walk. Finally, two organizations may diverge because they are in constant competition with each other, such as American, United, and Delta airlines for domestic air travel passengers. Each color on the map can also represent different types of organizations (for profit, nonprofit, local, national, international, financial, manufacturing, health/wellness, energy, etc.). Leaders and followers who find themselves needing to interact with people from other organizations must navigate the various transit options and make strategic decisions about when to cross paths with other organizations to achieve more than either can achieve individually.

Networks

Networks are a field of study all by themselves. For our purposes, we are going to talk about what networks are and how we, as competent followers and leaders, can navigate them to achieve success. **Networks** are combinations of people who interact with each other over time to achieve a

FIGURE 8.1 Public Transportation Map

communication goal. Each aspect of a network is called a **node**. If you were to make a list of all the people with whom you interact at work or in this class, who would be on the list? If you further distinguished them based upon how much time you spend interacting with each person, what might your network look like? Think about it the same way as you would think about a word cloud—the people with whom you interact most have the largest fonts and the people with whom you interact only occasionally or rarely have the smallest fonts.

Basic networking nodes include liaison/gatekeepers, central node, and boundary spanners. All of these roles appear in both individual and organizational networks. An additional node that exists in individual networks would be the isolate, the person who is only connected to one or two other persons in the organization and far removed from the center or organizational action. Liaisons and gatekeepers look very similar on a social networking visual representation because they connect two groups of people; the primary difference is what they do with the information power they possess—hoard (gatekeeper) or share (liaison) it. If a liaison leaves, a group of people could become isolated until someone else steps in to reconnect them to the other nodes. The central node is the person, role, or organization into which all other groups flow. Finally, boundary spanners connect multiple groups of nodes to each other and often connect the internal organization to external organizations or organization members.

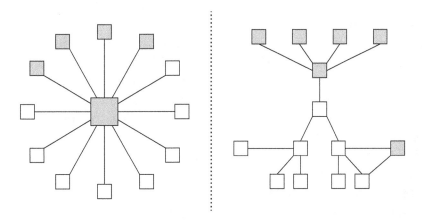

FIGURE 8.2   Organizational Network

Network roles are not specific to particular people—both leaders and followers can fulfill any of the network roles. Generally, isolates are followers. Looking at the images, it would be easy to assume that the boundary spanner and liaison/gatekeeper is going to be a manager or leader; however, that is not always the case. Just as your personal word cloud illustrated who is connected in your network, an organizational network often indicates where power is most prevalent.

Types of Networks

When we talk about organizational networks, most people think about the ways in which they are connected to each other. For example, if you are a restaurant server, you are connected to the people who work in the back of the house (e.g., cooks, dishwashers, management), people who work in the front of the house (e.g., host who seats people, bartender, other servers), and the people who become your customers. The connection to customers is fleeting as they may only spend an hour in your network; if you provide good service and are lucky, they may come back and request you, which makes them a larger part of your network. In this example, all of your interactions are with people who help you accomplish a task—making sure customers are satisfied with their dining experience! We refer to these as **operational networks** (Ibarra & Hunter, 2007), connections to other people who help us get the work done as efficiently as possible; these people are almost always internal members of our organizations. While these are an important, two other types of networks are just as important.

If anyone has ever told you about the importance of who you know in helping you secure a position, they were talking primarily about your personal networks (Ibarra & Hunter, 2007). **Personal networks** are the connections we build around shared interests to meet our individual and professional goals. These may include a neighbor, internship director, someone with whom we exchanged cards at a service-learning event, or even someone we followed online. Personal networks are generally broader than operational networks and primarily outside the organization for which we work, or want to work. Personal networks often have both information and referent power. The information power helps us understand the process and what we need to know to be successful in a particular industry or career. The referent power allows them to connect us to people we should know if we want to be successful—this is sometimes referred to as connection power because they have the contacts others need.

The last type of network may be the most important, and overlooked, one. **Strategic networks** (Ibarra & Hunter, 2007) are people who help us prepare for the future we envision. They include people who are both internal and external to the organization because different perspectives help us anticipate both the opportunities and challenges that may lie ahead. One of the most difficult things about strategic network members is that we cannot always know who will be relevant or when they may become relevant. This is why so many effective leaders live and die by their contact lists—there is always someone upon whom they can call to seek advice, serve as a sounding board, or share successes and setbacks.

TABLE 8.1   Three Types of Networking

	Operational	Personal	Strategic
Focus	Workplace functioning; productivity; efficiency & effectiveness	Develop professional skills (coaching or mentoring); exchange referrals and/or outside information.	Finding future opportunities; gaining stakeholder support
Location	Mostly Internal	Mostly External	Internal-External
Relationships & Relevance	Relations prescribed by task, organization, or organizational structure. It is clear who is relevant.	Relations are discretionary. It is not always clear who is relevant.	Relations can be nondiscretionary or discretionary. It is not always clear who is relevant.
Findings Network Members	Identify, who can block or support a project?	Professional associations, clubs, and interest communities	Identify, who outside of your immediate sphere can help you determine how your role and efforts contribute to the overall picture.

Adapted from Hill & Lineback, (2011); Ibarra & Hunter, (2007).

Representing your company as a leader, follower, or both involves working with others and making connections internally (coworkers) and externally (customers or consumers). Because many businesses work with other businesses to provide their service(s) or product(s), internal-external relationships are essential connections to cultivate and maintain. Think about the grocery store or supermarket where you buy your food and toiletries. That store relies on other businesses to sell the different food items you buy to make your meals or to offer your go-to hygiene products or cleaning supplies. These internal-external relationships, also referred to as business to business (b2b) relationships, are critical for optimal organizational functioning and meeting organizational goals. At the individual level, businesses themselves don't communicate with each other, the people representing those businesses, leaders and followers, communicate and connect with each other. Understanding this makes it easy for us to see why leaders' and followers' use of professional and social networking are key for successfully achieving both organizational and personal objectives.

Professional and Social Networking

Let's start this section by focusing on you. Be sure to circle your answer to the following question: On a scale of one to five, how important is having a good network to your ability to achieving your professional goals?

Not at all important = 1
Low importance = 2
Neutral = 3
Very Important = 4
Extremely Important = 5

Knowing that a good network can offer job support, information, learning, spark innovation, favors, or help you find your next job opportunity, most people answer in the four to five range (Ibarra, 2015). If you're not "most people," keep reading to find out why. Now, let's take a deeper look at your own network using the activity in Table 8.2.

Is the number you selected in step 4 of the audit activity lower than the number you selected for the question above the audit activity table? Most of us fall into this category. We know there is value in having a strong network, but we typically don't devote enough time and effort into developing those relationships as much as we should. Why? Well, maybe you dislike networking because it takes time and energy. You're a shy person or an introvert. You're new in town. You just started at a job and don't know many people yet. There are many reasons we can choose to focus on, but few of them constitute as a "good" excuse for not attending to your network.

When we move beyond the individual level to a broader collective level of relational leadership and followership, we begin to look at a bigger picture of inter-organizational or multi-organizational networks, as the leading, following, leadership, and followership of, among, and between organizational

TABLE 8.2   Network Audit Activity

Step 1: Think of 8 people you have discussed important work issues with in the past 4–6 months. These should be people you have really gone to recently for their help. Have you asked anyone for advice, pitched ideas to them for their feedback, asked for their opinion about changing jobs or positions, or asked for help in evaluating work-related opportunities? List their names in the spaces below.

1.

2.

3.

4.

5.

6.

7.

8.

Step 2: Looking at your network above, what are the top three strengths of your current network?

1.

2.

3.

Step 3: What are the top three weaknesses of your current network?

1.

2.

3.

Step 4: Based on your answers in steps 1 through 3, circle your answer to the following question.
How would you rate the quality of your current network?

Poor = 1
Fair = 2
Good = 3
Very Good = 4
Excellent = 5

Adapted from: Ibarra (2015).

entities. Think about some of today's leading companies—Apple, Samsung, IBM, or Microsoft—that have implemented inter-organizational teams with universities (or research institutions) as well as between R&D and suppliers to create or analyze new products (Gu et al., 2016). Next, we will examine leadership, followership, and this inter-organizational collaboration—moving from personal networks to larger professional types of networks (inter-organizational networks)—through coalition building.

Building Coalitions

Simply put, a **coalition** is a team of different people from different organizations (or walks of life) who come together to create a formalized alliance and achieve something none of them could have done alone (Regan & Garcia, 2020). Another term for this is **synergy**, where the whole is greater than the sum of its parts. Synergy is one of the reasons students often study in groups—what one person does not know or cannot figure out can usually be explained by another student. In the organizational world, well-designed and executed coalitions reach more people and accomplish greater goals than a single organization could ever imagine doing.

Coalition building requires people to have built their social and professional networks. Without a network, leaders and followers are reduced to making calls to strangers (aka cold calling in sales). Effective leaders depend not only upon their own networks, but also their followers' networks. Let's do a little quick math. Assume that everyone in your organization has a network of 25 people. Leaders who only use their own professional networks have access to 25 people, some of whom may work for the same organization, reducing the number of potential coalition members even further. If that same leader has 5 followers who each have networks of 25 people, the number of possible coalition partnerships grows to 150 (25 × 6 people). Now assume each of those 5 followers has an additional 5 followers with 25 people in their professional networks (we are up to 775 potential coalition members (31 × 25). That does not even include the next set of connections (think about it as a second-level connection in a professional social networking platform or a friend of a friend). The possibilities grow exponentially when we involve more people.

Preconditions for Coalition Building

Building a coalition is not a step that organizations take lightly; it is an involved process that sometimes yields no results. Before we get to the process of building coalitions, there are three conditions that lead to favorable coalition outcomes.

Dedicated Human and Financial Resources

When coalitions attempt to form without committing resources (people and money) to the project, they are setting themselves up to fail (National Institute for Nursing, n.d.). Think about it. If you were going to complete a project for this class and did not dedicate time in your schedule to that project, what happens? If you are like most students, you end up fitting it in when there is time, which means crunch time right before the deadline. Organizations are no different. Coalition building and execution require specific people, amounts of money, and time to be assigned to the project to be successful.

Recognizing the Role of Power

One of the fastest ways to ruin a coalition is for those in the dominant position to adopt an ethnocentric or egotistical perspective of being better than others (CommunityToolBox, n.d.). As we have talked about throughout, power can be used to benefit as well as hinder leaders and followers from accomplishing their goals. When it comes to coalitions, being aware of each person's role, understanding that everyone has an important role to play, and appreciating the value everyone brings to the decision-making table sets the coalition up for success.

Large Complex Problem

Coalitions address problems and issues that cannot be handled by a single organization. Sometimes they are emerging quickly and sometimes they impact large numbers of people who are not at the decision-making table (CommunityToolBox, n.d.). Think about COVID-19, Coronavirus, in 2020. Coalitions of medical personnel, businesspeople, private medical facilities, governments, educational leaders, and community leaders were best equipped to solve the problem. Medical personnel alone would only focus on how to handle people when they arrived at doctors' offices or hospitals. Governments focused on how they were going to get people home who were visiting their countries, prevent people from entering their borders who had been in affected areas, and minimize potentially spreading the virus when people returned home from overseas trips. Educational leaders highlighted the ways they could minimize spread by moving classes online and eliminating gatherings of more than 50 people.

None of these solutions alone would solve or eliminate the pandemic as it came to be known. These groups developed tunnel vision in which they did not think through the ramifications of the decisions they were making and how that would affect individuals in their communities and the local, national, and international economies. Eliminating imported products from affected areas and leading people to believe they could be quarantined in their homes decreased supply and increased demand—a recipe for higher prices and empty shelves (think toilet paper and sanitizing wipes that were nowhere to be found). Moving classes online for college students, eliminating sporting events, and cancelling conferences caused financial hardship for students, parents, and hourly workers who depended upon these events occurring for income, and organizations that did not have the financial reserves to handle the situation.

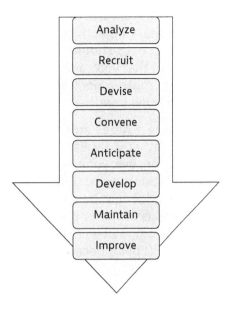

FIGURE 8.3   Coalition Building Process

Ultimately, those who were already at a disadvantage were further disadvantaged, as those who did not have to worry about these same issues made decisions without thinking through the implications that would have been considered with a diverse coalition of people, who could address the domino effect of each decision being made. Taking the time to make sure everyone affected is represented in the coalition has significant long-term positive effects (Regan & Garcia, 2020).

Building Process

As illustrated in Figure 8.3, coalition building is a process can easily be summarized in eight steps (Prevention Institute, n.d.). Let's take a brief look at each step and what competent communicators, regardless of whether they are leaders or followers, do at each step in the process (compiled from Berkowitz, n.d.; Electronic Frontier Foundation, n.d.; Myer, 2016; Prevention Institute, n.d.; Rabinowitz, n.d.; Smathers & Lobb, 2014).

1. **Ask Questions**. The first step in the process is to determine what objectives we are trying to achieve, whether a coalition is the best means to achieve those objectives, what resources we have available, whether this is the best use of our resources, and determine if the benefits of forming a coalition outweigh the costs. If the three preconditions above are not present, then a coalition is probably not the answer to the problem.

2. **Build a Team**. The second step is to recruit the most qualified people and organizations who can work with the initiator to achieve the desired outcomes. Just because organizations or individuals are a competitor in one area does not make them off-limits for a coalition—think strategically and long-term. Recruiting is a relationship-building exercise so utilizing the communication tactics we discussed in a relational model as well as those associated with responsible leadership are important.

3. **Work from the Ground Up**. While it is important to have some pre-liminary objectives to make the recruiting aspects easier, the final objectives should be determined by the team. These initial objectives that you communicate with potential partners should be broad and make a persuasive argument for what can be achieved when working together.

4. **Have a Meet and Greet**. Whether the first time everyone comes together is face to face or through technology-mediated communication, everyone needs to get to know each other and start building relationships so that the central node (the initial recruiter and convener) does not become the gatekeeper, liaison, and boundary spanner. This is also an opportunity to strengthen, clarify, and specify the coalition's objectives. Do not be surprised if some people walk away at this point because the coalition ends up heading in a direction they do not, or cannot, support for organizational culture reasons.

5. **Open the Coffers**. Coffers are where people keep their resources. Once the objectives are set, the team needs to determine what resources are necessary to achieve those objectives and who at the table will commit which resources. To minimize people walking away, think about resources broadly speaking (expertise, access to diverse communities, information) in addition to financial.

6. **Break out the Legos**. All coalitions must be built upon a strong foundation. Manage expectations by addressing who is going to participate, how they will communicate, how tasks will be determined and delegated, what the timeline is for completion, and how the group will respectfully and constructively handle issues that arise. Use all of the pieces you have to create a structure that is strong enough to withstand the process and adaptable enough to respond to environmental and other situational changes that will inevitably occur.

7. **Light the Candles or Uncork the Bottle**. Take the time to celebrate big and small accomplishments to keep people motivated and engaged. Continue sharing whatever will be beneficial to each other. Most importantly, continue recruiting people who can strengthen the coalition and bring new insights or diverse audiences to the project.

8. **Focus on the Big Picture**. Sometimes when we evaluate our processes and accomplishments, we become too focused on what needs to be changed instead of highlighting what we are doing well and should continue doing. Make sure all evaluation processes are fair, balanced, and conducted by people who do not have a vested interest in the outcome because they created it (outsiders and/or those who benefit from the coalition).

RESEARCH SUMMARY

Study: Endres and Weibler (2019) set out to examine network leadership in inter-organizational collaborative settings. As organizations seek to keep pace with the global economy in which they operate, more and more are seeking partnerships where the relationships are more collaborative rather than hierarchical. These authors wanted to determine what happens to leaders and followers when these inter-organizational networks are created and sustained to achieve broader goals than are possible in a single organization. They sought to answer three questions:

- "How and in what form, if at all, will leadership emerge in the networks?"

- "What might contribute to explain these different (non-)leadership phenomena?"

- "What are significant differentiation features in the network coordinators' main activities that might contribute to facilitating emerging different (non) leadership phenomena?"

They collected data in three different inter-organizational networks and used expert interviews, meetings, observations, informal conversations, and document analysis as their data. The analyses revealed a task and a joint motivational network identity. In the task identity network, there was a leadership void, no leader-follower relations emerged, and everyone behaved more like followers than leaders; in the motivational network identity, they found shared leadership with no single leader emerging.

Implications: Coming together as members of different organizations in a collaborative effort is not an easy task. No one wants to be viewed as bossy or egotistical—common when the only reason for multiple organizations to work together is to complete a task. This is especially true if one of the organizations, or potential leaders, is considered to be in the dominant position while all others are considered co-cultures, or those in minority positions. When organizations come together because they are creating something that is better than any one of them individually (think about synergy), shared leadership is effective because the "new" organization created by the network participants develops its own identity, relationship, and task goals that are best achieved through shared leadership in which everyone takes on leadership and followership roles through consensus-building practices.

Systems Theory

A systems theory perspective explains how a set of different interdependent objects work together to form a whole. There are many examples of systems occurring and experienced in our own lives and realities. A car, for example, has many parts making up the entire vehicle. Each part (motor, radiator, axels, battery, exhaust, etc.) has a job, working in relation to other parts allowing the car, as a whole, to be used for our transportation purposes. The human body is also made of many systems such as the cardiovascular system, respiratory system, and immune system. Leaders and followers have created other systems that you are familiar with such as school systems, systems of transportation, or government systems. Next, let's take a look at leadership, followership, and inter-organizational networks from a systems perspective as well as the role of communication within inter-organizational network systems.

A **system** is defined as a set of objects together with relationships between the objects and their attributes (Ruben, 2003). There are four characteristics of all systems. First, systems are wholes created from the sum of its parts. Distinct objects and their interrelations make up a system such as the ingredients of a cake or the members of a network. As a system, a network is built on the sum of its parts—the interdependence among the parts (i.e., network members) creates a structure where the outcome is more than the objects alone.

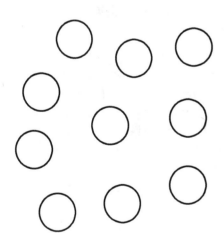

Like baking a cake, flour alone does not have all the parts to create a whole cake. You alone do not have all the parts to create the relationships making up your entire network. The parts in a system have unique qualities and characteristics. As members of a network, leaders and followers play different roles, have different backgrounds, areas of expertise, and relationships with other members. Think about your own network from our earlier activity in Table 8.2. How are members, as people, of your network unique? In what ways do their roles and relationships with you as well as other members within your network differ? In Figure 8.4, draw your network. Fill in each of the nodes (i.e., circles) with the initials of your network members, including your own. You may draw additional nodes if there are not enough provided. Then, draw lines connecting each of the nodes to represent the

FIGURE 8.4 Network Relational Communication Structure

communication relationships that exist, creating the structure of your network looks like.

As interdependent parts of a system, network members influence one another. According to Ruben & Gigliotti (2016), there are three social influence skills advantageous for leaders and followers within a network:

- **Attention and agenda setting skills**: Being able to identify shifting windows of opportunities to elevate items or actions to the status of an agenda item and influence the ways others think about these agenda items.

- **Managing meaning skills**: Being able to influence how events are seen and understood through the effective and appropriate use of verbal and nonverbal messages.

- **Sensemaking and sense-giving skills**: Being influential by offering sound explanations or interpretations of an uncertain environment or event.

Second, systems are hierarchical. The relationships between objects link them together in a system, which also creates subsystems and contributes to suprasystems. **Subsystems** refer to smaller units within a system. In your own network, subsystems may consist of the dyadic relationships that exist

TABLE 8.3 Inter-Organizational Network Types & Functions

Inter-organizational Network Type	Function
Information–information sharing and diffusion	Focuses on sharing information across organizational boundaries
Knowledge–generation, exchange, & management	Focuses on generating new knowledge and spreading ideas/practices between organizations
Capacity Building	Focuses on building social capital
Learning	Focuses on learning at the individual, organizational, and community levels
Problem Solving & Issue Management	Focuses on solving or improving responses to complex problems and issues
Effective Service-delivery, coordination, & action	Focuses on service delivery for services jointly produced by two or more organizations
Innovation	Focuses on creating an environment of diversity, collaboration, and openness to encourage creativity and enable innovation
Policy	Focuses on public decision within a particular area of policy
Collaborative Governance	Focuses on direction, control, and coordination of collective action between government agencies and non-public groups

Adapted from Popp et al. (2014).

between you and each of your network members, or between two or more of the members in your network. In your network structure, add different colors to each of the nodes that represent the various subsystems that exist in your network. In this same way, organizational systems can consist of many subsystems represented by the relationships among people in different departments (marketing, sales, product development, accounting, manufacturing, etc.) within the larger company. These relationships and the communication occurring among them can also combine with other systems making up a suprasystem.

Suprasystems are defined as larger units composed of subsystems that make up the next higher system. A suprasystem may be society as a whole or an inter-organizational network in business. **Inter-organizational networks** refer to two or more interconnected business relationships, which interact to negotiate to each other, share information, resources and activities (Muradli & Ahmadov, 2019). Inter-organizational networks involve multiple people, with multiple connections, working together "on cross-boundary, collaborative activities" (McGuire & Sylvia, 2009, p. 35). If we visualize what inter-organizational networks look like, it would be shifting constellations of people and units. Imagine your own network combined with all of the networks of your colleagues coming together to form an alliance that achieves something great (how do you think Facebook started?).

Third, systems try to maintain themselves within their environment by engaging in self-regulation (or homeostasis) processes. This characteristic of a system is often explained by using some sort of thermostat example, such as the thermostat in your home or in an oven. If you set your oven to 350 degrees, then the heating parts of the oven work to output heat until it reaches and maintains the desired goal of 350 degrees, as monitored by the thermostat input. Leaders and followers can act as the heating parts or the thermostat of the oven. They act as agents of an organizational system who bridge or broker connections within, between, and among other organizations. They are the building blocks for entire networks and the success of a network hinges upon their ability to communicate effectively with others.

Network members, and leaders and followers, practice shared leadership to manage the effectiveness of the entire network. Despite whether a person holds a leader or follower position, as a network member they can assume the role of a network leader in a given situation or context. According to McGuire and Sylvia (2009), there are four categories of network leader behaviors:

1. **Activation** behaviors involve identifying and integrating the right people and resources needed to achieve a goal.

2. **Framing** behaviors facilitate agreement on network members' roles, operating rules, and network values to organize and solidify the structure of a network.

3. **Mobilizing** behaviors involve developing and motivating network support from network members and external stakeholders.

4. **Synthesizing** includes a set of behaviors intended to enhance conditions favorable for creating and maintaining an environment of productive interactions among network members.

Together, the aggregated actions of network leaders and members impact the dynamics and outcomes of inter-organizational networks. Needless to say, there are various potential benefits and challenges of inter-organizational networking. They also contribute to a broader process: organizational leadership. Leadership, followership, and inter-organizational networks are complicated systems that involve complex processes.

TABLE 8.4 Inter-Organizational Networks Benefits & Challenges

Potential Benefits	Potential Challenges
Access to and leveraging of resources	Achieving consensus on commitments and network goals
Shared risk and shared accountability fostering creativity and collaboration	Culture clash
Efficiency	Loss of autonomy
Service quality and coordination	Coordination fatigue and costs
Advocacy	Developing trusting relationships
Learning and capacity building through knowledge sharing	Performance and accountability obstacles
Positive deviance (i.e., positive organizational change)	Power imbalance, conflict, and conflict management
Innovation	Collaboration
Flexibility and responsiveness toward unforeseen problems	Sustainability

Adapted from Popp et al. (2014).

Last, systems respond and adapt to the environment. Systems change, they grow, develop, and dissolve. In an open system, the parts (network members) are encouraged to interact with others (people outside of the system). The opposite occurs in a closed system, where members do not interact with others outside of their own network. Imagine if the subsystems (departments) of a company (marketing, sales, product development, accounting, manufacturing, etc.) operated in a closed system manner, only interacting with the members of their own department. What do you believe would happen? Regardless of whether a system such as an inter-organizational network is an open system or closed system, all systems receive feedback, both positive and negative, in an attempt to reduce error or amplify positive outcomes. Whether a system begins to fall apart or expand, attempts are made by leaders and followers to salvage the system or capitalize on what is working well. In business, these attempts to change, develop, or dissolve a particular system can be seen when mergers and acquisitions occur.

Mergers and Acquisitions

Mergers and acquisitions are common strategies organizations use to grow their business, reorganize their workforce, procure talent, and change their organization strategy. **Mergers** occur when two organizations combine their efforts to create a stronger organization. **Acquisitions** occur when one organization purchases another. Not all mergers or acquisitions result in one organization having to adapt to another or losing its organizational culture. For example, when Disney purchased Pixar, the two cultures and organizations operated differently enough that they maintained their own organizational cultures and identities as Disney became the parent company of Pixar—a successful endeavor. On the other hand, when Sprint and Nextel merged, they tried to unite the two organizational cultures. Nextel was a laid-back organization where executives came to work in khaki pants and polo shirts; Sprint was a conservative organization where executives came to work in suits, white shirts, and ties.

Mergers and acquisitions are a long-term process, consume more time, involve more employee resistance, and produce short-term poorer results (Heidari-Robinson et al., 2018). In their study of over 2,500 reorganizations (both internal and mergers/acquisitions), they found some astonishing statistics. Internal changes are when organizations implement large policy changes, change the organizational practices for how they do things, or strategically try to operate in a place they have not been previously. Let these numbers sink in. Mergers and acquisitions take, on average, 14 months compared to 12 months for internal changes. Approximately 40–60% of leaders' time is spent on mergers and acquisitions compared to 20–40% of their time on internal changes. In mergers and acquisitions, approximately two-thirds (66%) of followers and half of leaders are resistant to the change compared to 50% of followers and 40% of leaders for internal changes. Finally, over half of all mergers and acquisitions see the metrics by which they judge themselves drop significantly during the transition process.

Generally, mergers and acquisitions are kept quiet until the deal has been finalized. Executives in the C-Suite are aware of the process significantly earlier than middle- and low-level leaders and all followers. Often, lower-level leaders and all followers do not find out until immediately before it is announced on the news. If your campus has ever fired an administrator or athletic coach, then you have seen how this plays out. The people who work directly for the administrator and athletes who play for the coach find out immediately before the press release or news conference announcing the firing; the remainder of campus finds out through media/social media leaks before the official announcement, an email after the direct reports/players find out, or a media report on the announcement after it has occurred. Outside the C-Suite, organizational members do not have the same time to prepare for and process the change, which can lead to resentment and lack of trust.

Avoiding Disastrous Outcomes

What can you do as a leader or follower in organizations where mergers and acquisitions are almost inevitable? At the top of the list is preventing an "us vs. them" mentality (Fondrevay, 2018); this is especially dangerous in an acquisition where one organization (that one that was acquired) is in a one-down or non-dominant position. Think about it—if you were CEO of an organization that acquired another one, your implicit leadership theories would assume that you should remain in that position rather than allowing or appointing the CEO from the acquired organization to take on that role. In addition to perceiving that we are better, we also generally assume that our followers and workers are better than the ones in the other organization. If the other workers were better, would we be acquiring them? These perceptions lead to poor decision making and negatively impact both organizations because those who may be best able to move the new organization forward are also the ones who are most likely to leave or be let go.

Let's take a look at a recent acquisition that occurred—the organizational names are fictional to protect the acquiring organization. Medical Company acquired Screws and Pins in late 2019. Rather than creating a new organization, the Medical Company's president's goal was to leverage its own position and become the premier manufacturer and provider of all metal devices implanted into humans when their own bones, muscles, and joints are not working properly. Rather than creating a new company or allowing Screws and Pins to continue doing what it did well, the president announced that any Screws and Pins' employees who stayed on for six months (July 2020) would receive a significant severance package (a

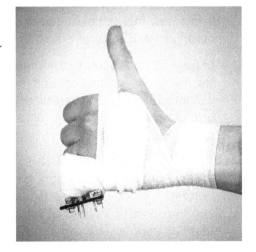

FIGURE 8.5   There are as many screws and pins used in people's bodies as used in home building. As badly as Medical Company wanted a share of this market, the way they went about getting it was not effective.

buyout of money to give people time to look for a new job). The six-month window was so that Medical Company could learn everything there was to know about manufacturing, marketing, and distributing medical devices; Screws and Pins, a small company, was excellent at what they did.

As you might imagine, the majority of Screws and Pins' employees began looking for other work and felt resentful because they were being treated as pawns in a chess game. In a chess game, people are willing to sacrifice their pawns to protect their more important pieces (queen, king, bishops). Essentially, Screws and Pins employees had information and expert power that Medical Company needed and wanted! Ultimately, the only people who stayed until the end were those who were nearing retirement and saw this as an opportunity to get paid for the first few months of their retirement. Medical Company did not achieve its goals because of their "us versus them" mentality and poor communication competence, which got in the way of progress—many of the most knowledgeable people left without sharing any expertise. If you worked for Screws and Pins, might you have considered leaving and applying at Medical Company as a consultant to help them with their transition, at a higher pay rate, of course?

Medical Company engaged in all three poor behaviors associated with an "us versus them" mentality (Fondrevay, 2018). These behaviors are primarily concerned with how we should be treating people when we find ourselves in leadership positions following a merger or acquisition; we would argue these are good practices to follow any time you are dealing with other humans.

- Consider each organization's culture to determine what aspects make the most sense to keep in the new organization and how everyone transitions into a new merged or acquired organizational culture. Remember that organizational cultures are also made up of people's personal identities.

- Engage in transparent communication about who is benefitting from the merger or acquisition, and in what ways. When frontline employees perceive that a decision was made to make upper-level employees richer or more powerful, they become resentful. Competent messages must be consistent—do what you say you are going to do and say what you are actually doing.

- Focus on vision and structure before addressing people. If the planning process involves a clearly articulated plan, leaders make decisions based upon rationality instead of relationships or emotions (i.e., "we need a team of people who can accomplish this—who in both organizations makes the most sense to achieve this part of our vision" versus "we have to keep these people because they work for me"). The difficulty here is that employment law prevents complete transparency to protect people's privacy.

Whatever you do, never say "Nothing will change" because the merger or acquisition would not have been necessary if nothing were going to change. People are smart and can see as well as sense the changes occurring around them.

Promoting Successful Outcomes

Because leaders are significantly more involved in mergers and acquisitions, they are the focus of how to improve the process and strengthen the outcome. That does not mean followers have no role to play. The primary way to enhance a merger and acquisition's success is to make sure that all decisions, communication, and relationship-building are consistent with the new organizational mission (Heidari-Robinson et al., 2018). Take the new mission to the streets and start asking people who are going to be affected by it what they think, how they can contribute, and what changes can be made to help them better meet the mission's goals. Using positively framed questions creates a positive mindset and minimizes the opportunities for unproductive venting, gossip, and resistance. Being willing to seek input and listening, not just hearing what is said, goes a long way toward the second success strategy.

The second success strategy for mergers and acquisitions is building and maintaining trust with both leaders and followers. As we have indicated in multiple places, trust is a very fragile concept that takes a long time to build and a single lapse to destroy. Competent communication is key. Take time to talk to people individually and in groups, face to face, or via webcast; this is not a time for email or texting because it leaves too many opportunities for misinterpretation or people rewriting the story in a negative way as they vent with each other. Continuing to proactively cultivate trust through positive, honest messages is crucial before, during, and after the merger and acquisition.

The last success strategy is the one that catches most leaders and followers off guard, and may even surprise you. Heidari-Robinson et al. (2018) indicate that it may be more important to change the leadership rather than the followership—between one-third and two-thirds of the current leadership should experience turnover in the process. Often, we assume that followers at lower levels are the ones most likely to leave the organization as it becomes more efficient; in reality, we should be looking at leadership turnover as a starting point. Why might that be the case? Think about it. If we have two leaders, one from each of the two original organizations, and we want them to lead the new organization, what are they most likely to do? That's right, treat it like the old organization for which they have worked all these years; it takes special leaders to change their mindset in ways that promote a new mission, vision, and structure.

CASE STUDY **Amazon–Whole Foods**

In 1995, founder and CEO, Jeff Bezos, his wife Mackenzie, and his first few employees launched Amazon working out of the Bezo's home garage. They packed books and shipped orders from their local post office themselves. Approximately 20 years later, Amazon has flourished into a Fortune 500 multinational technology company. Amazon's vision and mission statements clearly align with Bezos' goal for Amazon to be an "everything store."

- **Vision statement:** "To be Earth's most customer-centric company, where customers can find and discover anything they might want to buy online, and endeavors to offer its customers the lowest possible prices."

- **Mission statement:** "We strive to offer our customers the lowest possible prices, the best available selection, and the utmost convenience" (Gregory, 2019).

In 2017, Amazon added to its already healthy list of subsidiaries by acquiring its first grocery store chain, Whole Foods. Some immediate changes included: price cuts, tests of 2-hour delivery services, Whole Foods began selling Amazon tech products, Amazon Prime members received special discounts, third-party brand representatives were banned from stores, and Amazon lockers were put in stores for in-store pick up of online orders (Taylor, 2018). In February 2018, Amazon offered free two-hour delivery from Whole Foods stores for Prime members in select cities (Weise, 2018). By December 2018, Whole Foods announced it would no longer be working with the grocery delivery carrier, Instacart, which had been contracted in 2016 as Whole Foods' exclusive delivery carrier (Tobin, 2018). United Natural Foods Inc., the organic, natural, and specialty food distributor, appears to have survived, for now, as it remains contracted with Whole Foods until 2025.

Amazon's acquisition of Whole Foods emphasized its focus on organic and fresh food. For suppliers, that focus threatens big brands and opens doors for regional brands to sell products at Whole Foods. The problem for regional brands appears to lie in Amazon's push to change Whole Foods from a regional grocery chain to a national grocery chain, which complicates the process of local sellers supplying their product brands in Whole Foods stores. For Whole Foods employees, minimum wage was raised to $15.00 per hour in October 2018. Five months later, by March 2019, Whole Foods employees reported that their work hours had been reduced; however, Whole Foods denies cutting employees' hours (Cain, 2019). Employees taking steps to unionize and customers complaining about poorly stocked stores points to the challenge acquisitions face when companies with different values and organizational cultures come together (Gelfand et al., 2018).

Merely a month prior, by February 2019, Amazon had significantly expanded its physical presence in the retail industry through its owner-ship of Whole Foods stores, physical Amazon book stores, Amazon 4-star stores, and Amazon Go cashierless groceries and popular items stores (Kim, 2019), each of which continues to grow with plans for new stores in more locations. Some strategists suspect the acquisition of Whole Foods was used as a brick-and-mortar lab for Amazon to collect data and experiment for their separate grocery chain, Amazon Go (Simon, 2017). Amazon's acquisition of Whole Foods and ventures in capitalizing on the digital-physical integration of retail has sparked competitors—Walmart, Kroger, Costco, and Target—initiatives to implement similar supply chain and technology improvements (online delivery and in-store pick-up) (Mey-ersohn, 2018). Only time will tell the extent to which the Amazon-Whole Foods acquisition has changed the digital-physical landscape for inter-or-ganizational interaction.

DISCUSSION QUESTIONS

1. As Amazon implements major changes for Whole Foods stakeholders (leaders and followers), what challenges exist for internal and external stakeholders? In what ways can leaders and followers create win-win-win situations for each organization and the external stakeholders?

2. In this chapter, we talked about the importance of regulatory compliance. What are the potential compliance concerns associated with Amazon's use of data collected from Whole Foods stores and customers?

3. Given your own work experiences and knowledge, in what ways can lead-ers and followers use professional and social networking to address the challenges of blending two different organizational cultures during acquisi-tions or mergers?

ANALYSIS OPTIONS

A. Amazon is considered the second largest employer in the U.S. and con-tinues to grow through mergers and acquisitions. You have been hired to develop Amazon's new training program for both leaders and followers of newly acquired companies and mergers.

B. Because of CEO Jeff Bezos' vision of Amazon becoming an "everything store," the importance of professional and social relationships with exter-nal stakeholders is magnified. You have been tasked with anticipating and developing a set of key practices for leaders and followers' use of

(continued)

professional and social networking to build relationships with external stakeholders. Address what situations could happen, what messages would be appropriate, and what channels should be used to deliver messages that build stronger bonds.

C. Amazon has attempted to adapt to the needs and desires of Millennials and younger generations by introducing digital-physical improvements to the retail industry through the changes made to Whole Foods stores and operations. Not all internal and external stakeholders viewed these changes positively. Moving forward, what changes does Whole Foods need to make to ensure they are well positioned to meet the needs of both their leaders and followers as well as their shareholders, suppliers/partners, and customers?

ANALYSIS PROCESS

- Brainstorm a list of options for addressing the issue.

- Make a list of strengths and challenges for each of your brainstormed solutions.

- Choose the best solution for the issue.

- Develop an implementation plan for your chosen solution.

- Additional resources:

Amazon Corporate Site
https://tinyurl.com/yawuoc87

Word Cloud Generator
https://tinyurl.com/y89qsob5

Whole Foods Corporate Site
https://tinyurl.com/7emwla4

LEADER AND FOLLOWER DEVELOPMENT PRACTICES

1. Understand that every organizational move is part of a larger system; a change in one component creates a ripple effect of changes in other parts of the system.

2. Listen more and talk less during the process. Make sure you are listening to all stakeholders, not just the ones you think are important.

3. Focus on people who are asking tough and insightful questions because they may be the people who care the most about the new organization's future (O'Donnell, 2017).

4. Build diverse networks because different people can craft messages that speak to different audiences (Electronic Frontier Foundation, n.d.).

5. Be willing and able to delegate to the people who make the most sense to complete the task AND trust them to do their jobs well (Regan & Garcia, 2020).

DISCUSSION QUESTIONS AND ACTIVITIES

1. Using a free word cloud generator (e.g., https://www.wordclouds.com/), create an image of your network. For one day, keep track of every person you interact with. To make this meaningful, use a word processing program or spreadsheet to list every person you interact with. List each person you interact with (i.e., text, talk to for less than 5 minutes, email, etc.); if the interaction lasts for more than 5 minutes, list them once for each 5 minutes—if you spend 30 minutes together talking while eating lunch, put the person's name down 6 times). Upload the document into the word cloud generator and see if the people who come up as your strongest connections are the people with whom you believe you have the strongest connections. As you look at it, what network roles do you play? What network roles would you like to play?

2. Make a list of all of the people you know who are currently working in full-time jobs in the industry where you would like to find yourself. How many of them are leaders? How many of them are followers? What can you learn from each of these people about the industry and career possibilities between now and graduation? If there are not very many people in your network, what can you do to build a stronger professional network?

3. Given the difference in missions, what do you think happens when leaders from a large corporation located in multiple countries try to

team up with a local nonprofit (Habitat for Humanity) organization to engage in community service (e.g., build a house)? What might the leaders from both organizations have to consider regarding ethics, culture, and inclusion?

4. If you worked for Medical Company, what would you have done differently to avoid disastrous outcomes and promote a healthy culture? Be specific about the actual messages you would have used and who would have delivered them.

5. Choose an organization for which you would like to work or volunteer. Based upon what you know and research regarding the organization, with what other organizations would you suggest they build coalitions? How would you advise them to go about building those coalitions—address each of the 8 steps included in the chapter?

FIGURE CREDITS:

Fig. 8.1: Source: https://pixabay.com/photos/nyc-metro-plan-map-new-york-4328896/.

Fig. 8.5: Copyright © 2015 Depositphotos/Corepics.

CHAPTER 9

INTERNAL AND EXTERNAL PUBLICS

"A president must be on the job 24/7, ready for any contingency, any crisis, anywhere, anytime."

—GLORIA MACAPAGAL ARROYO

"When written in Chinese, the word 'crisis' is composed of two characters. One represents danger and the other represents opportunity."

—JOHN F. KENNEDY

There's an old saying in corporate communication regarding crises: *"It's not if; it's when."* No matter how good an individual or organization is and how well intentioned the practices might be—crises happen. How well the leadership team prepares for and responds to a potential crisis determines whether it is a bump in the road that protects the organization's brand or a full-blown crisis that harms the organization's brand and people's loyalty. Turn on the television, look at the Internet, or read a newspaper, and you'll see potential crises everywhere—product recalls, food contamination, data/security breaches, school shootings, health scares, wildfires, tsunamis/hurricanes, flooding, and more. Being prepared means being vocal, proactive, inquisitive, and strategic—all of which add up to being ready when a crisis hits.

If you look at the fireworks display, why do you think we chose it for a chapter dealing with how internal and external publics respond to individual and organizational brand crises? The quick and easy answer might be that crises are both aural (loud) and visual (must be seen to be appreciated). The less obvious answer would be that crises are something we celebrate in the way that fireworks often symbolize our independence on the Fourth of July in the United States or new beginnings on New Year's Eve around the world. In reality, the reason fireworks are associated with crises is because they can be a single incident (one firework shot off for effect) or a combination of incidents that spark an emotional reaction (the ones pictured above would be relatively boring if you did not have all of the different colors, shapes, and points in the explosion process). Additionally, all of the colors can be

FIGURE 9.1 Fireworks

thought of as representing the organization's various stakeholders (leaders/followers, customers/clients, shareholders, suppliers, partners, etc.). Finally, the various shapes and types of fireworks (firecracker, M80, Roman Candle, mortar, etc.) indicate that no two crises are identical just as no two fireworks are identical.

Brands

Organizational leaders and followers are the primary champions of a corporate brand as well as their own personal brands. Determining and controlling both your own or your organization's brand and its reputation is crucial for career success, especially when crises strike. Crisis situations are prime time for CEOs to experience character assassination attempts from the public (news media and stakeholders). Character attacks tend to target leaders' integrity, which can extend beyond the individual and impinge upon the organization itself; however, positive public perceptions of character traits and personal values linked to charisma can shield leaders and their organizations (Seiffert-Brockmann et al., 2018). That is, a good brand can be protective as a form of armor for crises. How impenetrable your armor is depends on how effectively you build your brand. In our digitally driven world, it is more important than ever for followers and leaders to be equipped with the knowledge and skills necessary to effectively develop and market their brands. This requires an understanding of what a brand is as well as how it is created and maintained. Together, this knowledge informs us about how to use media and technology to build successful brands and consumer-brand relationships as well as explains why some brands are more effective than others.

What Is a Brand?

There is no one best way to define what a brand is. According to the American Marketing Association (2020), a brand is a combination of the organization's name, sign, or symbol that helps people recognize it as different from others. The concern with this definition is that a brand can be more than just a name or design; it can be an organization or person—leader or follower—that stands for and offers something valuable to users and consumers. For this reason, scholars de Chernatony & McDonald (2003, p. 25) define brand as "an entity which offers customers (and other relevant parties) added value based on factors over and above its functional performance. These added values or brand values differentiate the offer and provide the basis for customer preference and loyalty." However, when we define a brand in this way, we fail to recognize both the creators' and consumers' roles in co-creating what a brand is, the promise it communicates to consumers, and how consumers perceive that promised offering. For this reason, we define a **brand** as a set of values embodied in an identifiable object, product, service, person, or place that communicates what it stands for and offers a functional, symbolic, and/or experiential promise to customers and other stakeholders (Anker et al., 2012).

We connect with organizational and personal brands. For personal brands, let's assess the personal leadership and followership brands of the movie or TV series characters listed in Table 9.1. What do they stand for (what promise do they make and fulfill to a user or consumer)? What value(s) do they offer? How would you answer these same questions for the organizational brands listed in Table 9.1?

TABLE 9.1 Evaluating Personal vs. Organizational Brands

Personal Brands (Leadership/Followership)	Organizational Brands
Frank Underwood & Doug Stamper (Netflix's House of Cards)	IKEA
Michael Scott & Dwight Schrute (NBC's The Office)	Apple
SpongeBob & Patrick (Nickelodeon's SpongeBob SquarePants)	Instagram
Albus Dumbledore & Harry Potter (J.K. Rowling's Harry Potter)	Patagonia
Katniss Everdeen & Peeta Mellark (Suzanne Collins's The Hunger Games)	Nike

What about your own personal brand? How would you define your leadership brand or followership brand? According to Ashkenas (2010), answering the following questions can help you formulate and crystallize your personal brand:

- What do you want to be known for online or offline? That is, what differentiates you—what skills, abilities, knowledge, and attitudes do you have that makes others want to work with you or follow you—from everyone else with a similar background or experience?

- What value can you create for others (friends, teammates, leader, or follower)?

- What will make you satisfied and feel as if you are making a meaningful contribution?

The ways in which people connect and interact with brands defines the relationship that they have with a brand. **Brand relationships** refer to the bonds that bring users or buyers and the provider together on a continuing basis (Schultz et al., 2015). When people build a relationship with a brand, the way they think about that brand and what promise it fulfills can vary among stakeholders in the same way that your answers about the brands in Table 9.1 and to your own personal brand questions above differ from your peers in class. Because we build relationships with the brands we use, there can be individual differences or overlap in the types of promise(s) a brand fulfills. For example, a brand of yogurt can fulfill the: a) functional value of having a positive impact on digestion, b) symbolic value of being associated with healthy living, and/or c) experiential value of being superior in taste or having that homemade taste like your grandmother used to make from farm-fresh milk (Anker et al., 2012).

According to Boncheck and France (2016), there are three ways stakeholders engage with a brand and think about the different kinds of promises (functional, symbolic, and experiential) a brand offers:

1. **Brand as an object** is based on seeing a brand as something that is made. Here, a brand is something attached to what you make; it can be seen or touched, but it is not alive. The brand as an object perspective emphasizes that we engage with a brand for its differential functional value.

2. **Brand as an idea** focuses on seeing a brand as something that has symbolic value in the minds and lives of users and buyers. It can offer additional self or identity-oriented benefits. When we build a relationship with a brand as an idea, we engage with the brand for its personally relevant and unique added value. The brand as an idea perspective stresses that we engage with a brand for its symbolic value.

3. **Brand as relationships** focuses on something that is experienced; it is emotionally or mentally sensory oriented. Brands are sometimes humanized (attributing human characteristics or behaviors) to influence or motivate consumers based on an interpersonal connection and emotion. Here, brands can be framed as fulfilling social roles or needs associated with meaningful interpersonal relationships. Uber and Lyft are examples of the guiding notion behind the brand as relationships perspective of fulfilling a social role. For example, as part of Uber's vision to create more job opportunities, drivers are encouraged to "build their business." This reframed the roles of driver-passenger to entrepreneur-supporter, whereas Lyft reframed this driver-passenger role as friend-friend by encouraging passengers to "sit up front." Airbnb is another example that focuses on the social need for belonging. Airbnb's mission of "belong anywhere" reframed the roles of host-guest to tap into neighbor-neighbor or human-human relationships. The brand as relationships perspective emphasizes that we engage with a brand for its experiential value based in the inherent human desire for social connection.

How a brand's promise and value is developed and perceived by customers is based on how well leaders and followers of an organization create and maintain a strong brand identity with unique communication attributes to connect internal and external aspects of organizations.

Creating and Maintaining a Successful Brand

Leaders and followers develop and maintain successful brands by defining their brand as their business. Adopting these brand-as-business perspective means organizations see managing their brand and managing their business as the same thing, its brand is its business and its business is its brand. According to Yohn (2014), leaders and followers can effectively develop and maintain brand identity by following seven principles of great brands.

1. **Great brands start inside.** Internal aspects of organizations such as vision and mission, organizational culture, and competencies extend to the customer or external stakeholder experience. Without cultivating these internal aspects, leaders and followers likely fail to execute and express a brand that makes a meaningful or lasting impact. Leaders and followers should feel informed and inspired by clear mission and vision statements, empowered by their work environment, and encouraged to use their skills and expertise for innovation.

2. **Great brands avoid selling products.** Successful brands sell promises and succeed by seeking and making emotional or interpersonal connections with stakeholders.

3. **Great brands ignore or challenge trends.** Brands that follow dominant trends in the industry place themselves in a one-down position.

Their value is consistently compared to that of "Brand X," rather than having their own inherent value. Chipotle became a great brand by challenging dominant societal and cultural conventions within the U.S. While there may be some benefits to jumping on the bandwagon (adopting or following trends), the long-term costs of following trends outweigh the advantages.

4. **Great brands don't chase customers.** A single brand cannot be all things for all people and successful brands do not try to be. Great brands focus on specific target markets and maintain the integrity of their brand's identity by taking a brand-centric approach rather than a customer-centric approach. For example, Lululemon remains a successful brand despite its aversion to putting products on sale in an attempt to preserve the company's brand identity as a "luxury" retail brand.

5. **Great brands sweat the small stuff.** Attention to detail matters for customer experience. The small stuff involves everything from product design and packaging to interacting with customers to fulfill their emotional or interpersonal needs and goals. Make the small stuff your business and you can make the small stuff big.

6. **Great brands commit and stay committed.** Focusing on the core of your brand and staying committed to that focus builds a strong brand identity and great brand. When your brand is your focus, organizations are less likely to get lost in a customer-driven reality that is financially or operationally unsustainable.

7. **Great brands never have to "give back."** "Giving back" implies you've taken something that needs to be paid back. Great brands challenge the idea of corporate social responsibility (CSR) and create shared value (CSV) for all stakeholders. Rather than engaging in socially responsible activities out of obligation (something to be done and checked off a list because it is expected), great brands engage in social initiatives for the opportunity (something you want to do because everyone can benefit). Leaders and followers develop and manage successful brands so that socially responsible practices are embedded in the brand's core identity.

Brand Identity

FIGURE 9.2   An example of a brand logo is the Cognella Propeller.

Successful brands highlight their brand identity at the business' centerpiece. **Brand identity** refers to the promises and core values that sum up what the person or organization stands for. According to Greyser and Urde (2019), a brand is composed of three layers of inter-organizational aspects: internal, external, and internal-external. Brand identity is shaped by internal aspects related to how an organization sees itself and operates. External aspects of brand identity relate to how the organization is perceived or wants to be seen by users, consumers, and other external stakeholders. What bridges internal and external aspects is the identity of a brand and its communicative attributes (communication style and characteristics). While we discuss the brand identity matrix (Table 9.2) in terms of an organizational brand, it is just as useful for and easily applied to leaders' or followers' personal brands.

TABLE 9.2   Brand Identity Matrix

External	**Value Proposition** What are our key offerings and how do they appeal to customers and stakeholders?	**Brand Relationships** What is the nature of our outside relationships with key customers and stakeholders?	**Brand Position** What is our intended position in the market and in the hearts and lives of customers and other stakeholders?
Internal–External	**Style** What is distinctive about the way we communicate and how we express ourselves?	**Brand Identity: Promise & Values** What do we promise? What are the core values that sum up what our brand stands for?	**Characteristics & Personality** What combination of human qualities forms our character?
Internal	**Vision & Mission** What we do and why or how we do it (mission)? Where do we aim to be (vision)?	**Culture** What are our attitudes, how do we work and behave?	**Competencies** What are we good at? What differentiates us from competitors?

Adapted from: Greyser & Urde (2019).

Internal Aspects

Brands start from within, with leaders and followers. A brand is founded on an organization's internal aspects: the vision and mission, culture, as well as competencies, all of which contribute to creating and maintaining brand identity. Mission and vision statements should guide and motivate followers' and leaders' decisions and behaviors as they bring the organization's mission and vision to life in their brand, daily and over time. The mission and vision generate the brand promise and core values. A brand identity's strength hinges on the extent to which leaders develop and enact a vision and both leaders and followers buy into the organization's mission.

An organization's culture, competencies, and brand identity become severely weakened when the vision and/or mission is not clear, does not exist, or there is a lack of agreement between leaders' and followers' perceptions/enactment and official statements provided to stakeholders. That is, the way followers and leaders create an organizational culture that extends beyond the internal tribe to external stakeholders remains important. Competencies (leaders and followers' motivations, skills, and knowledge used to make brands) are essential for creating and maintaining a brand identity with a competitive advantage. Knowledge competencies of leaders and followers are particularly advantageous. Matching product knowledge and expert knowledge of customers and competitors allows leaders and followers the upper hand in differentiating their brand above or ahead of competitors (Payne et al., 2016).

External Aspects

The external aspects of brand identity relate to how an organization is seen or wants to be seen by external stakeholders, including its value proposition, outside relationships, and positioning. External aspects highlight what the brand is known for by its users, consumers, and other external stakeholders. **Value proposition** refers to the brand promise(s) offered to customers. Leaders and followers should continually ask: are we delivering on our promise(s) from the eyes of the customer and stakeholder? Outside relationships involve the ways in which external stakeholders (sales reps, partners, service providers, community leaders, influencers) feel and behave toward a brand. Leaders and followers should focus on interacting with customers in ways that will make people want to engage and connect with the brand.

Brand position refers to the place in the minds and lives of customers and stakeholders that you want to own. Followers and leaders should strive to focus messages on customer relevancy and competitive differentiation to maximize value. For example, most people prefer one ride-share company over another. That ride-share company one prefers has a stronger brand position in people's minds than the one they will take only if their preferred one is not available.

Internal-External Aspects

The communication aspects of a brand bridge internal and external elements—its brand identity, communication style, and unique characteristics. As a brand's identity is created and maintained, leaders and followers should appropriately align a brand's identity, communication style, and characteristics/personality. Humanizing a brand, giving it distinct human qualities, can enhance consumer-brand relationships by increasing consumers' brand love (passionate emotional attachment to a brand), brand loyalty (feelings of allegiance, support, and commitment to a brand), and brand trust (strong belief or confidence in the reliability, truth, and, ability of a brand) (Kauffman et al., 2016). In terms of communication style, think about DISC styles. Leaders and followers can assign a brand's communication style to be results-oriented (driver), quality-oriented (contemplator), emotionally other-oriented (supporter), or socially other-oriented (influencer). What brands can you think of that have been humanized and successfully increased customers' love, loyalty, and trust for the brand?

Crisis

A **crisis** is:

- "A major unpredictable event that has potentially negative results. The event and its aftermath may significantly damage an organization and its employees, products, services, financial condition, and reputation" (Barton, 1993, p. 2).

- "A major occurrence with a potentially negative outcome affecting an organization, company or industry, as well as its public, products, services or good name" (Fearn-Banks, 1996, p. 1).

- "An event that brings, or has the potential for bringing, an organization into disrepute and imperils its future profitability, growth, and possibly, its very survival" (Lerbinger, 1997, p. 4).

Obviously, there are different definitions of crisis, but all these definitions contain similar themes (Figure 9.3). A crisis: disrupts business; builds in intensity; produces extreme negative results, such as death or destruction to human life and property; can damage the reputation of an organization's products and services; brings unwanted public attention from the media and the government; and may result in irreparable harm to the organization.

A *crisis* differs from a *problem* in two distinct ways. Problems occur in the natural course of business and can be solved/resolved through the normal course of business. In addition, problems don't disrupt the normal activities of an organization, and they generally don't garner unwanted media attention. Similarly, a crisis differs from bad publicity in three distinct ways: it can be managed through normal channels, has a tendency to fade quickly from the media's hot topics of the day, and can be quickly extinguished if the organization addresses the situation

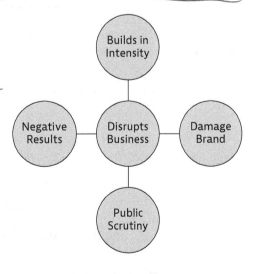

FIGURE 9.3   Star of Crisis Themes

proactively (i.e., takes responsibility, is willing to correct the situation, and makes restitution).

Types of Crises

Organizational leaders and followers can find themselves facing seven types of crises. Competent leaders and followers find themselves handling the various situations differently to meet internal and external publics' needs differently.

1. **Natural Crises. Natural crises** are hurricanes, tornadoes, floods, earthquakes, wildfires, blizzards, volcanic eruptions, and other disasters or "acts of God." In November 2016, a wildfire struck the Smokey Mountains in Tennessee. At the time, the mayor found himself thrust into the media spotlight as he not only dealt with the crisis that trapped and killed people, but also publicly handled the loss of his own house and property.

2. **Technological Crises.** When complex technology and human error collide, it can make for a dramatic **technological crisis** with explosions, crashes, and nuclear meltdowns. Think about the last time the server went down on your campus, the cell tower/satellite or electricity went out, or you had no Internet access. How did you respond? As we become more digitized each and every day, the opportunities for technology disasters continue to increase. Universities and other organizations are well aware of the importance of having backup systems in place for all their data as well as cyber walls that prevent unwanted intrusions into their organizational data. Organizational technology disasters involve primarily **internal stakeholders** (employees) and secondarily **external stakeholders** (customers and clients). Effective technological crisis preparation involves making sure someone is in charge of communicating with employees and someone else is in charge of communicating with customers and clients. Competent leaders need to think about all different types of contingencies as well as the following questions long before the crisis hits: How will employees continue working and access needed data if there is a server failure? How will customers and clients be able to access the website? How are the professionals going to keep everyone and the information they possess safe if they need to be evacuated?

3. **Confrontation Crises.** A **confrontation crisis** is human-made and occurs when people organize to fight a business or policy. Sometimes leaders and followers create these crises. For example, in August 2019, following a mass shooting at a Walmart in El Paso, Texas, and an employee on employee shooting in Southaven, Mississippi, about 40 white-collar leaders walked out to protest the company's policy to sell guns in about half of its American stores (Bhattarai & Bensinger, 2019). Walmart has

seen past confrontation crises by followers who have protested for better pay and to end racial discrimination (O'Connor, 2014).

4. **Malevolence Crises.** A **malevolence crisis** is instigated by individuals using criminal or violent means to vent their anger and possibly destroy an organization. Terrorism, kidnapping, firebombing, and product tampering are just some of the malevolent ways to induce a crisis. In early summer 2019, an employee follower entered a Virginia Beach city municipal building and shot at least 16 people (Almasay & Reiss, 2019). The shooter was listed on the website as a certified professional engineer and the municipal contact person for issues concerning local road projects. How quickly and well leaders responded to the shooting determined where followers and the public assigned blame for the unfortunate deaths and how safe they felt re-entering the building. A heartfelt statement from a leader concerning the situation caused by an individual's criminal or violent action can go a long way toward creating the perception that the organization could not have done anything to prevent the senseless act. On the other hand, a disorganized or inconsistent response from the organizational leader can create the perception of an ill-prepared team whom the public might blame for the senseless deaths.

5. **Skewed Management Values Crises.** A **skewed management values crisis** occurs when the spoken and unspoken culture of an organization is "profits at any cost." This type of short-term, get-it-while-you-can leadership dismisses the importance of customer, shareholder, and stakeholder interests. Monsanto, a company responsible for many of the genetically modified seeds used to grow the food we eat, and also responsible for the herbicides/pesticides used to protect those crops has been ranked among the companies with the worst reputations (Ausick, 2017). They have consistently been accused of putting profits above people's health and safety. Their recent merger with Bayer may turn those tides.

6. **Deception Crises.** When management hides information or misrepresents itself or its products, a **deception crisis**—another type of organizational misdeed—is guaranteed to follow. It may take years to uncover the deception, but it always comes out.

7. **Leadership Misconduct Crises.** The final type of organizational misdeed is the crisis stemming from leadership misconduct. A **leadership misconduct crisis** involves corporate skewed values, illegalities, and amoral behavior. Robert Kraft, owner of the New England Patriots, who allegedly attempted to solicit sex from an undercover officer posing as a prostitute is a recent example of leadership misconduct. While the activity was not specifically associated with his role in the Patriots' organization, his association with the professional football team made the headlines and brought the crisis to the public's knowledge.

FIGURE 9.4   No matter how big the crisis is, these feelings are always a likely outcome for the followers and leaders involved.

Surprising and Smoldering Crises

A **sudden/surprising crisis** is like the devastation created by a tornado ripping through a town with little to no warning. Organizations that can weather these types of storms have leaders and followers who have taken the time to develop a well-researched and practiced response plan. Once the ground winds begin swirling and the sky turns green, it's too late to conduct the research necessary to develop a sound message for the first responders.

To understand how a slow, smoldering crisis can happen, think of the Mississippi River. At its headwaters in Northern Minnesota, the river starts more as a brook than a mighty river. As it flows and meanders its way 2,320 miles down to the Gulf of Mexico, the Mississippi River picks up tributaries from the Ohio, Gallatin, Arkansas, and Illinois rivers, as well as several other smaller tributaries. By the time the Mississippi reaches New Orleans, it is a mighty river more than one mile across in some places. A **slow, smoldering crisis** often starts as a little problem, grows into a bigger problem, and eventually becomes a fast-moving disaster. In this case, the leaders and followers have time to react if they catch the initial little problem. Some of those little problems resolve themselves without intervention (for example, if the person creating the problem is asked to leave, agrees to leave, or is fired). If the problem does not resolve itself, the smoldering time is when a strong campaign should be built to prepare for what is to come.

Developing the Communication Plan

Once they break into the public arena, all crises have three things in common: a high degree of uncertainty, a short time to respond, and increased pressure for information. To handle the upsurge in expectations requires a lot of planning *and* practice. In fact, preparation is the most essential aspect of crisis communication management (Miller & Horsley, 2009). David Guth and Charles Marsh (2008) have identified four stages of crisis communication planning:

1. Risk assessment
2. Communication plan
3. Responders
4. Recovery

Each stage builds on the previous stage, so the entire process is systematically developed.

Stage 1: Risk Assessment

During stage 1, **risk assessment**, all phases of an organization must be analyzed for potential crises. You can create an assessment grid as an initial evaluation sheet for determining potential risk.

Stage 2: Communication Plan Development

After you have assessed and ranked the hazards, you're ready to develop a multi-layered **communication plan** in conjunction with the crisis management team. The communication plan must be devised with input from a variety of relevant personnel from senior management, legal, safety, sales and marketing, and human resources. The communication plan can be separated into four categories that should ultimately be integrated:

1. **Time frame**: You need a plan for staying on top of the situation before, during, and after the crisis: This is a 24-hour situation. There should be no monitoring, responding, or reacting to requests for information downtime.

2. **Internal messaging/External messaging**: A good communication plan includes information on who needs to know what when. Employees (followers and internal publics) should be the first to know what's going on. They are the primary public and will have the most questions. The internal messages can be crafted ahead of time based on the potential hazards and threats. External messages should be crafted to minimize ambiguity of what is happening and to provide guidance (for example, about safety issues) for the community and other stakeholders as the crisis unfolds.

3. **Delivery system**: Your communication also needs to consider how information will be delivered to interested parties. Will you communicate via traditional or social media? Information should be provided on an ongoing basis in every format possible: live briefings, videos uploaded to your home page, newspaper and television ads, and social media networks. The key is to develop and maintain a list of traditional and social media contacts to whom information/updates can be provided quickly and efficiently. In a crisis, an information vacuum leads to speculation, which can lead to rumors and then panic. New delivery systems also require that organizations be responsive to blog postings, tweets, and mobile platforms.

4. **Tracking and managing**: Before a crisis occurs, the team should know who the important influencers are and how to reach them. Online and offline, communication with these people needs to be tracked and managed. Developing relationships before a crisis is a key strategy that will extend the organization's reach and credibility during difficult times. If lists of key influencers and journalists have been made, the organization can immediately begin communication as soon as the crisis begins. In addition, it is important to assess what worked and what didn't work after the crisis has abated.

Stage 3: Responders

One of the single most important things the crisis communication team must have ready in stage 3 is the list of qualified **responders**. Will the CEO or another leader speak to the media? Who will be assigned to engage bloggers and tweeters? What role will employee followers play in communicating about the crisis? With so many avenues for communication distribution, controlling the message completely is impossible. This is why having a communication plan already in place with key spokespersons identified and trained and with corporate guidelines explained and defined is the best strategy for any organization facing a crisis. If you communicate first, clearly, and frequently, you have a better chance of having your responses be the ones people turn to for information.

Situational Crisis Communication Theory

According to situational crisis communication theory, the circumstance should determine the response. Because not all facets of a crisis are the same, only by understanding the particular situation can the PR team respond appropriately to its different aspects. Here are two different crisis situations that have been deemed on the negative and positive ends of the spectrum: Horizon Deepwater oil spill in the Gulf of Mexico and Southwest Airlines first airline fatality in its history.

TABLE 9.3 Crisis Responses

Crisis	Result	Response
British Petroleum: Worst U.S. environmental disaster on record when an oil rig in the Gulf of Mexico exploded and dispersed millions of gallons of oil into the area.	▪ Temporary destruction of fishing/shrimping ▪ Loss of tourism for the Gulf Coast states ▪ Death of 11 employees ▪ Loss of confidence in BP by investors ▪ Unwanted attention/ scrutiny (media/ government) ▪ Boycotting of franchises	▪ Television commercials to rebuild trust ▪ Offers to pay remuneration ▪ Removal of Tony Hayward as CEO ▪ No concrete response
Southwest Airlines: First fatality in airlines' 47-year flying history	▪ Emergency landing in Philadelphia for flight from New York to Dallas ▪ Broke an 8-year record of no U.S. airline fatalities ▪ Questions about maintenance and safety of mechanical system	▪ Immediate social media update of steps taken ▪ Heartfelt video response from the leader ▪ Met all passenger and crew needs (lodging, food, trauma counselling, travel arrangements) ▪ $5,000 to ease passenger burden; personal calls and notes to check on passengers ▪ Had a plan and executed it as written ▪ Team monitored social media in real time

Both of these responses were appropriate, but they were formulaic. **Formulaic** means that the responses lacked creativity or specificity to the situation. Formulaic responses are seldom seen as effective. Responses must be appropriate *and* authentic. The public must believe that the organization trying to quell the negativity from the crisis really does have the best interest of the community at heart. Without this trust, the best communication tactics sound hollow and empty. Situational crisis communication theory advises practitioners to make sure to tailor their responses to different crisis situations appropriately.

Stage 4: Recovery

Recovery is the stage that begins after the crisis has been addressed, but it may be the most important stage for communication because this is when credibility and trust are re-established. Organizations should ask for feedback from affected audiences, online influencers, and journalists on how well the company communicated during the crisis. From these data, you can develop better response systems for the next crisis.

Activism

While we expect organizations to respond to crises directly related to their organizations, do we expect them to use their first-amendment rights to speak out about issues unrelated to their core business? For example, what happens when the CEO of Johnson and Johnson talks about race relations and police brutality? Warren Buffett talks about issues affecting the LGBTQ+ community? The president of your college or university talks about environmental issues affecting third-world countries? Any time an organizational leader speaks out about issues that have no direct impact on their products or services, we are talking about **CEO activism** (Chatterji & Toffel, 2019).

At various times in history, phrases such as "There is no such thing as bad publicity" (Phineas T. Barnum, American showman and circus owner); "The only thing worse than being talked about is not being talked about" (Oscar Wilde, Irish poet and playwright); and "There's no such thing as bad publicity except your obituary" (Brendan Behan, Irish Republican with a self-proclaimed drinking problem) became popular. Unfortunately, in an age of social media and 24/7 access to information, publicity can be both beneficial and detrimental. Competent leaders and followers make strategic decisions about when, where, and how they are going to take a stand regarding social causes or promote social justice.

In addition to strategic leaders and followers, competent stakeholders weigh both the denotative and connotative meaning of these activist messages. Generally speaking, people are more influenced by messages that resonate with their own beliefs, come from a well-known organizational leader, and have at least an indirect connection to the organization's business (Gaines-Ross, 2016). The surface-level meaning of an activist message works well for employees, customers, and shareholders who support the position; it has the opposite effect for those who oppose the position.

At a deeper level, these same people often question the leader's motivation for making the statement—is it a publicity stunt to get the organization's name out in front of people, deflect attention from something else the organization does not want in the news, or promote the individual leader's reputation? While Millennials tend to be most open to, expect, and accept activist messages (i.e., support activist, message, and organization), other generations are more skeptical of their intent (Gaines-Ross, 2016). Only time will tell if iGen (those born in the last few years of the twentieth century up until now) will sustain those attitudes and beliefs.

More media coverage exists with respect to social issues and causes generally championed by liberal political views (e.g., racial and sexual equality); causes championed by more conservative political views are less common. Without research evidence, we can only speculate on why this may be the case. Are there fewer conservative CEOs, fewer who speak out, fewer issues about which they feel strongly ... ? In the last decade, two of the more prominent conservative leadership activists have been Hobby Lobby's (a national craft store chain) Founders David and Barbara Green and Chick-fil-A's Dan Cathy. The Greens opposed requiring employers to include contraception coverage as part of health insurance plans because of people's religious beliefs about procreation and when life begins. Cathy also cited religious beliefs when he spoke out against what was known at the time as same-sex marriage. In both cases, their strong stances have not negatively impacted their organizations as both are thriving.

Ultimately, two measures of activism matter for organizations: 1. The extent to which internal and external stakeholders respond positively; and 2. The extent to which attitudes, beliefs, and policies change. If a CEO activist were to speak out, what should the topic be—rate the ones below from most important (1) to least important (10) for Americans.

1. Climate change _____

2. Equal pay _____

3. Free speech _____

4. Gender equality _____

5. Gun control _____

6. Healthcare _____

7. Immigration _____

8. Privacy/Data protection _____

9. Race relations _____

10. Sexual harassment _____

Let's see how close you were to what Spring, Gaines-Ross, and Massey (2018) found. Their order was equal pay (79% of Americans), sexual harassment (77%), privacy/data protection (71%), healthcare (70%), gender equality (59%), free speech (54%), race relations (48%), climate change (39%), immigration

(38%), and gun control (35%). Stop and think about it—the first four are more closely aligned with doing business in the U.S. than the last six, where there is a significant drop in the percentage of Americans who believe organizational leaders should speak out on the topic. The same study found that people were more likely to boycott or stop supporting an organization when the leader engaged in activism than they were to increase their buying or support. This translates into significantly more risk than benefit for the organization and why it is critical that organizational leaders think strategically about speaking out before they do it.

Reaching the Masses Through Apologia

In chapter four, we talked about constructivism and creating person-centered messages tailored to the person with whom you are speaking. Because organizational leaders and, to a lesser extent, followers, find themselves communicating with larger groups of people, they need to choose their messages carefully. When was the last time you felt sorry for something you had done? When was the last time you genuinely apologized to someone—not one of those "I'm sorry" because a parent told you to apologize for misbehaving in public? How hard was it to do so? Insincere apologies are like perfume/cologne that people use to cover up the smell after smoking a cigarette—the pleasant scent lasts for a brief period of time and as soon as it wears off the nasty smell of the indiscretion returns. How about in your workplace—has another employee or leader apologized to you in the last 6 months … 12 months … ever?

Genuinely admitting to doing something wrong may be one of the most difficult forms of communication in which followers and leaders engage. In situations where there is wrongdoing (something as minor as not being polite by saying please or thank you or as major as taking credit for someone else's idea), many people will choose to avoid addressing the situation in the hopes that time will solve the problem because people will forget what happened. If anything, time actually makes it worse because additional situations are likely to pile up and increase one's negative impression. To adapt from Hallmark, apology is when you care enough to say the very best.

Apologia is a formal defense of an attitude, belief, or behavior. In 1973, Ware and Linkugel first developed a list of rhetorical messages one could use to defend, justify, or apologize for one's self; that list was later adapted to apply to organizations (Benoit, 1995, 1997).

Each of the strategies can be used effectively as long as it is situationally appropriate. For example, Tony Stewart could not use denial in Kevin Ward Jr.'s death after being struck by Stewart's car on a racetrack. Similarly, reducing the offensiveness of an act through bolstering is not going to be effective for Jim Beam when they were contaminating the local water supply with chemicals during a fire; no one cares how much they have donated to the local community or how much good bourbon has done for people's social lives when the cleanliness of their water is at stake.

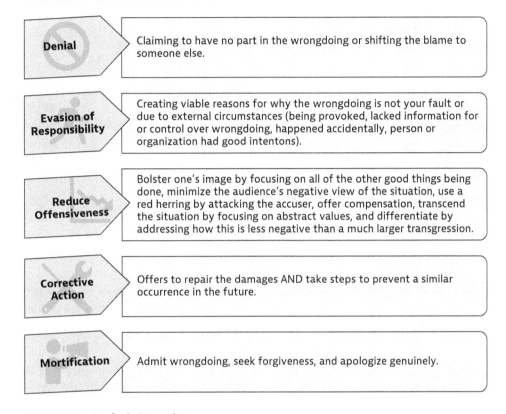

Denial — Claiming to have no part in the wrongdoing or shifting the blame to someone else.

Evasion of Responsibility — Creating viable reasons for why the wrongdoing is not your fault or due to external circumstances (being provoked, lacked information for or control over wrongdoing, happened accidentally, person or organization had good intentons).

Reduce Offensiveness — Bolster one's image by focusing on all of the other good things being done, minimize the audience's negative view of the situation, use a red herring by attacking the accuser, offer compensation, transcend the situation by focusing on abstract values, and differentiate by addressing how this is less negative than a much larger transgression.

Corrective Action — Offers to repair the damages AND take steps to prevent a similar occurrence in the future.

Mortification — Admit wrongdoing, seek forgiveness, and apologize genuinely.

FIGURE 9.5   Apologia Strategies

On the flip side, in 2019 Mario Lopez used mortification for insensitive comments he made about those who parent transgender children: "The comments I made were ignorant and insensitive, and I now have a deeper understanding of how hurtful they were. I have been and always will be an ardent supporter of the LGBTQ community, and I am going to use this opportunity to better educate myself. Moving forward I will be more informed and thoughtful" (Bacardi, 2019, par. 2).

Using Media and Technology to Build Relationships

In today's information- and technology-saturated world, brand success is significantly influenced by the way leaders and followers use media and technology to interact and build relationships both internally and externally. Media and technology allow people to cultivate, tailor, and/or adapt an effective brand when building relationships with coworkers internally, compared to building external relationships. Building internal relationships focuses on collaborating at a subcultural level, whereas external relationships focus on connecting at a broader cultural level. Regardless, interpersonal and organizational communication skills are at the core of connecting with others, particularly those who are culturally different, to form successful relationships that are becoming more technologically driven.

Building Internal Relationships

Collaboration and connected workforce—these are buzzwords infiltrating our workplaces. Workplaces rely on interactive communication technologies such as social collaboration tools to provide a platform for followers and leaders to build internal relationships. As many of you graduate and move into an increasingly globalized workforce, you may notice that approximately 9 out of 10 (89%) organizational employees use social collaboration tools to:

- Communicate with coworkers,
- Connect with geographically dispersed staff,
- Collaborate within teams and with outside departments,
- Improve revenue, productivity, and engagement (Harvard Business Review, 2018).

Knowing how to use interactive communication technologies is not enough; tomorrow's followers and leaders must be able to communicate, through both computer-mediated communication (CMC) and face-to-face interactions, in a competent and culturally sensitive manner (Ray & Violanti, 2019). For productive internal relationships, establishing rules of interaction is essential. Leaders and followers can capitalize on the advantages of interactive communication technology (ICT) for cultivating healthy relationships internally by discussing certain standards of engagement (Larson & Markarius, 2018; Ray & Violanti, 2019).

- Agreeing on the best channels for CMC (e.g., texting for quick responses or non-work discussions, email for work issues, and video-calling for long meetings or urgent matters). Generally, people prefer and engage in CMC with coworkers through similar ICT channels across cultures. After face-to-face interaction, people most prefer interacting through telephone, email, texting, and IM (Mao & Hale, 2015).
- Best times to connect, what time of day (and/or day of the week) is best to contact or avoid? Leaders and followers should also come to an understanding about expectations for their use of time (being on-time for meetings or appointments, delays in response time, etc.).

■ How to share information. How will we collaborate on, organize, and exchange files and documents? What file sharing system (e.g., Dropbox, Google Drive, Slack, OneDrive, internal cloud software, etc.) will we use and what will this process entail?

RESEARCH SUMMARY

Study: Xu (2018) set out to determine how communities come together to help each other make sense of, and cope with, a crisis situation. Specifically, the study examined what happens to the campus community during a crisis using chaos, uncertainty reduction, and sensemaking theories.

The research questions and hypotheses were:

RQ1.   How, if at all, does a crisis impact a campus community?

RQ2.   How, if at all, does a campus community function during a crisis?

RQ3.   What is a reliable and valid measurement of crises?

H1 & H2. Severity, urgency, and uncertainty of crises increase the importance of information (H1), and interpersonal communication needs (H2).

H3.   Information needs increase interpersonal communication (3a) and community preference (3b), and interpersonal communication increases community preference (3c).

H4.   Interpersonal communication, community preference, and information needs increase community as resource (4a), as well as community as knowledge (4b).

H5.   Community identification positively influences community preference, interpersonal communication, community as resource, and community as knowledge.

Using both qualitative (interviews) and quantitative (surveys) data, they found that collective sense-making happens in interpersonal relationships, regardless of what messages the organization puts out through social and traditional media. Specifically, the themes of vulnerability, strengthening one's ties to others, interpersonal communication, and other community members as a knowledge base to reduce uncertainty emerged as the qualitative themes. As predicted, information needs lead to interacting with others to meet those needs. The more one identifies with the larger community, the stronger their use of interpersonal communication to make sense of the crisis situation by seeking information and reducing uncertainty.

(continued)

Implications: It is important for leaders and followers to understand that external stakeholders have a role to play in a crisis situation. As long as they are strategically included in the communication plan, they can help each other make sense of the situation and engage in group coping mechanisms. Too often, organizations become too internally focused on which organization members are going to do what; effective organizations remember that there is a much larger community of people who can play an important role in helping protect the brand and reputation.

Building External Relationships

Think about a brand that engages and interacts with stakeholders through social media channels. What makes the interaction effective (or ineffective)? In what ways do you see aspects of the brand identity matrix being applied during these interactions? For the effective consumer-brand interaction that you thought of, how do you believe the social media strategy being used by the brand aligns with its business objectives? There should be a clear connection between social media actions and broader business goals. More often than we realize, brand success and brand relationships suffer from the disconnect between social media goals and business goals. According to Quesenberry (2018), two major social media mistakes that leaders and followers of an organization must avoid, include: a) starting with social media objectives and b) limiting brand presence to the most popular social media channels.

A brand's social media strategy should be based in its business objectives. Leaders and followers can take a channel (Facebook, Instagram, Twitter, etc.) and set goals for increasing their likes, comments, and shares. Sure, this makes sense, but our brand can get trapped like a hungry mouse in a social media-only wheel if we tunnel focus on seeing the cheese of likes-comments-shares. Starting with only social media goals can cause followers and leaders to lose sight of business goals. Business objectives range from increasing sales, generating brand awareness, improving customer experience, to gaining volunteers. To assess the strength of brand relationships and overall brand success, brands need to be able to evaluate how well social media efforts are contributing to the bottom line. For example, which of the following social media goals do you believe better allows leaders and followers to home in on the bottom line?

- "Increase engagement and our number of fans (friends and media followers) on Facebook by posting at least 4 times a week over the next 4 months."

- "Increase brand awareness by 15% for people ages 26–30 within 6 months."

Limiting brand presence to the most popular channels can also diminish consumer-brand relationship development. The most popular channel may not be the best platform for your brand; channels that you aren't on may be better for meeting your business goals (Quesenberry, 2018).

FIGURE 9.6 Social media channels are one tool for reaching external publics. They need to be used strategically to meet business goals and support the organizational mission.

Social Media Strategy

A good social media strategy is based upon on business objectives followed by target market, and analytics (metrics) (Quesenberry, 2018). Clearly defining your objective and target market is crucial for selecting appropriate platforms for building the long-term success of great brand relationships. Different channels and tools may be required for different objectives and certain target markets. Design message content so stakeholders actually read it. What works for Victoria's Secret won't work for Pampers or Sony. Doing this means grabbing attention by tapping into emotions and personal values. Stories and narratives often evoke emotion and resonate with beliefs. To retain the value of a good post (content that promotes action beyond viewing) or mediated interaction means tailoring messages to your audience and platform. Spoiler alert, the social media mistakes to avoid for nonprofits that we will talk about in the next chapter also apply here. Primarily, avoid posting the same content across all social media accounts. Developing an effective social media strategy starts with analyzing and answering questions embedded in three basic steps (Springman, 2011).

1. Identify your organization's stakeholder groups. Who are you specifically targeting? Who would you ideally like to work with? What are the advantages and disadvantages of your brand for each stakeholder group?

2. Foster a value proposition for each stakeholder group. Are you interacting in ways that deliver and satisfy your brand's value proposition(s)? What kind of added value will stakeholders extract from your communication and relationship with them in your attempts to deliver on your brand's promise? How does this value from each stakeholder group profit your organization in the long-term?

3. Determine a set of key performance indicators. How will you measure how effectively your company is creating value and living up to your brand's promise for each stakeholder group? How well is your business capturing value in return?

Social media and new technology can help improve customer relations, solutions, and fulfill customer needs (met or unmet) with more efficiency and effectiveness (Payne et al., 2017). Striving for ways to answer the question of how your business uses technology for innovation is becoming more of a requirement than an option. This means social media strategies also need to involve an assessment of how a certain brand relates to, fits in with, or contributes to specific crowdculture(s). A **crowdculture** refers to online communities that create or connect around certain ideologies, issues, practices, art, or entertainment (Holt, 2016). It is a subculture that leaders and followers will be wise to consider in developing a social media strategy; as crowdcultures gain momentum, they influence the masses across geographic boundaries.

CASE STUDY **Starbucks**

A company that started by buying coffee beans from a competing coffee maker and selling them in a single retail store in Seattle has blossomed into a Fortune 200 multinational firm. Over the last 45+ years, they have seen many economic changes; they are one of the few firms to weather those storms with their three founders leading the charge. In 2017, one of the founders retired and Starbucks continues to forge ahead. As a company focused on social causes such as recycling, fair trade, water safety in third-world countries, and most recently announcing the demise of the plastic straw in 2020 to protect wildlife, the issues associated with race relations in the last decade have caused the media and stakeholders to pause.

In 2015, Starbucks attempted to address issues of race that were dividing America with a campaign where baristas wrote "Race Together" on people's coffee cups. Howard, Schultz, then Chair and CEO, launched the campaign after conversations with the company's partners (aka employees or followers); the news release and accompanying videos can be accessed at https://stories.starbucks.com/stories/2015/race-together-conversation-has-the-power-to-change-hearts-and-minds/. The sentiment was designed to begin a conversation about race in coffee shops around the country and was part of a 100,000 Opportunities Initiative in which a coalition of companies agreed to hire youth who were disconnected from society because they were neither attending school nor working; the youth were disproportionately black, Hispanic, and Native American (Madhani, 2015).

The campaign was met with mixed reactions because people perceived that the company's intentions were not what was being portrayed to them. People took to social media to voice their primarily negative perspectives on the situation, especially regarding how the campaign was rolled out and lack of communication training baristas received with their three talking points (Abitbol et al., 2018). While the campaign did not unfold as the company and CEO intended, it did start a national conversation about race and Starbucks did not back down, despite the negativity expressed (Carr, 2015).

Fast forward to 2018 and the company once again finds itself at the center of a national discussion on race when two black men are arrested at a Philadelphia, PA, Starbucks. They had entered the establishment and asked to use the bathroom while they were waiting for another friend to arrive. The barista informed them that only paying customers could use it, so they sat down to wait for their friend. She asked them to leave and when they did not, she phoned police. When the friend, who happened to be white, arrived, police had already handcuffed the two black men to arrest them for trespassing. Once again, people took to social media to express their negativity about Starbucks and specifically about the apparent disconnect between their policies that promote everyone is welcome and practices that border on racial profiling and discrimination. Initially, the social media response mirrored the legalistic responses that occur in most situations.

(continued)

We apologize to the two individuals and our customers and are disappointed this led to an arrest. We take these matters seriously and clearly have more work to do when it comes to how we handle incidents in our stores. We are reviewing our policies and will continue to engage with the community and the police department to try to ensure these types of situations never happen in any of our stores.

Image 9.1

In the days that followed, CEO Kevin Johnson took to traditional media to adamantly state Starbucks' position and met with the two men who had been arrested. What differed in this response from others was Johnson's willingness to take responsibility for the situation ("the way that incident escalated, and the outcome, was nothing but reprehensible—and I'm sorry. And I believe that blame is misplaced. In fact, I think the focus of fixing this—I own it. This is a management issue and I am accountable to ensure we address the policy, and the practice and the training that led to this outcome.") and closed all of the stores for an afternoon to conduct racial and unconscious bias training with all of the partners, a move that was estimated to cost the company $7 million (McGregor, 2018). Only time will tell the extent to which Starbucks has changed the landscape for responding to crisis situations.

DISCUSSION QUESTIONS

1. In the reports associated with the Philadelphia racial incident, the followers appear to play little to no role in responding to the incident. How consistent is that with a company that refers to them as partners? What type of follower response would you have expected, especially after the half-day training?

2. In this chapter, we talked about the importance of personal and corporate brands. How would you describe the barista and Starbucks brands? How do you think your perspectives differ from those of your parents and grandparents?

3. Given your own work experiences, to what extent would you like to work for a company that is socially responsible in a very public way? What are the benefits and drawbacks of working for such a company?

ANALYSIS OPTIONS

A. Starbucks is considered the caffeine lifeblood of many Americans who cannot start their morning without a Starbucks coffee. The half-day training in which they closed all of their stores for a single day was deemed a first step. You have been hired to develop the "next steps" for both leaders and followers.

B. Because this organization is the exception rather than the norm, everything it does related to corporate social responsibility and CEO activism is magnified. As part of the executive team that includes people from all levels of the organization, you have been tasked with anticipating and developing a set of messages for potential crisis situations. Address what situations could happen, what messages would be appropriate, and what channels should be used to deliver those messages.

C. As people born after 1980 continue to shift the balance of power in organizations, we are also seeing a shift in the way people think about work. They increasingly want to belong in an organization that stands for something more than a paycheck. Moving forward, what changes does Starbucks need to make to ensure they are well positioned to meet the needs of both their leaders and followers as well as their shareholders, suppliers/partners, and customers?

ANALYSIS PROCESS

- Brainstorm a list of options for addressing the issue.

- Make a list of strengths and challenges for each of your brainstormed solutions.

- Choose the best solution for the issue.

- Develop an implementation plan for your chosen solution.

- Additional resources:

Starbucks Race Together Campaign
tiny.utk.edu/FCL9_1

Starbucks Corporate Site
https://tinyurl.com/b3rbbpr

(continued)

Starbucks Brand Success
tiny.utk.edu/FCL9_2

 LEADER AND FOLLOWER DEVELOPMENT PRACTICES

1. If you are going to engage in activism, be sure your personal and organizational values are crystal clear (Spring et al., 2018).

2. Be a competent communicator by creating messages appropriate for each of the internal and external audiences because they need to hear different messages from the organization's followers and leaders.

3. Avoid self-fulfilling prophecies where focusing on a specific set of stakeholders leads to them gaining more importance than they would have if the organization had made decisions based upon business strategy (Brockbank, 2016).

4. Make sure the message is appropriate for the channel. What you say to employees in small-group meetings is not the same as what you say to them in a company-wide email or what you post on one of your social media channels.

5. Be the bridge that connects various stakeholders and makes sure their voices are heard when important brand decisions are being made (Hack, 2017).

DISCUSSION QUESTIONS AND ACTIVITIES

1. Using the questions at the beginning of the chapter, craft your personal brand. How consistent is this brand with the career path you intend to take? What specific activities can you engage in before graduating to strengthen the followership aspects of your personal brand? The leadership aspects of your personal brand?

2. Choose an organization for which you worked or volunteered. If you have never worked or volunteered, use your college or university. As a member

of their internal publics, what do you see as your role with respect to promoting the organization on social media? In face-to-face interactions? Why? What policies exist when it comes to employees talking about the organization on social media? What types, if any, of training occur to help you be more effective in accomplishing these goals?

3. Choose a brand you support and one you do not support. Using the publicly available information, determine what their value propositions and brand relationships are. How are they different and similar? To what extent do their values and relationships help explain why you like one and dislike the other? Why?

4. Choose an organization that has recently experienced a crisis. How would you classify the crisis? Using the organization's website, social media channels, and/or traditional news media, find the ways in which the organization's leaders and followers have responded to the crisis. Pay particular attention to their actual messages and quotations. Based upon what you know about communicating competently and responding to a crisis situation, evaluate what they did well and what they could have done better (e.g., was their apologia appropriate for the crisis, was the message tailored to their various stakeholders, etc.)? Why did you draw the conclusions you did?

5. How do you feel about leaders, followers, and organizations that choose to engage in activism? How do you decide whether their activism is going to increase or decrease your loyalty to the brand? How close were your rankings of social justice causes to the research presented in the chapter? Why do you think that was the case?

FIGURE CREDITS:

CHAPTER 10

NONPROFIT AND ALTERNATIVE ORGANIZATIONS

"I would ask you to question who's at the table and who's not at the table and to think about those voices that aren't represented when you're making decisions."

—JAMES HALLIDAY, EMERGING PRACTITIONERS IN PHILANTHROPY

"We try to come alongside people and interact with our supporters so that they know that we see them, we're with them, and we're in this together."

—LINDSAY KOLSCH, TO WRITE LOVE ON HER ARMS

Nonprofit organizations are much like our brains. They are made up of five distinct groups of people: leaders/boards of directors, paid staff/followers, volunteers, donors, and service users. Looking at the image you see of the brain below, which area do you believe represents each group?

Donors   _____

Followers/Paid Staff   _____

Leaders/Boards of Directors   _____

Service Users   _____

Volunteers   _____

Why did you make the choices you did? Did you assume that one of the brain parts had to correspond to each group? Why or why not? In reality, service users are not actually represented in the image—they are part of the larger environment in which the brain operates. Service users influence the nonprofit and its members and are influenced by the nonprofit and its members. Knowing that about the service users, do you need to change any of your answers—go ahead, no one is going to collect and look at your book.

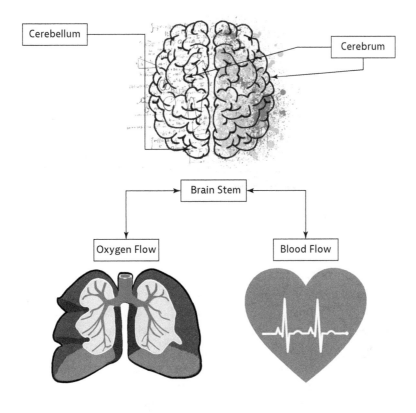

FIGURE 10.1   The Brain

Which of these groups serves as the connector between the nonprofit and its ability to act (the brain stem)? In nonprofits, followers/paid employees serve as the brain stem to connect the nonprofit to its vision and mission (the lifeblood circulating through the body and brain). Which of these groups best represents the nonprofit's ability to coordinate activity (cerebellum)? While this is the smallest portion of the brain, it is often the largest group of people involved in the nonprofit—its volunteers.

Which of these groups best represents the nonprofit's higher order functioning (the cerebrum)? While the leaders/board of directors are not the largest component of nonprofits, they are most akin to the way the cerebrum operates. So, what does that leave for the oxygen flow required to catalyze and allow the nonprofit's mission and vision to complete the system? It would be the donors; without resources, nonprofits would be unable to realize their vision and mission.

Defining Characteristics

Nonprofits have a separate chapter in this textbook because they are distinguishable from many of the organizations we have been discussing. While leaders and followers in these organizations must continue to communicate competently, perform their followership and leadership roles appropriately, and engage in effective relationship building, they must also recognize the mission, audience, and problem-solving differences between themselves and traditional "bottom-line" organizations (Norwich University, 2016; Renz, 2016). Specifically, nonprofits distinguish themselves in seven specific ways.

Mission

The goals and purpose of a nonprofit differ significantly. While a for-profit organization focuses on selling a product or service, a nonprofit fulfills a community need. Publishing houses as well as companies such as Amazon seek your business and discretionary income, whether it is for physical or electronic books and resources. Dolly Parton's Imagination Library, a nonprofit organization focused on promoting love of reading and catalyzing children's literacy, provides a book a month free of charge to all children born in the state of Tennessee from birth through age five. While one could argue that publishing houses and Amazon also want to promote literacy, the reality is that *selling* books and other reading materials to strengthen their profits takes priority over promoting literacy—only those who can afford to purchase the books and other reading materials have access to increasing their literacy and love of reading. In the last 20 years, for-profit organizations have attempted to blur these lines. When someone mentions TOMS® Shoes, what is the first thing that comes to mind? If you said that they provide a pair of shoes to someone in need for every pair they sell, you can see how the line between for-profit and nonprofit missions becomes more difficult to distinguish. While they have this philanthropic aspect to their business, that cannot exist without charging enough for their shoes to keep the business and charitable giving possible.

Funding

Whereas for-profit organizations develop a business plan and go to the bank to take out a loan, or apply to appear on Shark Tank, where rich business people fund new start-ups for a percentage of the business, to start their organizations, nonprofit organizations often begin in people's homes on a minimal budget. Nonprofit organizations originate organically, are generally funded by "start-up" donations, and depend upon print, broadcast, and social media to promote themselves. If they are lucky, online retweets, shares, and likes as well as face-to-face word-of-mouth conversations also promote nonprofits. Sometimes nonprofits come into existence because a national organization paves the way by providing all of the non-financial resources such as materials, software, training, and name recognition. Name recognition alone can save a new nonprofit an immense amount of time getting the word out about their services. For example, the Rotary Club has over 35,000 locations (https://my.rotary.org/en), which means they have helped countless communities begin their own Rotary Clubs and can help local people interested in starting a rotary club to recognize youth leadership and promote clean drinking water for all. The new local club that someone begins does not have to develop processes for handing out leadership awards or helping students participate in educational exchange programs around the world because that work has already been done at the national and international level—all the new club has to do is raise the donations necessary to fulfill those parts of the organizational mission.

Feedback Processes and Audiences

Nonprofit organizations serve multiple audiences and they must be able to adapt their communication to meet those various audiences' needs. For example, internally, nonprofits have both their employees and volunteers; externally, they still have their volunteers who are part of the larger community, users of their products and services, donors and potential donors, followers and leaders in organizations with which they might ally. By continuing to purchase goods and services, followers and leaders receive direct feedback in their organizational settings. Because nonprofits have so many audiences, they must infer feedback. For example, Susan G. Komen (https://ww5.komen.org/) raises money to fight breast cancer every year. People can participate in local walks to raise funds or they can create their own fundraisers by asking people to make a contribution in one's name in lieu of flowers at a funeral; older couples getting married may also choose donations in lieu of wedding gifts. Organizational members must infer that these people are supporting the organization and them because it is possible that they feel more strongly about breast cancer than they do specifically about the Komen Foundation. Another way of thinking about the indirect nature of organizational feedback is that the for-profit receives direct feedback every time their organic fruits and vegetables sell at the local grocery store; the nonprofit receives indirect feedback when they grow and distribute organic vegetables to people in need and then must make the pitch to potential donors that supporting their efforts to feed the poor are worthy of one's charitable dollars.

Goodwill Reigns Supreme

Nonprofit organizations must depend upon the goodwill they create in the community to remain viable. **Goodwill** refers to behaviors perceived as compassionate, other-serving, and generous. Donations alone will not sustain nonprofits over the long haul. They must build goodwill among members of the community to ensure they continue to have people who utilize their services, volunteer to sustain the organization's mission, and donors who monetarily support those services. Children's lemonade stands illustrate how goodwill can break down over time. The first time you drive home and see a child selling lemonade to help provide drinking water for victims of a natural disaster, you will probably stop and buy a glass, even if you do not typically drink lemonade. You do it to support the child and the cause. You may even stop and buy lemonade for the next few days. By week two or three, the child still has goodwill because the cause's importance has not changed; however, people are not going to continue buying lemonade because the leadership is not building goodwill in the community by encouraging children in other neighborhoods (the volunteers or followers) to set up similar lemonade stands. There is no diversification—people can only drink or pour down the sink so much lemonade and we quickly forget about the victims of natural disaster—so our affinity for donating to that cause also wanes.

Leadership and Followership Roles

We have talked extensively about how people engage in role switching between leadership and followership behaviors depending upon the context. In nonprofit organizations, the leadership and followership roles are even more fluid than they are in other organizational structures. For example, a chief executive officer (CEO) in a for-profit organization is replaced with a board of directors in a nonprofit organization. The board is composed of people who all support the organization's mission even though they may be doing it for different reasons. The local face of the organization must carry out the board's wishes as best as possible—is this person performing leadership or followership behaviors? To answer this question, think about what distinguishes leaders and followers. Who drives the nonprofit's vision in this case? The person who is the organization's face is also the leader. If it is the board, they serve as a collective leader and the face of the organization serves as a follower. In cases where the board's role is almost exclusively one of fund raising, the face of the organization is more likely to be the leader and the board, while the employees and volunteers serve as followers.

Federal Status

All organizations, both for-profit and nonprofit, must file annual income taxes even though the nonprofits do not have to provide a portion of their revenue to the government in the form of income taxes. Donating money to a nonprofit may result in a tax deduction as long as the organization is registered as charitable (Note: stay tuned as this distinction may be changing as the current tax codes change). Not all nonprofits are registered as charitable and as such your donations may not be tax deductible. For example, the American Civil Liberties Union, Democratic and Republican National Committees, and purchasing tickets for children of fallen soldiers or first responders to attend an event are not tax deductible. Even though these are all honorable causes, they do not qualify as charitable.

Organizational Culture

Values drive an organization's culture. Whereas a for-profit's primary value is long-term sustainability through profits and innovation, a nonprofit's primary value is service to others. Nonprofits are more likely to have **clan cultures** where organizational members operate similar to a family in a friendly work environment; people create long-term bonds with others, and leaders and followers focus on mentoring, team-building, and facilitative behaviors. Some nonprofits also operate as **person cultures** where the individual members are more important than the organization; as such, there are few hierarchical layers with most members operating as equals. In person cultures, how employees, volunteers, and the larger community are treated is of critical importance.

Followers, Leaders, and Volunteers

While some for-profit organizations have volunteers as part of their workforce, the number of volunteers required to operate the organization is a small percentage of the total workforce. For example, if you were potentially interested in medicine, you may have volunteered or interned at a hospital to gain experience. On the other hand, many nonprofit organizations cannot operate successfully without their volunteers or interns. For example, think about the public library in your community. Most U.S. libraries are part of the county government system and operate on a shoestring budget. Because of their limited resources, they must depend upon volunteers who are willing to check in/out and shelve books, catalog donated books, and run book sales that fund the purchase of new titles for the library. If people stopped donating their previously read books to sell them at used bookstores or online, then public libraries would have a difficult time continuing to operate with current materials for people to read, view, and use for research. Donations combined with volunteer workforces distinguish nonprofit organizations.

FIGURE 10.2   The number of volunteers in an organization grows as long as the leaders and paid followers continue to treat the volunteers with respect.

Power Bases

Throughout the text, we have talked about reward and coercive power; while they are not the ideal power bases for most leaders to use for long-term success in for-profit organizations, their effectiveness is even more limited in nonprofit and volunteer-rich organizations. Volunteers are tied to the nonprofit primarily by their belief in its vision, mission, and values and can continue to support those principles without necessarily volunteering in the organization. For example, consider someone who volunteers at Khan Academy, a nonprofit organization helping to educate Kindergarten through 12th-grade students with learning modules. If the person decided that Khan Academy were espousing views with which the individual did not agree (e.g., evolution, content included in or excluded from American History, etc.), it would be easy to leave the organization and begin volunteering elsewhere (e.g., a literacy group, the Boys and Girls Clubs, a museum's educational programming, or even with the Boy Scouts or Girl Scouts). Thus, if a leader chooses to utilize coercive power or withhold rewards, then the volunteers can more easily choose not to continue their relationship with the nonprofit—it is not their means of income/survival and they are likely to be able to find additional organizations where their volunteer talents can be put to good use. People who volunteer in nonprofit organizations are generally more internally motivated; they are committed to the cause more than to the organization. Thus, they need to be treated well, find that referent power is significantly more effective than either reward or coercive power, and thanked for their service.

Tensions in the Staff–Volunteer Relationship

Both volunteers and paid staff generally choose nonprofit organizations for intrinsic rather than extrinsic reasons. **Intrinsic reasons** for choosing a particular workplace or volunteer organization reflect people's internal motivations to succeed; these may include satisfaction with helping others, championing a cause, or even increasing one's sense of belonging to something that is bigger than they are. As long as these internal motivations remain, the staff member or volunteer is likely to continue with the organization. If and when those motivations are replaced by extrinsic reasons (e.g., pay so that one can meet safety or security needs) or conflict, people's intentions to leave the organization and their choice to actually leave the organization increase. Rimes et al. (2017) identify four aspects of conflict that can decrease satisfaction and increase turnover.

- **Different Expectations**: With different obligations and functions within the organization, paid staff and volunteers can have different perceptions of each other's roles or how the work should be accomplished.

- **Behavioral and/or Emotional Differences**: Volunteers and paid staff may create in-groups and out-groups that negatively impact their relationships. They may also view organizational and personal politics, infighting, or the pressure of being part of the organization as creating conflict.

- **Position Security**: Paid staff may feel they need to exert themselves and strengthen their position within the organization to justify the amount of money the organization is paying them. They may also experience conflict if they believe the organization is attempting to operate with more volunteers and cut paid positions to save money. Even though they are volunteers, conflict can arise if they believe the paid staff do not value them and are attempting to minimize their role in the organization. It can become a vicious cycle of paid staff and volunteers each trying to assert their necessity to the organization that results in continual conflict. Both types of positions are necessary and need to operate harmoniously for effective organizational functioning.

- **Communication Issues**: Inadequate or ineffective communication in nonprofit organizations may magnify conflicts because of the paid staff-volunteer relationship. Volunteers often feel as if they do not receive enough information, do not have clear role expectations or goals, and must guess if they are doing a good job because there is little feedback.

Communicating Competently With Volunteers

Whereas leaders tend to communicate with employees in for-profit organizations, both leaders and followers find themselves communicating with volunteers as they become an additional level in the organization's functioning. Some organizational paid followers find themselves taking on leadership roles without being well trained to do them. Becoming a competent communicator prior to entering the nonprofit organization serves both leaders and followers well. Poor relationships with people in the organization, lack of support, and ineffective professional interactions are primary reasons volunteers leave (Brodie et al., 2011).

Think back to your own experiences as a volunteer if it were required as part of your high-school education, religious missionary work, or personal fulfillment. If you do not have volunteer experience, think about the first time you entered a new organization where you were both the newest and lowest on the organizational chart. If leaders and paid staff treated you as if you were dispensable and could be replaced at any moment, then you were less likely to remain committed to the organization and its goals or purpose. When employees or leaders in these organizations take the time to get to know you—what catalyzed you to volunteer (your why) with this particular organization (perhaps it was their mission), and what you hope to achieve while you are there—they are in a better position to support you and adapt their messages to better meet your needs and expectations. Additionally, acting ethically in these organizations generally follows the outcome ethical perspectives: utilitarianism, epicureanism, and altruism. Nonprofits are generally geared toward providing benefit for others (utilitarianism and altruism) and many volunteers find themselves choosing to participate in nonprofits for their own tranquility and benefit (epicureanism); thus, these three ethical approaches are consistent with their missions and values.

While communicating competently is convenient shorthand for how leaders and followers should interact with volunteers, what does that mean in practice? First, it means there should be at least one person or small group of people responsible for serving as liaison between volunteers and paid staff (Rimes et al., 2017). Volunteers need to understand their roles in the organization and have someone to whom they can turn when conflict seems to be arising. Similarly, paid staff need to understand how volunteers believe they fit into the organizational structure. Second, it means making sure that everyone, both volunteers and paid staff, are prepared to communicate with diverse others. Because people with visible (e.g., diminished sight or physical)

and invisible disabilities (e.g., chronic or recurring illness, sensory processing, diminished hearing), or other differences (e.g., English as their second language, cultural or generational differences) may choose to work, volunteer, or utilize services of a nonprofit organization, everyone involved needs to be capable of interacting with these diverse others. Third, volunteers and paid staff need to have time to build relationships and trust if they are going to be working together long-term: it would be the difference between people who are there for a one-time event or transition and people who are an integral part of the organization's functioning. Communicating competently can diffuse the potential for conflict and promote amicable relationships.

Building Partnerships

To survive, nonprofit organizations need to form partnerships with the community around them as well as potential funding sources. Nonprofits need to connect with potential donors, service users, and people to serve on their board of directors; communication is a critical component of building these relationships. In today's multimedia world, being able to utilize social media strategically moves from desirable to required. Both followers and leaders need to engage in these relationship-building processes.

Collaborating With Others

Nonprofits often find themselves collaborating with for-profit corporations as sponsors for events. While these partnerships are beneficial, they are primarily one-sided (the nonprofit benefits from the monetary infusion) and short-term (when the event ends, the partnership ends, sometimes until the next year when the event is held again). Two emerging forms of collaboration involve nonprofits working with volunteer cadres (Follman et al., 2016) and skills-based volunteers (Letts & Holly, 2017).

Volunteer cadres are groups of people who agree together to help multiple organizations. Unlike traditional volunteers, they develop their own organizational culture and build relationships among the volunteers before entering a nonprofit organization. Anyone is free to participate in the cadre and choose with which nonprofits to collaborate. Because the volunteers already know each other before arriving at the nonprofit, they can more efficiently complete the necessary tasks. Similarly, they have likely engaged in these tasks at another nonprofit. Athletic teams on many college campuses could constitute volunteer cadres. For example, the women's basketball team may work together to build a house for Habitat for Humanity one week, run a skills clinic for the Boys and Girls Clubs another week, and serve as grand marshals for a local parade another week. Because the team members already have familiarity with each other and know how to work together, much of the time spent on getting to know each other at a volunteer site or trying to determine the best way to accomplish the task is minimized.

Not all volunteer cadres must be intact groups or teams. Envision a future where people interested in volunteering locally sign up with an agency. Imagine a volunteer version of Kelly Services, Randstad, or Adecco where volunteers complete a profile with the types of volunteering they are interested in doing, their availability to volunteer, and how far they are willing to travel to volunteer. A volunteer coordinator would then be responsible for assigning groups or teams of volunteers to meet specific needs of local nonprofits. One week, they may be helping at a national park with educational programming; another week they may be handing out water during a half marathon benefitting a local charity; and another week, they may be trying out new messaging strategies for the local United Way. These types of volunteer cadres build comradery and cohesion by working together on multiple projects; they become committed to each other and the volunteer organizations for which they are working. From the nonprofit's perspective, it allows them to request volunteers who have worked with their staff before and begin solidifying the follower-volunteer relationships.

Skills-Based Volunteering occurs when for-profit or educational organizations partner with nonprofits to provide a specific set of needed services with the goal of teaching followers and volunteers in the nonprofit how to do the task in the future. It follows the adage of "Give a poor person a fish and the person is fed for a day. Teach a poor person to fish and the person is fed for life." Because nonprofits may not need a particular skill set continuously, they do not want to hire someone to perform the task, so they bring in volunteers from another organization to help them do it. Skills-based volunteering is not designed for simple tasks and is most appropriate when the nonprofit is being proactive. Many partnerships between nonprofits and for-profits are reactionary in nature or allow the outside organization to dictate what it provides to the nonprofit (this is sometimes referred to as *pro bono* work). Lawyers and their firms as well as medical personnel are often portrayed in the media as providing free legal or medical services for local nonprofits. These services are *pro bono* because they come free of charge and what services are going to be provided are determined by the providers.

Unlike *pro bono* work, skills-based volunteering involves determining what the nonprofit will need in the short- and long-term. Generally, these needs are complex (how to engage in strategic planning) rather than basic (creating a spreadsheet of all volunteers and their skills). Because the non-profit drives the skills-based volunteering, they must be proactive, strategic, and possess both employee and volunteer buy-in for participation. When the consulting, educational, or for-profit organization chooses its lead, they must choose someone who is committed to making the nonprofit stronger and not someone who is looking for a day away from the office or a new line to add to one's résumé. Instead of a flash, one-day visit to the nonprofit, skills-based volunteering involves spending concentrated time (possibly up to a week) in the nonprofit. As the skills-based volunteers are helping the nonprofit address their challenge, they are also helping followers, leaders, and volunteers develop skills to approach similar challenges in the future. Both *pro bono* and skills-based volunteering benefit nonprofit organizations.

Social Media Usage

While the first nonprofit websites are nearly 30 years old, the .org web extension (used almost exclusively for nonprofits) is among the most used and trusted behind .com (reserved for for-profit organizations), .net (purchasable by anyone), and three others unique to different countries (Germany, China, and United Kingdom) (https://iwantmyname.com/blog/top-10-global-domain-extensions-statistics-numbers). Fundraising, building relationships with various stakeholders, and raising awareness about the organization's mission occur at unprecedented levels on social media. This trend is likely to increase, rather than decrease, over the next decade. Social media are an inexpensive way to reach service users, potential volunteers and paid staff, organizations with which to partner, and donors/funding agencies. Like all forms of communication, this can be a double-edged sword: because it is so easy to push a message out, organizations and their members sometimes forget to stop and think about the ethical and long-term reputation implications of those messages (see Table 10.1 for a list of social media errors nonprofits make).

When working with social media, organizations benefit from having social media policies in place. These policies serve to make sure everyone involved (leaders, boards of directors, followers/paid staff, and volunteers) behave ethically when engaging with others on the platform. Of the nonprofits examined that had social media policies, they highlighted the following aspects of social media usage (Gilstrap & Minchow-Proffitt, 2017).

- **Engagement:** Statements that help people interact with others on social media. Sample phrases might include "Talk to your audiences and let them talk to and about you" and "Build relationships."

- **Responsibility:** Statements that help people interact with respect and restraint. Sample phrases might include "The creation and maintenance of these channels requires forethought, care, and responsibility"; "Content should be as accurate and reliable as possible"; or "Be careful to brand your affiliate properly."

- **Privacy:** Statements that ensure everyone's public image is meant for public consumption. Sample phrases might include: "Keep personal information private" and "Use of audio, photos, and video requires a signed consent form."

TABLE 10.1   Top Mistakes Nonprofits Make on Social Media

Reason	Example
Using the wrong approach for the medium	People turn to Instagram for pleasing images to escape the moment and look to other sources for hard news. They want to like images and find it difficult to like images of tragedies.
Using so many platforms that none of them is done well	Each form of social media has its own language, culture, and target audience. Organizations err when they try to use all of the different social media without unique, specific strategies. Choosing one or two social media that can be done well and strategically utilizes resources effectively and efficiently. People who want to find and follow the organization will go searching for it.
Not engaging with followers	Nonprofits thrive on likes, shares, and follows. If people in the organization are not willing to respond when someone posts a comment, then people will quickly stop posting comments, eliminating the opportunity to engage, and likely stop following or sharing.
"Knot Spell Chekking"	Even though abbreviations and shorthand are an important component of social media, people are still turned off by poor spelling and grammar. People do pay attention and may perceive that an organization is not worth their time and attention if they cannot spell- or grammar-check their messages. Mistakes happen, but they need to be minimized by having multiple eyes for visual posts and ears for oral/video posts.
Boring posts	Each year Villanova University does an 1842 one-day fundraising campaign. 1842 is the year the school was founded. Prior to September 18th (1842 Day), they send out the following tweets: "One month until 1842 Day"; "One week until 1842 Day"; "1842 Day is tomorrow"; and "1842 Day starts now!" There is nothing engaging about these text-based posts. How much stronger would their campaign be with a video of last year's donations being used, a testimonial from a student or community member who benefitted from one of those donations; a competition chart breaking down the previous year's top donors by college on campus or graduation year; and one text-based message? Each of those could still carry the #1842Day. Giving people similar information in multiple ways will keep them engaged.

Adapted from Ibele, (2018).

- **Protection:** Statements that minimize negative consequences. Sample statements might include: "In all cases, employees or volunteers should respect applicable law, including copyright and trademark laws" and we do "not seek to limit the rights of individuals to communicate in a free and open manner, however certain materials and language will not be tolerated … such as libelous, defamatory, false, obscene, indecent, lewd, violent, abusive, threatening, harassing, discriminatory behavior, in violation of the law of that constitutes hate speech."

- **Transparency:** Statements that keep a nonprofit and its members real in the eyes of others. Sample statements include "Build trust by being open and transparent" or "employees and volunteers … [should] state facts accurately and cite appropriate sources."

- **Respect:** Statements that likely represent the "Treat others as you want to be treated" adage. Sample statements might include: "Be courteous", "Employees and volunteers may not use slurs, personal insults or obscenity"; and "The tone should not be overly informal or use slang, jargon, profanity."

Even though social media are a lifeline for many today, they are diminishing our attention spans and turning people off rather than invigorating them. Decreased attention spans mean that nonprofits must grab and maintain their followers' attention. Today's nonprofits operate both globally and locally; knowing which social media to use where is critical to success. For example, based upon number of subscribers, Facebook, and its Reddit counterpart, remains the social media king in Africa, Asia, and North America; however, email subscribers are critical in Australia/Oceania, Europe, and South America (Global NGO Technology Report, 2018).

Creating, Communicating, and Living a Vision

In chapters 2 and 3, we talked about theoretical approaches to leadership. In this chapter, we are going to get down to the nuts and bolts of what it means to live as a leader—everyone interested in adopting this mindset can become a leader to those around them. Dudley, who was a college student in Canada, forwarded this perspective. On orientation day, he made an exaggerated Harry Potter-like hat (twice the size) and took a friend with him to hand out lollipops to new students. Parents and their college-bound children walked nervously on campus. He described himself as peacocking (strutting one's stuff ostentatiously) the way twenty-something males are prone to do. As one nervous woman and her parents walked by, he asked the man next to him to "give this beautiful woman a lollipop" and when she took it, Dudley said to the parents, "First day away from home and already she is taking candy from a stranger." The laughter that ensued set everyone at ease. The parents and their new college student went on to other orientation activities and Dudley continued handing out lollipops.

FIGURE 10.3   Lollipops add smiles to people's faces with their bright colors and long-lasting flavors.

When he graduated, the young woman who received the lollipop came up to him to thank him for his generosity. Because of that one interaction, she decided to stay on campus rather than returning home with her parents that day; her fear had been significantly reduced. Why did the simple gesture of giving someone a lollipop have such a profound impact on her life? Because turnabout is fair play; her comment back to Dudley had a profound impact on his view of leadership. Leadership, according to Dudley, "fundamentally, is identifying and living what you want to stand for on a daily basis. I think most of us hope to matter. I think hoping to matter isn't leadership. My type of leadership is saying, 'Don't let days go by where all you did was be here. Don't be reactive. Actually plan to matter.'"

Dudley's view of leadership fits perfectly with how nonprofit followers and leaders create a vision of how they are going to matter in the lives of others and live that vision every day. If nonprofit organizational members bought into his philosophy, they would have to engage in more of those "lollipop" moments instead of sitting behind their desks and computer screens every day. As a group, the nonprofit would have to determine what organizational values support the mission and vision they want to enact each and every day. Think about it this way: if someone followed you around for a month and observed all of your interactions (with potential donors, service users, volunteers, and coworkers) to do a feature story for the local news on your nonprofit, what three values would they say you and your nonprofit stand for—how close would they be able to get? From that list of values, each member would choose one (starting with just one is plenty) and consciously think about how to enact that value. Now that you have chosen the value, create a question that requires you to DO something each day to demonstrate you are living the value. For example, if your value is respecting diverse others, the question you ask each day might be "How did I make someone feel welcome or included today?"

Dudley's perspective is consistent with the advice offered for future nonprofit leaders (Matsushita, 2017). Her recommendations for the competencies future leaders need include:

- Build strong adaptive nonprofit organizations with clear missions and values.

- Anticipate and embrace change by understanding the dynamics at work in the environment around you.

- Support the growth and development of others by being resilient in a changing environment.

- Tell the organization's story early and often to establish the nonprofit's identity for the outside world.

- Be willing to innovate and take reasonable risks to reduce uncertainty.

- Serve as the connector between the nonprofit by building relationships with others.

- Be a responsible steward of the nonprofit's resources.

Why would these competencies only be necessary for leaders? Couldn't followers and volunteers also benefit from possessing the competencies listed?

The concept is a powerful one that you will likely never see in another textbook and the reason is because it is not based upon the rational models of leadership so prevalent in our society. The concept relies upon emotional intelligence, actively adapting to the environment around you, and behaving ethically, especially from an ethic of care advanced by those focused on character and individual actors. If you like what you are reading, check out this TedTalk on everyday leadership (https://www.ted.com/talks/drew_dudley_everyday_leadership?language=en#t-50708).

RESEARCH SUMMARY

Study: Buse et al. (2016) set out to study the relationships among diversity, inclusion, governance practices, policies, and effectiveness for nonprofit boards. Most nonprofit organizations have a board of directors that oversees the organization's functioning. Almost all of the board members

(continued)

come from outside the organization and support the nonprofit's mission and values. They are also among the many donors who keep a nonprofit organization functioning. Given that many, especially group and team scholars, have argued more diversity leads to better decision making and team functioning, this study examined the ways in which age, racial, and sexual (number of males and females) diversity as well as inclusion behaviors impacted governance practices. They hypothesized positive relationships between diversity and governance practices as well as between inclusion behaviors and governance practices. They completed a secondary analysis using data collected by Boardsource as part of their biannual survey. For this study, the researchers analyzed data provided by over 1400 CEOs who have fundraising as a primary part of their mission. Results indicated that board membership diversity, inclusion behaviors, and diversity policies positively impact effective governance; age, race, and sex diversity positively impact the creation and implementation of diversity policies; and the relationship between governance practices and racial diversity is complex and a function of other factors such as policies, behaviors, and practices.

Implications: Simply placing diverse people on boards because of their diversity is not going to guarantee effective governance. When composing nonprofit boards, the creators need to ensure that the diverse members genuinely represent diverse views, can express those views, and other board members are willing to listen and seriously consider diverse views. Creating diversity policies and procedures for organizational and board functioning is one step toward maximizing the benefit of having a diverse board. Another step is to train nominating committees to look beyond simple outward appearance diversity to garner the benefits of creating a board composed of diversity of thought. Finally, strengthen the nonprofit's culture regarding inclusion behaviors so diverse viewpoints are seen as the norm rather than the exception.

4D Model of Followership and Leadership

The 4D model of followership and leadership is a useful resource for non-profits to assess how followers and leaders interact and react to stressors within an organizational setting. According to Adair (2008), there are four categories of behavior (disciple, doer, disengaged, and disgruntled), reflecting how followers and leaders think and feel about an organization and their position within it. These four categories specify the general focus (or source), attitude, and type of involvement associated with each behavior. Unlike personality, 4D behaviors are not enduring or fixed traits. Followers and leaders may naturally gravitate toward demonstrating disciple or doer behaviors, and at times cross over to enact the other for some length of time; however, when stress rises, leaders' or followers' behavior will move from the natural quadrants of disciple or doer (quadrant I or II) to a stress quadrant (quadrant III or IV) behavior, disengaged or disgruntled (Adair, 2008). This is depicted in Table 10.2, along with ways in which these behaviors can shape leaders' and followers' expressions relative to their preferred DISC communication style.

TABLE 10.2   4D Followership and DISC

DISC Style	4D Followership & Leadership Model		DISC Style
Driver: What outcome is the bare minimum? ——————▶			**Driver:** What outcome will help me avoid this place entirely? ◀——————
Influencer: How can I do the least amount while working with others? ——————▶	**III Disengaged** (Passive or apathetic reaction to stress)	**IV Disgruntled** (Active reaction to stress)	**Influencer:** How can I delegate my responsibilities to others? ◀——————
Supporter: Who will help me complete tasks? ——————▶	"Do the job to keep job." Uninvested	"Anyplace is better than here." Avoidant (or neglectful)	**Supporter:** Who cares? ◀——————
Contemplator: Why do this in this way? ——————▶			**Contemplator:** Why am I still here? Why do this? ◀——————
Driver: What outcome is best for us? ——————▶			**Driver:** What is the best outcome for my resumé? ◀——————
Influencer: How can we work together better? ——————▶	**I Disciple** (Serving others' needs)	**II Doer** (Serving own needs)	**Influencer:** How can I use work with others for personal gain? ◀——————
Supporter: Who will contribute to our success? ——————▶	"Our work is the best of the best." Fully committed	"Grass is always greener." Invested	**Supporter:** Who will benefit? ◀——————
Contemplator: Why are our efforts more successful than others? ——————▶			**Contemplator:** Why is this important for me? ◀——————

4D quadrants and involvement type adapted from Adair (2008) and Gilstrap & Morris (2015).

The first quadrant, **disciple behavior**, refers to focusing on serving the needs of others while conveying a high interest in pursuing tasks and goals, buying into the organization's mission (and/or vision), and seeing one's personal efforts as valuable to (or valued by) the organization. This includes followers and leaders who are engaged, productive, and motivated to stay with the organization for an extended period of time. The source or focus of this behavior is a drive to serve the needs of others. People enacting disciple behavior maintain the general attitude that this organization is home, where they belong, and they go above and beyond to help the collective fulfill the organization's mission. As such, the disciple behavior is associated with a fully committed type of involvement. Fully committed involvement includes consistently and actively adapting efforts, taking on either followership and/or leadership duties to complete what needs to be done, and showing consistent motivation to be (or become) a leader within the organization.

Second, leaders and followers who are motivated and productive but always looking for the next best opportunity reflect the doer behavior. **Doer behavior** refers to focusing on serving one's own needs while demonstrating an interest in pursuing tasks and goals, buying into the organization's mission at one's own benefit, and believing personal efforts are valuable to (or valued by) the organization. Because doers are first and foremost concerned with their own personal mission and vision, their buy-in to the organization's mission is slightly less than that of disciples. It is having the gumption to get things done that will benefit the organization, second to benefiting one's own endeavors. The general attitude of doer behavior is the grass is always greener, which is reflected in a hard-work ethic, competitive nature, and continuous propensity to update one's résumé. This behavior is associated with an invested involvement, that is, there is a clear personal investment, a motivation to aid in attaining organizational goals, and the flexibility to assume leader roles or duties when other leaders are not available. Whether serving the needs of others or serving one's own needs, disciple and doer behaviors are proactive, whereas disengaged and disgruntled behaviors are reactive.

The focus of the third and final 4D behaviors, disengaged and disgruntled, direct attention to leaders' and followers' reactions to stress rather than natural tendencies. **Stress** means experiencing mental, emotional, or physical strain or tension; it does not always equate to or require crisis to occur. Just as any employee or volunteer, nonprofit followers' and leaders' behaviors are susceptible to experiencing stress aroused by competing demands (professional, financial, or personal) at the individual level. However, nonprofit employees (and volunteers) are particularly prone to experiencing stress caused by relational aspects of the work environment, specifically a lack of perceived support (Knapp et al., 2017). Perceptions of insufficient organizational support diminish one's beliefs in the organization; chronic stressors lead to burnout.

Burnout is described as mental, physical, and/or emotional exhaustion resulting in disengagement and lack of personal accomplishment (Olinske & Hellman, 2017), such as when a someone becomes disengaged. As a passive (apathetic) reaction to stress, **disengaged behavior** involves being disinterested in pursuing tasks and goals, not buying into the organization's mission (and/or vision), but still believing one's personal efforts are valuable to (or valued by) the organization. Perceiving little to no value in an organization's mission or vision yet maintaining some minimum level of value in keeping one's position or activity results in the half-hearted attitude of disengaged behavior—doing just enough to keep the job. This behavior is associated with an uninvested involvement. Uninvested involvement may include making donations or donating the least amount of effort and time necessary to complete tasks without being a reliable member.

The final 4D behavior, disgruntled behavior, is typically based in thoughts and feelings of being wronged (rejected, subbed, devalued, etc.). Unlike the passive reaction to stress seen in the disengaged behavior, **disgruntled behavior** is an *active* reaction to stress referring to the act of being highly disinterested in pursuing tasks and goals, not buying into the organization's mission (or vision), and believing one's personal efforts and the organization have little to no value to one another. The general attitude of this behavior is: any place is better than here. Disgruntled behavior is associated with avoidant (or neglectful) involvement, which is enacted through a tendency to evade, abandon, or discredit one's own or others' efforts and those of the organization.

A primary difference between behaviors in natural and stress quadrants is the visibility of leaders' and followers' degree of passion and motivation in their activity. Regulatory fit theory explains why leaders and followers may move from behaviors in the natural quadrants to behaviors in the stress quadrants. More specifically, regulatory fit theory helps identify leaders' and followers' motivation orientation and assess the level of motivation orientation involvement based on the degree to which the way people pursue tasks and goals (valence of behavior) fits with their personal beliefs and values. There are two motivation orientations guiding peoples' behavior: promotion-focus and prevention-focus. When leaders or followers assume a **promotion-focus** motivation orientation, they are interested (passionate or eager) in pursuing tasks and goals to promote positive outcomes in terms of achieving hopes, wishes, and aspirations (Higgins, 2000, 2005). By contrast, leaders or followers who assume a **prevention-focus** motivation orientation seek to prevent negative outcomes concerning their duties, obligations, and responsibilities while being disinterested (apathetic or unconcerned) in pursuing tasks and goals.

Losing sight of the organization's mission (and/or vision) while holding on to one's work motivated by a sense of duty, obligation, or responsibility negatively impacts nonprofit functioning in terms of recruiting, fundraising, and morale. Burnout (exhaustion and lack of personal accomplishment) coupled with a lack of organizational support create disgruntled behavior. Burnout experienced by leaders who feel a lack of organizational support (e.g., supportive board of directors) to offer resources or support (e.g., leadership development) to others (followers or volunteers) become fed up feeling incapable and unmotivated to perform duties, obligations, or responsibilities. When leaders, followers, or volunteers reach this point, they feel ineffective and take on a dysfunctional attitude (Olinske & Hellman, 2017). They are no longer driven to prevent, but to instead promote negative outcomes related to their duties, obligations, and responsibilities. As a result, disgruntled behavior leads to termination or voluntarily quitting, thus emphasizing the high turnover intentions and turnover rates of nonprofits (Knapp et al., 2017). This holds true to the predictions made by the 4D followership and leadership model and shows how regulatory fit theory can be used as a resource for understanding followers' or leaders' motivation to contribute to nonprofit organizations.

Organizational Information Theory

Originally forwarded and tested by Karl Weick (1979), the heart of organizational information theory is that organizations are process- rather than structurally driven; that is, how information flows within a dynamic organization. OIT seeks to reduce ambiguity and complexity from organizational functioning and messages. As information-rich environments, nonprofits benefit from adopting Weick's perspective. **Organizational information theory (OIT)** involves the ways in which nonprofits and other entities collect, manage, use, and repackage the data they collect. Ideally, the repackaging process minimizes the opportunities for misunderstanding and equivocality. .

Reducing equivocality or ambiguity is a three-step process that includes enactment, selection, and retention. **Enactment** occurs when organizational members bring their past experiences to bear on the situation as they try to create and attach meaning to a new experience. Attaching meaning is an iterative process of trial and error until an acceptable meaning is achieved. **Selection** involves further evaluating the available information to continue reducing ambiguity and determining what additional information is necessary to minimize ambiguity. While traditional organizations may leave this step to their leaders, nonprofits allow everyone involved to participate in selection. Finally, **retention** encompasses the long-term storage of information that the nonprofit deems important to adapting to their environment and reducing opportunities for misunderstanding. Any information deemed tangential or unnecessary is discarded in favor of more useful information.

Just as Weick believes the gap between theory and practice disappears when using this theory (Langenberg & Wesseling, 2016), nonprofit organizations find the gap between their organization and the outside environment dissolving around them. As they create messages appropriate for their various stakeholders (service users, donors, volunteers, members of the Board of Directors, community government), they must engage in trial and error processes to determine how they can help each group attach the intended meaning to their messages. Because these people are bombarded with continuous messages every minute of every day, they can often experience information overload and fatigue. The easier a nonprofit makes it for them by reducing ambiguity and equivocality, the more likely they are to act upon and store the information for future retrieval.

CASE STUDY   **Roman Catholic Church**

The Roman Catholic Church, or Catholic Church as it's more commonly referred to in the U.S., is one of the largest and oldest religious institutions today. Structurally, the Catholic Church has levels of leadership: The Pope, based in Vatican City, Italy, oversees all Catholic ministries around the world; Archbishops oversee a geographical region composed of multiple bishops; the episcopate are bishops who oversee a diocese of churches, priests lead an individual church parish; and diaconate oversee ministries carried out at individual churches. With the exception of the Pope, each of these layers is both a leader and follower. Like other nonprofit organizations, the Catholic Church relies upon volunteers to carry out their ministries (working with youth, taking care of the sick and homebound, religious education, aiding the poor, etc.). What makes this organization unique in many ways is that they also have a congregation of followers who do not fit into the typical organizational structure and still look to the leadership for vision and guidance on how to carry out that vision. Over the course of time, the Catholic Church has been criticized for its patriarchal approach that only allows men to become leaders and stance on birth control, homosexuality, and sanctity of marriage until death do them part.

Over the course of the last 30 years, the Catholic Church has been involved in a series of sexual abuse scandals dating back at least 50 years. For the purposes of this case, we are specifically focusing on the state of Pennsylvania. In August 2018, a grand jury released a report that details

(continued)

sexual abuse of minor children and how various bishops and priests covered up the abuse.

In 2002, at the height of the sexual abuse accusations, Pope John Paul sent the following letter (excerpted here for analysis purposes and available at http://w2.vatican.va/content/john-paul-ii/en/speeches/2002/april/documents/hf_jp-ii_spe_20020423_usa-cardinals.pdf) to the Cardinals, who are the second layer in the hierarchy and leaders of regional bishops.

"Dear Brothers,

1. Let me assure you first of all that I greatly appreciate the effort you are making to keep the Holy See, and me personally, informed regarding the complex and difficult situation which has arisen in your country in recent months. I am confident that your discussions here will bear much fruit for the good of the Catholic people of the United States ... Like you, I too have been deeply grieved by the fact that priests and religious, whose vocation it is to help people live holy lives in the sight of God, have themselves caused such suffering and scandal to the young. Because of the great harm done by some priests and religious, the Church herself is viewed with distrust, and many are offended at the way in which the Church's leaders are perceived to have acted in this matter. The abuse which has caused this crisis is by every standard wrong and rightly considered a crime by society; it is also an appalling sin in the eyes of God. To the victims and their families, wherever they may be, I express my profound sense of solidarity and concern.

2. It is true that a generalized lack of knowledge of the nature of the problem and also at times the advice of clinical experts led Bishops to make decisions which subsequent events showed to be wrong. You are now working to establish more reliable criteria to ensure that such mistakes are not repeated ...

3. The abuse of the young is a grave symptom of a crisis affecting not only the Church but society as a whole. It is a deep-seated crisis of sexual morality, even of human relationships, and its prime victims are the family and the young. In addressing the problem of abuse with clarity and determination, the Church will help society to understand and deal with the crisis in its midst. It must be absolutely clear to the Catholic faithful, and to the wider community, that Bishops and superiors are concerned, above all else, with the spiritual good of souls. People need to know that there is no place in the priesthood and religious life for those who would harm the young. They must know that Bishops and priests are totally committed to the fullness of Catholic truth on matters of sexual morality, a truth as essential to the renewal of the priesthood and the episcopate as it is to the renewal of marriage and family life ...

I beg the Lord to give the Bishops of the United States the strength to build their response to the present crisis upon the solid foundations of faith and upon genuine pastoral charity for the victims, as well as for the priests and the entire Catholic community in your country. And I ask Catholics to stay close to their priests and Bishops, and to support them with their prayers at this difficult time.

The peace of the Risen Christ be with you!"

Fast forward to 2018 and the Pope, Francis this time, is once again responding to issues surrounding the Catholic Church's sexual abuse and cover-up allegations.

Pope Francis responded to the grand jury findings with a 2000-word letter (available at https://www.washingtonpost.com/news/acts-of-faith/wp/2018/08/20/read-the-popes-letter-to-the-faithful-on-abuse-in-catholic-church/?noredirect=on&utm_term=.b22689d28f58) and excerpted here for analysis purposes.

"If one member suffers, all suffer together with it" (1 Corinthians 12:26). These words of Saint Paul forcefully echo in my heart as I acknowledge once more the suffering endured by many minors due to sexual abuse, the abuse of power and the abuse of conscience perpetrated by a significant number of clerics and consecrated persons. Crimes that inflict deep wounds of pain and powerlessness, primarily among the victims, but also in their family members and in the larger community of believers and non-believers alike. Looking back to the past, no effort to beg pardon and to seek to repair the harm done will ever be sufficient. Looking ahead to the future, no effort must be spared to create a culture able to prevent such situations from happening, but also to prevent the possibility of their being covered up and perpetuated. The pain of the victims and their families is also our pain, and so it is urgent that we once more reaffirm our commitment to ensure the protection of minors and of vulnerable adults.

1. If one member suffers … In recent days, a report was made public which detailed the experiences of at least a thousand survivors, victims of sexual abuse, the abuse of power and of conscience at the hands of priests over a period of approximately seventy years. Even though it can be said that most of these cases belong to the past, nonetheless as time goes on we have come to know the pain of many of the victims. We have realized that these wounds never disappear and that they require us forcefully to condemn these atrocities and join forces in uprooting this culture of death; these wounds never go away. The heart-wrenching pain of these victims, which cries out to heaven, was long ignored, kept quiet or silenced. But their outcry was more powerful than all the measures meant to silence it, or sought

(continued)

even to resolve it by decisions that increased its gravity by falling into complicity. The Lord heard that cry and once again showed us on which side he stands—With shame and repentance, we acknowledge as an ecclesial community that we were not where we should have been, that we did not act in a timely manner, realizing the magnitude and the gravity of the damage done to so many lives. We showed no care for the little ones; we abandoned them ...

2. ... all suffer together with it ...

The extent and the gravity of all that has happened requires coming to grips with this reality in a comprehensive and communal way. While it is important and necessary on every journey of conversion to acknowledge the truth of what has happened, in itself this is not enough. Today we are challenged as the People of God to take on the pain of our brothers and sisters wounded in their flesh and in their spirit. If, in the past, the response was one of omission, today we want solidarity, in the deepest and most challenging sense, to become our way of forging present and future history ... A solidarity that summons us to fight all forms of corruption, especially spiritual corruption ...

I am conscious of the effort and work being carried out in various parts of the world to come up with the necessary means to ensure the safety and protection of the integrity of children and of vulnerable adults, as well as implementing zero tolerance and ways of making all those who perpetrate or cover up these crimes accountable. We have delayed in applying these actions and sanctions that are so necessary, yet I am confident that they will help to guarantee a greater culture of care in the present and future. ...

May the Holy Spirit grant us the grace of conversion and the interior anointing needed to express before these crimes of abuse our compunction and our resolve courageously to combat them.

Francis
Vatican City, Aug. 20, 2018"
Acts of Faith newsletter

To make sure voices at all levels are heard in this matter, the quotations below come from members of the various congregations in Pennsylvania after finding out about the 300 priests who have been accused of engaging in inappropriate sexual behavior, primarily with minors.

At St. Ursula's near Pittsburgh, the priest took it upon himself to address the grand jury findings during his weekly mass: "he said that the responsibility for the various allegations rests with the people of the Catholic church. He added that the actions of his fellow priests and the church leadership are shameful. 'The revelations of this past week compel us to recognize the ways in which we've failed as Christians,' Adams said. His message to his parish was clear and simple: they need to confront the horrific abuse and recognize that the church exposed the most vulnerable people in the community to pain and suffering." (https://www.npr.org/2018/08/19/639997915/pennsylvania-priests-respond-to-abuse-report). The article went on to quote two parishioners with differing viewpoints:

- "It's part of life, the church is an organization like any other organization. It's going to have its problems. It draws from the world, so it draws from the problems of the world."

- "Things happen. It happened, it's over. We need to move on."

- "I just feel sorry for [the priests]. Because it happens in all religions. It's not just the Catholic. And they're bringing the Catholic out. And there's other people who are doing it."

- "I'm not gonna leave the church. I'll always be a Catholic. But my kids won't. My daughter especially. It's sad, it's really sad and I think a lot of people are going to leave."

On social media, people responded to the story when it broke in the Scranton area https://www.thetimes-tribune.com/news/bishop-defends-level-of-detail-scranton-diocese-disclosed-1.2375990):

- "The fact that [Bishop] Timlin and Cardinal Wuerl have not yet been formally dismissed and defrocked for their part in allowing these monsters to continue to rape and abuse the most defenseless members of their parishes is enough evidence for me to determine that those in the Vatican and in the hierarchy here in the US do NOT have the best interests in mind or heart for those that have been abused and those still being abused … its VERY clear that the Catholic Church leadership is completely in CYA mode still at this time from their LACK of action."

- "Gotta love the sheeple that got on the news tonight and said 'Hey, who doesn't have something bad in their past?' OMG, sheeple, we are talking sexual abuse of children. That is not acceptable no matter WHO you are. And, we are talking about clergy, bishops, archbishops, who look down on divorced parents—yet some of those very same clergy are the biggest hypocrites of all. As a divorced parent, I couldn't even sponsor my own kids at their confirmations. WISE UP! You don't need a building to say your prayers. And you don't have to PAY to have the Lord listen to you."

- "Without ANY doubt, the Church needs to make changes, and FAST! But I'm wondering what those changes should be?? The Church is such a huge, bureaucratic organization, where do you begin? Wait for direction from the

(continued)

Pope? Or should each Bishop just take the 'bull by the horns' and begin locally? I listened to Cardinal Dolan do a radio interview a few days ago. And he was adamant that the time is now to come clean regarding abuse cases. Get everything out in the open. (He gave a rather graphic analogy, that was spot on.) Really tragic that the many hard-working, holy priests are looked upon as potential abusers. Being thought of as pariahs."

DISCUSSION QUESTIONS

1. What similarities and differences do you see in the way Pope Francis responded today and the way the Pope John Paul responded after the early allegations? In what ways and to what extent do those responses reflect competent leadership?

2. What additional information would you want to know before drawing conclusions about what is happening today with regard to sexual abuse in the Catholic Church? What information might the media be withholding from the public? How might the media be using statistics to present a more negative picture of the situation?

3. The NPR article presents two sides of how members of the Catholic Church might respond. What other potential responses exist and how might people's roles in the Catholic Church impact their reactions?

ANALYSIS OPTIONS

A. As a religious organization, church members expect this to be a safe haven where they can reveal their greatest vulnerabilities and seek acceptance. You have been charged with training the diaconate and volunteers to be competent followers as well as leaders among the church members. Address how they may go about rebuilding the trust that has been lost.

B. Because this organization has almost exclusively men in positions of leadership and minimal numbers of women in followership roles, addressing issues of diversity and inclusion can be more difficult. How can the Catholic Church work to make all who identify as Catholic, regardless of their sex or sexuality, feel welcome and valued members of the organization?

C. As with many crisis situations, individuals on social media and the mainstream media are calling for the leaders to resign. If all who were directly involved in perpetrating and/or covering up the abuse were to resign, it would leave a significant void in an organization already struggling to attract enough people to address the organization's needs. Determine how the Catholic Church should choose and develop the next generation of leaders, followers, and volunteers.

ANALYSIS PROCESS

- Brainstorm a list of options for addressing the issue.

- Make a list of strengths and challenges for each of your brainstormed solutions.

- Choose the best solution for the issue.

- Develop an implementation plan for your chosen solution.

- Additional resources:

Rotary Site
https://tinyurl.com/mfg72sl

Pope Francis Letter
tiny.utk.edu/FCL10_4

Susan G. Komen Site
https://tinyurl.com/ycngbbka

PA Priests Respond
tiny.utk.edu/FCL10_5

Global Domain Names
tiny.utk.edu/FCL10_1

Scranton-area Response
tiny.utk.edu/FCL10_6

Everyday Leadership
tiny.utk.edu/FCL10_2

News Articles
tiny.utk.edu/FCL10_7

(continued)

Pope John Paul Letter
tiny.utk.edu/FCL10_3

News Articles
tiny.utk.edu/FCL10_8

News Articles
tiny.utk.edu/FCL10_9

News Articles
tiny.utk.edu/FCL10_12

News Articles
tiny.utk.edu/FCL10_10

News Articles
tiny.utk.edu/FCL10_13

News Articles
tiny.utk.edu/FCL10_11

 LEADER AND FOLLOWER DEVELOPMENT PRACTICES

1. Seek out someone who has your dream job and a community member
    involved with an issue that is important to you. Working in nonprofit
    organizations requires skills to effect changes that are not present in
    for-profit organizations (Weaver, 2017).

2. Pay attention to the idioms you prefer and how they downplay useful communication strategies that you may be avoiding, spend a day doing the antithesis of what you normally do (focus on tasks if you normally focus on relationships or listen if you normally talk the majority of the time), and be present in the moment instead of thinking about the past and future.

3. Make sure you, and everyone involved with the nonprofit organization, can name and define the vision, mission, values, and purpose.

4. Understand that your personal reputation and the reputation of your nonprofit are synonymous—you must live the vision and values of the nonprofit both personally and professionally (*Forbes* Nonprofit Council, 2018).

5. Because burnout is so prominent in nonprofits due to their life-changing missions, make sure everyone is cared for and has the time necessary to refuel (Burke, n.d.).

DISCUSSION QUESTIONS AND ACTIVITIES

1. Find someone you know who works or volunteers at a nonprofit organization. If you do not know anyone who does, use the halo you have as a student to request an informational interview with someone in the organization. Develop a set of questions that you would like answered about communication in the organization (make sure to collect information about all of the stakeholders discussed at the beginning of the chapter); relationships among leaders, followers (paid staff), and volunteers; and information about why people have chosen this particular nonprofit over others. Use the information in this chapter to analyze the strengths and places where they could improve.

2. Choose a nonprofit organization that you find interesting or one for which you might like to volunteer or work. Collect at least five messages from their website (and/or social media) that represent their communication with potential donors. Using what you know about persuasion and social influence, determine what they might do better to reach their potential donors.

3. One of your goals in life is to successfully lead a nonprofit organization. Based upon what you have learned, what steps should you be taking now to prepare yourself for this career path? How are those steps similar to and different from a for-profit leadership path?

4. If you completed the DISC analysis in chapter 1, go back to those results and see how accurately they represent how you believe you would

respond in the 4D model of followership. Looking at the model, where would you have placed yourself if you were not aware of your DISC results? Why? If they are the same, why do you think that is the case?

5. What could you, or a group to which you belong, do on campus to make others feel more included? What would it take to carry out such a plan? How do you think other students, faculty, staff, and administrators would respond to your efforts (their responses may be different)?

FIGURE CREDITS:

Fig. 10.1a: Source: https://pixabay.com/illustrations/brain-mind-psychology-idea-drawing-2062057/.

Fig. 10.1b: Source: https://pixabay.com/vectors/lungs-human-anatomy-bronchia-296392/.

Fig. 10.1c: Source: https://pixabay.com/vectors/ekg-electrocardiogram-heart-art-2069872/.

Fig. 10.2: Source: https://pixabay.com/photos/volunteers-hands-tree-grow-2729695/.

Table 10.1a: Source: https://pixabay.com/photos/mobile-phone-smartphone-keyboard-1917737/.

Fig. 10.3: Source: https://pixabay.com/vectors/lollipop-sweets-colorful-sugar-161512/.

CHAPTER 11

ORGANIZATIONS AROUND THE WORLD

"Cultural leaders are responding to a climate of fear and exclusion with visions of inclusiveness and balance."

—HILDE SCHWAB

"Who does not desire such a victory by which we shall join places in our Kingdom, so far divided by nature, and for which we shall set up trophies in another conquered world?"

—ALEXANDER THE GREAT

What makes leaders and followers competitive gladiators of organizations operating within multicultural, multinational, international, and global arenas is doing what they do and doing it well within their dome of influence in a given type of organizational arena. Unlike domestic organizations (companies that identify and reside in one country with little, *if any*, international interests), these four arenas cross beyond domestic boundaries and embrace cultural diversity. With the exception of multicultural organizations, the extent to which these four types of organizations invest and manage business internationally varies and can often easily be confused with one another (Stohl, 2001).

- A **Multicultural** organization identifies with the values of one country (nationality), but and recognizes the need for a diverse workforce and diverse contracts outside the company. Anchoring and identifying in one country with a culturally diverse set of employees, multicultural organizations are primarily importers and exporters. Examples include local retail shops selling imported products (e.g., exotic teas and spices) or local manufacturers who export to nearby countries.

- A **Multinational** organization identifies with one country while doing business across several countries. Multinational organizations retain their nationality of origin; however, products and management models are responsive to the local cultural values of their foreign locations. For example, McDonald's identifies with American culture, but you won't be able to buy their staple cheeseburger in India where cows are considered sacred.

- **International** organizations (i.e., global) identify with two or more countries with different cultural qualities. The different culturally based values exist among employees, customers, and management. International organizations typically build their largest and most powerful arena in their home country to keep a strong headquarters, while also having locations in other countries. Google is considered an international organization as its headquarters is located in the U.S., while also having locations in Latin America, Europe, Asia Pacific, Africa, and the Middle East.

- **Global** organizations (i.e., transnational) identify with the worldwide system rather than any particular country. Global organizations maintain a national "home" headquarters while also maintaining many other national headquarters and distributing decision-making power across these various national headquarters. Examples include General Electric (GE), Toyota, and Nestlé.

The type of organization plays an important part in determining expectations for how leaders and followers communicate at work. For example, the parent organization determines the primary language to be used, the national culture to which leaders and followers are expected to adapt and adhere, and the communication channels leaders and followers are expected to use to work and interact. Within the parameters of these expectations, keep in mind that *people*, not organizations; leaders and followers working within and across organizations communicate with each other to function as a system and create the organization's culture.

After looking at the solar system and seeing the definitions above for multicultural, multinational, international, and global, what parts of the solar system would you expect to represent each?

Global   _____

International   _____

Multicultural   _____

Multinational   _____

In space, the solar system serves as today's global organizations where people work. Each planet is its own culture. These cultures may be bound by geographical or value-based borders. Just as every individual in a given culture is not identical, there are differences in terrain on each planet. Craters on Mars may represent regional differences in dialect or values. After being down-graded to a dwarf planet, Pluto shows what can happen when an organization or geographical area loses its cultural identity. While the planets are different cultures, the sun allows all of those cultures to coexist and

FIGURE 11.1   The Solar System of Leadership and Followership

represents the similarities that exist between and among different cultures. Even though there are similarities among people from all different cultures, they do not always have successful interactions. It may be because of their cultural values or their other differences are so great. Think about black holes—leaders and followers within a single organization or across organizations attempt to interact but find themselves sucked into the black hole of incompetence.

Because moons are confined to a given planet, or culture, they would be considered multicultural organizations associated with a specific set of cultural values. With the stars each representing organizations made up of leaders and followers, the ones visible from multiple planets would be considered multinational organizations. If you have ever been a stargazer, maybe something you had to do for physics or astronomy class, you know that different planets are visible from Earth at different times; when these planets inhabit the same visual plane, they signify international organizations. Finally, shooting stars or asteroids would be the global organizations that operate comfortably in multiple cultures because they are not bound to a single planet or culture.

As we watch our places of work and the people with whom we work become increasingly diverse through globalization and migration, we also witness technology becoming more sophisticated and appealing for organizations to connect people (near or far) and reduce costs. Followers and leaders find themselves expressing and interpreting messages more through technology-mediated communication (TMC), an ability that is now a job requirement rather than a conditional asset for effective workplace communication. The demands, pressures, and reliance on TMC for work purposes incrementally modifies and elevates the standards defining effectiveness in terms of leaders' and followers' abilities to engage in competent communication, especially in situations characterized by cultural differences.

To keep up with the increasingly co-cultural and technologically driven requirements of our globally hungry workforce, followers and leaders must develop and foster co-culturally competent communication skills, with specific emphasis on facilitating cultural sensitivity. As such, leaders and followers of today, tomorrow, and five years from now first need to develop a sound understanding of the way culture influences one's own communicative behaviors as well as the behaviors of coworkers (or others) living and working next door, in virtual office(s), telecommuting, and across many other areas of the world. Understanding diversity in terms of cultural variation and variability better prepares leaders and followers to engage in rhetorically sensitive, co-culturally competent communication; it also equips them with the fundamental knowledge necessary to begin utilizing cultural diversity and TMC as tools, rather than tasks on a to-do list.

The advantage of leaders and followers who work and interact with wider sets of culturally diverse others and environments is they are afforded more opportunities to learn, practice, strengthen, and influence others. However, not all followers or leaders *want* to work for multicultural, multinational, international, or global organizations. Working within these arenas is neither desirable nor suitable for every human; in fact, it would be problematic if it were. Regardless, engaging in efforts to better understand cultural variation and the ways culture influences our own, as well as others' behaviors to develop and improve co-cultural competence and cultural sensitivity should be a regular practice. Similar to how often you practice personal hygiene in one day—washing your hands, brushing your teeth, bathing—these abilities should be practiced often, if not daily, to be effective! Competence and sensitivity are relationship-building tools readily available every day in the pockets of one's tool belt, hidden under your daily attire. Yes, you read that correctly—*daily*. Social skills need to be practiced and exercised often to reach their maximum potential and be truly useful.

Cultural Meanings Activity

Let's ease into culture with an easy icebreaker exercise. Take a look at the following words, and in the space below each word, describe what the word means or represents to you.

1. Gift   2. LOL

_____   _____

3. Thongs   4. Kiss

_____   _____

For each of these pictures, describe what you see or believe is occurring

IMAGE 11.1

IMAGE 11.2

Now, look at the words below and draw a picture in the empty box underneath illustrating what each word means or represents to you.

6a. Pear

6b. Pair

Look at your descriptions for the first four words. You probably described a "gift" as a present, even though in German it means poison and in Norwegian it means married. "LOL" is a commonly (probably overly) used acronym used in English meaning "laugh out loud," whereas in Dutch it means fun. "Thongs" in English refers to underwear; in Australia it means summer-style sandals. "Kiss" in English refers to a touch with the lips; in Sweden it means pee.

Moving on, what do you believe is going on in the car images? One of the images appears to be driving on the opposite side of the road because the steering wheel is on the right. While this may be different from the driving behavior of your own culture, it does not mean it is "wrong." About one-third of the countries in the world drive on the left side of the road. For the last word set, pear–pair, most of you probably drew the fruit or something similar to the curvy oval-like shape of a pear under the word "pear."

What did you draw under the word "pair"? A couple? A couple of what? This illustration will vary for most people; it could be a picture of two people, animals, shapes, objects, or none of those things—maybe you drew a pair of sunglasses. The point is, there are different ways of thinking, doing, and interpreting objects, behaviors, and situations.

Our ways of thinking and being are influenced by culture, cultural norms and values. As we talk about culture differences, remember how natural and normal it is to see, think, describe, believe, or perceive things completely differently or with alternative meanings then that of another person or even yourself in terms of what you know (or thought you knew). Different is not synonymous with bad or wrong; different is just different and it can be simply variation without an attached valence.

Cultural Values and Variability: Dimensions of National Culture

Do you remember how we defined culture, all the way back in chapter one? We defined culture as the shared assumptions that impact people's behaviors, feelings, perceptions, and thoughts. As a leader or follower, being effective in the international and global arenas of work life involves understanding broadly held cultural values to better learn how to: understand different ways of thinking, adapt to differences in uncertainty and behavioral limits, adjust your role to adequately navigate power differentials to support leader-follower relationships, and learn appropriate communicative behaviors across cultures. As such, four dimensions of national culture are held under a spotlight with these particular points in mind.

Geert Hofstede (2001) developed a six-dimension model of culture based on national culture, three of which are discussed here: individualism-collectivism, uncertainty-avoidance, and power distance. Hofstede (2001) emphasizes the way each dimension focuses on national culture (broadly held norms and values) and emphatically cautions against confusing or assigning these values to followers and leaders at the individual level. Not everyone who comes from an individualistic culture agrees or holds values related to independence with the same intensity as the society at the collective level. The last dimension discussed is Edward Hall's (1976) high–low context communication dimension.

Individualism–Collectivism
Individualistic cultures "emphasize personal rights and responsibility, privacy, voicing one's own opinion, freedom, innovation, and self-expression" (Anderson et al., 2002, p. 93). In direct opposition to individualistic cultures, **collectivistic cultures** place higher value on the group rather than the individual by emphasizing "community, collaboration, shared interests, harmony, tradition, the public good, and maintaining face" (Anderson et al., 2002, p. 93). Individualism encourages leaders and followers to think in terms of

independence, autonomy, and critical thought, whereas collectivism encourages more dependent and non-critical thinking, leading to higher expectations for conformity and obedience (Can & Aktas, 2012). Individualistic cultures, typically Western or European, include: the U.S., Australia, the United Kingdom, the Netherlands, New Zealand, Italy, Belgium, Denmark, France, and Sweden. Collectivistic cultures, typically Eastern or South American, include: Guatemala, China, Japan, Ecuador, Panama, Venezuela, Colombia, Pakistan, Indonesia, Costa Rica, Peru, and Taiwan.

Although culture certainly influences our beliefs, values, and behaviors, that is not to say that every leader or follower of the same nationality or culture believes and expresses a culture's broadly held values with the same intensity, degree, or extent as that culture at the national level. Unlike other dimensions of cultural values, individualism–collectivism exists at the cultural (national) and individual level. A leader or follower may live or come from an individualistic culture yet think in terms of collectivism or vice versa.

Research suggests leaders and followers may experience thinking of self in relation to others in both ways (independent and interdependent), however, one way of thinking will predominate (Gudykunst & Lee, 2002). Independent self-construal (IndSC) aligns with individualistic cultural values and interdependent self-construal (InterSC) aligns with collectivism. For example, imagine someone bumps into you in a hallway toward the end of a term: what are your immediate thoughts? Thoughts along the lines of "how rude—*I* was standing still" or "how could someone not see *me* standing here" reflect an IndSC way of thinking, whereas thinking in terms of "*they* must be in a hurry" or "final exams are making all of *us* tired, that must've been an accident" reflects an InterSC. How might these different ways of thinking influence leaders' and followers' thoughts and attitudes regarding belonging (diversity and inclusion) within an organization—is a person a part of our in-group or out-group—or what is right and wrong (ethical)?

Uncertainty–Avoidance

Uncertainty-avoidance deals with how well a society handles ambiguity and unstructured environment. Generally, **high uncertainty avoidance cultures** tend to think "what is different is dangerous," whereas **low uncertainty avoidance cultures** think "what is different is curious" (Hofstede, 2001, p. 161). Countries high in uncertainty avoidance include: Greece, Portugal, Guatemala, Uruguay, Belgium, El Salvador, Poland, Japan, Peru, Argentina, and France. Countries low in uncertainty avoidance include: Singapore, Jamaica, Denmark, Sweden, Hong Kong, the United Kingdom, Ireland, Malaysia, India, and China.

TABLE 11.1   Individualism–Collectivism Dimension

Messages and behaviors highlight self and personal goals; More use of "I," "me," and "mine" pronouns.	Messages and behaviors highlight others and goals of the group; More use of "we," "our," "us," and "they" pronouns.
Employees perform best as individuals; Employees and managers report working individually.	Employees perform best in in-groups; Employees and managers report team-work and personal contacts.
Hiring and promotion decisions should be based on skills and rules; Belief in individual decisions.	Hiring and promotion decisions take employee in-groups into account; Belief in collective decisions.
Management is management of individuals.	Management is management of groups.
Leadership is the property of the leader.	Leadership is inseparable from the context.
Direct appraisal of performance improves productivity; Incentives to be given to individuals.	Direct appraisal of performance is a threat to harmony; Incentives to be given to in-groups.
Relationships with colleagues depend less on their group identity.	Relationships with colleagues is cooperative for in-group members, hostile for out-group.
Treating friends better than others is nepotism and unethical: Universalism.	Treating friends better than others is ethical and normal: Particularism.
In business, task and company prevail over personal relationships.	In business, personal relationships prevail over task and company.

Adapted from Hofstede (2001, pp. 244–245).

TABLE 11.2   Uncertainty–Avoidance Dimension

Low Uncertainty-Avoidance	High Uncertainty-Avoidance
Managers should be selected on criteria other than seniority; Appeal of transformational leader role	Managers should be selected on basis of seniority; Appeal of hierarchical control role
Individual decisions, authoritative management, and competition among employees acceptable; Top managers involved in strategy	Preference for group decisions, consultative management, and against competition among employees; Top managers involved in operations
Optimism about employer's motives; admit dissatisfaction with employer; weak loyalty to employer; less hesitation to change employers	Pessimism about employer's motives; don't admit dissatisfaction with employer; strong loyalty to employer; tendency to stay with same employer
More ambition for advancement and management positions	Lower ambition for advancement and preference for specialist positions
If necessary, employers may break rules	Company rules should not be broken
Acceptance of foreigners as managers; less resistance to change	Suspicion of foreigners as managers; more resistance to change
Power of superiors depends on position and relationships; Relationship orientation	Power of superiors depends on control of uncertainties; Task orientation
Tolerance for ambiguity in structures and procedures	Highly formalized conception of management
Superiors optimistic about employees' ambition and leadership capacities; Precision and punctuality have to be learned and managed	Superiors pessimistic about employees' ambition and leadership capacities; Precision and punctuality come naturally

Adapted from Hofstede (2001, pp. 160–170).

The reliance on cultural rules and rigidity can be explained by the uncertainty-avoidance (UA) dimension. For cultures high in UA, uncertainty causes feelings of discomfort and anxiety, making high UA cultures less likely to take risks. As such, developing and upholding tight rules reduces risk, uncertainty, and anxiety. In the business world, there are times when followers and leaders must take risks to pursue innovative or creative ideas, particularly during organizational change; the tendency to avoid uncertainty suppresses creative thinking (Can & Aktas, 2012). This can pose an obstacle for leaders and followers when cultural values are guided by high UA. As a leader, it is important to build trust and reduce anxiety aroused by pursuing and engaging in change, innovation, and creativity. As a follower, analyze and understand how culture influences your ethical perspective when evaluating how much you are willing to stretch your ethical position to meet the needs and activities necessary for successful change, innovation, and creativity.

Cultures with high uncertainty-avoidance (UA) also tend to show more emotions and are more suspicious of strangers (Anderson et al., 2002). Understanding high UA in this way highlights the importance of self and other awareness when attempting to develop and foster trust among leaders and followers within co-cultural organizations. Awareness misperceptions stymie opportunities to build closeness, openness, and mutuality among leaders and followers.

Let's examine a general example, such as the commonly held reciprocal claims of rudeness between America and France. People from France claiming Americans are rude and Americans who claim people from France are rude is an awareness misperception rooted in and explained by the UA differences of each culture's influence. In France, interpersonal relationships are highly valued and showing emotions is reserved for people in one's close interpersonal network (think family and close friends). Therefore, it is unusual, suspicious, dangerous, offensive, or rude for a stranger to approach and begin asking questions out of curiosity or in an attempt to get to know you. On the other hand, the low UA American culture asks questions out of curiosity; developing a relationship with strangers is not rude, as it is expected, typical behavior.

Imagine a follower who is transitioning from living and working in an American culture to working on an international assignment in France, begins trying to make small talk with the new leader by asking about hobbies, past experiences, and beliefs. Given your knowledge of UA, what kind of reaction might that follower expect to receive? How can this follower adapt the communication, style, and/or approach to reduce the uncertainty and anxiety associated with the leader's suspicious reactions? As a leader, what would be important to communicate to this follower? How could you use communication to avoid offending the follower who believes this is how to indicate a level of friendliness and build a relationship before focusing exclusively on the task that needs to be completed?

Power Distance

Power Distance refers to how people in lower positions anticipate that influence and control are unequally distributed (Hofstede, 2011, p. 9). High power distance cultures (HPDC) adhere to hierarchically based social systems where control and influence are given and limited to a select few members, compared to being equally distributed among leaders and followers. At the extreme end of the continuum, they view the limited number of leaders, those who hold top positions in the hierarchical structure, as the primary vision developers and implementers. Everyone else is a follower who accepts large distances in power distribution as typical.

Followership and leadership in HPDC are full of color and completely lacking color—there is no gray or in-between and the clear division across leaders and followers based on power differentials is expected, accepted as normal, and preferred. As leaders have ultimate power, authority and status, they decide what is right and wrong, make the decisions and dictate how followers should act based on strong obedience expectations. Followership in HPDC means deference and conformity. A leader tells a follower to jump and rather than asking why or resisting this request, the follower asks how high, when, and acts on command. High power-distance countries include: Malaysia, Guatemala, Panama, Philippines, Mexico, Venezuela, China, Egypt, Iraq, and Kuwait. Low power distance countries include: Austria, Israel, Denmark, New Zealand, Ireland, Sweden, Norway, Finland, Switzerland, and the United Kingdom.

TABLE 11.3   Power Distance Dimension

Low Power Distance	High Power Distance
Flat pyramid organization; decentralized decision structures; less concentration of authority	Hierarchical pyramid organization; centralized decision structures; more concentration of authority
Managers rely on personal experience and on subordinates.	Managers rely on formal rules.
Subordinates expect to be consulted.	Subordinates expect to be told.
Consultative leadership leads to satisfaction, performance, productivity.	Authoritative leadership and close supervision lead to satisfaction, performance, and productivity.
Superior–subordinate relations are pragmatic.	Superior–subordinate relations polarized, often emotional.

Adapted from Hofstede (2001, pp. 107–108).

People in HPDC see power as a pervasive aspect of everyday life and prefer coercive and reward power; members of low power distance cultures prefer expert or legitimate power (Anderson et al., 2002). For leaders, understanding a culture's impact on followers' preferences for certain types of power provides opportunities to empower followers. Developing and exercising referent power with followers who tend to assume passive roles influenced by high power distance can encourage followers to voice their opinions and express dissent openly and comfortably.

Although coercive power generally involves using communication to manipulate or threaten force against another, HPDC followers may perceive this type of power as reassuring rather than threatening. Coercive power, used with good intentions, can strengthen followers' confidence in a leader's vision and decisions. Followers must understand how leaders' cultures influence perceptions and preferences for certain power bases. Values of obedience and dependency associated with high power distance can potentially pose a threat to creativity and collaboration when interacting with coworkers

(Blair & Bligh, 2018). Expressing and utilizing any type of power requires careful consideration of what one's nonverbal communication means and how appropriate use influences others.

The meaning behind nonverbal communication differs as a result of power distance values, particularly nonverbal behaviors related to voice and eye behavior. For instance, high voice volume and strong eye gaze convey and establish power in HPDC. As a follower, avoiding eye contact with others is a sign of respect for that person's authority or status, whereas avoiding eye contact in some low power distance cultures is a sign of deception, disrespect through disconfirmation, or not listening. Therefore, effective leaders are able to use nonverbal behaviors appropriately to establish competent power use as well as distinguish differences in what others' nonverbal cues mean. Similarly, effective followers are able to use and pick up on these nonverbal indicators of power to better support, teach, and foster relationships with co-workers and leaders.

High Context–Low Context

Culture shapes the tendency to rely more or less on context when communicating, an important aspect of leading and following when international or global organizations communicate with each other. **High context communication**, also known as connotation, relies on people's knowledge of the situation and the other person to convey meaning (Hall, 1976, p. 79). **Low context communication**, also known as denotation, uses language or other cues to carry the message's meaning (Hall, 1976, p. 70).

Imagine a situation where Pat, a new employee, witnesses coworkers Chris and Jerome interacting. Jerome says to Chris, "Hey fat boy, get me a copy of last month's report stat." Chris chuckles and replies "You got it, Jerome." A week later, Pat sees Chris and says, "Hey fat boy, can I get a copy of last month's report?" Whereas Jerome's high-context (HC) comment relied on the unspoken long-term friendship with Chris, where friendly banter and running jokes are typical during exchanges, Pat's comment is most likely perceived as highly inappropriate and incompetent because they do not share the same type of work relationship.

Followers and leaders working in international or global organizations are particularly prone to experiencing communication differences influenced by culture. Therefore, effective leadership and followership involves being able to pick up on the ways other people differ in their reliance on context during interaction to adapt one's own communication to reduce misunderstandings. HC cultures include: Japanese, Chinese, Indian, Russian, Arabic, African, Greek, Spanish, and Italian-speaking countries. Low-context (LC) cultures include: German, Belgian, Scandinavian, American-English, British-English, Australian, Canadian, and French-speaking countries.

To complicate things even more, there is variation and variability across HC and LC cultures—not all HC cultures use or rely on context in the same way. For example, both Japan and Russia are HC cultures, yet expressing refusal or saying "no" differs between the two. In Russia, it is normal and acceptable to directly refuse a leader's offer or invitation, whereas saying no directly is avoided in Japan. In fact, in Japan, "yes" does not necessarily indicate agreement, acceptance, or permission; it may mean "no" or serve as confirmation/acknowledgement of another's offer or request. The following HC and LC responses refusing a leader's invitation to an anniversary party this coming Sunday due to a previously planned engagement, let's say a daughter's birthday for this example, illustrate this point.

From this example, we see even when two or more cultures lean towards HC communication, the meaning of a message and the way messages rely on context can differ. While there is no right or wrong response, a lack of understanding and awareness about both general and specific differences in cultural values is often the source of misunderstanding and conflict. For leaders and followers alike, being effective means attending to these differences, especially when engaging in intercultural communication situations vulnerable to misunderstanding, conflict, and emotion. Acquiring knowledge about values related to face (identity and self-image), which is influenced

TABLE 11.4   Context Dimension

Low Context	High Context
Explicit language and direct messages; Rely on the message(s) itself for information and meaning.	Implicit language and indirect messages; Rely on context (and relationship) for information and meaning of behaviors.
More specific, what is important is said; less expectations for others to "read between the lines"; High reliance on written communication.	Less specific, what is important is understood; more expectations for others to "read between the lines"; Low reliance on written communication.
Less use of nonverbal communication.	More use of nonverbal communication.
Less distinctions between in-group and out-group members; individualistic leaning.	More distinctions between in-group and out-group members; leaning.
Responsibility is dispersed throughout leaders and followers within the system.	Leaders are personally responsible for the actions of all followers within a system.
Business relationships less dependent on connections and relationships.	Business relationships more dependent on connections and relationships.
Less avoidance of direct and open confrontation to express and defend self; More use of confrontational approaches to resolve conflict; Criticisms are more direct.	Avoid direct and open confrontation to maintain harmony and social bonds; More nonconfrontational approaches used to resolve conflict; Criticisms are subtle.

Adapted from Hall (1976).

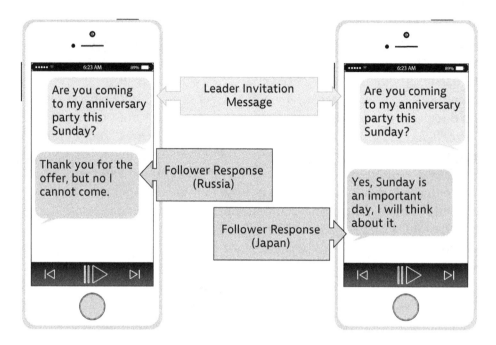

FIGURE 11.2   HC Follower Response Examples

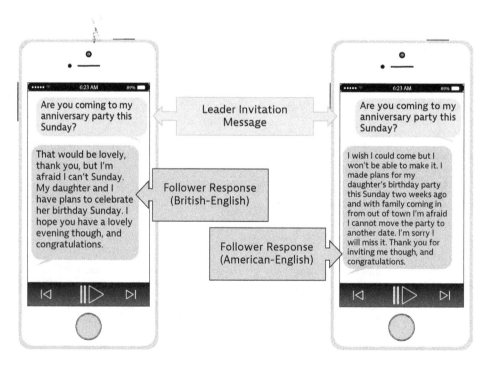

FIGURE 11.3   LC Follower Response Examples

by culture, is equally important for understanding meaning and engaging in effective intercultural communication.

RESEARCH SUMMARY

Study: Researchers from 6 different continents and over 20 different countries set out to develop and validate a scale that examined leadership identity (Van Dick, 2018). After administering surveys to over 5000 participants, they developed a prototype for four different types of leadership that cut across geographical and cultural boundaries. The researchers start with the premise that leadership and followership are social activities that each exists in relation to the other in a specific context (social identity theory). Leaders must not only manage the group and its activities, but also help to mold and shape the group's identity by working with the followers. At the center of their approach is social identity (the sense of "we" and "us" within the group). Four types of leadership identity influence and are influenced by social identity. These are impresarioship (we matter), prototypicality (we are a team), entrepreneurship (we create who we are), and advancement (we are doing it for us). All four leadership identities successfully predicted follower identification with the team (the extent to which members feel they are part of the group), follower trust in the leader, and follower job satisfaction. In combination, they also successfully predicted innovation, organizational citizenship behaviors (engaging in voluntary behaviors that are beneficial to the organization, not part of one's contractual obligations, and not officially recognized in the reward system), and burnout; however, in each of these cases, all four leadership identities were not statistically significant predictors (entrepreneurship and impresarioship for innovation; prototypicality and advancement for organizational citizenship behaviors; and advancement for burnout). When the full scale is used (combining all four leadership identities), it successfully predicts everything (team identification, trust, job satisfaction, innovation, and organizational citizenship behaviors) except burnout, beyond what transformational and authentic leadership from chapter 3 would predict. That is, transformational and authentic leadership are viable explanations for these key organizational indicators across geographical and cultural borders, *and* leadership identity strengthens a researcher's ability to predict those important outcome variables.

Implications: In Chapter 2 with historical approaches to leadership, we saw leaders who exerted power over their followers. In Chapter 3, we saw leader-follower relationships where both groups exert mutual influence. This research takes our conceptualization of leadership and followership one step further to associate leadership with one's identity and follower

(continued)

outcomes. Understanding leaders' identities allows organizations and team followers to both experience positive outcomes regardless of Hofstede's and Hall's dimensions. Essentially, approaching leadership from a "we" or "us" mentality is equivalent to behaving in a co-culturally communicatively competent manner, something to which all leaders should seek to aspire. Future research would benefit from a similar analysis of followers' identities to see how well they have adopted the "we" and "us" mentalities present in this social identity approach to cross-cultural leadership.

Communication Accommodation Theory

Because people have similar and different patterns of interacting with each other, Howard Giles and colleagues (1973) developed speech accommodation theory, which later became communication accommodation theory. According to the theory, language, context, identity, and power interact as people decide what communication behaviors to use during an interaction (Gallois et al., 2005). We use those four factors to develop messages with the goal of having others perceive us as being in tune with them. If you have ever tried to use humor and had it fall flat or generate dismay rather than laughter, you were likely out of tune with those around you.

Accommodation

As followers and leaders who seek social approval from others, we strive to recognize when it is considered competent to alter our own communication behaviors to better match (convergence) or mismatch (divergence) the communication behaviors of others. **Convergence** is the process of altering one's communication behaviors to reduce the social distance between oneself and other(s). On the flip side, **divergence** is the process of altering one's communication behaviors to exaggerate or maximize the social distance between oneself and other(s). Communication behaviors may include language, nonverbal cues, channel, and message characteristics. While working at a Jewish Community Center summer camp, we spoke English about 90% of the time so that everyone who came to camp could participate in the activities. When people wanted to argue or disagree, they would switch to speaking in Yiddish or Hebrew to exclude most of the children and other adults who were considered outsiders from the conversation. English was one way to engage in convergence and switching to Yiddish or Hebrew allowed the counselors to participate in divergence.

When leaders and followers engage in convergence during a co-cultural interaction, they make others feel as if they are part of the in-group. Followers with less power are more likely to use accommodation strategies to present themselves as belonging with those who have more power. In the camp example, using English helps Christians, Muslims, and Buddhists who attend the camp feel as if they belong and are just another camper regardless of their religious beliefs. Accentuating similarities in co-cultural interactions by using accommodation promotes positive perceptions, attraction, and future interaction likelihood. If they have a positive experience where their religious beliefs are not condemned by the camp leaders, then they are more likely to talk positively about their experiences and return for other community events.

Non-Accommodation

Non-accommodation occurs when people do not alter their communication behaviors to meet the needs of other(s) and thus maintain or increase social distance. Leaders with formal power are more likely to use non-accommo-dation strategies because they do not need to accommodate to maintain the power structure. Divergence, one aspect of non-accommodation, highlights where the in-group ends and the out-group begins. When followers and leaders employ this strategy, it may be to preserve their own/group's identity, ensure they remain a viable part of the organization, or exert their power over others.

Under-accommodation involves attempting to engage in adaptive communication behaviors without achieving the goal of convergence. For example, in the camp example, counselors may use a combination of Yiddish and English or refer to God, which meets the needs of those who practice Judaism or Christianity and not those who worship Allah or Buddha, or focus on serving others at the expense of interpersonal relationships (Sharabi, 2017). **Over-accommodation** occurs when leaders and followers engage in so many communication behaviors to promote convergence that they actually end up patronizing or condescending those who are part of the out-group. While there are ways to do it in the camp example, you are likely more familiar with over-accommodation in other settings where people talk extremely loudly in a room of elderly people even if none is wearing a hearing aid, over-annunciate each word and speak at an excruciatingly slow rate when they encounter someone who speaks a different native language, or avoid making any eye contact with someone from a culture where direct eye contact is seen as disrespectful.

Transcending Cultural Differences

Because interacting with people from different cultures is inevitable in today's global environment, followers and leaders must be aware of how they view and interact with people from other cultures, regardless of whether they are within or outside geographical boundaries. As organizations were becoming more global and technologically connected, Bennett (1986) developed a stage model for becoming more interculturally sensitive to others. While the "stages" may no longer be as concrete and linear as he proposed, they provide a framework for understanding people's perspectives on co-cultural interactions and becoming more culturally sensitive. For our purposes, we are going to call them "states" because people may change based upon context and may regress back.

Cultural Ethnocentrism

When leaders and followers are not interested in acknowledging cultural differences exist, they are said to be in the **ethnocentrism** stages.

- **Denial State:** People who only recognize their own culture; they may stereotype other cultures or interact only with their in-groups. While participation is an engaging way to learn, Western faculty in the denial state may attach a large portion of a student's grade to participation. This faculty member may be in the denial state because there are many Eastern cultures where faculty are considered experts and it is therefore impolite to talk and take time away from their ability to share their expertise. It may be tempting to try and convince your instructor to take away the participation points for a class—just realize that their educational argument may outweigh your cultural argument. Organizational members in the denial state may say, "Why can't they just speak English and make this process easier?" or "Why do I have to learn about their culture—can't they just travel here for meetings instead of us having to go there?"

- **Defense State:** People who recognize there are other cultures and believe theirs is the best. In the United States, the Ku Klux Klan is a historical example of a defense state organization. Members knew there were other cultures because without other cultures there would be no one against whom to fight and no one against whom to claim their superiority. Organizational members in the defense state may say, "Why did we have to open an office in Spain? When I was there last week, they kept putting their hand on my forearm while we were talking. I also got more hugs in one day than I have in all of my working years combined."

- **Minimization State:** People who acknowledge cultural differences and believe they are being culturally sensitive. While awareness is an important part of the process, it is not sufficient for communicating competently. In your elementary and middle school, you may have learned to ignore or look past differences in skin color, physical ability, or even mental ability as a sign that you accept everyone as they are. In reality, this is a minimization state that can become harmful when those differences make a difference in whether we can interact competently (it is important to know that someone is deaf and needs to be able to read lips or have a sign interpreter; it is also important to recognize there are differences among dark-skinned people depending upon their family heritage and experiences). Organizational members in the minimization state may say, "We are all people" or "We all just want to be accepted as members of the human race."

FIGURE 11.4   Cultural Sensitivity Development (adapted from Bennett, 1986)

Cultural Ethnorelativism

When followers and leaders are interested in and motivated to seek out cultural differences, they are said to be **ethnorelative**.

- **Acceptance State:** People who are motivated to learn about other cultures and recognize the same communicative behavior can have different meanings in different cultures. Even though they may not agree with the cultural practices or meanings of others, they are genuinely curious about how other cultures operate. If your world civilizations teacher in high school made you do presentations on another culture, you could certainly spot students who were still in the ethnocentrism group in comparison to those who had progressed to the acceptance state. Organizational members in the acceptance state may say, "How do they do it in Trinidad and Tobago?" or "I don't think consensus decision making is for me or my group, but I am glad it works for others."

- **Adaptation State:** People who have learned to use the norms and can empathize with people from another culture. In this state, people recognize their own values and respect the values of other cultures. Organizational members may have the following interaction,

  "I am meeting Tuilika for a breakfast meeting. Even though we set it for 8:30, I expect she will arrive at 9:15."

  "Doesn't it bother you to sit there for 45 minutes waiting for her?"

"No, we respect each other. When I am there, she respects my sense of time and arrives 45 minutes early. When she is here, I respect hers and bring a book to read or something to do until she arrives."

▪ **Integration State:** People who seamlessly transition from one set of cultural norms to another. People who have achieved this state of cultural sensitivity are often multilingual, multiracial, and or, multicultural, having spent significant amounts of formative time in multiple cultures. Unlike others whose cultural sensitivity state can be determined by what they say, these people are more recognizable by their actions. They can be comfortable and competent at a breakfast meeting with their Japanese counterparts, a mid-morning strategy meeting with their on-site Anglo coworkers, and a lunch interview with the cultural training team from Costa Rica.

Cultural Sensitivity

We defined co-cultural communication competence (CCC) as the process of exchanging symbolic information between people, who as a result of culture can simultaneously share the same, similar, and different orientations toward the world. Two key elements of CCC necessary for facilitating cultural sensitivity include: 1) cognitively controlling attention and 2) pro-social perspective taking (taking the perspective of another). **Cultural sensitivity** refers to the ability to assume a perspective of "understanding and appreciating cultural differences that promotes appropriate and effective behavior in co-cultural communication" (Chen & Starosta, 2000, p. 5). Broadly, cultural sensitivity requires 1) knowledge (self and other awareness and willingness to learn), 2) openness (open-mindedness, empathy, and non-judgment), and 3) interaction involvement (being responsive, willing to listen, and being receptive). For leaders, each of these elements must be utilized while paying attention to, and engaging in, prosocial perspective taking in terms of the cultural, individual, relational, and environmental factors at play as well as the uniqueness of a given situation.

Cultural sensitivity benefits include increased trust, satisfaction, empowerment, morale, motivation, follower voice (upward feedback), and sense of community. In theory and practice, it is helpful to remember that "we can't control how another interprets our message, but we can influence how it is interpreted" (Lee, 2018, p. 5). To enhance this ability, organizations develop and implement training programs and offer continuous learning opportunities to followers. Leaders themselves should attend and explore continuous training opportunities individually as well as alongside followers (company retreats, conferences, company-wide online forums analyzing experiences and re-examining assumptions, practices, policies etc.).

Language Differences and Technical Aspects of TMC

While much research has focused on leader-follower, face-to-face communication (e.g., Sueda, 2014), culture differences in the context of TMC complicate our understanding of language use and exponentially increase the likelihood of misunderstandings and conflict. How do you think unintentional misunderstandings affect another's impression of us? If the misunderstanding aroused a negative impression, what does it take for leaders or followers to recover face and regain their lost positive impression from another person when engaging in TMC? The answer to both questions is, it depends. When using TMC to analyze and construct messages with culturally different coworkers, the depressed presence or complete absence of nonverbal communication and language style (verbal linguistic cues) are two of the most prominent technical aspects for leaders and followers to take into consideration.

First, we need to address the potential absence of nonverbal cues available in TMC interactions. The meanings expressed through nonverbal communication are often lost when interacting through TMC. Think about the last time you sent a text message that was received in the wrong context, tone of voice, intensity, or interpreted differently than you intended it to be. For example, "Thought U promised 2 b on time today" has multiple potential interpretations. It could be seen as a scolding for being late in a low-context relationship and sarcasm in a high-context relationship. Simply adding an emoji, JK, or LOL could each indicate a high-context relationship. The lack of nonverbal cues is more likely to pose problems for followers and leaders in HC communication cultures given their high use and reliance on nonverbal communication.

HC communication and collectivism dimensions are related. Research examining multinational and international companies around the world suggests members of HC and collectivistic cultures prefer to interact using certain forms of TMC, including (in descending order): e-mail, face-to-face, cell phone (audio phone call), landline telephone, online chat tools, text message (instant message), audio conferencing, video conferencing, fax, postal mail, and voice mail (Mao & Hale, 2015). Members of collectivistic cultures are less likely to be willing to help others when using TMC compared to members of individualistic cultures (Hansen et al., 2015). Therefore, followers seeking help from colleagues who are members of collectivistic cultures are more likely to receive assistance when using face-to-face, audio phone call, or audio conferencing tools compared to e-mail. Video conferencing tools may also be a useful resource for requesting help over e-mail in some cases. However, this may not necessarily apply to leaders requesting help from followers in the same way due to power differences, especially when working in HPDC.

Let's now shift our focus to examining how technical aspects of verbal communication linguistic style affects impressions when using TMC. In terms of power, the way followers and leaders accommodate (alter language use to be more like that of the other) messages impacts impressions related to social liking and task reliability. For follower-follower interactions, accommodating language (e.g., using pronouns such as "I" and "we") is associated with positive impressions (social, task, and rapport), whereas leaders' accommodating language is associated with followers' negative social liking, task reliability, and rapport impressions (Muir et al., 2017). Two other aspects of style, emoticons and errors, also have profound impacts on impressions of competence and should be carefully considered during TMC. The use of emoticons is a double-edged sword. While they can be helpful in forming positive impressions of social competence, they also form depressed impressions of functional competence (task competence), which are more difficult to recover or regain positive impressions, more than the initial negative impressions formed from a sender's messages containing errors (Brown et al., 2016). Therefore, to make a good first, or lasting, impression, leaders and followers should be especially aware of power differentials, use of emoticons, and errors when constructing messages.

CASE STUDY   Hon Hai Precision & Sharp Corporation

The electronic devices that rule our individual, social, and work lives such as, Apple products (iPhone, iPad, etc.), BlackBerry, Nintendo, Nokia devices, Wii, Xbox, and PlayStation gaming systems have one commonality: their parts. The parts that make up some of our most beloved electronic devices have a common manufacturer and supplier, Hon Hai Precision (i.e., FoxConn Technology Group). Hon Hai Precision is a multinational Taiwanese electronics contract manufacturing company headquartered in New Taipei City, Taiwan. Hon Hai Precision manufactures, assembles, and sells electronic equipment and products for the 3C (computer, communication, and consumer electronics). Products include power supplies, cables, connectors, LCD monitors, motherboards, and PC (personal computer) components (nanoPC and desktop). The company focuses on nanotechnology, heat transfers, wireless connectivity, material sciences, and green manufacturing process. To better serve its customers (e.g., Apple, Dell, Sony, Blackberry, etc.), Hon Hai Precision has invested in several research centers and testing laboratories globally as well as logistic planning and an e-supplying system for chain management, computer software development, and computer programming services. In 2016, buying majority stake, Hon Hai Precision became the parent company of another worldwide leader in design and manufacture of electronics company, Japan's Sharp Corporation. Although Sharp Corporation has built a reputation as a global leader in electronics, prior to the Hon Hai Precision bailout, the company had been teetering on the edge of bankruptcy for years, struggling to develop a successful restructuring plan.

In August 2016, the Taiwanese Vice President of Hon Hai Precision, Mr. Tai, was appointed President, CEO, and Chairman of Sharp Corporation based in Osaka, Japan. From the get-go, Mr. Tai announced that he would hand over the reins (step down) once he restored Sharp Corporation's earnings growth in the Tokyo Stock Exchange. Immediately, Mr. Tai began making restructuring changes in personnel management, specifically in terms of the performance-incentive program. Two weeks into the job, Mr. Tai offered monetary rewards to followers according to how well they achieved their goals. By November of 2016, Mr. Tai implemented a performance-based evaluation system based on leaders and followers' type of work and responsibilities. Under Mr. Tai's new system, Sharp employees are given tasks (assignments) and subsequently evaluated based on the scope and difficulty of the task as well as level of achievement. Leaders and followers who complete tasks that fulfill or exceed goal expectations receive higher evaluation grades and rewarded more authority. This new type of system functions in direct opposition of the traditional Japanese management practice of Sharp Corporation's performance-based evaluation system based on age and seniority. As a result, Sharp Corporation employees maintaining leadership positions were demoted to followership positions if they were deemed to have failed their responsibilities, and vice versa for employees assuming followership positions. Mr. Tai's intent was to boost morale, productivity, engagement, and recruit foreign talent by rewarding work contributing to the company's bottom line, while also enforcing punishment for work that did not. However, in April 2017, there were mixed feelings among Sharp Corporation employees about Mr. Tai and his personnel management changes. During a press conference one month earlier, in March 2017, when asked to comment about employees quitting because of the changes in management practices Mr. Tai replied, "I am not worried at all because I want employees to stay if they want to work with me." Those who embraced the changes saw this as an opportunity for growth potential and felt their work was finally receiving the appreciation it deserved. However, not everyone felt this way. Others, mostly employees in managerial and mid-level positions, and those who were accustomed to the old management practices, found it difficult to support and adapt to Mr. Tai's new system.

Given Mr. Tai's recent changes, managers began looking more closely at the output of employees they were responsible for overseeing within their departments. One of Sharp Corporation's Japanese managers, Mr. Z, took notice of a Taiwanese expatriate employee, Mr. A, working under his

(continued)

authority. Mr. Z noticed Mr. A making many careless mistakes and missing several deadlines for written tasks assigned to him within the past 3 months. To address Mr. A's mistakes, Mr. Z scolded Mr. A in front of everyone else, and he even hit the desk with his fist. However, Mr. A's mistakes and missed deadlines were not a result of laziness or lack of effort, rather his Japanese writing skill insufficiency. While Mr. A spoke fluent Japanese, his Japanese writing skills were equivalent to that of a ninth-grade high schooler (freshman in high school). In fact, when Mr. A was hired, he was only supposed to be given assignments requiring him to write reports in his native language, Mandarin Chinese, mostly used for meetings and presentations for the parent company, Hon Hai Precision. Thus, in this case, Mr. Z might have thought that "taking care" of Mr. A's careless mistakes was important for the new performance system in terms of maintaining his own position as well as Mr. A's position within the department. He could have warned Mr. A in a separate room, but this idea never occurred to him.

Despite departmental misunderstandings, in the first week of December 2017, only 9 months since Mr. Tai's Taiwanese style reforms were in question, Sharp Corporation began trading on the Tokyo Stock Exchange First Section for large companies. Mr. Tai's restructuring changes (cutting costs, revising budgets, and personnel management reforms) worked. In less than two years, "We've finally reached our goal" said Mr. Tai. Within days, Mr. Tai announced he would uphold his pledge to step down once his restructuring efforts restored Sharp Corporation's earnings. There was only one problem. The leaders and followers of Sharp Corporation Japan protested; they did not want Mr. Tai to leave just yet. "We will be in a tough spot if Tai-san leaves us," the words of a senior executive echoing the leaders and followers of Sharp Corporation's sentiments calling Mr. Tai "irreplaceable." The Japanese speaking Mr. Tai stated, "The board members said it is not right to elect a new president when the company is recovering, so we have started to think about the possibility of a co-CEO system." It is Mr. Tai's belief that this arrangement will let him hand over some control while cultivating his successor. Mr. Tai agreed to stay on as CEO, with a co-CEO, until 2020. In July 2018, Sharp Corporation announced its plans to acquire Toshiba Client Solutions (Toshiba's PC-related subsidiary) by October 2018. Sharp Corporation purchased Toshiba's personal computer business on October 1, 2018. Mr. Tai is confident Toshiba Client Solutions can be revived with the same management methods used with Sharp Corporation.

*Based upon research by Sueda (2014)

DISCUSSION QUESTIONS

1. Use the information about cultural values (culture dimensions) as well transcending cultural differences, what do you believe occurred with Mr. Tai and his followers in this scenario? And with Mr. Z and Mr. A?

2. Given what you read about communication accommodation theory, co-cultural competence and cultural sensitivity, in what ways would you have communicated differently if you were the leader (Mr. Z) and the follower (Mr. A) in this scenario?

3. As a communication consultant, what advice about utilizing TMC to communicate about issues would you offer to the leader (Mr. Tai) and followers in this case?

ANALYSIS OPTIONS

A. Sharp Corporation has decided to invest in opening another branch in another country. You have been hired to find the top five countries whose values align most closely with both Taiwan and Japan using Hofstede's dimensions.

B. You have been hired to implement new TMC resources for Sharp Corporation to improve communication among employees. Develop training scenarios for employees to role-play and learn from using Hall's high-low context communication.

C. Using communication accommodation theory and cultural sensitivity, develop a training plan for leaders and followers to be accommodative without becoming over-accommodative and sensitive without stereotyping.

ANALYSIS PROCESS

- Brainstorm a list of options for addressing the issue.

- Make a list of strengths and challenges for each of your brainstormed solutions.

- Choose the best solution for the issue.

- Develop an implementation plan for your chosen solution.

- Additional resources:

(continued)

Hoifstede Culture
https://tinyurl.com/
yy3pm5k4

 LEADER AND FOLLOWER DEVELOPMENT PRACTICES

1. Engage in positive indifferences by recognizing the cultural differences and optimistically approaching the practices that initially seem "foreign" (Neely, 2017).

2. Learn, listen, and ask questions about other cultures to better understand your own cultural biases (Markman, 2018).

3. Leaders and followers participate, seek/provide feedback, and engage in conflict differently across cultures so the cross-cultural teams needs to establish norms and revise them as people become more comfortable in the co-cultural environment (Toegel & Barsoux, 2017).

4. See the world as others see it without losing sight of how you see it (Rowland, 2016).

5. Learn enough of the other culture's, organization's, and/or person's verbal and emotional expression (Molinsky, 2015).

DISCUSSION QUESTIONS AND ACTIVITIES

1. Choose an organization for which you would like to work. Using their company webpage and any news articles/press releases you can find, classify the type of organization they are (domestic, global, international, multicultural, or multinational). See what conclusions you can draw about their cultural dimensions based upon the ways in which leaders and followers are talked about.

2. Of the five types of organizations, which one is most appealing to you as a future employee? Why?

3. What do you see as the similarities and differences in followership across the five different types of organizations?

4. Choose a second organization for which you would like to work. Using the news articles available, social media, and corporate website, find an example of a time when the leaders did not meet people's cultural dimension expectations (e.g., they used high-context when they should have been low-context communication; they used low power distance when they should have used high power distance). How did people respond on traditional and social media? What should they have done differently?

5. Leaders often find themselves in the news for engaging in cultural ethnocentrism. Choose one of those leaders and develop a message strategy that would have indicated cultural ethnorelativism and cultural sensitivity.

FIGURE CREDITS:

Fig. 11.1: Source: https://pixabay.com/photos/solar-system-sun-mercury-venus-439046/.

Img. 11.1: Source: https://pixabay.com/photos/auto-ford-mustang-cockpit-oldtimer-3331349/.

Img. 11.2: Source: https://pixabay.com/photos/oldthimer-right-hand-drive-england-101825/.

Img. 11.3: Source: https://pixabay.com/illustrations/stairs-silhouettes-human-upward-70509/.

Img. 11.4: Source: https://pixabay.com/illustrations/mechanics-gear-gears-blue-551265/.

Fig. 11.2: Source: https://pixabay.com/illustrations/iphone-apple-smartphone-mobile-1203419/.

Fig. 11.3: Source: https://pixabay.com/illustrations/iphone-apple-smartphone-mobile-1203419/.

Fig. 11.4a: Source: https://pixabay.com/illustrations/world-globe-earth-planet-blue-1303628/.

Fig. 11.4b: Source: https://pixabay.com/illustrations/globe-world-earth-planet-1339833/.

CHAPTER 12

POLITICAL AND PUBLIC ARENAS

"I think it's a good thing for a president or political leaders to want to put their values or their faith into action. Desmond Tutu did that in South Africa. Martin Luther King Jr. did that here. This is a good thing."

—JIM WALLIS

"These days there are not enough of such intermediary groups, between the state and the individual, with the result that political leaders are often unduly guided by opinion polls."

—JACQUES DELORS

The chameleon. It is an animal distinguished by its eyes, tail, and feet. Because they have the capacity to change colors, chameleons often are associated with cowards who lack confidence and change their personalities or views to meet the situation. The primary function of color change for chameleons is communication. Like chameleons, leaders and followers may change their colors when communicating in the political and public arenas. If you are a pessimist, you might see politicians and other public figures as chameleons who change the persona they portray every time they encounter new people or a new situation just so they can fit in; if you are an optimist, you might see politicians and other public figures as chameleons who change their message to meet the audience's needs on any given occasion. Regardless of your perspective, the changing nature of chameleons and their vast repertoire of physical features are what allow them to survive in their natural habitat. Leadership and followership in political and public arenas can blend in or stand out in a grassroots movement, in competent ways, as a well-known identity, or in toxic disguise, but they cannot hide.

FIGURE 12.1   Chameleons

Political and Public Influence

Just as organizational leaders use vision and mission statements to inspire and motivate followers and stakeholders, public figures (e.g., political candidates, celebrities) convince citizens to accept their vision and mission. These visions and missions might be for a local municipality, state, country, charity, or even a social justice cause. Table 12.1 reminds us about the differences between vision and mission statements.

Political and Public Brands

A **brand** is a promise. That promise is built from a vision and mission. What leaders are doing when they communicate a powerful vision is influencing others to buy-in to what they are selling. What they are selling is a promise for the future through a particular type of personal brand, either as a: human (person), celebrity, businessperson, or politician. In this way, a brand captures and represents a vision for the future and its associated values.

Based upon the idea of brands being promises, what brands come to mind for you? Were they individual, celebrity, organizational, or political? If Lolly Daskal is not a name you know, it is one you need to learn. Over a million people follow her leadership tweets (they are always consistent and about how to be a better leader) and her tagline is "We are here to be our most valuable" (https://www.lollydaskal.com/). As founder and CEO of Mirasee, Danny Iny has created a brand that is all about being personable. From his books on marketing to his podcasts, he emphasizes "audience first." In

TABLE 12.1   Mission & Vision Statement Differences

	Mission	Vision
Answers	Why are we here? What do we do–why or how do we do it?	Where do we aim to be?
Function	To inform	To inspire
Time-Orientation	Focuses on the present, leading to the future	Focuses on the future
Describes	Reason for being (Purpose)	Ideal future state
Features	Purpose and Values; Grounds brand identity	Goals and Values; Directs brand identity evolution
Necessitates	Embracing/Creating shared meaning impacting culture and competencies	Aligning values with culture and competencies

Adapted from Kopaneva and Sias (2015).

fact, his audience is so important to him that he writes all of his own email messages and they come from his personal address (Danny Iny), rather than the corporate email address. Most people know Oprah Winfrey by her first name because she has created a strong celebrity brand. Her brand is very similar to the Army's—challenge yourself to achieve all that you can—reach your full potential. Whether it was her talk show, her current affiliation with WW (formerly Weight Watchers), or her television channel (OWN–Oprah Winfrey Network), she provides a consistent, positive, uplifting brand message that has made her a billionaire.

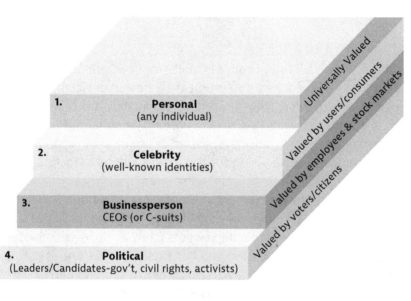

FIGURE 12.2   4 Levels of Personal Brands

Leaders and followers can use rhetoric to effectively communicate a vision and mission that inspires, motivates, and convinces others to rally in support. Presidential candidates effectively influence and mobilize the masses by using eight dimensions of charismatic rhetoric (Baur et al., 2016).

- **Collective focus** refers to employing more references to the group and less to personal self-interests. The benefit is creating a sense of community and unity to promote trust and motivation.

- **Temporal orientation** involves making more references to the connections between the past and the present. This is useful for explaining a current position and substantiating a compelling vision for the future.

- **Followers' worth** refers to spotlighting the supporters' value to the leader and the collective. This type of motivational language and praise is beneficial for leaders to inspire others to strive for goals, increase support, and enhance followers' self-efficacy.

- **Similarity to followers** involves downplaying differences between leaders and supporters while drawing attention to the benefits of communality. The advantage of this kind of rhetoric is building on the sense of community, which can be done by referencing shared experiences.

- **Values and moral justifications** involve referring to ethical beliefs and ideals. The goal is to inspire followers, which may be done by creating and expressing messages that both complement and challenge followers' values to align collective goals with the values of the individual followers.

- **Tangibility** involves the use of flowery or grandiose language that creates an intangible and less concrete vision of the future. The goal is to maintain followers' commitment, yet not diminish motivation as certain goals are met.

- **Action** refers to verbalizing and enacting a consistent, powerful, and meaningful vision. There is a difference between "telling" and "doing." Verbalizing and enacting behaviors that mimic the core values embedded in a vision can be highly influential. This should be visible to followers through a leader's actions. Leaders can compel others to do the same by expressing confidence the vision can be attained in a manner that will excite and motivate followers.

- **Adversity** involves convincing followers that the leader's vision of the future is superior to their perceptions of the present. A leader may emphasize hardships or highlight current negative conditions to contrast with the vision or promote that following the vision is more of a necessity, rather than a desire.

Use Figure 12.3 below, to see how well you know your charismatic rhetoric dimensions in practice. Match each of the quotes (on the left side) with the most appropriate charismatic rhetoric dimension (on the right side).

"America is strongest when we are working with real alliances, when we are sharing the burdens of the world by working through our statesmanship at the highest levels and our diplomacy to bring etherisations to our side."—John Kerry, 2004

A. Collection focus

"When we compare these two records in the areas that Senator Kennedy has–has discussed tonight. I think we find that America has been moving ahead. Let's take schools. We have built more schools in these last seven and a half years than we built in the previous seven and a half, for that matter in the previous twenty years."—Richard Nixon, 1960

B. Temporal orientation

"I have a deep religious Faith. Our family does. It is fundamental. It's probably the reason that I'm in politics. I think our faith tells us, instructs us, about the moral life that we should lead.''—Walter Mondale, 1984

C. Followers worth

"The governor wants to divert $1 out of every $6 off into the stock market, which means that he would drain a trillion dollars out of the Social Security Trust Fund in this generation over the next ten years, and Social Security under that approach would go bankrupt within this generation."—Al Gore, 2000

D. Similarity to followers

"I think it will depend in great measure upon what we do here in the United States, on the kind of society that we build, on the kind of strength that we maintain."—John F. Kennedy, 1960

E. Value/ Morals

"Now one of the reasons I was able to get so many good women to be part of that team was because of our recruiting effort."—Mitt Romney, 2012

F. Tangibility

"As Governor of California, I took charge of passing the strictest air pollution laws in the United States—the strictest air quality law that has even been adopted in the United States."—Ronald Reagan, 1980

G. Action

"... to inspire our people to reach for greatness, to correct our defects, to answer difficult questions, to bind ourselves together in a spirit of unity."—Jimmy Carter, 1976

H. Adversity

Adapted from Baar et al. (2016)

FIGURE 12.3 Charismatic Rhetoric Activity

Interested in knowing what combinations of charismatic rhetoric dimensions have been used by U.S. presidential candidates, which is the most effective for successful influence, as well as when it was used and by whom? Check out the research summary below to find out!

RESEARCH SUMMARY

Study: Baur et al. (2016) set out to study how eight charismatic strategies may be used in conjunction with one another to form distinct profiles of leadership influence by content analyzing the 1960–2012 United States presidential debates. Charismatic rhetoric is an important tool for leaders to inspire and motivate followers when they express a vision. The two major research questions guiding this study asked: 1) do different configurations of charismatic rhetoric dimensions emerge when leaders articulate their vision, and 2) if so, are certain configurations more effective than others? Results show four distinct configurations of charismatic rhetoric dimensions (listed left to right from highest to lowest use):

- Cluster 1: tangibility, collective focus, and action

- Cluster 2: adversity, temporal orientation, and follower worth

- Cluster 3: collective focus, action, and values and moral justifications

- Cluster 4: follower similarity, follower worth, and temporal orientations

Results indicated presidential candidates using cluster four were more successful in convincing followers to support their vision than were leaders using the other three clusters. Presidential candidates who were members of Cluster 4 in this study include: Barak Obama (2008, 2012); Bill Clinton (1992, 1996); George W. Bush (2000, 2004); Bob Dole (1996); Al Gore (2000); John Kerry (2004); and John McCain (2008). Candidates of cluster 3 include Ross Perot (1992 and Mitt Romney (2012). Candidate members of cluster 2 include John F. Kennedy (1960) and George H. W. Bush (1988, 1992). Candidates of cluster 1 include Jimmy Carter (1976) and Gerald Ford (1976). Additionally, these findings showed that using a balanced configuration of rhetoric dimensions, and not just specific individual dimensions, enables leaders to be effective when influencing followers to adopt their vision.

Implications: While certain influential factors may be out of leaders' control (debate-specific factors and campaign-year factors), leaders can control how much they intentionally tailor their use of rhetoric to include charismatic elements to effectively articulate a vision. For both politicians and organizational leaders, a balanced use of charismatic rhetoric dimensions is crucial for communicating vision, especially when responding to

(continued)

crises as well as announcing and executing changes. Message content and message delivery (presentation style) remain key aspects of influencing followers to support a vision for the future. Putting in the time and effort to enhance one's communication skills is a priority for leaders and followers to effectively influence others, especially politicians.

Social Media in Political and Public Persuasion

Social media offer a platform for leaders and followers to promote a particular brand and persuade others to engage with favorable brands. Think about Ashton Kutcher's use of Twitter in promoting and integrating the personal and celebrity aspects of his brand. The same applies to politician and businessperson brands, like Barack Obama's and Donald Trump's uses of Twitter to post and engage with the masses. Tweets are a powerful vehicle for politicians' self-promotion—a balance between professional and personal tweets can increase interest in a politician's party and intention to vote for the party (Colliander et al., 2017). Using social media networking sites as a medium for interacting with followers and the masses appears to be another advantage for political leaders. Looking at the 2016 U.S. presidential election, Donald Trump utilized user-generated content as sources of his tweets significantly more often than Hilary Clinton; 50% of his tweets were retweets of, and replies to citizens, while three quarters of Clinton's tweets were original content focused more on self-promotion (Lee & Lim, 2016). Whether we like, dislike, or feel indifferently about the person, the importance of using social media as a platform for influence cannot be discounted. We look to people with strong brands for information and often find we are influenced by their opinions. In research, this is the **opinion leader phenomenon**.

Opinion leaders who are followers are one of the most valuable assets any leader can have. They are the not-so secret weapon on the front lines arousing other followers' support and bringing a leader's vision to life. They are simultaneously followers themselves and influential leaders within their own network. Opinion leader followers can encourage others to get involved or persuade them to change their minds or attitude about an issue. They are popular within their social sphere networks, and they know it. Most social networking sites allow account holders to see how many followers someone has and how many people like the posts based on content across several discussion topics. Their opinion leader accolades stem from their expertise more than their social status; they are informed and actively disperse their knowledge regarding certain events, news, and relevant stories (Park, 2013). They frequently use social media to communicate about issues and are the ones creating or producing content that others are sharing, retweeting, and commenting on (Weeks et al., 2017).

The beauty of opinion leadership and social media is exposure of a wide variety of ideas and information. Followers and leaders are no longer limited to information from a single source. People are increasingly getting their news from their peers and through social media (Pew, 2019). By the same token, the pitfall of obtaining news from peers and/or social media apps is selective exposure. **Selective exposure** involves favoring information that reinforces one's own pre-existing views while avoiding contradictory information. In our digitally driven world, most of us engage in selective exposure without even realizing it. Think about the last time you got your news by opening up a news or social networking app to find "most popular stories," "most shared stories," or "suggested for you" categories of information. While having our preferences categorized for us makes it easier to find information, we risk limiting ourselves to a single perspective, the viewpoint that we ourselves prefer or already have. In terms of social media and influence, a big question for leaders, followers, and opinion leader followers is: how much do we actually seek out, and select, more diverse content? Opinion leaders are usually well-known identities because they achieve celebrity status.

Agenda Setting and Framing Theory

As originally conceived, the **agenda-setting function** of media indicated that mass media tell us not what to think, but rather what to think about (McCombs & Shaw, 1972). Based upon what news stories they cover, how they position those in the media (e.g., lead story), and how they present them (e.g., bold headline above the newspaper fold or with accompanying visuals) people come to attach meaning to a topic's importance (aka. **issue salience**). When they label a topic as important, they pay more attention to it and also talk more with others about the topic. So, at the time of the original research, they were interested in whether it made a difference what stories newspapers covered about each of the election issues. They concluded that the news stories prompted people to think about politics and the election, but not necessarily which side to take on each issue. America and technology have come a long way in the last 50 years since those initial studies.

In the second wave of agenda setting, researchers began to ask about the ways media influence how we think about issues

FIGURE 12.4   What do you see here? Is it a chalice or the heads of two people facing each other? In agenda setting, people see what the media want them to see.

(aka **attribute salience**; Balmas & Shaefer, 2010). In this case, the media may either choose to present a particular perspective on the topic or frame it in a particular way. Think about the difference between two headlines that read "Terrorist Attack" and "Nightclub Shooting." They may be portraying the same incident, such as the one that occurred at Pulse nightclub outside Orlando, Florida in 2016. If you live or grew up in a large city, shootings are a relatively common occurrence on the news so the fact that 49 people died is downplayed by the headline, "Nightclub Shooting." If you have grown up hearing about the ways our country and views of freedom, safety, and security have changed since September 11, 2001, the label, "terrorist" automatically elevates the shooting's seriousness. Thus, the frames, or lenses, through which the headlines portray the incident matter in terms of how people think about the situation or issue.

We have added social media to our news repertoire and also become more critical of the possibility that news outlets are not presenting the whole, unbiased truth. In the third wave of agenda setting, we have begun examining the interconnected nature of media and social media outlets. Think about how much of what you know regarding the news has been aggregated for you. The AP wire has long served as an aggregator for traditional media; online news aggregators such as BuzzFeed are where many turn when they first access their cellphones in the morning. These aggregators engage in priming as they, often over time, serve as gatekeepers for what information people can access (Scheufele & Tewksbury, 2007). Known as **intermedia agenda setting**, the most recent version of the original theory examines the ways in which different forms of media interact with each other. For example, how do bloggers and traditional or social media interact to help us determine what to think about and how to think about issues; a recent study examined how "fake news" sites interact with traditional media, which are assumed to be factual (Guo & Vargo, 2018).

As interesting as media history may be, what relevance does it have for followers and leaders, especially political and public ones, in today's world? The answer is simple: think about how former President Obama and President Trump used Twitter to their advantage during the election and their time in office. Getting people to think about healthcare or immigration would be the first level of agenda setting. Helping the media highlight stories about universal healthcare and the need for a wall illustrate second-level agenda setting or framing. While neither of them specifically controlled or orchestrated third-level or intermedia agenda setting, the number of tweets helped the media determine what agenda they would portray, and that was reflected in the number of times their posts were retweeted or discussed. Organizational leaders and followers can also help build the media's agenda for social causes, branding, and political decision making.

Celebrity Leadership

Celebrity status when it comes to leadership is not always something con- ferred on a person or group of people for life. For example, some people achieve celebrity status because of their connection to the music or enter- tainment industries (a very traditional definition of celebrity); others achieve celebrity status because of their experiences that elevate their social position in the eyes of others (a more contemporary definition of celebrity). Only in the last two decades have YouTubers achieved celebrity status; the same can be said for blogging and vlogging social influencers. Elementary-school children can name their favorite YouTubers and push notifications ensure they never miss a new video post. Regardless of how one achieves celebrity status, they all share social capital. **Social capital** is all about the relation- ships, resources, and relative impact a person or group of people has on the larger society.

Relationships form because these individuals communicate competently to build connections with others. In this case, the Parkland School shooting survivors built virtual relationships with other high-school students to create a day in which students across the country protested school violence and shootings. These surviving students developed celebrity status because they were willing to speak out about law enforcement, mental health, and the fear they have each and every day when they go to public school. While the mobilization effort was not taken as seriously as it might have been if it did not involve students skipping class to participate and had been better organized, the message was clear—even as minors in this country, we have a stake and interest in what happens with important topics such as gun control and mental health.

Resources can be both tangible (money, access to media/social media outlets, space on which to put forward a platform) and intangible (status, ready-made follower relationships, expertise). What do the following names mean to you: Tina Tchen, Roberta Kaplan, Hilary B. Rosen, and Fatima Goss Graves? If you are like most Americans, very little. These four women started an organization called Time's Up Legal Defense Fund. As President and CEO of the National Women's Law Center, Fatima Goss Graves helps administer the funds raised to benefit women's fight against the injustices that occur in their workplaces. Hilary Rosen currently works as an analyst for CNN. Pre- viously, she headed the Recording Industry Association of America. Roberta Kaplan is a litigator and lawyer who addresses public interests and civil rights. Finally, Tina Tchen is also a lawyer who served as an assistant to President Obama and Executive Director of the White House Council on Women and Girls. Together, they and their organization, which has received donations and solidarity support from star celebrities, have raised over $20 million and helped countless women battle inequities in workplaces across industries from farm workers to Hollywood.

Relative impact is about reaching as many people as possible, finding a way to make social justice issues ring true for those who may not be directly involved with the issue. For example, many people know very little about safe drinking water in America and around the world. Celebrities bring these social and human rights issues to light. Terry Crewes, former NFL star and current actor, added legitimacy to the #MeToo movement to indicate that it was not just women looking for attention and a payday when he came out about his own experiences with sexual assault. The relative impact of the sheer number of voices associated with the movement and the fact that it is not just a "woman's" issue significantly increased the movement's impact on our nation.

Celebrity leaders interested in making a difference through their philanthropy efforts must recognize that their efforts might be more like a boomerang, or dud firework, than a rocket launched into outer space. If they truly want their work to have long-term success, five strategies should be at the heart of their work to change the world (Ditkoff & Grindle, 2017).

1. **Shared Understanding**: Competent communication involves ensuring appropriate framing of the social issue being addressed for potential supporters. In our instant-gratification American society, followers need to understand that the mission and vision involve longer-term efforts than a single event or donating lots of resources (time and money) to a problem for a short period of time. Social injustices can take decades to show significant improvements.

2. **Set Winnable Milestones**: Competent leaders and followers set incremental, achievable goals. Creating opportunities to celebrate successes along the way maintains, and may even increase, the movement's momentum. While eradicating hunger among public school students may be the ultimate goal, that may not be achieved in some people's lifetimes, so there has to be a reason for them to participate. Winnable

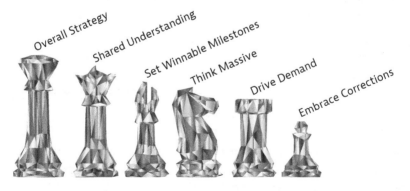

FIGURE 12.5 Strategies for Long-Term Celebrity Activism Success

milestones may involve choosing some of the poorest public schools or areas where many of the children who attend the school are with-out permanent homes. Each implementation in that area (making sure all children have free breakfast and lunch at school, creating a sustainable way to send them "home" with backpacks of food to get through the evening or weekend, helping caregivers find meaningful work that will allow them to provide basic shelter and safety needs) becomes a winnable milestone.

3. **Think Massive**: Whatever the scale of the problem being addressed, the solution must match. Think about the natural disasters we have seen over time (e.g., hurricanes; flooding). Philanthropic organizations, celebrity leaders and followers, and individuals donate millions of dollars to help the victims, yet years later the people affected are still struggling to get back to where they were before the disaster. Why is that? The simple answer is that money is only a small slice of the solution. These people need others to help them recover emotionally, physically, and psychologically from the event. They also need people and resources that will help them feel psychologically safe, return to work, or rebuild their homes. We can also go back to our example above about public schools. What may work for one or two schools in a single area has to be able to be scaled up to solving hunger problems for all school-age children. Can the winnable moments listed above be repeated at schools across the country? If the answer is no, the effort will fail because it does not meet the scalable criterion.

4. **Drive Demand**: One of the most difficult aspects of being competent in these situations is making sure to meet the needs of those involved in the situation. There is nothing worse than donating large amounts of resources to address a problem with a solution the people affected by the issue do not want. For example, if we go back to the school hunger example, developing the backpack program is not going to be successful if those involved see the weekend or evening backpacks of food in a negative light. Some people are offended if outsiders believe they cannot take care of their families, especially when they are working multiple part-time jobs to buy groceries and put gas in the car. Working with these families to develop solutions that allow them to save face and maintain their dignity is a critical component leaders and followers must consider.

5. **Embrace Corrections**: In reality, most attempts to solve a social problem fail on the first, and possibly the second or third, attempt. Competent leaders and followers must be willing to evaluate the situation and change direction when necessary. What worked in one school in an area may not be what is effective in another school in the same area, so those involved must be willing to consider alternative approaches and go back to working with those impacted to develop additional solutions. Trial and error can become a critical component for progress to occur.

Transparency and Operating in a Mediated World

Because today's organizational world operates in a highly politicized environment, leaders and followers must be armed with the knowledge to successfully face political risk, preserve their reputation and brand with the public, and hone their individual political skills.

Political Risk

Many organizations are increasingly finding a need for evaluating and preparing for political risk. For organizational leaders and followers, **political risk** refers to the probability that a governmental or activist action will significantly—positively or negatively—impact their business or brand. Governments and political leaders are not the only players contributing to political risk in our technology-hungry world. Political activities that can impact businesses happen everywhere—on our streets, in our homes, social media chat or forum sites, local bars and restaurants, etc.—as we see a rise in people using personal devices to record and post videos, terrorist threats or attacks, and changes in laws or regulations.

Rice and Zegert (2018) identify several types of political risk highlighting just how real this issue is today. They further suggest four competencies for managing political risk.

- **Step 1: Understand**. Evaluate ways in which your company's brand or product lends itself to being served on the political risk plate. For example, companies in the oil and gas industry are prone to long-term overseas investments, political uncertainty, and social unrest. These companies have a bigger political risk appetite then Disney, whose political risk appetite is set close to zero with their shared understanding that "nothing hurts the mouse." However, even Disney needs to think about the "what if": what if they are wrong? What if something can or does hurt the mouse? Leaders and followers can better understand their organization's political risk appetite by analyzing their answers to three questions: What is my organization's political risk appetite? Is there a shared understanding of our risk appetite? How can we reduce blind spots?

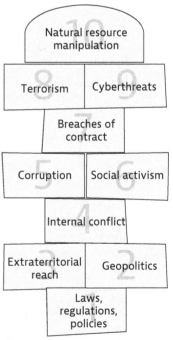

FIGURE 12.6 Forms of Political Risk

- **Step 2: Analyze**. Information is key and quality information likes to play hide-and-seek. Do the research, be sure to hunt for good information, and test for groupthink. As leaders and followers analyze their political risk appetite, they must put into practice two acts: 1) distinguishing between valuable and vulnerable assets, and 2) integrating risk analysis into formal practice during decision-making. The three primary questions to ask in this step are: How can we get good information about the political risk we face? How can we ensure rigorous analysis? How can we integrate political risk analysis into business decisions?

- **Step 3: Mitigate**. To preemptively minimize the potential damage of political risk, leaders and followers should ensure they have built strong relationships with external stakeholders as well as established protocols and ways to monitor awareness. Know when political risk is on the horizon; a good warning system is key. Before, during, or after political risk strikes, your external stakeholders and even competitors can be your strongest allies in preserving your business and its reputation. How can we reduce exposure to the political risks we have identified? Do we have a good system and team in place for timely warning and action? How can we limit the damage when something bad happens?

- **Step 4: Respond**. To preemptively prepare for political risk responses, reflecting on past failures, crises, and learning opportunities are critical for success. Leaders and followers should assess whether they are: a) capitalizing on near misses, b) reacting effectively to crises, and c) developing mechanisms for continuous learning.

Public Reputation

Should CEOs speak up or take a stand on political issues? It is a simple yes or no question. The push for transparency in today's highly politicized environment makes it not as simple to answer. Speaking up or taking a stance has worked well for some and backfired for others. Large companies and well-known brands, even those whose track records are clean, are more at risk for being targeted for protest (Graves, 2017). This research also indicates businesses (small or large) that are more active in their communication with the public are more likely to be singled out by activists. So, they should, or they shouldn't? When it comes to politics, the saying "you can run but you can't hide" generally does not apply. Business leaders are beginning to have less of a choice; it may no longer be an option to refrain from speaking up or taking a stance. For this reason, let's look at Gaines-Ross's (2017) guidelines for how CEOs should act to preserve their companies' reputation.

- Be ready to respond.

- Personalize your narrative.

- There is strength in numbers.

- Be consistent.

Kenneth Frazier, CEO of pharmaceutical giant Merck, may not have been ready to react when the White House responded after one woman was killed during the 2017 racially-motivated shooting in Charlottesville, Virginia. Prior to responding, Frazier talked with the Board of Directors to give them a heads-up and seek their approval before going public with the message that appears below. The narrative was personal for him; his grandfather had been born into slavery and a message that did not condemn white supremacy aroused concern (Gelles, 2018). Additionally, the Board of Directors supported his decision to resign from the White House's American Council on Manufacturing. Following his public statement, many other CEOs began speaking out about the response (strength in numbers). What remains to be seen is the extent to which his message will remain consistent as other opportunities for responding to public statements of neutrality on white supremacy and racial tension arise.

MerckVerified account @Merck

Statement from Kenneth C. Frazier, chairmen and chief executive officer, Merck:

"I am resigning from the President's American Manufacturing Council.

Our country's strength stems from its diversity and the contributions made by men and women of different faiths, races, sexual orientations and political beliefs.

America's leaders must honor our fundamental values by clearly rejecting expressions of hatred, bigotry and group supremacy, which run counter to the American ideal that all people are created equal.

As CEO of Merck and as a matter of personal conscience, I feel a responsibility to take a stand against intolerance and extremism,"

IMAGE 12.1   Forms of Political Risk

Political Skill

Politics and the public—two things that both leaders and followers cannot escape from in the workplace. A leader's or follower's individual political skill is essential to success, now more than ever. **Political skill refers to the** ability to effectively understand others and use such knowledge to influence others to act in ways that promote one's personal and/or organizational objectives

(Kimura, 2015). Political skill is a mix of social competencies necessary for social influence (Ferris et al., 2017).

- **Social astuteness** refers to the ability to adapt informally, understand one's own and others' behaviors while being keenly attuned to diverse situations. This aspect of political skill is important for leaders and followers to effectively choose among a variety of appropriate behaviors. It plays a critical role in breaking glass ceiling barriers for women's and minority's career progression.

- **Interpersonal influence** involves the ability to exert powerful influence to adapt one's own behavior to the situation and alter another's attitudes, behaviors, or beliefs. This aspect of political skill is the foundation for followers' and leaders' capability in forming coalitions and relationships with others that result in personal status gains.

- **Networking ability** is the capacity to develop a diverse set of connections for personal and professional success. Successful companies tend to have effective leaders and followers with strong networks.

- **Apparent sincerity** refers to the ability to appear to others as possessing high levels of integrity, authenticity, and genuineness. This aspect allows leaders and followers to manage divergent interests in a manner that inspires consistent and positive ratings of both task-oriented and relationship-oriented performance.

Researchers who have studied political skill to answer "how" and "why" influence tactics are effective have found leaders and followers high in political skill know what to do in different social situations at work and know how to do it in a manner that appears to be less self-serving and more sincere (Ferris et al., 2017). In practice, this research indicates that political skill works to perfect the influence manner, presentation style, and execution to ensure its success.

RESEARCH SUMMARY

Study: Steffens et al. (2018) set out to examine the relationships among social identity theory, implicit followership theories, and social influence. Social identity addresses 1) the attitudes and behaviors people engage in as a result of the ways in which they define themselves as members, or not members, of collective groups and 2) the ways in which they come to view appropriate follower behaviors based upon implicit followership theories. They proposed four hypotheses:

1. The more people identify with a group, the more they regard followers in that group as representing the followership prototype.

(continued)

2. The less people identify with a group, the less they regard followers in that group as representing the followership prototype.

3. The more people identify with a group, the more they endorse persuasion strategies aimed at changing followers' behavior.

4. The less people identify with a group, the less they endorse coercion strategies aimed at changing followers' behavior.

To test these hypotheses, they conducted two experiments. In the first experiment, they asked people to talk about the leaders and followers of a group with which the person identified, or did not identify. As expected, those who were part of the in-group saw followers as representing the followership prototype and those who were part of the out-group saw followers as representing the followership anti-prototype. In the second experiment, people classified themselves as either Republican or Democrat. They were randomly assigned to one of two scenarios involving Republican or Democratic followers. After assessing these followers, they also allocated a budget to both persuasion and coercion strategies. All four hypotheses were supported: members of the in-group used more persuasion strategies and characterized followers as exhibiting the prototype; members of the out-group used more coercion strategies and characterized followers as exhibiting the anti-prototype of followers.

Implications: Similar to LMX in Chapter 5, these results show the importance of positive behaviors and perceptions associated with members of the in-group and negative behaviors and perceptions associated with members of the out-group. This is in large part why political candidates are more successful with members of their own political party and less successful with members of other political parties. Republican and Democrat are deep social identities for many people; those who view their political social identities as revolving around issues rather than parties are the ones who are more persuadable and often impact election results.

While political skill can, and *should*, be used with good intentions to prevent or avoid causing harm, we know all too well that this is not always the case. Political skill has a dark side. Some have even included this toxic aspect in describing what political skill is, referring to it as the ability to effectively exercise influence during negotiation, persuasion, and manipulation (Mintzberg, 1985). Generally, all competencies have the potential to venture to the dark side when taken to extremes. Political skill, however, is especially susceptible to toxicity, as it teeters between light and dark (good and bad) at the hand who wields it.

Toxic Leadership and Followership

Before we go to the dark side, take a few moments to think about some possible positive connections between transformational leadership and charismatic rhetoric as well as authentic leadership and political skill. What connections did you make or find? Now that you have these theories or concepts freshly reviewed in your mind, think about how these could be used in a negative or toxic way. Jot down your thoughts in Table 12.2.

Sure, we can all think of famous toxic leaders (Hitler, Stalin, Jim Jones, etc.). Because some of these leaders brought harm and suffering to many, the historical evidence indicating that they engaged in effective leadership communication is often overlooked. Oh, no no followers, not so fast: you get an equal turn in the hot seat here. You, toxic followers, don't get to hide anymore. Think about it, and allow us to provide some sense-giving. We know that for as long as leadership has existed, followership has existed. We also know people have had and continue to have an insatiable attraction to leadership, but we are now beginning to focus on followers and study followership. Leaders and leadership have captured the spotlight for so long, bad followers have avoided catching the heat for their own toxicity or role in toxic leadership. Toxic followers have been masked in the shadows, protected from exposure, by both good and bad leaders.

TABLE 12.2   Dark Side Activity

Theory/Concept	Possible Dark Side Uses/Examples
Transformational Leadership	
Charismatic Rhetoric	
Responsible Leadership	
Political Skill	

In reality, a lot of the famous leaders everyone knows wouldn't be nearly as famous for being "toxic" if it weren't for their followers' toxicity. Another disappointing truth is we don't have to rely on lists of bad leaders and followers when they exist in our everyday lives. Just because they aren't in the news or in history books doesn't mean people don't come face-to-face with or haven't experienced harmful leaders and followers in their lived realities. While we may use well-known examples of toxic leaders and followers throughout this discussion, we should all be aware that you and many others will resonate with some of these examples for the simple reason that they have happened (or are happening) in your own life.

When we say toxic leadership or toxic followership, what exactly do we mean? Leadership and followership on their own are theoretical concepts. It is people's characteristics and behaviors that make leadership (or followership) transformational, authentic, charismatic, or toxic. The word toxic has several synonyms, including bad, destructive, narcissistic, evil, and dark side. According to Lipman-Blumen (2005, p. 2) **toxic leaders are** "individuals who, by virtue of their destructive behaviors or their dysfunctional personal characteristics, inflict serious and enduring harm upon the individuals, groups, organizations, communities and even the nations that they lead or follow." We can identify good versus toxic leaders and followers based on destructive behaviors (see Figure 12.7; Heppell, 2011; Lipman-Blumen, 2005).

Lack of integrity & honesty
- lying to followers to bolster a powerful vision; misleading followers through lies; subverting justice system and committing crimes

Outsized ambition putting the leader's quest for glory above the well-being of others
- making an overthrow a trigger for downfall of the system

Egotism and arrogance that foster incompetence & corruption
- building a totalitarian/dynastic regime; failing to nurture other leaders

Actions that "intimidate, demoralize, demean, & marginalize" others
- playing on fears and needs; setting one group against another; fostering hatred of other groups among followers; identifying or using scapegoats

Breaching opponents' and followers' basic human rights & stifling criticism
- violating the rights of followers or non-followers; blocking constructive criticism

Holding tight to power by undermining potential successors
- critically, feeding unrealistic illusions to followers, and thereby fueling dependency; glass ceiling phenomenon

FIGURE 12.7 Destructive Behaviors of Toxic Followers and Leaders

For toxic followers, there are two additional destructive behaviors, conforming (doing whatever the leader says without thinking through the implications) and colluding (sharing the values and worldview of a toxic leader).

We can also distinguish between good and toxic leaders or followers based on dysfunctional personal characteristics (Kellerman, 2004), including:

- **Incompetent**: lack the communication and political skill required to use power positively.

- **Rigid**: lack the ability to adapt and accept new or different ideas, information, and changing circumstances.

- **Intemperate**: forceful and lack self-control.

- **Callous**: disconfirming; ignore or put down others with a clear disregard for others' thoughts and feelings.

- **Corrupt**: driven by their own self-interest, rather than the interests of the collective, to the extent that they justify lying, cheating, and stealing.

- **Insular**: either lack adequate concern or awareness for others' well-being or those who may be affected by their decisions.

- **Evil**: commit psychological and/or physical harm to others by using pain and suffering as an instrument of power.

All of this, so far, may be information that you already know or have heard before. Have you noticed how opposite these toxic behaviors are to the key behaviors and characteristics effective leaders and followers share? The real questions of interest are often, why—why do toxic leaders and followers do what they do and why do they get away with it? What attracts people to these toxic behaviors?

According to Popper (2014), there are three reasons why people are attracted to toxic leaders (or followers). First, the **psychoanalytic explanation of toxic behaviors** is grounded in our basic evolutionary needs for an authority figure to fulfill our needs and desires for protection and security. People may be drawn to a toxic follower to fulfil their esteem needs or to reach their own personal goals. This explanation is most obvious when people are less mature, less competent, inexperienced, have insecure forms of attachment, or lack basic needs for survival.

Second, the **cognitive-psychological explanation of toxic behaviors** is based in how people make sense of reality. People are drawn to toxic leaders and followers because they match their own implicit theories of leadership and followership. This explanation is most obvious when people attempt to reduce uncertainty or have no other comparative alternatives available. Last, the **social-psychological explanation of toxic behaviors** is anchored in identity, specifically social identity, which is the need for identity and the need to belong. People can be drawn to toxic leaders or followers because they confirm or effect one's self-concept, its crystallization and development, which touches on people's emotions. This explanation is most obvious when people feel the need to belong or the need for identity.

Grassroots Leadership and Followership

As our journey together comes to a close, we end where we began—the over-whelming similarities between leaders and followers. Grassroots organizing and implementation is a mindset as much as it is a process. To be effective, everyone involved must be empowered to make a difference; power is dis-tributed and shared among everyone, rather than located within a specific position such as leader (Keyser, 2016). Listening, role modelling, and trusting each other are the cornerstones of grassroots organizing. If the people involved do not engage in all three of these communication behaviors, the grassroots efforts are not going to be successful. Sometimes, grassroots organizing occurs when the community wants to support a particular political candidate. The community may rally to encourage the candidate to seek office and then knock on doors, build a social media presence, and organize public appearances for the candidate. The same can happen when an important social issue arises. Earlier we talked about sexual misconduct in the workplace, equality with respect to pay, and gun violence—all of these are social issues best addressed through grassroots organizing rather than top-down policy decisions.

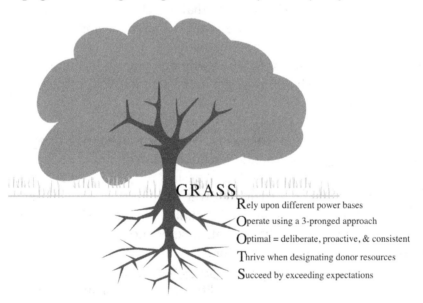

GRASS
Rely upon different power bases
Operate using a 3-pronged approach
Optimal = deliberate, proactive, & consistent
Thrive when designating donor resources
Succeed by exceeding expectations

FIGURE 12.8   Grassroots Approaches

Grassroots approaches to handling public social problems merge leader-ship and followership behaviors (W. K. Kellogg Foundation, 2003). First, they rely upon different power bases (referent more than legitimate, reward, or coercive). Second, they use a three-pronged approach by focusing on the individual, organization, and community. Third, these processes are most effective when they are deliberate, proactive, intentional, and consistent.

Fourth, grassroots efforts thrive when those involved in implementation determine how donor resources are going to be used rather than the donor dictating how the funds are going to be used. Finally, grassroots efforts exceed expectations when the community or social issue, rather than the leaders and followers, is prioritized.

CASE STUDY **Theresa May and Brexit**

Prime Minister Theresa May served in that role and as leader of the conservative party in Great Britain from 2016 to 2019. She survived two no-confidence votes in 2018 and 2019. While her political career is long, this case focuses on her leadership during the time in which the United Kingdom negotiated to withdraw from the European Union, known as Brexit. In case you did not follow this political situation, Brexit is shorthand for "British exit" and Brexiters are those who support the region's separation from the European Union (EU). Primarily, the United Kingdom joined the EU for economic reasons—it gave the region a level of economic and trading security. Rewind to 2016: The public voted to withdraw from the EU. From 2016 to 2019, Theresa May attempted to broker a deal that would be acceptable to both the EU and the Labour Party (akin to the Democratic party in the U.S.); the Conservative Party (akin to the Republican party in the U.S.) had always been supportive of divorce from the EU. During 2017 and 2018, Parliament agreed to withdraw in 2019 and voted to prevent the EU from making future laws for the UK.

In March 2018, PM May addressed Parliament with the following words as part of her plan for future UK-EU relations (https://www.bbc.com/news/uk-politics-43256183):

> "The government I lead will be driven not by the interests of the privileged few, but by yours. We will do everything we can to give you more control over your lives. When we take the big calls, we'll think not of the powerful, but you. When we pass new laws, we'll listen not to the mighty but to you. When it comes to taxes, we'll prioritise not the wealthy, but you. When it comes to opportunity, we won't entrench the advantages of the fortunate few. We will do everything we can to help anybody, whatever your background, to go as far as your talents will take you.

> We are living through an important moment in our country's history.

> As we leave the European Union, we will forge a bold new positive role for ourselves in the world, and we will make Britain a country that works not for a privileged few, but for every one of us.

> That pledge, to the people of our United Kingdom is what guides me in our negotiations with the EU."

(continued)

In November, 2018, she addressed the House of Commons regarding the withdrawal plan (https://www.gov.uk/government/speeches/pm-statement-on-brexit-negotiations-15-november-2018):

"With permission, Mr Speaker, I would like to update the House on our negotiations to leave the European Union.

First, I want to pay tribute to my Rt Hon Friends the Members for Esher and Walton and Tatton.

Delivering Brexit involves difficult choices for all of us.

We do not agree on all of those choices but I respect their views and thank them sincerely for all that they have done.

Mr Speaker, yesterday we agreed the provisional terms of our exit from the European Union, set out in the Draft Withdrawal Agreement.

We also agreed the broad terms of our future relationship, in an Outline Political Declaration.

President Juncker has now written to the President of the European Council to recommend that 'decisive progress has been made in the negotiations.'

And a special European Council will be called for Sunday 25th November.

This puts us close to a Brexit deal.

Mr Speaker, what we agreed yesterday was not the final deal.

It is a draft treaty that means we will leave the EU in a smooth and orderly way on 29 March 2019 and which sets the framework for a future relationship that delivers in our national interest.

It takes back control of our borders, laws and money.

It protects jobs, security and the integrity of the United Kingdom.

And it delivers in ways that many said could simply not be done."

In March 2019, PM May had to seek an extension because the UK and EU had not been able to broker a successful deal (https://www.gov.uk/government/speeches/pm-statement-on-brexit-20-march-2019):

"Nearly three years have passed since the public voted to leave the European Union. It was the biggest democratic exercise in our country's history. I came to office on a promise to deliver on that verdict. In March 2017, I triggered the Article 50 process for the UK to exit the EU—and Parliament supported it overwhelmingly. Two years on, MPs have been unable to agree on a way to implement the UK's withdrawal. As a result, we will now not leave on time with a deal on 29 March. This delay is a matter of great personal regret for me. And of this I am absolutely sure: you the public have had enough. You are tired of the infighting. You are tired of the political games and the arcane procedural rows. Tired of MPs talking about nothing else but Brexit when you have real concerns about our children's schools, our National Health Service, and knife crime. You want this stage of the Brexit process to be over and done with. I agree. I am on your side. It is now time for MPs to decide … Do they want to leave the EU with a deal which delivers on the result of the referendum—that takes back control of our money, borders and laws while protecting jobs and our national security? Do they want to leave without a deal? Or do they not want to leave at all, causing potentially irreparable damage to public trust—not just in this generation of politicians, but to our entire democratic process? It is high time we made a decision … I passionately hope MPs will find a way to back the deal I have negotiated with the EU. A deal that delivers on the result of the referendum and is the very best deal negotiable. I will continue to work night and day to secure the support of my colleagues, the DUP and others for this deal. But I am not prepared to delay Brexit any further than 30 June. Some argue that I am making the wrong choice, and I should ask for a longer extension to the end of the year or beyond, to give more time for politicians to argue over the way forward. That would mean asking you to vote in European Elections, nearly three years after our country decided to leave. What kind of message would that send? And just how bitter and divisive would that election campaign be at a time when the country desperately needs bringing back together? Some have suggested holding a second referendum. I don't believe that is what you want—and it is not what I want. We asked you the question already and you gave us your answer. Now you want us to get on with it. And that is what I am determined to do."

DISCUSSION QUESTIONS

1. In our society, language is an important tool. What language choices did PM May make that were effective? Ineffective? Why? Similarly, some accounts refer to her as PM May and others refer to her as Mrs. May. What difference do these titles make in how people perceive her and her message? Would you expect a male prime minister to be referred to as Mr.? Why?

2. If you were a citizen of the United Kingdom, to what extent would you side with PM May and to what extent would you side with those who oppose withdrawal? In what ways does your in-group or out-group status with the Conservative Party and Labour Party contribute your view?

3. Beyond in-group and out-group status, what other factors would likely contribute to your perceptions of PM May's rhetorical effectiveness? Why are these characteristics or qualities important?

(continued)

ANALYSIS OPTIONS

A. Traditional and social media have had much to say about the Brexit withdrawal situation. You are part of PM May's communication cabinet and have been tasked with developing strategies to help set a desirable agenda. Be sure to consider the first, second, and third levels of agenda setting.

B. In her March 2019 speech, PM May appealed to the people. Assume you heard the message and were moved to organize a grassroots effort to convince Parliament to vote on a plan, either for withdrawal or no withdrawal.

C. The Labour Party has hired your communication firm to help them develop a message that responds to PM May's criticism (see March 2019 message) and lays the groundwork for removing her from office so that she can be replaced by a Labour candidate. Strategize how you would reach the UK people and convince them that your approach is more effective for them and the region as a whole.

ANALYSIS PROCESS

- Brainstorm a list of options for addressing the issue.

- Make a list of strengths and challenges for each of your brainstormed solutions.

- Choose the best solution for the issue.

- Develop an implementation plan for your chosen solution.

- Additional resources:

Lolly Daskal Website
https://tinyurl.com/y42kro5u

PM May Address to Parliament
tiny.utk.edu/FCL12_1

House of Commons
tiny.utk.edu/FCL12_2

2018 Withdrawal Speech
tiny.utk.edu/FCL12_4

PM May Extension Request
tiny.utk.edu/FCL12_3

Labour Party
https://tinyurl.com/ycyf2ggt

Theresa May on Twitter
https://tinyurl.com/zn9r6lv

Conservative Party
https://tinyurl.com/kc9hx5x

 LEADER AND FOLLOWER DEVELOPMENT PRACTICES

1. Use clear language, short statements, and speak with conviction (Thatcher, 2016).

2. Serve as a role model for integrity and loyalty without falling prey to the temptations that exist within political and public spaces (Cohen, 2018).

3. Build resilience so you have the strength to resist personal attacks (Ellen, 2016).

4. Know more about your political rivals than they know about you (Shah, 2017).

5. Put the good of others above personal gain by listening and being self-aware.

DISCUSSION QUESTIONS AND ACTIVITIES

1. Choose a political or celebrity figure with whom you agree. Find at least five examples of messages that illustrate the person's beliefs and values. Find examples of each type of charismatic rhetoric the person uses. Which types does the person use most frequently? Least frequently? Why do you think that is the case? Complete the same task for a political or celebrity leader with whom you disagree. What are the similarities and differences between the rhetoric each uses? What might that say about why you agree with one and disagree with the other?

2. Open your favorite news app. Scroll through until you find a story about a celebrity or political leader. Pay particular attention to how they frame the leader. After reading the story, choose a news source you do not usually read (e.g., CNN, FOXNews, MSNBC) and find its coverage of the same story. Finally, find the leader's social media and see how the story is framed there. What similarities and differences exist in the ways the two news sources and individual's social media frame the story? Why do you think these similarities and differences exist?

3. Are you an opinion leader follower? Do you know an opinion leader follower? How much of what we have discussed holds true for you or an opinion leader follower you know? Using yourself, or another opinion leader follower you know/find online, use specific examples to explain how they tell you what to think about. IF they also tell you what to think or do, include examples of those as well.

4. Choose a toxic follower you have known (think back to some of those group projects you have worked on in college). Which of the less-than-competent communication behaviors we have discussed did this person engage in? What impact did those behaviors have on the group or team? How will you avoid this from happening the next time you are in a leadership or followership situation?

5. Grassroots campaigns are everywhere. Find one in your local area. Attend an event, day of service, meeting, etc. What did you learn about yourself, the people who are part of the movement, and the movement itself? What did they do that inspired you and what did they do that could create barriers between themselves and others in the local community or government?

FIGURE CREDITS:

References

Chapter 1

Braun, S., Stegman, S., Hernandez Bark, A. S., Junker, N. M., & van Dick, R. (2017). Think manager—think male, think follower—think female: Gender bias in implicit followership theories. *Journal of Applied Social Psychology, 47*(7), 377–388. https://doi.org/10.1111/jasp.12445

Carnes, A., Houghton, J. D., & Ellison, C. N. (2015). What matters most in leader selection?: The role of personality and implicit leadership theories. *Leadership and Organization Development Journal, 36*(4), 360–379. https://doi.org/10.1108/LODJ-06-2013-0087

Carsten, M. K., Harms, P., & Uhl-Bien, M. (2014). Exploring historical perspectives of followership: The need for an expanded view of followers and the follower role. In L. M. Lapierre & M. K. Carsten (Eds.), *Followership: What is it and why do people follow?* (pp. 3–25). Emerald Group Publishing.

Deal, T. E., & Kennedy, A. A. (1982). *Corporate cultures: The rites and rituals of corporate life.* Basic.

Fayol, H. (1916/1949). *General and industrial management* (C. Storrs, Trans.). Sir Isaac Pitman & Sons.

Flanagin, A. J. (2017). Online social influence and the convergence of mass and interpersonal communication. *Human Communication Research, 43*(4), 450–463. https://doi.org/10.1111/hcre.12116

Foti, R. J., Hansbrough, T. K., Epitropaki, O., & Coyle, P. T. (2017). Dynamic viewpoints on implicit leadership and followership theories: Approaches, findings, and future directions. *Leadership Quarterly, 25*(2), 261–267. http://dx.doi.org/10.1016/j.leaqua.2014.02.004

French, J., & Raven, B. (1959). The bases of social power. In D. Cartwright (Ed.), *Studies in social power* (pp. 150–167). Research Center for Group Dynamics, Institute for Social Research, University of Michigan.

Hartman, J. L., & McCambridge, J. (2011). Optimizing millennials' communication styles. *Business Communication Quarterly, 74*(1), 22–44. https://doi.org/10.1177%2F1080569910395564

Kuppler, T. (2014). *Culture fundamentals: 9 important insights from Edgar Schein.* Culture Institute. https://www.humansynergistics.com/blog/culture-university/details/culture-university/2018/07/26/culture-fundamentals---9-important-insights-from-edgar-schein

Lee, Y., & Kramer, A. (2016). The role of purposeful diversity and inclusion strategy (PDIS) and cultural tightness/looseness in the relationship between national and organizational culture. *Human Resource Management Review, 26*(3), 198–208. https://doi.org/10.1016/j.hrmr.2016.01.001

Marston, W. (1928). *Emotions of normal people.* Harcourt, Brace.

Maslow, A. H. (1943). A theory of human motivation. *Psychological Review, 50*(4), 370–396. https://psycnet.apa.org/doi/10.1037/h0054346

Mok, P. (1975). *Interpretation manual for communicating styles and technology.* Training Associates Press.

Phillips, J. S., & Lord, R. G. (1986). Notes on the practical and theoretical consequences of implicit leadership theories for the future of leadership measurement. *Journal of Management, 12*(1), 31–41. https://doi.org/10.1177%2F014920638601200104

Raven, B. H. (1965). Social influence and power. In I. D. Steiner & M. Fishbein (Eds.), *Current studies in social psychology* (pp. 371–382). Holt, Rinehart and Winston.

Schriesheim, C. A., & Hinkin, T. R. (1990). Influence tactics used by subordinates: A theoretical and empirical analysis and refinement of Kipnis, Schmidt, and Wilkinson subscales. *Journal of Applied Psychology, 75*(3), 246–257. https://psycnet.apa.org/doi/10.1037/0021-9010.75.3.246

Smircich, L. (1983). Concepts of culture and organizational analysis. *Administrative Science Quarterly, 28*(3), 339–358. https://www.jstor.org/stable/2392246

Yukl, G., Chavez, C., & Seifert, C. F. (2005). Assessing the construct validity and utility of two new influence tactics. *Journal of Organizational Behavior, 26*(6), 705–725. https://doi.org/10.1002/job.335

Chapter 2

Blake, R., & Mouton, J. (1974). What's new with the grid? *Training and Development Journal, 25*(5), 473–476.

Cote, R. (2017). A comparison of leadership theories in an organizational environment. *International Journal of Business Administration, 8*(5), 28–35. https://doi.org/10.5430/ijba.v8n5p28

Drea Zigarmi, T., & Roberts, P. R. (2017). A test of three basic assumptions of Situational Leadership® II Model and their implications for HRD practitioners. *European Journal of Training and Development, 41*(3), 241–260. https://doi.org/10.1108/EJTD-05-2016-0035

Evans, M. (1970). The effects of supervisory behavior on the path-goal relationship. *Organizational Behavior and Human Performance, 5*(3), 277–298. https://doi.org/10.1016/0030-5073(70)90021-8

Fiedler, F. E. (1967) *A Theory of Leadership Effectiveness.* McGraw-Hill.

Hersey, P., & Blanchard, K. H. (1974). So, you want to know your leadership style? *Training & Development Journal, 28*(2), 22–37.

House, R. (1971). A path-goal theory of leader effectiveness. *Administrative Science Quarterly, 16*(3), 321–339. https://doi.org/10.2307/2391905

House, R. (1996). Path-goal theory of leadership: Lessons, legacy, and a reformulated theory. *The Leadership Quarterly, 7*(3), 323–352. https://doi.org/10.1016/S1048-9843(96)90024-7

House, R. J., & Mitchell, T. R. (1974). Path-goal theory of leadership. *Journal of Contemporary Business, 9*, 81–97.

Lewin, K. (1939). Field theory and experiment in social psychology: Concepts and methods. *American Journal of Sociology, 44*(6), 868–896. https://doi.org/10.1086/218177

Mann, R. D. (1959). A review of the relationship between personality and performance in small groups. *Psychological Bulletin, 56*(4), 241–270.

Martins, R. (2015, Feb 24). Rats remember who's nice to them—and return the favor. *National Geographic*. https://www.nationalgeographic.com/news/2015/2/150224-rats-helping-social-behavior-science-animals-cooperation/#close

Stogdill, R. (1949). Personal factors associated with leadership: A survey of the literature. *Journal of Psychology, 25*(1), 35–71.

Stogdill, R. (1974). *Handbook of leadership: A survey of theory and research.* The Free Press.

Taylor, F. W. (1911). *The principles of scientific management.* Harper & Brothers.

Vandegrift, R., & Matusitz, J. (2011). Path-goal theory: A successful Columbia Records story. *Journal of Human Behavior in the Social Environment, 21*(4), 350–362. https://doi.org/10.1080/10911359.2011.555651

Weber, M. (1922). *Economy and Society. An Outline of Interpretative Sociology.* University of California Press.

Wiener-Bronner, D. (2017, December 18). The ranks of women CEOs got even smaller this year. *CNN Money*. http://money.cnn.com/2017/12/18/news/women-ceos-2017/index.html

Chapter 3

Baker, S. (2007). Followership: The theoretical foundation of a contemporary construct. *Journal of Leadership & Organizational Studies, 14*(1), 50–60. https://doi.org/10.1177/0002831207304343

Bass, B. M. (1985). *Leadership beyond expectations.* Free Press.

Bass, B. M. (1996). *A new paradigm for leadership: An inquiry into transformational leadership.* State University of New York at Binghamton.

Carsten, M. K., Harms, P., & Uhl-Bien, M. (2014). Exploring historical perspectives of followership: The need for an expanded view of followers and the follower role. In L. M. Lapierre & M. K. Carsten (Eds), *Followership: What is it and why do people follow?* (pp. 3–25). Emerald Group Publishing.

Chaleff, I. (2008). Creating new ways of following. In R. E. Riggio, I. Chaleff, & J. Lipman-Blument (Eds), *The art of followership: How great followers create great leaders and organizations* (pp. 67–88). Jossey–Bass.

Chaleff, I. (2009). *The courageous follower: Standing up to & for our leaders* (3rd ed.). Berrett-Koehler Publishers, Inc.

Chaleff, I. (2016). In praise of followership style assessments. *Journal of Leadership Studies, 10*(3), 45–48. https://doi.org/10.1002/jls.21490

de Bettignies (2014, Nov 11). *The five dimensions of responsible leadership.* INSEAD: The Business School for the World. https://knowledge.insead.edu/responsibility/the-five-dimensions-of-responsible-leadership-3685

Epitropaki, O., Sy, T., Martin, R., Tram-Quon, S., & Topakas, A. (2013). Implicit leadership and followership theories "in the wild": Taking stock of information-processing approaches to leadership and followership in organizational settings. *The Leadership Quarterly, 24*(6), 858–881. https://doi.org/10.1016/j.leaqua.2013.10.005

Kellerman, B. (2007). What every leader needs to know about followers. *Harvard Business Review, 85*(12), 84–91. https://hbr.org/2007/12/what-every-leader-needs-to-know-about-followers

Kelley, R. E. (1988). In praise of followers. *Harvard Business Review, 66*(6), 142–148. https://hbr.org/1988/11/in-praise-of-followers

Kelley, R. E. (2008). Rethinking followership. In R. Riggio, I. Chaleff, & J. Lipman-Blumen (Eds.), *The art of followership: How great followers create great leaders and organizations* (pp. 5–15). Jossey-Bass.

Kouzes, J. M., & Posner, B. Z. (1987). *The leadership challenge: How to get extraordinary things done in organizations.* Jossey-Bass.

Lin, C., Huang, P., Chen, S. & Liang, C. (2017). Pseudo-transformational leadership is in the eyes of the subordinates. *Journal of Business Ethics, 141*, 179–190. https://doi.org/10.1007/s10551-015-2739-5

Lin, S., Scott, B., & Matta, F. K. (2019). The dark side of transformational leader behaviors for leaders themselves: A conservation of resources perspective. *Academy of Management Journal, 62*(5), 1556–1582. https://doi.org/10.5465/amj.2016.1255

Liu, C., & Lin, C. (2018). Assessing the effects of responsible leadership and ethical conflict on behavioral intentions. *Review of Managerial Science,12*(4), 1003–1024. https://doi.org/10.1007/s11846-017-0236-1

Miska, C., & Mendenhall, M. E. (2018). Responsible leadership: A mapping of extant research and future directions. *Journal of Business Ethics, 148*, 117–134. https://doi.org/10.1007/s10551-015-2999-0

Smith, A. M., & Green, M. (2018). Artificial intelligence and the role of leadership. *Journal of Leadership Studies, 12*(3), 85–87. https://doi.org/10.1002/jls.21605

Tepper, B., Duffy, M., Shaw, J., & Murphy, Kevin R. (2001). Personality moderators of the relationship between abusive supervision and subordinates' resistance. *Journal of Applied Psychology, 86*(5), 974–983. http://doi.org/10.1037/0021-9010.86.5.974

Tsui, A. S. (2019 pre-print). Guidepost: Responsible research and responsible leadership studies. *Academy of Management Discoveries.* https://journals.aom.org/doi/pdf/10.5465/amd.2019.0244

Uhl-Bien, M., Riggio, R. E., Lowe, K. B., & Carsten, M. K. (2014). Followership theory: A review and research agenda. *Leadership Quarterly, 25*(1), 83–104. http://doi.org/10.1016/j.leaqua.2013.11.007

Venus, M., Stam, D., & van Knippenberg, D. (2013). Leader emotion as a catalyst of effective leader communication of visions, value-laden messages, and goals. *Organizational Behavior and Human Decision Processes, 122*(1), 53–68. https://psycnet.apa.org/doi/10.1016/j.obhdp.2013.03.009

Violanti, M. T., & Ray, C. A. (2019, Nov). Co-cultural audiences matter: A communication approach to responsible leadership. *Academy of Management Global Proceedings, Slovenia.* https://doi.org/10.5465/amgblproc.slovenia.2019.0446.abs

Yaslioglu, M. M., & SelenayErden, N. (2018). Transformational leaders in action: Theory has been there, but what about practice? *The IUP Journal of Business Strategy, 15*(1), 42–53. https://www.researchgate.net/publication/324602033_Transformational_Leaders_in_Action_Theory_Has_Been_There_But_What_About_Practice

Chapter 4

Amundsen, S., & Martinsen, O. (2014). Empowering leadership: Construct clarification, conceptualization, and validation of a new scale. *Leadership Quarterly, 25*(3), 487–511. https://doi.org/10.1016/j.leaqua.2013.11.009

Bandura, A. (1991). Social cognitive theory of self-regulation. *Organizational Behavior and Human Decision Processes, 50*(2), 248–287. https://doi.org/10.1016/0749-5978(91)90022-L

Bodie, G., Gearhart, C., Denham, J., & Vickery, A. (2013). The temporal stability and situational contingency of active-empathic listening. *Western Journal of Communication, 77*(2), 113–138. https://doi.org/10.1080/10570314.2012.656216

Burleson, B. R. (1987). Cognitive complexity and person-centered communication: A review of methods, findings, and explanations. In J. McCroskey & J. A. Daly (Eds.), *Personality and interpersonal communication* (pp. 305–349). Sage.

Burleson, B. (2009). Understanding the outcomes of supportive communication: A dual-process approach. *Journal of Social and Personal Relationships, 26*(1), 21–38. https://doi.org/10.1177/0265407509105519

Campbell, N. (2016). Ethnocentrism and intercultural willingness to communicate: A study of New Zealand management students. *Journal of Intercultural Communication, 40*. https://immi.se/intercultural/nr40/campbell.html

Carsten, M., Uhl-Bien, M., & Huang, L. (2018). Leader perceptions and motivation as outcomes of followership role orientation and behavior. *Leadership, 14*(6), 731–756. https://doi.org/10.1177/1742715017720306

Carver, C. S., Johnson, S. L., Oormann, J. F., & Scheier, M. (2015). An evolving view of the structure of self-regulation. In G. H. E. Gendolla, M. Topps, & S. L. Koole (Eds.), *Handbook of biobehavioral approaches to self-regulation* (pp. 9–23). Springer.

Clark, R., & Delia, J. (1979). TOPOI and rhetorical competence. *Quarterly Journal of Speech, 65*(2), 187–206. https://doi.org/10.1080/00335637909383470

Disque, B. M. (2018, May 30). Commentary: Followership, or how to avoid being a toxic subordinate. *Noncommissioned Officer Journal*: Army University Press. https://www.armyupress.army.mil/Portals/7/nco-journal/docs/Followership-May-2018.pdf

Ellingsworth, H. W. (1988). A theory of adaptation in intercultural dyads. In Y. Y. Kim & W. B. Gudykunst (Eds.), *International and intercultural communication annual* (Vol. 12, pp. 259–279). Sage.

Giles, S. (2016, Mar 15). The most important leadership competencies, according to leaders around the world. *Harvard Business Review*.https://hbr.org/2016/03/the-most-important-leadership-competencies-according-to-leaders-around-the-world

Greene, J. O. & McNallie, J. (2015). Competence knowledge. In A. Hannawa, & B. H. Spitzberg (Eds.), *Communication competence* (pp. 213–236). Walter de Gruyter GmbH.

Guerrero, L. & Ramos-Salzar, L. (2015). Nonverbal skills in emotional communication. In A. Hannawa, & B. H. Spitzberg (Eds.), *Communication competence* (pp. 131–152). Walter de Gruyter GmbH.

Hale, C., & Delia, J. (1976). Cognitive complexity and social perspective taking. *Communication Monographs, 43*(3), 195–203. https://doi.org/10.1080/03637757609375932

Kassing, J. W. (1997). Development of the intercultural willingness to communicate scale. *Communication Research Reports, 14*(4), 399–407. https://doi.org/10.1080/08824099709388683

Lapierre, L. M. (2014). Why and how should subordinates follow their managers? In L. M. Lapierre & M. K. Carsten (Eds.), *Followership: What is it and why do people follow?* (pp. 157–169). Emerald Group Publishing Limited.

Lee, F., Sheldon, K., & Turban, D. (2003). Personality and the goal-striving process: The influence of achievement goal patterns, goal level, and mental focus on performance and enjoyment. *Journal of Applied Psychology, 88*(2), 256–265. https://doi.org/10.1037/0021-9010.88.2.256

Lee, A., Willis, S., & Tian, A. (2018a). Empowering leadership: A meta analytic examination of incremental contribution, mediation, and moderation. *Journal of Organizational Behavior, 39*(3), 306–325. https://doi.org/10.1002/job.2220

Lee, A., Willis, S., & Tian, A. (2018b, March 02). When empowering employees works, and when it doesn't. *Harvard Business Review Digital Articles*, 2–6. https://hbr.org/2018/03/when-empowering-employees-works-and-when-it-doesnt

Lian, H., Yam, K. C., Ferris, D. L., & Brown, D. (2017). Self-control at work. *Academy of Management Annals, 11*(2), 703–732. https://doi.org/10.5465/annals.2015.0126

Miller, G. R. & Steinberg, M. (1975). *Between people: A new analysis of interpersonal communication*. Science Research Associates.

Randel, A. E., Galvin, B. M., Shore, L. M., Ehrhart, K. H., Chung, B. G., Dean, M. A., & Kedharnath, U. (2018). Inclusive leadership: Realizing positive outcomes through belongingness and being valued for uniqueness. *Human Resource Management Review, 28*(2), 190–203. https://doi.org/10.1016/j.hrmr.2017.07.002

Riggio, R. (1986). Assessment of basic social skills. *Journal of Personality and Social Psychology, 51*(3), 649–660. https://doi.org/10.1037/0022-3514.51.3.649

Salovey, P., & Mayer, J. D. (1990). Emotional intelligence. *Imagination, cognition and personality, 9*(3), 185–211. https://doi.org/10.2190%2FDUGG-P24E-52WK-6CDG

Sawyer, C. R. & Richmond, V. P. (2015). Motivational factors and communication competence. In A. Hannawa, & B. H. Spitzberg (Eds.), *Communication competence* (pp. 193–212). Walter de Gruyter GmbH.

Spitzberg, B. H. (2015). The composition of competence: Communication skills. In A. Hannawa, & B. H. Spitzberg (Eds.), *Communication competence* (pp. 237–271). Walter de Gruyter GmbH.

Spitzberg, B. H. & Changnon, G. (2009). Conceptualizing intercultural competence. In D. K. Deardorff (Ed.), *The Sage handbook of intercultural competence* (pp. 2–52). Sage Publications.

Steele, G., & Plenty, D. (2015). Supervisor–subordinate communication competence and job and communication satisfaction. *International Journal of Business Communication, 52*(3), 294–318. https://doi.org/10.1177%2F2329488414525450

Suda, L. (2013). *In praise of followers*. Paper presented at PMI® Global Congress 2013—North America, New Orleans, LA. Project Management Institute. https://www.pmi.org/learning/library/importance-of-effective-followers-5887

Troth, A., Jordan, P., Lawrence, S., & Tse, H. (2012). A multilevel model of emotional skills, communication performance, and task performance in teams. *Journal of Organizational Behavior, 33*(5), 700–722. https://doi.org/10.1002/job.785

Wong, S., & Giessner, S. (2018). The thin line between empowering and laissez-faire leadership: An expectancy-match perspective. *Journal of Management, 44*(2), 757–783. https://doi.org/10.1177%2F0149206315574597

Zenger, J. & Folkman, J. (2014, July 30). The skills leaders need at every level. *Harvard Business Review.* https://hbr.org/2014/07/the-skills-leaders-need-at-every-level

Zorn, T., & Violanti, M. (1996). Communication abilities and individual achievement in organizations. *Management Communication Quarterly, 10*(2), 139–167. https://doi.org/10.1177%2F0893318996010002001

Chapter 5

Birch, J. (2018, Jan 3). Leadership advice goes beyond 140 characters [blog post]. *The Globe and Mail.* https://www.theglobeandmail.com/report-on-business/careers/leadership-lab/leadership-advice-goes-beyond-140-characters/article37454218/

Buber, M. (1956). *I and thou* (Ronald Gregor Smith, Trans.). Charles Scribner's Sons.

Buehler, K. (2017, November 21). Challenges faced by leaders of remote teams [Weblog]. https://www.hrtechnologist.com/articles/mobile-workforce/challenges-faced-by-leaders-of-remote-teams/

Byron, K., & Baldridge, D. C. (2007). E-mail recipients' impression of senders' likability. *Journal of Business Communication, 44*(2), 137–160. https://doi.org/10.1177%2F0021943606297902

Cialdini, R. B. (2001). *Influence: Science and practice.* Allyn & Bacon.

Citigroup. (2014, Oct 28). New Citi/LinkedIn survey reveals men struggle with work-life balance—but may not be telling women their concerns [News release]. https://www.citigroup.com/citi/news/2014/141028a.htm

Coleman, J. (2018, April 16). The power of relational leadership. *Forbes.* https://www.forbes.com/sites/johncoleman/2018/04/16/the-power-of-relational-leadership/#7432d1ed369d

DeRosa, D. (2018, Jan 4). The 6 fundamentals of an efficient virtual team [weblog]. onpoint Consulting. https://www.onpointconsultingllc.com/blog/the-6-fundamentals-of-an-efficient-virtual-team

Erdogan, B. & Bauer, T. (2014). Leader-member exchange (LMX) theory: The relational approach to leadership. In D. Day (Ed.), *The Oxford Handbook of Leadership and Organizations* (pp. 407–433). Oxford University Press.

Fibuch, E., & Robertson, J. J. (2018, Nov/Dec). Bringing value: Leading by coaching and mentoring others. *Physician Leadership Journal.*

George, W., & Sims, P. (2007). *True north: Discover your true authentic leadership.* San Francisco, CA: Jossey-Bass.

Graen, G. B., & Scandura, T. A. (1987). Toward a psychology of dyadic organizing. In L. L. Cummings & B. M. Staw (Eds.), *Research in organizational behavior* (Vol. 9, pp. 175–208). New York, NY: JAI Press.

Graen, G. B. & Uhl-Bien, M. (1995). Relationship-based approach to leadership: Development of leader-member exchange (LMX) theory of leadership over 25 years:

Applying a multi-level multi-domain perspective. *The Leadership Quarterly, 6*(2), 219–247. doi:10.1016/1048-9843(95)90036-5

Grenny, J. (2017, Sept 25). Great storytelling connects employees to their work. *Harvard Business Review.* https://hbr.org/2017/09/great-storytelling-connects-employees-to-their-work

Ha, P. (2017, Jun 8). How to manage virtual teams throughout the projects [weblog]. https://medium.com/teamdeck/how-to-manage-virtual-teams-throughout-the-projects-4b473e9ae4d7

Hoy, W. K., & Smith, P. A. (2007). Influence: A key to successful leadership. *International Journal of Educational Management, 21*(2), 158–167. https://doi.org/10.1108/09513540710729944

Jiang, H., & Luo, Y. (2016). Crafting employee trust: From authenticity, transparency to engagement. *Journal of Communication Management, 22,* 138–160. doi:10.1108/JCOM-07-2016-0055

jurczak, I. p., & Violanti, M. T. (2019). Geographically dispersed leadership. In S. E. Kelly (Ed.), *Computer-mediated communication for business: Theory into practice* (pp. 55–66). Cambridge Scholars Publishing.

Komives, S. R., Lucas, N., & McMahon, T. R. (1998). *Exploring leadership: For college students who want to make a difference.* Jossey-Bass.

Morgan, J. (2016, Aug 30). Building an organization with truly human leadership: How Barry-Wehmiller treats their employees like family members. *Inc.* https://www.inc.com/jacob-morgan/building-an-organization-with-truly-human-leadership.html

Neeley, T. (2015, Oct.) Global teams that work. *Harvard Business Review.* https://hbr.org/2015/10/global-teams-that-work

Porcelli, M. (2019, July 15). 6 qualities of relational leaders: Welcome to the relational dimensions of leadership. *The StartUp.* https://medium.com/swlh/6-qualities-of-relational-leaders-94b60ee964d7

Short, J., Williams, E., & Christie, B. (1976). *The social psychology of telecommunications.* Wiley.

Whiteley, P., Sy, T., & Johnson, S. K. (2012). Leaders' conceptions of followers: Implications for naturally occurring Pygmalion effects. *The Leadership Quarterly, 23*(5), 822–834. doi: 10.1016/j.leaqua.2012.03.006

Wilson, K., Sin, H., & Conlon, D. (2010). What about the leader in leader-member exchange? The impact of resource exchanges and substitutability on the leader. *Academy of Management Review, 35*(3), 358–372. doi:10.5465/amr.35.3.zok358

Wright, K. B. (2004). On-line relational maintenance strategies and perceptions of partners within exclusively internet-based and primarily internet-based relationships. *Communication Studies, 55*(2), 239–253. https://doi.org/10.1080/10510970409388617

Zak, P. J. (2017, Jan-Feb). The neuroscience of trust: Management behaviors that foster employee engagement. *Harvard Business Review,* 1–8. https://hbr.org/2017/01/the-neuroscience-of-trust

Zumaeta, J. (2019). Lonely at the top: How do senior leaders navigate the need to belong? *Journal of Leadership & Organizational Studies, 26,* 111–135. doi: 10.1177/1548051818774548

Zurer, R. (2018, April 12). How this 2.8 billion dollar company wins by caring for workers [Blog Post]. Conscious Company Media. https://consciouscompanymedia.com/workplace-culture/developing-talent/how-this-2-8-billion-company-wins-by-caring-for-workers/

Chapter 6

Bang, H., & Midelfart, T. N. (2017). What characterizes effective management teams?: A research-based approach. *Counseling Psychology, 69*(4), 334–359. https://doi.org/10.1037/cpb0000098

Bergman, J. Z., Rentsch, J. R., Small, E. E., Davenport, S. W., & Bergman, S. M. (2012). The shared leadership process in decision-making teams. The Journal of Social Psychology, 152(1), 17–42. https://doi.org/10.1080/00224545.2010.538763

Chiu, C., Balkundi, P., & Weinberg, F. J. (2017). When managers become leaders: The role of manager network centralities, social power, and followers' perception of leadership. *The Leadership Quarterly, 28*(2), 334–348. https://doi.org/10.1016/j.leaqua.2016.05.004

Forsyth, D. R. (2006). *Group dynamics* (5th ed.). Wadsworth.

Humphrey, S. E., Federica, A., Cushenbery, L., Hills, A. D., Fairchild, J. (2017). Team conflict dynamics: Implications of a dyadic view of conflict for team performance. *Organizational Behavior and Human Decision Processes 142*, 58–70. https://doi.org/10.1016/j.obhdp.2017.08.002

Janis, I. L. (1972). *Victims of groupthink*. Houghton Mifflin.

Jarvenpaa, S., Knoll, K., & Leidner, D. (1998). Is anybody out there? Antecedents of trust in global virtual teams. *Journal of Management Information Systems, 14*(4), 29–64. https://doi.org/10.1080/07421222.1998.11518185

Lu, L., Yuan, Y. C., & McLeod, P. L. (2012). Twenty-five years of hidden profiles in group decision making: A meta-analysis. *Personality and Social Psychology Review, 16*(1), 54–75. https://doi.org/10.1177/1088868311417243

McNeil, K. L. (2016, January 1). Work group trust: Differences between individualist and collectivist cultures. *Proceedings of the Academy of Organizational Culture, Communications and Conflict Allied Academies International Conference, 21*, 40–45. http://www.alliedacademies.org/pdfs/AOCCC_Proceedings_Spring_2016.pdf

Newell, S., & Swan, J. (2000). Trust and inter-organizational networking. *Human Relations, 53*(10), 1287–1329. https://doi.org/10.1177/a014106

Oetzel, J., & Ting-Toomey, S. (2013). *The SAGE handbook of conflict communication: Integrating theory, research, and practice* (2nd ed.). Sage.

Oetzel, J., Ting-Toomey, S., Masumoto, T., Yokochi, Y., Pan, X., Takai, J., & Wilcox, R. (2001). Face and facework in conflict: A cross-cultural comparison of China, Germany, Japan, and the United States. *Communication Monographs, 68*(3), 235–58. https://doi.org/10.1080/03637750128061

Pruitt, D. G. & Rubin, J. Z. (1986). *Social conflict: Escalation, stalemate, and settlement.* McGraw-Hill.

Rousseau, D. S., Sitkin, S., Burt, R., & Camerer, C. (1998). Not so different after all: A cross-discipline view of trust. *Academy of Management Review, 23*(3), 387–393. https://doi.org/10.5465/AMR.1998.926617

Stasser, G., & Titus, W. (1985). Pooling of unshared information in group decision making. *Journal of Personality and Social Psychology, 48*(6), 1467–1478. https://doi.org/10.1037/0022-3514.48.6.1467

Sueda, K. (2014). *Negotiating multiple identities: Shame and pride among Japanese returnees.* Springer International.

Ting-Toomey, S. (2005). The matrix of face: An updated face-negotiation theory. In W. B. Gudykunst (Ed.), *Theorizing about intercultural communication* (pp. 71–92). Sage.

Tuckman, B. W. & Jensen, M. A. (1977). Stages of small-group development revisited. *Group and Organization Studies, 2*(4), 419–427. https://doi.org/10.1177/105960117700200404

Van de Ven, A., & Poole, M. (1995). Explaining development and change in organizations. *Academy of Management Review, 20*(3), 510–540. https://doi.org/10.5465/AMR.1995.9508080329

Wakabayashi, D. (2017, August 7). Google fires engineer who wrote memo questioning women in tech. *New York Times.* https://www.nytimes.com/2017/08/07/business/google-women-engineer-fired-memo.html

Wang, D., Waldman, D. A., & Zhang, Z. (2014). A meta-analysis of shared leadership and team effectiveness. *Journal of Applied Psychology, 99*(2), 181–198. https://doi.org/10.1037/a0034531

Weingart, L. R., Behfar, K. J., Bendersky, C., Todorova, G., & Jehn, K. A. (2015). The directness and oppositional intensity of conflict expression. *Academy of Management Review, 40*(2), 235–262. https://doi.org/10.5465/amr.2013 0124

Chapter 7

Amarantou, V., Kazakopoulou, S., Chatzoudes, D., & Chatzoglou, P. (2018). Resistance to change: An empirical investigation of its antecedents. *Journal of Organizational Change Management, 31*(2), 426–450. https://doi.org/10.1108/JOCM-05-2017-0196

Anderson, N. (2018, May 3). University of Tennessee chancellor fired in unusually blunt letter. *The Washington Post* online edition. https://www.washingtonpost.com/news/grade-point/wp/2018/05/03/university-of-tennessee-chancellor-fired-in-unusually-blunt-letter/?noredirect=on&utm_term=.b713702b7b68

Ashforth, B., Saks, E., & Lee, A. (1998). Socialization and newcomer adjustment: The role of organizational context. *Human Relations, 51*(7), 897–926. https://doi.org/10.1023/A:1016999527596

Bridges, W. (2003). *Managing transitions* (2nd ed). Perseus Books.

Burke, S. (2018, May 10). *Vote of confidence for University of Tennessee president.* AP News online. https://www.apnews.com/fd49010f897c4ccf8ee56eaecdaddb67

Burgoon, J. K. (1993). Interpersonal expectations, expectancy violations, and emotional communication. *Journal of Language and Social Psychology, 12*(1–2), 30–48. https://doi.org/10.1177=026192X93121003

Burgoon, J. K., & LePoire, B. A. (1993). Effects of communication expectancies, actual communication, and expectancy disconfirmation on evaluations of communicators and their communication behavior. *Human Communication Research, 20*(1), 67–96. https://doi.org/10.1111=j.1468-2958.1993.tb00316.x

Burgoon, J. K., & Ebesu Hubbard, A. S. (2005). Cross-cultural and intercultural applications of expectancy violations theory and interaction adaptation theory. In W. B. Gudykunst (Ed.), *Theorizing About Intercultural Communication* (pp. 149–171). Sage.

Burgoon, M. (1995). Language expectancy theory: Elaboration, explication, and extension. In C. R. Berger & M. Burgoon (Eds.), *Communication and social influence processes* (pp. 29–52). Michigan State University Press.

Burkus, D. (2017, July 20). How adobe structures feedback conversations. *Harvard Business Review Digital Articles*, 2–4. https://hbr.org/2017/07/how-adobe-structures-feedback-conversations

Fulghum, R. (2004). *All I needed to know I learned in kindergarten: Uncommon thoughts on common things*. Ballantine Books.

Geertz, C. (1973). *The interpretation of cultures: Selected essays*. New York, NY: Basic.

Heyden, M. L. M., Fourné, S. P. L., Koene, B. A. S., Werkman, R., & Ansari, S. (2017). Rethinking 'top-down' and 'bottom-up' roles of top and middle managers in organizational change: Implications for employee support. *Journal of Management Studies, 54*(7), 961–985. https://doi.org/10.1111/joms.12258

Jablin, F. (2001). Organizational entry, assimilation, and disengagement/exit. In F. Jablin & L. Putnam (Eds.), *The new handbook of organizational communication: Advances in theory, research, and methods* (pp. 732–818). Sage.

Jablin, F., & Krone, K. J. (1987). Organizational assimilation. In C. R. Berger & S. H. Chaffee (Eds.), *Handbook of communication science* (pp. 711–746). Sage.

Jablin, F., & Miller, V. (1990). Interviewer and applicant questioning behavior in employment interviews. *Management Communication Quarterly, 4(1)*, 51–86. https://doi.org/10.1177/0893318990004001004

Jones, G. R. (1986). Socialization tactics, self-efficacy, and newcomers' adjustments to organizations. *Academy of Management Journal, 29*(2), 262–279. https://doi.org/10.2307/256188

Kotter, J. P., & Cohen, D. (2002). *The heart of change: Real-life stories of how people change their organizations*. Harvard Business Press.

Lederman, D. (2018, May 3). Tennessee chancellor ousted, blasted. *Inside Higher Education* online. https://www.insidehighered.com/news/2018/05/03/tennessee-chancellor-dismissed-abruptly-president-cites-poor-performance

Luhmann, N. (1995). *Social systems*. Stanford University Press.

Luna, T., & Cohen, J. (2017, December 20). To get people to change, make change easy. *Harvard Business Review*, 2–5. https://hbr.org/2017/12/to-get-people-to-change-make-change-easy

Megargee, S. (2018, May 2). University of Tennessee chancellor being forced out of post. AP News online. https://www.apnews.com/0f10768c5e894ba6b253a86121d5f7af/University-of-Tennessee-chancellor-being-forced-out-of-post

Pacanowsky, M., & O'Donnell-Trujillo, N. (1982). Communication and organizational cultures. *Western Journal of Speech Communication, 46(2),* 115–130. https://doi.org/10.1080/10570318209374072

Pacanowsky, M. E., & O'Donnell-Trujillo, N. (1983). Organizational communication as cultural performance. *Communication Monographs, 50(2)*, 126–147. https://doi.org/10.1080/03637758309390158

Sandberg, J., & Tsoukas, H. (2015). Making sense of the sensemaking perspective: Its constituents, limitations, and opportunities for further development. *Journal of Organizational Behavior, 36*(S1), S6–S32. https://doi.org/10.1002/job.1937

Schein, E. (2004). *Organizational culture and leadership* (3rd ed.). Jossey-Bass.

Sparr, J. L. (2018). Paradoxes in organizational change: The crucial role of leaders' sensegiving. *Journal of Change Management, 18*(2), 162–180. https://doi.org/10.1080/14697017.2018.1446696

Stripling, J. (2018, May 2). A stunning ouster in Tennessee gets ugly and feels like political payback. *Chronicle of Higher Education* online. https://www.chronicle.com/article/A-Stunning-Ouster-in-Tennessee/243321

Van Maanen, J., & Schein, E. H. (1979). Toward a theory of organizational socialization. In B. M. Staw & L. L. Cummings (Eds.), *Research in organizational behavior* (Vol. 1, pp. 209–264). JAI.

Wanberg, C. (2012). *The Oxford handbook of organizational socialization.* Oxford University Press.

Weick, K. E., Sutcliffe, K. M., & Obstfeld, D. (2005). Organizing and the process of sensemaking. *Organization Science, 16*(4), 409–421. https://doi.org/10.1287/orsc.1050.0133

West, R., & Turner, L. H. (2018). *Introducing communication theory: Analysis and application.* McGraw Hill Education.

White, C. (2015). Expectancy violations theory and interaction adaptation theory: From expectations to adaptation. In D. O. Braithwaite & P. Schrodt (Eds.), *Engaging Theories in Interpersonal Communication: Multiple Perspectives* (pp. 216–228). Sage.

Whittle, A., Mueller, F., Gilchrist, A., & Lenney, P. (2016). Sensemaking, sense-censoring and strategic inaction: The discursive enactment of power and politics in a multinational corporation. *Organization Studies, 37*(9), 1323–1351. https://doi.org/10.1177/0170840616634127

Zamudio-Suaréz, F. (2018, May 2). Chancellor of Tennessee flagship is suddenly fired after only one year. *Chronicle of Higher Education* online. https://www.chronicle.com/article/Chancellor-of-Tennessee/243316

Chapter 8

Berkowitz, B. (n.d.). *Section 6. Coalition building II: Maintaining a coalition.* University of Kansas Community Toolbox. https://ctb.ku.edu/en/table-of-contents/assessment/promotion-strategies/maintain-a-coalition/main

Cain, A. (2019, July 29). A secret internal memo reportedly outlined Amazon's plans for a new grocery-store chain that could thrive in areas where Whole Foods struggles. *Business Insider.* https://www.businessinsider.com/amazon-whole-foods-new-grocery-chain-report-2019-7

Rabinowitz, P. (n.d.). Section 5. Coalition building I: Starting a coalition. University of Kansas Community Toolbox. https://ctb.ku.edu/en/table-of-contents/assessment/promotion-strategies/start-a-coaltion/main

Electronic Frontier Foundation (n.d.). Basic steps & tips to building a coalition. https://www.eff.org/electronic-frontier-alliance/coalition-tips

Endres, S., & Weibler, J. (2019). Understanding (non)leadership phenomena in collaborative interorganizational networks and advancing shared leadership theory: An interpretive grounded theory study. *Business Research*. https://doi.org/10.1007/s40685-019-0086-6

Fondrevay, J. J. (2018, May 21). After a merger, don't let "us vs. them" thinking ruin the company. *Harvard Business Review*. https://hbr.org/2018/05/after-a-merger-dont-let-us-vs-them-thinking-ruin-the-company

Gelfand, M., Gordon, S., Li, C., Choi, V., & Prokopowicz, P. (2018, October 2). One reason mergers fail: The two cultures aren't compatible. *Harvard Business Review*. https://hbr.org/2018/10/one-reason-mergers-fail-the-two-cultures-arent-compatible

Gregory, L. (2019, Feb 3). Amazon.com Inc.'s mission statement & vision statement (an analysis). *Panmore Institute*. http://panmore.com/amazon-com-inc-vision-statement-mission-statement-analysis

Gu, J., Chen, Z., Huang, Q., Liu, H., & Huang, S. (2016). A multilevel analysis of the relationship between shared leadership and creativity in inter organizational teams. *Journal of Creative Behavior*, *52*(2), 109–126. https://doi.org/10.1002/jocb.135

Heidari-Robinson, S., Heywood, S., & Pless, J. (2018, June 13). How to make your post-merger re-org a success. *Harvard, Business Review*. https://hbr.org/2018/06/how-to-make-your-post-merger-reorg-a-success

Hill, L., & Lineback, K. (2011, March 3). The three networks you need. *Harvard Business Review*. https://hbr.org/2011/03/the-three-networks-you-need

Ibarra, H. (2015, February 3). How to revive a tired network. *Harvard Business Review*. https://hbr.org/2015/02/how-to-revive-a-tired-network

Ibarra, H., & Hunter, M. L. (2007, January). How leaders create and use networks. *Harvard Business Review*. https://hbr.org/2007/01/how-leaders-create-and-use-networks

Kim, E. (2019, February 19). Amazon changed how it reports its retail footprint—and now it's not as clear. *CNBC*. https://www.cnbc.com/2019/02/19/amazon-changes-reporting-on-physical-stores.html

McGuire, M., & Silvia, C. (2009). Does leadership in networks matter?: Examining the effect of leadership behaviors on managers' perceptions of network effectiveness. *Public Performance & Management Review*, *33*(1), 34–62. https://doi.org/10.2753/PMR1530-9576330102

Meyersohn, N. (2018, August 28). Amazon-Whole Foods one year later: The grocery business will never be the same. *CNN Business*. https://money.cnn.com/2018/08/28/technology/business/amazon-whole-foods-365-walmart-kroger-costco-grocery/index.html

Muradli, N., & Ahmadov, F. (2019). Managing contradiction and sustaining sustainability in inter organizational networks through leadership: A case study. *Entrepreneurship and Sustainability Issues*, *6*(3), 1255–1269. https://doi.org/10.9770/jesi.2019.6.3(14)

Myer, T. (2016, Nov 29). *Becoming a change leader—building guiding coalition*. Govloop. https://www.govloop.com/community/blog/becoming-change-leader-building-guiding-coalition/

National League for Nursing (n.d.). *Coalition-building*. http://www.nln.org/docs/default-source/advocacy-public-policy/coalition-building-pdf.pdf?sfvrsn=0

O'Donnell, S. (2017, Dec 5). How to avoid losing people, productivity, and profit during mergers and acquisitions. *Forbes*. https://www.forbes.com/sites/forbescoachescouncil/2017/12/05/

how-to-avoid-losing-people-productivity-and-profit-during-mergers-and-acquisitions/#-113ca5ce75c2

Popp, J. K., Milward, H. B., MacKean, G., Casebeer, A. & Lindstrom, R. (2014). Inter-organizational networks: A review of the literature to inform practice. *IBM Center for The Business of Government.* http://www.businessofgovernment.org/report/inter-organizational-networks-review-literature-inform-practice

Rabinowitz, P. (n.d.). Section 5. Coalition building I: Starting a coalition. University of Kansas Community Toolbox. https://ctb.ku.edu/en/table-of-contents/assessment/promotion-strategies/start-a-coaltion/main

Regan, C., & Garcia, M. D. (2020, Jan 23). *Your guide to coalition building* [blog]. The Campaign Workshop. https://www.thecampaignworkshop.com/blog/campaign-strategy/coalition-building

Ruben, B. D. (2003). General systems theory. In R. Budd & B. D. Ruben (Eds.), *Interdisciplinary approaches to human communication* (2nd ed., pp. 95–118). Transaction Publishers.

Ruben, B., & Gigliotti, R. (2016). Leadership as social influence: An expanded view of leadership communication theory and practice. *Journal of Leadership & Organizational Studies, 23*(4), 467–479. https://doi.org/10.1177/1548051816641876

Simon, H. (2017, September 12). Whole Foods is becoming Amazon's brick-and-mortar pricing lab. *Harvard Business Review.* https://hbr.org/2017/09/whole-foods-is-becoming-amazons-brick-and-mortar-pricing-lab

Smathers, C., & Lobb, J. (2014, Nov 18). *Establishing a new* coalition. The Ohio State University Extension. https://ohioline.osu.edu/factsheet/CDFS-3

Taylor, S. (2018, June 25). Amazon expands Prime member savings to all Whole Foods locations across U.S. *Geekwire.* https://www.geekwire.com/2018/amazon-expands-prime-member-savings-whole-foods-locations-across-u-s/

Tobin, B. (2018, December 14). Amazon-owned Whole Foods ends partnership with Instacart. *USA Today.* https://www.usatoday.com/story/money/2018/12/14/amazon-ends-instacart-partnership-whole-foods/2309370002/

Weise, E. (2018, February 8). Amazon starts free, 2-hour Whole Foods deliveries in fresh test of grocery model. *USA Today.* https://www.usatoday.com/story/tech/news/2018/02/07/amazon-launches-whole-foods-deliveries-four-cities/318337002/

Chapter 9

Abitbol, A., Lee, N., Seltzer, T., & Lee, S. Y. (2018). #RaceTogether: Starbucks' attempt to discuss race in America and its impact on company reputation and employees. *PR Journal, 12*(1). https://prjournal.instituteforpr.org/past-issues/

American Marketing Association. (2020). *Branding.* https://www.ama.org/topics/branding/

Anker, T. B., Kappel, K., Sandøe, P., & Eadie, D. (2012). Fuzzy promises: Explicative definitions of brand promise delivery. *Marketing Theory, 12*(3), 267–287. https://doi.org/10.1177/1470593112451379

Ashkenas, R. (2010, January 22). Define your personal Brand with simple questions. *Harvard Business Review.* https://hbr.org/2010/01/define-your-personal-brand-wit

Bacardi, F. (2019, July 31). *Mario Lopez apologizes for transgender parenting comments.* https://pagesix.com/2019/07/31/mario-lopez-apologizes-for-transgender-parenting-comments/?_ga=2.233412759.803227450.1566397346-2068966868.1566397346).

Benoit, W. L. (1995). *Accounts, excuses and apologies: A theory of image restoration strategies.* State University of New York Press.

Benoit, W. (1997). Image repair discourse and crisis communication. *Public Relations Review, 23*(2), 177–186. https://doi.org/10.1016/S0363-8111(97)90023-0

Boncheck, M. & France, C. (2016, May 9). Build your brand as a relationship. *Harvard Business Review.* https://hbr.org/2016/05/build-your-brand-as-a-relationship

Brockbank, W. (2016, March 29). 3 keys to internal and external stakeholder management for HR professionals. *Inside HR.* https://www.insidehr.com.au/3-keys-to-successful-stakeholder-management-for-hr/

Carr, A. (2015, June 15). The inside story of Starbucks's race together campaign, no foam. FastCompany. https://www.fastcompany.com/3046890/the-inside-story-of-starbuckss-race-together-campaign-no-foam

Chatterji, A. K., & Toffel, M. W. (2019). Assessing the impact of CEO activism. *Organizations and Environment, 32*(2), 159–185. https://doi.org/10.1177/1086026619848144

de Chernatony, L. & McDonald, M. (2003). *Creating Powerful Brands in Consumer, Service and Industrial Markets* (3rd ed.). Elsevier/Butterworth-Heinemann.

Gaines-Ross, L. (2016). Is it safe for CEOs to voice strong political opinions? *Harvard Business Review.* https://hbr.org/2016/06/is-it-safe-for-ceos-to-voice-strong-political-opinions

Greyser, S. A. & Urde, M. (2019, January/February). What does your corporate brand stand for? *Harvard Business Review.* https://hbr.org/2019/01/what-does-your-corporate-brand-stand-for

Hack, N. *Co-creation through engagement* [blog post]. https://www.because.net/co-creation-through-engaging/

Harvard Business Review Analytic Services. (2018, September 7). The digitization of collaboration: New social tools can empower better ways of working together. *Harvard Business Review.* https://hbr.org/resources/pdfs/comm/workplace/TheDigitizationOfCollaboration.pdf

Holt, D. (2016, March). Branding in the age of social media. *Harvard Business Review.* https://hbr.org/2016/03/branding-in-the-age-of-social-media

Kaufmann, H., Loureiro, S., & Manarioti, A. (2016). Exploring behavioural branding, brand love and brand co-creation. *Journal of Product & Brand Management, 25*(6), 516–526. https://doi.org/10.1108/JPBM-06-2015-0919

Larson, B. Z. & Markarius, E. E. (2018, October 5). The virtual work skills you need— Even if you never work remotely. *Harvard Business Review.* https://hbr.org/2018/10/the-virtual-work-skills-you-need-even-if-you-never-work-remotely

Madhani, A. (2015, July 15). Starbucks-led coalition commits to hiring 100,000 disconnected youth. *USA Today.* http://www.usatoday.com/story/news/2015/07/13/starbucks-howard-schultz-coalition-100000-jobs/30052691/

Mao, Y. L., & Hale, C. (2015). Relating intercultural communication sensitivity to conflict manage-ment styles, technology use, and organizational communication satisfaction in multinational organizations in China. *Journal of Intercultural Communication Research, 44*(2), 132–150. https://doi.org/10.1080/17475759.2015.1025090

McGregor, J. (2018, April 19). Anatomy of a PR response: How Starbucks is handling its Phila-delphia crisis. *Washington Post.* https://www.washingtonpost.com/news/on-leadership/wp/2018/04/19/anatomy-of-a-pr-response-how-starbucks-is-handling-its-philadelphia-cri-sis/?noredirect=on&utm_term=.98688d258419

Payne, A., Frow, P., & Eggert, A. (2017). The customer value proposition: Evolution, development, and application in marketing. *Journal of the Academy of Marketing Science, 45*(4), 467–489. https://doi.org/10.1007/s11747-017-0523-z

Quesenberry, K. A. (2018, January 2). The basic social media mistakes companies still make. *Harvard Business Review.* https://hbr.org/2018/01/the-basic-social-media-mistakes-companies-still-make

Schultz, D. E., Barnes, B. E., Schultz, H. F., & Azzaro, M. (2015). *Building Customer-brand Rela-tionships.* Routledge.

Seiffert-Brockmann, J., Einwiller, S., & Stranzl, J. (2018). Character assassination of CEOs in crises—Questioning CEOs' character and values in corporate crises. *European Journal of Communication, 33*(4), 413–429. https://doi.org/10.1177/0267323118763860

Spring, M., Gaines-Ross, L., & Massey, P. (2018). *CEO activism in 2018: The pur-poseful CEO.* Weber Shandwick. https://www.webershandwick.com/news/ceo-activism-in-2018-half-of-americans-say-ceo-activism-influences-government/

Springman, J. (2011, July 28). Implementing a stakeholder strategy. *Harvard Business Review.* https://hbr.org/2011/07/implementing-a-stakeholder-str

Ware, B. L., & Linkugel, W. A. (1973). They spoke in defense of themselves: On the generic criticism of apologia. *Quarterly Journal of Speech, 59*(3), 273–283. https://doi.org/10.1080/00335637309383176

Xu, S. (2018). Crisis communication within a community: Bonding, coping, and making sense together. *Public Relations Review, 44*(1), 84–97. https://doi.org/10.1016/j.pubrev.2017.10.004

Yohn, D. L. (2014, April 23). Think differently about protecting your brand. *Harvard Business Review.* https://hbr.org/2014/04/think-differently-about-protecting-your-brand

Chapter 10

Adair, R. (2008). Developing great leaders, one follower at a time. In R. Riggio, I. Chaleff, & J. Lipman-Blumen (Eds.), *The art of followership: How great followers create great leaders and organizations* (pp. 137–154). Jossey-Bass.

Burke, E. (n.d.). 14 nonprofit management tips for a growth mindset. *Classy.* https://www.classy.org/blog/nonprofit-management-tips-growth-mindset/

Buse, K., Bernstein, R. S., & Bilmoria, D. (2016). The influence of board diversity policies and practices, and board inclusion behaviors on nonprofit governance practices. *Journal of Business Ethics, 133*(1), 179–191. https://doi.org/10.1007/s10551-014-2352-z

Follman, J., Cseh, M., & Brudney, J. L. (2016). Structures, challenges, and successes of volunteer programs co-managed by nonprofit and public organizations. *Nonprofit Management & Leadership, 26*(4), 453–470. https://doi.org/10.1002/nml.21206

Forbes Nonprofit Council. (2018, February 5). New to nonprofit leadership: Here are seven tips for success. *Forbes.* https://www.forbes.com/sites/forbesnonprofitcouncil/2018/02/05/new-to-nonprofit-leadership-here-are-seven-tips-for-success/#2c32c5763d15

Gilstrap, C. & Minchow-Proffitt, H. (2017). The ethical frameworks of social media policies among U.S. nonprofit organizations: Legal expectations, dialogic prescriptions, and a dialectical model. *Journal of Nonprofit & Public Sector Marketing, 29*(2), 169–187. https://doi.org/10.1080/10495142.2017.1326337

Gilstrap, C. A., & Morris, A. (2015). Role fluidity and emergent followership. *Journal of Nonprofit Education & Leadership, 5*(3), 153–173. https://js.sagamorepub.com/jnel/article/view/6530

Higgins, E. T. (2000). Making a good decision: Value from fit. *American Psychologist, 55*(11), 1217–1230. https://doi.org/10.1037/0003-066X.55.11.1217

Higgins, T. E. (2005). Value from regulatory fit. *Current Directions in Psychological Science, 14*(4), 209–213. https://doi.org/10.1111/j.0963-7214.2005.00366.x

Ibele, T. (2018, March 9). *The top 5 social media fails you are still making (and how to #win instead).* https://www.wildapricot.com/blogs/newsblog/2018/03/09/social-media-fails

Langenberg, S. & Wesseling, H. (2016). Making sense of Weick's organizing: A philosophical exploration. *Philosophy of Management, 15*, 221–240. https://doi.org/10.1007/s40926-016-0040-z

Letts, C., & Holly, D. (2017). The promise of skills-based volunteering. *Stanford Social Innovation Review,15*(4), 40–47. https://ssir.org/articles/entry/the_promise_of_skills_based_volunteering

Matsushita, S. (2017). Fulfilling missions and serving communities: Seven key leadership roles nonprofits will need to succeed. *HR Professional, 34*(11), 29–31. http://hrprofessionalnow.ca/leadership-matters/501-fulfilling-missions-and-serving-communities

Nonprofit briefs. (2018, April/May/June). *Nonprofit World, 36*(2), https://www.snpo.org/publications/sendpdf.php?id=2293

Norwich University. (2016, December). *7 key differences between nonprofit and for-profit organizations.* https://online.norwich.edu/academic-programs/masters/public-administration/resources/articles/7-key-differences-between-nonprofit-and-for-profit-organizations

Renz, D. O. (2016). The future of nonprofit leadership and management. In Renz, D. O. and R. D. Herman (Eds.,), *The Jossey-Bass Handbook of Nonprofit Leadership and Management* (4th ed.) (pp. 734–745). John Wiley and Sons.

Rimes, H., Nesbit, R., Christensen, R. K., & Brudney, J. L. (2017). Exploring the dynamics of volunteer and staff interactions: From satisfaction to conflict. *Nonprofit Management and Leadership, 28*, 195–213. https://doi.org/10.1002/nml.21277

Weaver, M. L. (2017, January). Strategies to advance your leadership skills. *Nonprofit Communications Newsletter.* https://doi.org/10.1002/NPCR

Weick, K. (1979). *The social psychology of organizing.* New York, NY: McGraw Hill.

Your Public Registry and Nonprofit Tech for Good. (2018). *2018 global NGO report*. http://techreport.ngo/wp-content/uploads/2018-Tech-Report-English.pdf

Chapter 11

Anderson, P. A., Hecht, M. L., Hoobler, G. D., & Smallwood, M. (2002). Nonverbal communication across cultures. In W. B. Gudykunst & B. Mody (Eds.), *Handbook of international and intercultural communication* (2nd ed.) (pp. 89–106). Sage Publications.

Bennett, M. (1986). A developmental approach to training for intercultural sensitivity. *International Journal of Intercultural Relations, 10*(2), 179–196. https://doi.org/10.1016/0147-1767(86)90005-2

Blair, B., & Bligh, M. (2018). Looking for leadership in all the wrong places: The impact of culture on proactive followership and follower dissent. *Journal of Social Issues, 74*(1), 129–143. https://doi.org/10.1111/josi.12260

Brown, S., Fuller, R., & Thatcher, S. (2016). Impression formation and durability in mediated communication. *Journal of The Association for Information Systems, 17*(9), 614–647. https://aisel.aisnet.org/jais/vol17/iss9/1

Can, A., & Aktaş, M. (2012). Cultural values and followership style preferences. *Procedia-Social and Behavioral Sciences, 41*(1), 84–91. https://doi.org/10.1016/j.sbspro.2012.04.012

Chen, G. M., & Starosta, W. J. (2000). The development and validation of the intercultural sensitivity scale. *Human Communication, 3*(1), 1–15. http://digitalcommons.uri.edu/com_facpubs/36/

Gallois, C., Ogay, T., & Giles, H. (2005). Communication accommodation theory: A look back and a look ahead. In W. B. Gudykunst (Ed.), *Theorizing about intercultural communication* (pp. 121–148). Sage.

Giles, H., Taylor, D., & Bourhis, R. (1973). Towards a theory of interpersonal accommodation through language: Some Canadian data. *Language in Society, 2*(2), 177–192. https://doi.org/10.1017/S0047404500000701

Gudykunst, W. B., & Lee, C. M. (2002). Cross-cultural communication theories. In W. B. Gudykunst & B. Mody (Eds.), *Handbook of international and intercultural communication* (2nd ed.) (pp. 25–50). Sage.

Hall, E. (1976). *Beyond culture*. Anchor Press.

Hansen, M., Fabriz, S., & Stehle, S. (2015). Cultural cues in students' computer-mediated communication: Influences on e mail style, perception of the sender, and willingness to help. *Journal of Computer Mediated Communication, 20*(3), 278–294. https://doi.org/10.1111/jcc4.12110

Hofstede, G. (2001). *Culture's consequences: Comparing values, behaviors, institutions, and organizations across nations* (2nd ed.). Sage.

Hofstede, G. (2011). Dimensionalizing cultures: The model in context. *Online Readings in Psychology and Culture, 2*(1), 1–26. https://doi.org/10.9707/2307-0919.1014

Iliadi, P. L. L., & Larina, T. V. (2017). Refusal strategies in English and Russian. *RUDN Journal of Language Studies, Semiotics and Semantics, 8*, 531–542. https://doi.org/10.22363/2313-2299-2017-8-3-531-542

Lee, D. (2018) *A great example of how to deal with an upset employee: How to respond to employee complaints in a way that boosts trust, morale, and their willingness to be honest in the future.* Human Nature at Work. http://humannatureatwork.com/wp-content/uploads/2016/03/A-Great-Example-of-How-to-Deal-With-An-Upset-Employee.pdf

Neely, T. (2017, Aug. 29). How to successfully work across countries, languages, and cultures. *Harvard Business Review.* https://hbr.org/2017/08/how-to-successfully-work-across-countries-languages-and-cultures

Mao, Y., & Hale, C. (2015). Relating intercultural communication sensitivity to conflict management styles, technology use, and organizational communication satisfaction in multinational organizations in China. *Journal of Intercultural Communication Research, 44*(2), 1–19. https://doi.org/10.1080/17475759.2015.1025090

Markman, A. (2018, June 15). 3 ways to identify cultural differences on a global team. *Harvard Business Review.* https://hbr.org/2018/06/3-ways-to-identify-cultural-differences-on-a-global-team

Molinsky, A. (2015, Jan. 15). The mistake most managers make with cross-cultural training. *Harvard Business Review.* https://hbr.org/2015/01/the-mistake-most-managers-make-with-cross-cultural-training

Muir, K., Joinson, A., Cotterill, R., & Dewdney, N. (2017). Linguistic style accommodation shapes impression formation and rapport in computer-mediated communication. *Journal of Language and Social Psychology, 36*(5), 525–548. https://doi.org/10.1177%2F0261927X17701327

Rowland, D. (2016). Leading across cultures requires flexibility and curiosity. *Harvard Business Review.* https://hbr.org/2016/05/leading-across-cultures-requires-flexibility-and-curiosity

Sharabi, M. (2017). Work ethic among Jews and Muslims: The effect of religiosity degree and demographic factors. *Sociological Perspectives, 60*(2), 251–268. https://doi.org/10.1177%2F0731121416650403

Stohl, C. (2001). Globalizing organizational communication. In F. Jablin & L. Putnam (Eds.), *The new handbook of organizational communication: Advances in theory, research, and methods.* Sage.

Sueda, K. (2014). *Negotiating multiple identities: Shame and pride among Japanese returnees.* Springer.

Ting-Toomey, S. (2005). The matrix of face: An updated face-negotiation theory. In W. B. Gudykunst (Ed.), *Theorizing about intercultural communication* (pp. 71–92). Sage.

Toegel, G. & Barsoux, J. (2017, June 8). 3 situations where cross-cultural communication breaks down. *Harvard Business Review.* https://hbr.org/2016/06/3-situations-where-cross-cultural-communication-breaks-down

Van Dick, R., Lemoine, J. E., Steffenss, N. K., Kerschreiter, R., Akfirat, S. A., Avanzi, L., Dumont, K., Epitropski, O., Fransen, K., Giessner, S., González, R., Kark, R., Lipponen, J., Markovits, Y., Monzani, L., Orosz, G., Pandey, D., Roland-Levy, C., Schuh, S., ..., & Haslam, S. A. (2018). Identity leadership going global: Validation of the identity leadership inventory across 20 countries. *Journal of Occupational and Organizational Psychology, 91*(4), 1–32. https://doi.org/10.1111/joop.12223

Chapter 12

Balmas, M., & Sheafer, T. (2010). Candidate image in election campaigns: Attribute agenda setting, affective priming, and voting intentions. *International Journal of Public Opinion Research, 22*(2), 204–229. https://doi.org/10.1093/ijpor/edq009

Baur, J., Parker Ellen, B., Buckley, M., Ferris, G., Allison, T., Mckenny, A., & Short, J. (2016). More than one way to articulate a vision: A configurations approach to leader charismatic rhetoric and influence. *The Leadership Quarterly, 27*(1), 156–171. https://psycnet.apa.org/doi/10.1016/j.leaqua.2015.08.002

Cohen, H. (2018, Oct 29). *A political leader* [blog]. Leadership Expert. http://www.leadership-expert.co.uk/political-leader.html

Colliander, J., Marder, B., Lid Falkman, L., Madestam, J., Modig, E., & Sagfossen, S. (2017). The social media balancing act: Testing the use of a balanced self-presentation strategy for politicians using twitter. *Computers in Human Behavior, 74*, 277–285. https://doi.org/10.1016/j.chb.2017.04.042

Ditkoff, S. W., & Grindle, A. (2017). Audacious philanthropy. *Harvard Business Review.* https://hbr.org/2017/09/audacious-philanthropy

Ellen, S. (2016, May 7). Election survival guide: 9 tips for politicians and one for us. *The Conversation.* https://theconversation.com/election-survival-guide-nine-tips-for-politicians-and-one-for-us-59003

Ferris, G., Perrewé, P., Daniels, S., Lawong, D., & Holmes, J. (2017). Social influence and politics in organizational research: What we know and what we need to know. *Journal of Leadership & Organizational Studies, 24*(1), 5–19. https://doi.org/10.1177%2F1548051816656003

Gaines-Ross, L. (2017, February 17). What CEOS should know about speaking up on political issues. *Harvard Business Review.* https://hbr.org/2017/02/what-ceos-should-know-about-speaking-up-on-political-issues

Gelles, D. (2018, Feb. 18). The CEO who stood up to President Trump: Ken Frazier speaks out. *The New York Times.* https://www.nytimes.com/2018/02/19/business/merck-ceo-ken-frazier-trump.html

Graves, C. (2017, February 7). Why every ad today feels political (even if it isn't). *Harvard Business Review.* https://hbr.org/2017/02/why-every-ad-today-feels-political-even-if-it-isnt

Guo, L., & Vargo, C. (2018). "Fake news" and emerging online media ecosystem: An integrated intermedia agenda-setting analysis of the 2016 U. S. presidential election. *Communication Research, 47*(2), 178–200. https://doi.org/10.1177%2F0093650218777177

Heppell, T. (2011). Toxic leadership: Applying the Lipman-Blumen model to political leadership. *Representation, 47*(3), 241–249. https://doi.org/10.1080/00344893.2011.596422

Kellerman, B. (2004). *Bad leadership: What it is, how it happens, why it matters.* Harvard Business School Press.

Keyser, J. (2016, July 26). Grassroots leadership. *Common Sense Leadership.* http://www.commonsenseleadership.com/grassroots-leadership/

Kimura, T. (2015). A review of political skill: Current research trend and directions for future research. *International Journal of Management Reviews, 17*(3), 312–332. https://doi.org/10.1111/ijmr.12041

Kopaneva, I., & Sias, P. (2015). Lost in translation: Employee and organizational constructions of mission and vision. *Management Communication Quarterly, 29*(3), 358–384. https://doi.org/10.1177%2F0893318915581648

Lee, J., & Lim, Y. (2016). Gendered campaign tweets: The cases of Hillary Clinton and Donald Trump. *Public Relations Review, 42*(5), 849–855. https://doi.org/10.1016/j.pubrev.2016.07.004

Lipman-Blumen, J. (2005). Toxic leadership: When grand illusions masquerade as noble visions. *Leader to Leader, 2005*(36), 29–36. https://doi.org/10.1002/ltl.125

McCombs, M. E., & Shaw, D. L. (1972). The agenda-setting function of mass media. *Public Opinion Quarterly, 36*(2), 176–187. https://doi.org/10.1086/267990

Park, C. (2013). Does Twitter motivate involvement in politics? Tweeting, opinion leadership, and political engagement. *Computers in Human Behavior, 29*(4), 1641–1648. https://doi.org/10.1016/j.chb.2013.01.044

Pew Research Center (2019, March 26). *For local news, Americans embrace digital but still want strong community connection.* https://www.journalism.org/2019/03/26/overall-social-media-plays-a-moderate-role-in-local-news/

Popper, M. (2014). Why do people follow? In L. L. Lapierre & M. K. Carsten (Eds.), *Followership: What is it and why do people follow?* (pp. 109–120). Emerald Group Publishing Limited.

Rice, C., & Zegart, A. (2018, May). Managing 21st century political risk. *Harvard Business Review.* https://hbr.org/2018/05/managing-21st-century-political-risk

Scheufele, D., & Tewksbury, D. (2007). Framing, agenda setting, and priming: The evolution of three media effects models. *Journal of Communication, 57*(1), 9–20. https://doi.org/10.1111/j.0021-9916.2007.00326.x

Shah, J. (2017, Aug 10). *11 digital marketing tips for an effective political campaign* [blog]. Designhill. https://www.designhill.comdesign-blog/11-digital-marketing-tips-for-an-effective-political-campaign/

Speed, R., Butler, P., & Collins, N. (2015). Human branding in political marketing: Applying contemporary branding thought to political parties and their leaders. *Journal of Political Marketing, 14*(1–2), 129–151. https://doi.org/10.1080/15377857.2014.990833

Steffens, N., Haslam, S., Jetten, J., & Mols, F. (2018). Our followers are lions, theirs are sheep: How social identity shapes theories about followership and social influence. *Political Psychology, 39*(1), 23–42. https://doi.org/10.1111/pops.12387

Thatcher, M. (2016, Sept 13*). 6 tips for writing a power campaign speech.* Write Limited. https://write.co.nz/6-tips-for-writing-a-powerful-political-campaign-speech/

Weeks, B., Ardèvol-Abreu, A., & Gil de Zúñiga, H. (2017). Online influence? Social media use, opinion leadership, and political persuasion. *International Journal of Public Opinion Research, 29*(2), 214–239. https://doi.org/10.1093/ijpor/edv050

W. K. Kellogg Foundation. (2003). *Grassroots leadership development: A guide for grassroots leaders, support organizations, and funders.* https://www.wkkf.org/resource-directory/resource/2003/01/grassroots-leadership-development-a-guide-for-grassroots-leadership-support-organizations-and

Index

CPSIA information can be obtained
at www.ICGtesting.com
Printed in the USA
LVHW011132010922
727320LV00001B/4

9 781516 537778